40 Lessons

to speak

French

Les langues pour tous

Collection dirigée par Jean-Pierre Berman,
Michel Marcheteau et Michel Savio

FRENCH

To start learning or revise your French:

- **40 lessons**
  (Coffret livre + 2 CD également disponible)
  (Pack containing book + 2 CD also available)
- **Instant French**
  (Coffret livre + 1 CD également disponible)
  (Pack containing book + 1 CD also available)

■ Dictionnaries:

- **Dictionnaire de l'anglais d'aujourd'hui**
  (English/French – French/English)
- **Dictionnaire bilingue de l'argot d'aujourd'hui**
  Bilingual Dictionary of Today's Slang

■ Specialised bilingual dictionaries:

- **Dictionnaire de l'anglais économique, commercial et financier**
  (English/French – French/English)
- **Dictionnaire de l'anglais des médias et du multimédia**
  Dictionary of Medias and Multimedia
  (English/French – French/English)
- **Dictionnaire de l'Internet et du multimédia**
  Internet and Multimedia Bilingual Dictionary
  (English/French – French/English)
- **Dictionnaire de l'environnement et du développement durable**
  (English/French – French/English)
- **Dictionnaire de l'anglais de l'informatique**
  French/English – Dictionary of computing
- **Dictionnaire des vins, bières et spiritueux du monde**
  Bilingual dictionary of wine, beers and spirits
  (English/French – French/English)
- **Dictionnaire de l'anglais juridique**
  (English/French – French/English)

Autres langues disponibles dans les séries
de la collection **Langues pour tous :**
anglais, allemand, arabe, chinois, espagnol, grec moderne,
hébreu, hongrois, italien, japonais, latin, néerlandais, occitan,
polonais, portugais, russe, tchèque, turc, vietnamien

Consultez notre site Internet : www.languespourtous.fr

ISBN : 978-2-266-18052-8

40 lessons

to speak French

by

Sylviane Nouschi

and

Nicole Gandilhon

with the assistance of

Elinor Sigler

Head, office of International Education

Ecole Centrale de Paris

CD

5th edition

POCKET

Table of contents

Table of contents

Foreword

This book is meant to provide everyone who wants to start learning French or to brush up memories of French with **a simple and handy tool.**

The authors' main concern has been to meet the requirements of those who aim for **good understanding and easy handling** of the language. Their purpose has been to enable everyone to progress step by step and reach an operational level.

In order to achieve this end, they have focused on **the basic elements and structures.** Rather than attempting to describe every mechanism, quote all exceptions or irregular forms, they have tried to give **clear, precise and reliable landmarks.**

Having in mind a concern for **efficiency**, they have deliberately restricted the number of grammatical terms to the sheer minimum and have chosen **accurate but simple explanations.**

The approach is gradual throughout the lessons and throughout the book, so as to deal with the main points one by one, in a constructive manner. The aim is to make sure that the use of every item is mastered before proceeding to the next one.

Every structure studied is illustrated by sentences **in current use in everyday French.** In order to avoid ambiguity, they are **all related to a situation** or context which is briefly indicated in English.

The book consists of:

- Simple and easily assimilated units, dealing with only one difficulty at a time so as to secure mastery of the point studied.
- Explanations and remarks which, in addition to translations into English, make clear the basic structures.
- Exercises in which the structures and vocabulary are repeatedly practised to secure complete understanding.
- Concise explanations of typical expressions and practical information, connected with the points studied, widening the scope to aspects of everyday France.

How to use this book

The following description and explanations will help you organize your time and get the most out of this book.

The book includes :

– 40 lessons of eight pages each ;
– a short grammar summary.

All of the lessons are organized along the same lines in order to facilitate self-learning. They include four parts, A, B, C and D, each two pages long. This is to help you work at your own pace. Even if you don't have time to learn an entire lesson, you can start one and study only part of it, without having the impression you're wasting your time.

Lesson outline

Part A is subdivided into four sections : A1, A2, A3, A4.

A1 : Presentation

The first section introduces the new information (in grammar, vocabulary and pronunciation) you will need to learn and use to make sentences in French.

A2 : Examples

This section, based on the material introduced in A1, presents examples which you should then reconstruct by yourself.

A3 : Comments

Additional comments regarding the sentences in A2 clarify points of grammar, vocabulary or pronunciation.

A4 : Translation

The final section includes the complete translation of part A2.

Part B is subdivided into four sections : B1, B2, B3, B4, and follows the same outline as Part A, adding further explanation to the points of grammar and some new vocabulary.

Part C The four sections C1, C2, C3 and C4 include exercices, practical information and some comments on life in France.

C1 : Exercises
You should use the exercises to verify that the points of grammar learned in Parts A and B are understood.

C2 : Answers
All the correct answers to the exercises of Part C1 are given, so that you can check your work.

C3 and C4 : Practical information and notes on French life civilization
These sections focus on common expressions as well as on information about life and culture in France and the evolution of the French language.

Part D is also subdivided into four section :

D1 - D3 propose a living dialogue using the vocabulary acquired in A and B.

D2 - D4 are devoted either to vocabulary and grammar commentaries, usual expressions, practical facts.
➔ The dialogues start only from lesson 6.

Lessons 10 bis, 20 bis, 30 bis, 40 bis

- Do each series of 10 tests in less than five minutes without referring to the lesson.
- Refer to the corrigé and study the points where you were mistaken.
- GRAMMAR SUMMARY reviews all of the basic grammar points.

The **bilingual glossary** gives you all the vocabulary of part A and B.

Some advice

- **Study on a regular basis**

It is more effective to work at regular intervals, even for a short period of time, than to try to learn several lessons at the same time at widely-separated intervals. Studying for a half hour every day, even if it is only one of the four parts of a lesson, is more effective than skimming over several lessons for three hours every ten days.

- **Programme your efforts**

Work on each lesson in turn, and don't go on to B without having learned and understood A.
This principle applies equally to the different lessons : don't begin a new lesson without having thoroughly understood the previous one.

- **Go back over the lessons**

Don't hesitate to review the lessons you have already learned and repeat the exercises. Make sure you have understood and remember them.

Suggested work method

- **For parts A and B :**

1. After studying A1 (or B1), read the series of sentences in A2 (or B2) several times.
2. Read the comments in A3 (or B3).
3. Go back to A2 (or B2) and translate the sentences into English, without looking at A4 (or B4).
4. Check the accuracy of your translation by reading A4 (or B4).
5. Try to reconstruct the sentences in Part A2 (or B2) starting from A4 (or B4) without looking at A2 (or B2). Then verify your accuracy, and so forth.

- **For part C and D**

1. Each time you can, write out the answers to the exercices in C1 before comparing them to the corrected lesson in C3.
2. Study a lesson until you can:
   – translate A4, B4 and D3 into French without looking at A2, B2, or D1:
   – do all of the exercises in C1 without any errors.

Recording of the book

A recording is the natural audio-oral companion to the book ; it will make it possible for you to practise speaking and comprehension.
The **40 lessons** kit is composed of **2 CDs** recorded in digital sound.
On each of them you will find:
– the whole of parts A2, B2 and D1 (with the symbol).
– a selection of exercices C (with the symbol).

Recording

➡ On the **CD recording** there are **no blanks** for repetition, but using the "pause" key will give you time for repeating. The CDs will help you develop your **listening comprehension**. It also gives you **fast access** to lessons or passages you want to listen again.

1 Regardez là-bas !

A1 PRESENTATION

Grammar

- Imperative

The French imperative form is one of the simplest verbal forms.

The second person plural is used to address either a person you don't know well or several persons.

It usually ends with **ez**.

Regardez !	*Look, look at!*
Regardez Anne !	*Look at Anne!*

Vocabulary

où ?	*where?*
là	*there*
là-bas	*over there*
oui	*yes*
et	*and*

- **Notre-Dame** is the Paris cathedral.
- **Anne, Louis** are first names.

A2 EXAMPLES *(Visiting Paris)* CD

1. **Regardez !**
2. **Louis, regardez !**
3. **Regardez Notre-Dame !**
4. **Où ?**
5. **Là !**
6. **Là-bas ?**
7. **Oui, là-bas !**
8. **Regardez là-bas !**
9. **Anne et Louis, regardez !**
10. **Regardez Notre-Dame, là-bas !**

A3 COMMENTS

Pronunciation

- The French **r** is produced at the back of the mouth as if gargling.
- The nearest English equivalent to **e** in **regardez** is *e* in *open*, with lips slightly rounded.
- **ez (regardez)** and **et** have the sound of: *A* in *A B C*.
- **a** or **à** is pronounced like *a* in *father*.
- **o** is pronounced like *o* in *not* **(Notre-Dame).**
- **ou** is pronounced like *oo* in *cool.*
- **oui** is pronounced like *we.*
- The final **e** is silent **(Anne, Notre-Dame).**

⟶ Final consonants are not usually pronounced in French: **Pari(s), Loui(s), ba(s).**

Grammar

⟶ Note that the object following **Regardez !** is not introduced by any preposition: **Regardez Notre-Dame !** *Look* ***at*** *Notre-Dame!*

A4 TRANSLATION

1. Look!
2. Louis, look!
3. Look at Notre-Dame!
4. Where?
5. There!
6. Over there?
7. Yes, over there!
8. Look over there!
9. Anne and Louis, look!
10. Look at Notre-Dame, over there!

1 Hélène, reste ici !

B1 PRESENTATION

Grammar

imperative	singular	plural
2nd person	**reste / regarde** *stay / look*	**restez / regardez** *stay / look*

- When speaking to a relative, a friend, or someone you know well, use the second form singular of the imperative:
  Ex.: **regarde !** *look!* **reste !** *stay!*

Vocabulary

reste ! *stay!*
à côté de *beside*
ici *here*
s'il te plaît *please* (to a person you know well)
s'il vous plaît *please* (to a person you don't know well)
merci *thank you*

Hélène is a feminine first name.

B2 EXAMPLES *(Taking a photograph)* CD

1. **Hélène, reste ici !**
2. **Anne, reste là !**
3. **Reste là, s'il te plaît !**
4. **Hélène, reste à côté de Louis !**
5. **Hélène et Anne, restez là !**
6. **Hélène, regarde Louis !**
7. **Regarde Louis, s'il te plaît !**
8. **Anne et Hélène, regardez Louis !**
9. **Regardez Louis, s'il vous plaît !**
10. **Merci.**

B3 COMMENTS

Grammar

- Remember: the second person plural is used to address either a person you don't know well or several persons (see lesson 1, A1).
- Remember to say:

s'il te plaît	to a person you know well.
s'il vous plaît	to several persons or to a person you don't know well.

Pronunciation

- in **reste** or **restez**, the first **e** is pronounced like *e* in *pet.*
- **ai** has the sound of *A* in *A B C* : **plaît**.
- **i** has the sound of *ee* in *see* : **ici**.
- **o** in **côté** is pronounced like **o** in *note.*
- in **merci, er** is pronounced like *air.*
- **c** followed by **e** or **i** is pronounced like *s* in *set* : **merci**.
- **h** is always silent when it is the first letter of a word.

B4 TRANSLATION

1. Hélène, stay here!
2. Anne, stay there!
3. Stay there, please!
4. Hélène, stay beside Louis!
5. Hélène and Anne, stay there!
6. Hélène, look at Louis!
7. Look at Louis, please!
8. Anne and Hélène, look at Louis!
9. Look at Louis, please!
10. Thank you.

1 Exercises

C1 EXERCISES

A. Put the verb in the imperative form :

1. Anne, (regarder) ! (You know Anne very well.)
2. Anne et Hélène, (rester) là !
3. Hélène, (regarder) Louis ! (You don't know Hélène well.)
4. Louis, (rester) là ! (Louis is a relative.).

B. (CD) You know all of them very well :

1. Tell Anne to stay beside Louis.
2. Tell Louis and Hélène to look at Anne.
3. Tell Anne to look over there.
4. Tell Hélène to look at Anne.

C2 ANSWERS

A. 1. Anne, regarde !
2. Anne et Hélène, restez là !
3. Hélène, regardez Louis !
4. Louis, reste là !

B. 1. Anne, reste à côté de Louis !
2. Louis et Hélène, regardez Anne !
3. Anne, regarde là-bas !
4. Hélène, regarde Anne.

C3 VERBS

Imperative		Infinitive	
regarde/regardez !	*look !*	**regarder**	*to look (at)*
reste/restez !	*stay !*	**rester**	*to stay*

• **er** is the ending of the infinitive of a great number of verbs. They all belong to the same group and are conjugated the same way.

• **er** is pronounced like *A* in *A B C.*

C4 OUR ANCESTORS : THE GAULS

• **Gallia** is the name the Romans gave to the region bordered by the Rhine River to the north, the Alps to the east, the Mediterranean and the Pyrenees to the south, and the Atlantic Ocean to the west. It was originally inhabited by the Celts, who were of Indo-European origin. Celt society was divided into three orders : druids, warriors and common people. The Greek colonization that followed began at the Rhone River delta and extended to the shores of the Mediterranean, and numerous cities such as Massalia (**Marseilles**) and Nikaia (**Nice**) came into existence at that period. In the second century BC, the conquering Romans established a "Roman Province" in the vicinity of **Narbonne** and, little by little, some one hundred different peoples were unified into tribes. The total population of Gaul at that time is estimated at between five and thirteen million inhabitants.

• The Gauls, who were good farmers, propagated viniculture, invented the barrel, drank barley beer, produced pork products, and shod their horses. They were skilled craftsmen who worked with metal and leather as well as with wood. They were also fearless warriors. However, since they lacked any political institutions to bind them together, there was constant warfare among the various tribes. Each of these elected a military chief or king from among the nobles.

• The only thing that united the peoples of the different tribes was religion. The druids were invested with a triple religious, pedagogical and political role. The Gauls practiced the worship of natural phenomena and the adoration of the gods ; their most important ceremony involved the harvest of the mistletoe growing in oak trees, which symbolized the immortality the soul.

• In 52 BC, Julius Caesar crushed the revolt of the tribes led by **Vercingétorix** and increasingly romanized Gaul by encouraging urbanism. Several cities such as **Orange, Autun** and **Troyes** today bear traces of the period in basilicas, thermal baths, triumphal arches, theaters, and aqueducts.

• An astute policy of assimilation was pursued, and after the Edict of Caracalla in 212 AD, the free Gauls became full-fledged citizens, speaking the Latin of their conquerors.

1 D1 Map of France

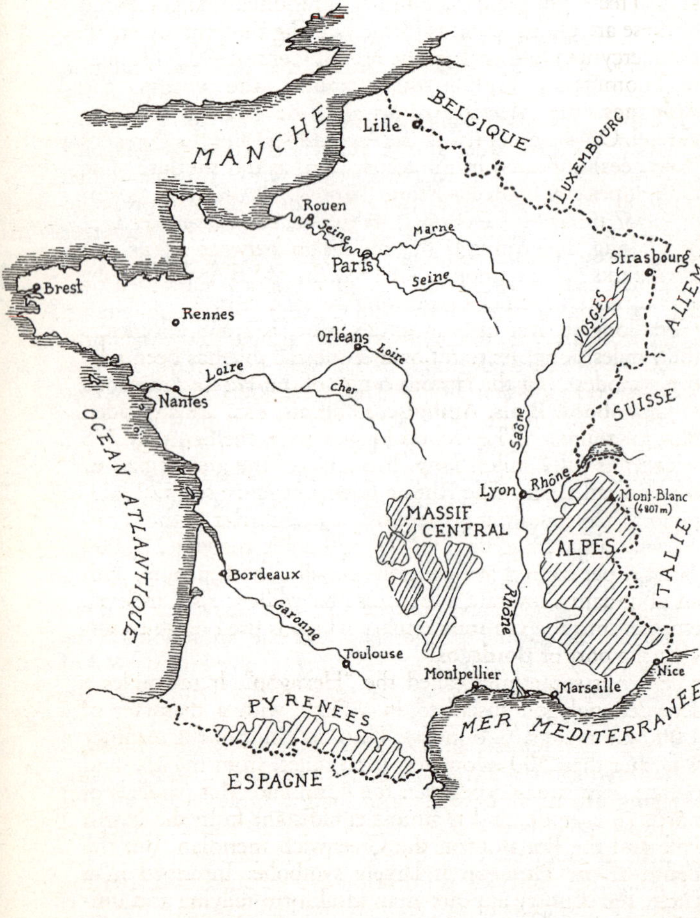

D2 FRANCE

• France covers an area of 551,695 square kilometers (213,000 square miles).
• The average altitude in continental France is 342 meters (1,120 feet), but there is a number of mountain ranges. Some of these are old mountains formed during the primary era of the Hercynian fold such as the **Massif Central** (90,000 square kilometers ; 35,000 square miles), the **Vosges**, the **Ardennes**, the **Massif Armoricain**, the **Maures** and the **Estérel**. On the other hand, the Alps (**Alpes**) and the Pyrenees (**Pyrénées**) appeared in the tertiary era, as did the **Jura**. The highest peak in France is **Mont Blanc** which reaches a height of 4,807 meters (15,770 feet). A tunnel 11.6 kilometer (7.2 mile) long dug through the mountain between 1959 and 1965 links the Chamonix Valley to the **Val d'Aoste** in Italy, and 21 million vehicles go through it each year.
• The longest river in France, the **Loire**, is 1,008 kilometers (626 miles) long. Its traditional economic role has been relatively modest, but the famous castles of the ***Val-de-Loire*** such as **Chambord, Blois, Amboise, Langeais**, etc., are a decided plus for tourism. The second longest river, the **Seine**, is 776 kilometers (482 miles) long. It drains off the greater part of the Parisian Basin. The **Rhône** flows in France for 520 kilometers (323 miles) ; it is the most powerful river of the country with an average flow rate of 820 cubic meters (217,000 gallons) per second at **Beaucaire**. Finally, the **Garonne**, with an abundant flow rate and occasional violent rises in level, empties into the **Gironde** estuary which is used by ships serving the port of **Bordeaux**.
• France is sometimes called the "Hexagon". It resembles a six-sided polygon inscribed in a circle with a diameter of 1,000 kilometers (620 miles). Thus no point of the territory is farther than 500 kilometers (310 miles) from the seas and oceans. It is situated between the 42nd and 51st parallels of northern latitude, and is almost equidistant from the North Pole and the Equator, on the Greenwich meridian. But the figure of the Hexagon is largely symbolic. Inscribed in a circle, the country appears as an ideal form rallying and unifying the French on a land with a regular outline.

2 N'écoute pas Antoine !

A1 PRESENTATION

■ Grammar

ne reste pas / **ne restez pas**	→ *don't stay*

• The negative of the imperative is formed with: (CD)

ne ... pas *do not, don't ;*
n' ... pas (with verbs starting with a vowel or **h**),

on either side of the verb.

■ Vocabulary

écouter *to listen / to listen to*
chanter *to sing*
ne... pas encore *don't... yet*
maintenant *now*

Antoine is a masculine first name.

A2 EXAMPLES *(On the stage, before the show)* (CD)

1. **Reste ici !**
2. **Ne reste pas là !**
3. **Restez ici, s'il vous plaît !**
4. **Ne restez pas là !**
5. **Hélène, écoute, s'il te plaît !**
6. **N'écoute pas Antoine !**
7. **Hélène et Anne, écoutez, s'il vous plaît !**
8. **Ne chantez pas !**
9. **Ne chantez pas maintenant !**
10. **Ne chantez pas encore !**

2 Don't listen to Antoine!

A3 COMMENTS

■ Grammar: negative imperative

singular	**ne reste pas**	*don't stay*
plural	**ne restez pas**	
singular	**n'écoute pas**	*don't listen*
plural	**n'écoutez pas**	

■ Pronunciation

- **an / en :** two spellings for one sound **(chantez, encore).** This nasal vowel doesn't exist in English. The nearest English equivalent is the vowel sound in *swan* (without pronouncing the **n**).
- **ain :** the nearest equivalent is *an* in *bang* (without pronouncing the **ng**). Ex.: **maintenant.**
- **oi** is pronounced like *wo* in *won.* Ex.: **Antoine.**
- **ch** in **chante** is pronounced like *sh* in *shoe.*
- **c + a, o, u** is pronounced like *c* in *car* **(encore, écoutez).**

A4 TRANSLATION

1. Stay here!
2. Don't stay there!
3. Stay here, please!
4. Don't stay there!
5. Hélène, listen, please!
6. Don't listen to Antoine!
7. Hélène and Anne, listen, please!
8. Don't sing!
9. Don't sing now!
10. Don't sing yet!

2 Parlons français ensemble.

B1 PRESENTATION

■ Grammar

- The first person plural of the imperative always ends with: **-ons**.

reste	*stay*
restons	*let's stay*
restez	*stay*

■ Vocabulary

parler *to speak*
français *French*
ensemble *together*
ou *or*
avec *with*

B2 EXAMPLES *(To speak or not to speak)* CD

1. **Parlons français.**
2. **Parlons français ensemble.**
3. **Parlons avec Anne ou Louis.**
4. **Parlons français avec Anne ou Louis.**
5. **Restons ensemble.**
6. **Ne restons pas ici.**
7. **Ne parlons pas ici.**
8. **Ne parlons pas maintenant.**
9. **Chantons !**
10. **Chantons ensemble !**

B3 COMMENTS

Pronunciation

- **on**, in **restons,** is a nasal vowel. The nearest vowel sound in English is the *o* in *long* (without pronouncing the *ng*).
- **em** is pronounced like **en (ensemble).**
- **ç** + vowel is pronounced like *s* in *set* **(français).**
- in **avec**, the final **c** is heard; it is pronounced like *k* in *deck*.
- **s** between a vowel and a consonant is pronounced like *s* in *set* **(dansons, ensemble).**

Remember

où = *where* but ⟶ **ou** = *or*.

B4 TRANSLATION

1. Let's speak French.
2. Let's speak French together.
3. Let's speak with Anne or Louis.
4. Let's speak French with Anne or Louis.
5. Let's stay together.
6. Let's not stay here.
7. Let's not speak here.
8. Let's not speak now.
9. Let's sing!
10. Let's sing together!

C1 EXERCISES

A. (CD) **Giving orders (in French) :**

1. Tell Anne and Louis to sing together.
2. Tell Antoine not to listen.
3. Tell Hélène and Anne to listen.
4. Tell Hélène not to look yet.
5. Tell Louis and Anne not to sing.

B. (CD) **Turn into the first person plural :**

1. Regardez !
2. Reste !
3. Écoute !
4. Parlez !

C. (CD) **Translate into French :**

1. Let's stay here !
2. Let's not speak !
3. Let's look over there !

C2 ANSWERS

A. 1 Chantez ensemble !
2. N'écoute pas !
3. Écoutez !
4. Ne regarde pas encore !
5. Ne chantez pas !

B. 1. Regardons !
2. Restons !
3. Écoutons !
4. Parlons !

C. 1. Restons ici !
2. Ne parlons pas !
3. Regardons là-bas !

C3 THE DEPARTMENTS

• From **Ain** to **Val d'Oise**, metropolitan France includes 95 departments, which are the main administrative districts of the country. Departments are often identified by a number corresponding to their place on the alphabetical list (with the exception of those of the Paris region which were created more recently). The numbers on license plates include the number of the department in which the vehicle is registered, indicated by the last two numbers of the plate.

• Departments were created by decree in 1790. They were conceived of as areas that would be small enough to maintain a human dimension : one day on horseback was supposed to suffice to reach the county town (today called préfecture).

In each department, power is shared between the General Council (**Conseil Général**) elected for six years by universal suffrage and the Prefect (**Préfet**), a high-ranking civil servant who is appointedby the Council of Ministers.

THE HIT PARADE OF THE DEPARTMENTS :

• The largest outside of metropolitan France : **Guyane**

• The largest in metropolitan France : **Gironde**

• The smallest : **Paris**

• The one with the most inhabitants : **Nord**

• The one with the fewest inhabitants : **Lozère**

• The one with the greatest population density : **Paris**

• The one with the least population density : **Lozère**

2 D1 Map of "départements"

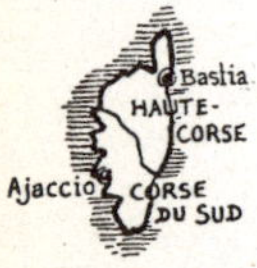

2 D2 The "départements"

01	Ain
02	Aisne
03	Allier
04	Alpes-de-Haute-Provence
05	Hautes-Alpes
06	Alpes-Maritimes
07	Ardèche
08	Ardennes
09	Ariège
10	Aube
11	Aude
12	Aveyron
13	Bouches-du-Rhône
14	Calvados
15	Cantal
16	Charente
17	Charente-Maritime
18	Cher
19	Corrèze
2A	Corse du sud
2B	Haute-Corse
21	Côte-d'Or
22	Côtes-du-Nord
23	Creuse
24	Dordogne
25	Doubs
26	Drôme
27	Eure
28	Eure-et-Loir
29	Finistère
30	Gard
31	Haute-Garonne
32	Gers
33	Gironde
34	Hérault
35	Ille-et-Vilaine
36	Indre
37	Indre-et-Loire
38	Isère
39	Jura
40	Landes
41	Loir-et-Cher
42	Loire
43	Haute-Loire
44	Loire-Atlantique
45	Loiret
46	Lot
47	Lot-et-Garonne
48	Lozère
49	Maine-et-Loire
50	Manche
51	Marne
52	Haute-Marne
53	Mayenne
54	Meurthe-et-Moselle
55	Meuse
56	Morbihan
57	Moselle
58	Nièvre
59	Nord
60	Oise
61	Orne
62	Pas-de-Calais
63	Puy-de-Dôme
64	Pyrénées-Atlantiques
65	Hautes-Pyrénées
66	Pyrénées-Orientales
67	Bas-Rhin
68	Haut-Rhin
69	Rhône
70	Haute-Saône
71	Saône-et-Loire
72	Sarthe
73	Savoie
74	Haute-Savoie
75	Paris (Ville de)
76	Seine-Maritime
77	Seine-et-Marne
78	Yvelines
79	Deux-Sèvres
80	Somme
81	Tarn
82	Tarn-et-Garonne
83	Var
84	Vaucluse
85	Vendée
86	Vienne
87	Haute-Vienne
88	Vosges
89	Yonne
90	Belfort (Territoire de)
91	Essonne
92	Hauts-de-Seine
93	Seine-Saint-Denis
94	Val-de-Marne
95	Val-d'Oise
971	Guadeloupe
972	Martinique
973	Guyane
974	Réunion
975	Saint-Pierre-et-Miquelon

3 J'habite Nice.

A1 PRESENTATION

Grammar

- Personal pronouns: subject / singular

je, j' (1st person)	**tu** (2nd person, used to address close friends, relatives, children)
I	*you*

- **je** becomes **j'** when preceding a vowel or **h**:
  j'habite..., *I live in...*
- **Present tense**
  In French, the endings of verbs vary according to the person and number of the subject:
  Je parle. *I speak.*
  Tu parles. *You speak.*

Vocabulary

habiter *to live in*
allemand *German*
italien *Italian*
anglais *English*
bonjour *good morning / good afternoon*
non *no*
en *in*

Nice is a French town on the Riviera.

A2 EXAMPLES *(Places and languages)* (CD)

1. **Bonjour !**
2. **J'habite en France.**
3. **J'habite Nice.**
4. **Je parle français et italien.**
5. **Tu parles allemand ?**
6. **Non.**
7. **Non, je ne parle pas allemand.**
8. **Tu parles anglais ?**
9. **Oui.**
10. **Oui, je parle français et anglais.**

A3 COMMENTS

Pronunciation

- **j** is pronounced like *su* in *pleasure* (ex.: **je, bonjour**).
- The sound of **u** in **tu** doesn't exist in English. It is pronounced like the double *ee* of *cheers* said with pursed lips.

Grammar

- In spoken French, the simplest way to turn a statement into a question is to modify the intonation into a rising one.
  Ex.: **Tu parles allemand ?** — *Do you speak German?*
- **oui, non** are often used alone.
  Ex.: **Tu parles anglais ? — Oui.**
  Do you speak English? — Yes, I do.
- Remember in the negative, **ne** and **pas** are used on either side of the verb (see lesson A2, 7).
- In French, adjectives referring to nationality are not capitalized.
  Je parle italien. *I speak Italian.*

A4 TRANSLATION

1. Good morning!
2. I live in France.
3. I live in Nice.
4. I speak French and Italian.
5. Do you speak German?
6. No, I don't.
7. No, I don't speak German.
8. Do you speak English?
9. Yes, I do.
10. Yes, I speak French and English.

3 Nous visitons Paris.

B1 PRESENTATION

■ Grammar

- Personal pronouns subjects plural.

nous (1st person plural)	**vous**	for both singular and plural subjects (like *you* in English)
we	*you*	

- Present tense:

nous parlons	*we speak*
vous parlez	*you speak*

⟶ In French, the present tense conveys the meanings of both the English simple present and progressive present. In other words:

je parle ⟶ *I speak* / *I am speaking*

■ Vocabulary

aimer bien	*to like*
visiter	*to visit*
trouver	*to think, to find*
très	*very*
bien	*well*
aussi	*too*

boulevard Saint-Germain	(a well-known Left-Bank boulevard)
Saint-Germain-des-Prés	(*Saint-Germain-in-the-fields*, part of the Paris Latin Quarter)

B2 EXAMPLES *(Living in Paris)* (CD)

1. **Nous visitons Paris.**
2. **Vous visitez Paris aussi ?**
3. **Non, nous habitons ici.**
4. **Nous habitons boulevard Saint-Germain.**
5. **Vous habitez près de Saint-Germain-des-Prés ?**
6. **Oui, très près.**
7. **Vous parlez très bien français !**
8. **Vous trouvez ? Merci !**
9. **Vous aimez bien Paris ?**
10. **Oui, nous aimons bien Paris.**

B3 COMMENTS

Pronunciation

- **o, au** : two spellings for one sound pronounced like *o* in *note* **(aussi, côté).**
- **ien** in **bien** is pronounced like *y* in *yes* followed by the sound of *an* in *bang.*
- **g** before **e** and **i** is pronounced like *j* **(Germain)**.
- **s** between two vowels is pronounced like *z* in *zoo* **(visiter)**.
- **ss** between two vowels is pronounced like *s* in *set* **(aussi)**.

Grammar

- Rappel : **Vous aimez bien Paris ?** *Do you like Paris?*
  A rising tone turns a statement into a question.

B4 TRANSLATION

1. We are visiting Paris.
2. Are you visiting Paris too?
3. No, we live here.
4. We live on boulevard Saint-Germain.
5. Do you live near Saint-Germain-des-Prés?
6. Yes, very near.
7. You speak French very well!
8. You think so? Thank you!
9. Do you like Paris?
10. Yes, we like Paris.

3 Exercices

C1 EXERCISES

A. **Match the pronouns with the verbs :**
je, j', tu, nous, vous ;
regarde - visitez - chantons - habite - regardes - écoutons - parlez

B. **Put the verb between brackets in the correct form :**
1. Nous (habiter) là bas.
2. Je (rester) ici.
3. Vous (danser) ?
4. Tu (regarder) Louis.

C. **Turn the sentences into the negative :**
(using **ne… pas** or **n'…pas**)

D. (CD) **Translate into French :**
1. We are looking at Anne.
2. You are not singing together.
3. I speak Italian and French.
4. I'm visiting Paris too.

C2 ANSWERS

A. Je regarde - J'habite - Tu regardes - Nous chantons
Nous écoutons - Vous visitez - Vous parlez.

B. 1. Nous habitons là-bas.
2. Je reste ici.
3. Vous dansez,
4. Tu regardes Louis.

C. 1. Nous n'habitons pas là-bas.
2. Je ne reste pas ici.
3. Vous ne dansez pas ?
4. Tu ne regardes par Louis.

D. 1. Nous regardons Anne.
2. Vous ne chantez pas ensemble.
3. Je parle italien et français.
4. Je visite Paris aussi.

C4 THE ORIGINS OF THE FRENCH LANGUAGE

■ Although place-names often retain a Gallic imprint (**Lyon** and **Verdun** are Gallic names), French did not evolve from a Celtic language. It is first and foremost an evolution of Latin which definitively overcame its rivals around the second century. Scholarly terms, especially, have Latin roots. French was also enriched by contact with neighboring tongues. A variety of Germanic words was added to the layers of Celtic and Latin of the Roman vocabulary. This is due to the presence, starting in the second century, of Franks and Alemanni in the northern and eastern parts of the country. This influence can particularly be seen in the vocabulary linked to warfare, in the pronunciation or the use of what is called an aspirate « h » (as in **hanche**), or in grammar with the adjective placed before the noun (as in **Neufchâtel**).

■ Under the reign of **Charlemagne**, there was a revival of Latin culture. All members of the clergy once again learned the Latin of the Church, which forms the basis for religious and philosophic vocabulary in French.

■ Nonetheless, the Old French of the Middle Ages was still divided into distinct dialects (Picard, Normand, Champenois, etc.) that differed from one another both in pronunciation and in vocabulary. It was finally the **Langue d'oïl**, from the northern part of France, that would become French, even if the **Langue d'oc**, which was more latinized, also played an important role. In the 16th century, with the Edict of **Villers-Cotterets**, **François I** decreed that from then on all administrative texts would be published in French, instead of Latin. This was a milestone : French became the language of the state.

■ At the end of the 17th century, French was also the language of the cultivated European elite. Theaters popularized the works of **Molière**. As a vector of communication, the French of the period integrated foreign expressions but remained faithful to a classical version of the language, even under the French Revolution. At that period, only one Frenchman in ten spoke French fluently, and the abolition of provincial dialects was envisaged. But it was largely due to the spread of schools in the 19th century that French came to be spoken by the working classes and in rural areas. Today, in spite of having borrowed numerous terms from English, French remains faithful to its Latin origins and to its talent for assimilation.

D1 Map of French "regions"

D2 ATTRACTIVE REGIONS

■ The different French regions, with their rich and varied architectural and cultural heritage, and the vastly diverse coasts and the "white gold" of the mountains are veritable poles of tourist attraction.

■ The Loire country appeals to roving travelers because it provides the greatest concentration of Renaissance castles in the world, such as **Chambord** and **Chenonceau. Bourgogne** combines the interest of its Romanesque architecture as seen in **Vézelay** and **Cluny**, with the allure of its famous gastronomy. In Provence, the cities of **Avignon**, **Arles** and **Aix-en-Provence** are famous for their theater and music festivals. The medieval monastery of **Mont-Saint-Michel** in Normandy receives more than one million visitors a year.

■ France has the unique advantage in Europe of having a lengthy coastline, and each of its coastal regions has a specific appearance and clientele. The Opal Coast is the summer destination of those who live in the north of the country, as well as of tourists from Belgium and Great Britain. Seaside resorts in Normandy draw Parisians each weekend and tourists from all over the world in the summertime. The south of Brittany particularly appeals to families because of its varied scenery and its temperate climate. **Vendée** and **Charentes**, which are very sunny, have seen an increase in housing development and campgrounds. And the prestigious resorts of the **Basque** country such as **Biarritz**, or the Riviera with **Nice** and **Cannes**, are known all over the world.

■ The mountains draw tourists both in summer and in winter. The **Arcs** and **Val d'Isère** in **Savoie**, with their vast network of trails and snow cover six months out of the year, are world ski capitals.

■ An additional advantage is that the majority of the French regions possess an excellent hotel and restaurant network. The French Secretariat of Tourism has divided hotels into five categories from one to four stars and luxury, according to the facilities and comfort they offer. The number of vacation villages and youth hostels is growing, and it is frequently possible to stay with the locals for a very attractive price.

4 Ils visitent Paris aujourd'hui.

A1 PRESENTATION

Grammar

- Personal pronouns subject : 3rd person

	masculine	feminine
singular	**il** *(he, it)*	**elle** *(she, it)*
plural	**ils** *(they)*	**elles** *(they)*

Ex.: **il parle,** *he speaks* **elle parle,** *she speaks*
ils parlent, *they speak* **elles parlent,** *they speak*

Pronunciation

- In **il** and **ils**, the **l** is heard.
- In **elle** and **elles**, the first **e** is pronounced like **è**, the last one is glided over.
- Note that **-e/ -es/ -ent**, verb endings of the present tense, are all considered like a final **e** and are therefore silent.

Vocabulary

aimer *to love*
voyager *to travel*
aujourd'hui *today*
souvent *often*
parfois *sometimes*
mais *but*

Agnès and **Philippe** are first names.

A2 EXAMPLES *(Travelling)* (CD)

1. **Agnès et Philippe habitent en Angleterre.**
2. **Ils habitent ensemble.**
3. **Elle voyage souvent.**
4. **Il voyage souvent aussi.**
5. **Ils ne restent pas souvent ici.**
6. **Ils voyagent parfois ensemble.**
7. **Il parle très bien français, mais il ne parle pas espagnol.**
8. **Elle parle anglais.**
9. **Ils visitent Paris aujourd'hui.**
10. **Elle aime Paris.**

4 They are visiting Paris today.

A3 COMMENTS

Grammar

- Verbs ending in **er** in the infinitive have the same conjugation:

aimer	*to love*	**rester**	*to stay*	**écouter**	*to listen*
parler	*to speak*	**danser**	*to dance*	**visiter**	*to visit*
habiter	*to live*	**chanter**	*to sing*	**voyager**	*to travel*

They belong to the 1st group. Present tense:

singular			plural	
je parle	*I*	*speak*	**nous parlons**	*we speak*
tu parles	*you*	*speak*	**vous parlez**	*you speak*
il, elle, parle	*he, she, it*	*speaks*	**ils, elles, parlent**	*they speak*

- When there are several subjects and at least one of them is masculine, the pronoun is always: **ils**.
  Ex.: **Anne et Louis parlent français = ils parlent français.**

Pronunciation

- Note that **oy** in **voyage** is pronounced like **oi** + the sound of *y* in *yes*.
- Remember: **en** in **souvent** is a nasal sound which does not exist in English. The nearest equivalent is the vowel sound in *swan* (without pronouncing the *n*).

A4 TRANSLATION

1. Agnès and Philippe live in England.
2. They live together.
3. She often travels.
4. He often travels too.
5. They don't often stay here.
6. They sometimes travel together.
7. He speaks French very well, but he doesn't speak Spanish.
8. She speaks English.
9. They are visiting Paris today.
10. She loves Paris.

4 On arrive demain.

B1 PRESENTATION

Grammar

- **on**

  In conjugation, **on** is considered as a 3rd person singular.
  In colloquial French, **on** is often used instead of **nous**.

  Ex. : **On habite ici.** *We live here.*

Vocabulary

arriver	*to come / to arrive*
déjeuner	*to have lunch*
demain	*tomorrow*
dix heures	*ten o'clock*
du matin (see C4)	*a.m.*
midi	*noon*
après	*after*

B2 EXAMPLES *(Arrival)* (CD)

1. **On arrive !**
2. **On arrive demain.**
3. **On arrive demain à dix heures.**
4. **On arrive demain à dix heures du matin.**
5. **On déjeune ensemble.**
6. **On déjeune ensemble à midi.**
7. **On visite Paris demain après-midi.**
8. **On ne visite pas Notre-Dame.**
9. **On ne parle pas très bien français.**
10. **On ne parle pas encore très bien.**

B3 COMMENTS

Grammar

- The present can be used to express a future action when a word in the sentence indicates the future.

  Ex.: **On arrive demain.** *We are coming tomorrow.*

Expressions

- **À dix heures du matin :** see C4, p. 33.

Pronunciation

- **jeu** in **déjeune** is pronounced like **je.**
- Note the liaisons:

  on arrive (n) **dix heures** (z)

- Remember: the sound in **on** is the sound of a nasal vowel. The nearest vowel sound in English is the *o* in *long* (without pronouncing the *ng*).
- Remember: the nearest English equivalent of **ain** in **demain** is the sound of *an* in *bang* (without pronouncing the *ng*).

B4 TRANSLATION

1. We are coming!
2. We are coming tomorrow.
3. We are coming tomorrow at ten o'clock.
4. We are coming tomorrow at ten a.m.
5. We are having lunch together.
6. We are having lunch together at twelve.
7. We are visiting Paris tomorrow afternoon.
8. We are not visiting Notre-Dame.
9. We don't speak French very well.
10. We don't speak very well yet.

C1 EXERCISES

A. Choose the correct form :

1. Il (parlons, parles, parle) français.
2. Elles (visitent, visitez, visites) Nice.
3. Elle ne (voyages, voyagent, voyage) pas souvent.
4. Ils (aimons, aimes, aiment) Paris.

B. (CD) **Use <u>ils</u> or <u>elles</u> to replace the names :**

1. Antoine et Louis habitent Paris.
2. Agnès et Philippe ne parlent pas espagnol.
3. Hélène et Agnès arrivent demain.
4. Hélène, Agnès et Antoine déjeunent ensemble.

C2 ANSWERS

A. 1. Il parle français.
2. Elles visitent Nice.
3. Elle ne voyage pas souvent.
4. Ils aiment Paris.

B. 1. Ils habitent Paris.
2. Ils ne parlent pas espagnol.
3. Elles arrivent demain.
4. Ils déjeunent ensemble.

C3 NOMBRES/ *NUMBERS* (see also lesson 6, C4) (CD)

un	**deux**	**trois**	**quatre**	**cinq**	**six**	**sept**	**huit**	**neuf**	**dix**	**onze**	**douze**
1	**2**	**3**	**4**	**5**	**6**	**7**	**8**	**9**	**10**	**11**	**12**

→ Note that :

- **sept** is pronounced like *set.*
- **ui** has nearly the sound of *we* with tightened lips (**huit**).
- The sound **eu** in **neuf, heure,** is pronounced like *ur* in *hurt.*
- In **cinq, huit, neuf,** the final consonant is pronounced.
- In **six, dix** the final **x** is pronounced like *s* in *set.*

C4 THE SYMBOLS OF FRANCE

■ **The cock** is the symbol of vigilance, and of the French, no doubt because of the Latin word **Gallus** which means both cock and Gaul. It is often found as a weathervane on church belfries. Since 1848, it appears on the seal of the French Republic : Liberty holds a helm adorned with a cock. Starting in 1899, the cock also appeared on the 20-franc gold piece. Today, it is also frequently seen as the emblem of France in international sports competition.

■ **The French tricolor flag** has, since July 17th, 1789, symbolized the union of the crown and the people : white was the color of the royal standard while blue and red appeared in the coat of arms of the city of Paris. This choice was legally consecrated in 1793.

As time went by, the flag would undergo several modifications. The royal eagle which appeared on the pole was replaced during the Restoration (1815-1830) by the royal fleur-de-lis, then made a come-back in 1852, replacing the symbols of the Republic. Since 1871, the pole has been topped by a copper plaque sometimes adorned with a low relief decoration bearing the initials RF, for **République Française**. In the middle, white section of the flag, supplementary symbols have on occasion been added. This was the case of the **Vichy** emblem under **Pétain** (1940-1944) or of the Lorraine Cross, sometimes presented in the shape of a V, the symbol of those rallying to the cause of **Général de Gaulle.**

■ **The Marseillaise** was composed in 1792 by Captain **Rouget de Lisle.** A battalion of soldiers from Marseille marched into Paris singing it on July 30th, 1792. The **Marseillaise** became the symbol of revolutionary France, representing the opposition to the princes and rulers of Europe gathered to support the monarchy. In 1795, after the Republican battles at **Valmy** and **Fleurus**, the **Convention** declared it the national anthem.

In 1915, the president of the Republic, **Raymond Poincaré**, wrote about it : "Everywhere it resounds, the Marseillaise evokes the idea of a sovereign nation with a passion for independence whose sons all make a deliberate choice : liberty or death."

4 Map of "Dom-Tom"

D2 THE DOM-TOM

■ The overseas departments (the DOM, **Départements d'outre mer**) and the overseas territories (TOM, **Territoires d'outre-mer**), are left over « dust » from the French colonial empire which covers 120,000 square kilometers (45,000 square miles) and has a population of over two million inhabitants. They are scattered across all latitudes, throughout the world's oceans, and encompass a variety of geographical reliefs and climates : from the frigid ice fields of **Adélie** to the lunar summits of the **Fournaise** in **Guadeloupe**, from the jungles of French Guyana to the lichen-covered rocks of **Saint-Pierre-et-Miquelon.**

■ Three main groups can nonetheless be distinguished :

• the Antilles of the Caribbean : Guadeloupe, Martinique, Saint-Martin, and a small part of the Amazonian forest, French Guyana. Kourou, in the DOM of French Guyana, lends itself particularly well to the launching of satellites into orbit and is well known as the departure base for Ariane IV and Ariane V.

• the Pacific Islands : New Caledonia, French Polynesia, Wallis and Futuna.

• on the Antarctic continent : **Terre Adélie** and the western islands of **Saint-Paul**, **Kerguelen**, **Crozet** and New Amsterdam.

■ France's other possessions are scattered throughout the Atlantic Ocean (**Saint Pierre-et-Miquelon**) and the Indian Ocean (**Réunion, Mayotte**).

These overseas territories make it possible for France to have at its disposal a flourishing maritime domain rich in fishing resources.

■ However, in spite of important subsidies from metropolitan France, these territories and domains face difficulties, partially due to the destabilization of traditional societies. These tropical paradises are today fighting a battle against the decline of agriculture, the difficulties of scholarization, the consequences of a high birth rate, unemployment, and confrontations between different ethnic groups.

5 Tu vas trop vite !

A1 PRESENTATION

■ Grammar

• **aller** *(to go)* is an irregular verb. Present tense:

		simple present		progressive present
je	**vais**	*I*	*go*	*am going*
tu	**vas**	*you*	*go*	*are going*
il, elle	**va**	*he, she, it*	*goes*	*is going*
nous	**allons**	*we*	*go*	*are going*
vous	**allez**	*you*	*go*	*are going*
ils, elles	**vont**	*they*	*go*	*are going*

■ Vocabulary

monsieur (M.) *Mr.*
madame (Mme) *Mrs.*
trop *too*
vite *fast*
loin *far*
à *to*
toujours *always*

Tours is a town on the **Loire** river.

A2 EXAMPLES *(Going places)* (CD)

1. **Je vais à Tours.**
2. **Je vais souvent à Tours.**
3. **Tu vas trop vite !**
4. **Il ne va pas à Paris.**
5. **Ils vont souvent à Paris.**
6. **On ne va pas souvent à Rome.**
7. **Nous allons parfois à Paris.**
8. **Vous allez à Rome ?**
9. **Vous allez loin ?**
10. **M. et Mme Martin ne vont pas loin.**
11. **Ils vont à Nice.**
12. **Ils vont toujours à Nice.**

A3 COMMENTS

Grammar

- Adverbs indicating frequency like **parfois, souvent, toujours** are usually placed after the verb in the affirmative or after **pas** in the negative. Ex.:
  Je vais souvent en Allemagne. *I often go to Germany.*
  On ne va pas souvent à Rome. *We don't often go to Rome.*
  On va parfois à Paris. *We sometimes go to Paris.*
- Remember: in French, the present tense conveys the meanings of both the English simple present and progressive present.

Pronunciation

- **oin** is pronounced like *w* (in *west)* followed by the French nasal vowel **in (loin).**
- **ain, in:** two spellings for one sound **(maintenant, Martin).** (See lesson 2, A3.)

A4 TRANSLATION

1. I'm going to Tours.
2. I often go to Tours.
3. You are going too fast!
4. He isn't going to Paris.
5. They often go to Paris.
6. We don't often go to Rome.
7. We sometimes go to Paris.
8. Are you going to Rome?
9. Are you going far?
10. Mr. and Mrs. Martin are not going far.
11. They are going to Nice.
12. They always go to Nice.

5 Mlle Smith va travailler en France.

B1 PRESENTATION

Grammar

- **Aller,** followed by a verb in the infinitive, expresses either an intention or the immediate future. It is the French equivalent of *to be going to.*

Ex.:

je	**vais**	**rester**	*I*	*am*	*going to stay*
tu	**vas**	**travailler**	*you*	*are*	*going to work*
nous	**allons**	**parler**	*we*	*are*	*going to speak*

Vocabulary

travailler	*to work*
mademoiselle (Mlle)	*Miss*
octobre	*October*
décembre	*December*
juillet	*July*
bientôt	*soon*
puis	*then*

B2 EXAMPLES *(Plans)* CD

1. **Mlle Smith va travailler en France.**
2. **Elle va bientôt travailler à Paris.**
3. **Elle va travailler avec Mme Lenoir.**
4. **Elles vont travailler ensemble.**
5. **Vous allez habiter Paris ?**
6. **Oui, je vais habiter Paris.**
7. **Je vais habiter boulevard Saint-Germain, avec Hélène.**
8. **Nous allons parler ensemble.**
9. **Nous allons parler français ensemble.**
10. **Je vais rester à Paris en octobre.**
11. **Puis je vais aller en Italie.**
12. **Je vais rester en Italie en décembre.**

B3 COMMENTS

Grammar

• **à / en**

— Generally **à**, meaning *in* or *to*, is used with the name of a town:

à Paris	*in* or *to Paris*
à Nice	*in* or *to Nice*
à Rome	*in* or *to Rome*

— **en**, meaning *in* or *to*, is used with the name of a country:

en Italie	*in* or *to Italy*
en Allemagne	*in* or *to Germany*
en France	*in* or *to France*

Pronunciation

• Note that in spoken French the **e** in the middle of a word is often glided over.

Ex.: **mademoiselle, boulevard.**

B4 TRANSLATION

1. Miss Smith is going to work in France.
2. She is going to work in Paris soon.
3. She is going to work with Mrs. Lenoir.
4. They are going to work together.
5. Are you going to live in Paris?
6. Yes, I am going to live in Paris.
7. I am going to live on Boulevard Saint-Germain, with Hélène.
8. We are going to speak together.
9. We are going to speak French together.
10. I am going to stay in Paris in October.
11. Then I am going to go to Italy.
12. I am going to stay in Italy in December.

5 Exercises

C1 EXERCISES

A. Use the correct form of the verb aller :

1. Vous (aller) loin.
2. Tu (aller) vite.
3. Je (aller) là-bas.
4. Nous (aller) à Paris.
5. Il (aller) parler.
6. Elles (aller) écouter Louis.

B. Use a or en :

1. Je vais... Tours.
2. Il voyage... Espagne.
3. Ils vont souvent... Allemagne.
4. Nous travaillons... Nice.

C2 ANSWERS

A.
1. Vous allez loin.
2. Tu vas vite.
3. Je vais là-bas.
4. Nous allons à Paris.

B.
1. Je vais à Tours.
2. Il voyage en Espagne.
3. Ils vont souvent en Allemagne.
4. Nous travaillons à Nice.
5. Il va parler.
6. Elles vont écouter Louis.

C3 INSTITUTIONS OF THE FIFTH REPUBLIC

■ While the United States has known only one constitution since 1787, France is now living under the fifth one of her history.

■ The Constitution of the Fifth Republic, written in 1958, has led to a stability that all the French profit from, but it is linked to an ambiguous logic.

■ The President of the Republic is elected through direct universal suffrage for a period of seven years. This type of election gives him an authority that is essential for the defense of the institutions. His « reserved domain » includes diplomacy and national defense. He is the guardien of the constitution, and names the Prime Minister and the high-ranking civil servants. In addition, he has the power to dissolve Parliament.

■ But the system is also a parliamentary one, since the National Assembly, composed of around 480 deputies, elected via universal suffrage for five years, votes the laws and has some control over the executive branch. The Prime Minister is a member of the majority party in the National Assembly. He manages national policy according to the orientations of his party. His government can be held responsible by the Parliament, whose deputies can vote a motion of censure that obliges the government to resign.

■ Both presidential and parliamentary, the Fifth Republic is a hybrid. It may occur, as it did between 1986 and 1988, and again in 1997, that the parliamentary majority is not of the same party as the president : this is referred to as a period of "**cohabitation.**"

5 D1 Map of the Francophone world

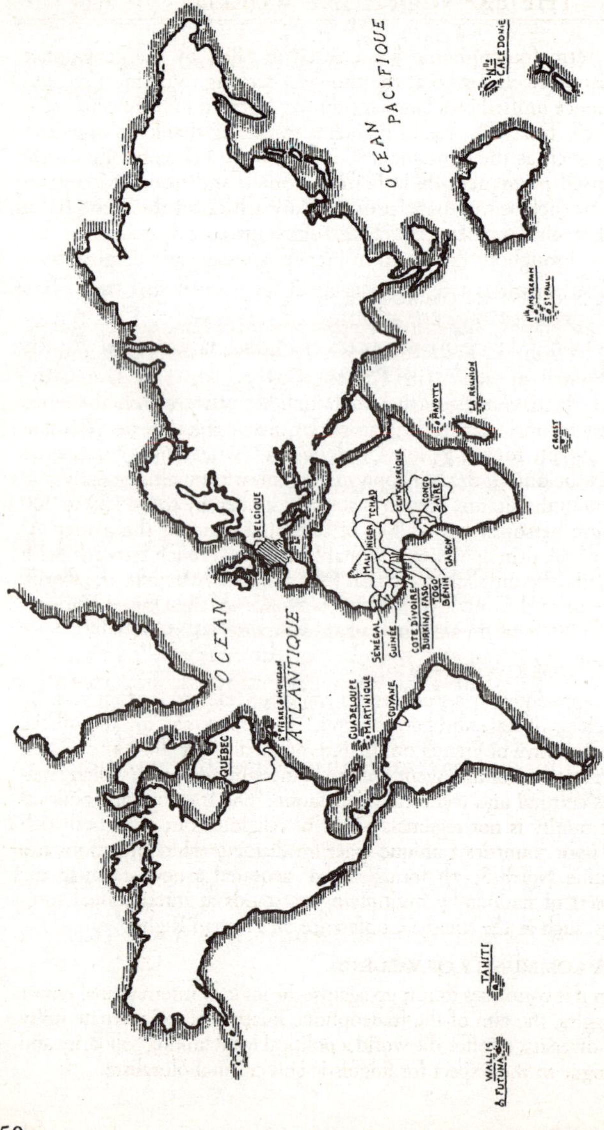

D2 THE FRANCOPHONE WORLD

The term **francophonie** was created in 1882 by the geographer **Onésime Reclus**, who at the time was seeking to define a zone of influence unified by a language during a period of triumphal colonialism. Today, the use of French is spreading thanks to organizations such as the Permanent Council of the Francophone World (**Conseil permanent de la Francophonie**), and to on-site organizations such as the Association of Universities for the Teaching of the French Language (**AUPELF**) which instruct thousands of students throughout the world in French language and civilization.

■ A LINGUISTIC COMMUNITY :

Vast geographic dispersion creates a variety of linguistic categories, ranging from the first, which includes the traditional communities of French speakers (in France, **Québec**, or French-speaking Switzerland) to the fourth, which includes countries where French is taught only to a small portion of the population (in Vietnam and Egypt, for example). Consequently, while the 47 countries which belong to the francophone organization include nearly 500 million inhabitants, French is actually spoken by some 160 to 200 million persons, that is, 3 % of the inhabitants of the planet. As one of the principal international languages, French remains, with English, the only language that is taught everywhere in the world, and one of the only two working languages of the United Nations, where 20 % of the delegates express themselves in French.

■ A POLITICAL COMMUNITY :

It is represented by a secretary general who is elected for four years by the chiefs of state and governments. As a spokesman for and official representative of French on the international scene, he is the highest representative of the Agency of the Francophone World, which organizes cultural and technical cooperation. The francophone political community is not regional, ethnic or religious, but gives both rich and poor countries a unique space for dialogue which functions as a genuine North/South forum. It has acquired a new status in the concert of nations by multiplying its stands at international meetings, such as the Vienna Conference on Human Rights.

■ A COMMUNITY OF VALUES :

Even if it continues to run up against the logic of international power struggles, the aim of the francophone iniatives is to incarnate unity and diversity, to offer the world a political ideal linking solidarity and dialogue to the respect for linguistic and cultural pluralism.

6 Elle est très jolie.

A1 PRESENTATION

Grammar

Être		To be	
je	suis	*I*	*am*
tu	es	*you*	*are*
il, elle	est	*he, she, it*	*is*

- In French, an adjective generally has both masculine and feminine forms. It agrees in gender with the noun or the pronoun it refers to.
  Ex.: **Il est français.** *He is French.*
  Elle est française. *She is French.*

Vocabulary

français(e)	*French*
anglais(e)	*English*
irlandais(e)	*Irish*
grand(e)	*tall*
joli(e)	*pretty*
blond(e)	*fair, blond*
intelligent(e)	*intelligent*
sympathique (masc. and fem.)	*nice*

A2 EXAMPLES *(People)* (CD)

1. **Je suis français.**
2. **Je suis française.**
3. **Tu es sympathique.**
4. **Tu es intelligent.**
5. **Tu es intelligente.**
6. **Nicolas n'est pas anglais.**
7. **Il est irlandais.**
8. **Il est grand et blond.**
9. **Il est très sympathique.**
10. **Anne est anglaise.**
11. **Elle est très jolie.**
12. **Elle n'est pas très grande.**

A3 COMMENTS

Grammar

- The usual way to form a feminine adjective in the singular is to add an **e** to the masculine adjective:

	masculine	feminine
pretty	**joli**	**jolie**
fair	**blond**	**blonde**

- When the masculine adjective ends with a silent **e**, it isn't modified in the feminine form:

	masculine	feminine
nice	**sympathique**	**sympathique**

- When a masculine adjective ends with a consonant, the consonant is not pronounced. But when the feminine adjective ends with an **e**, the final consonant is pronounced:

	masculine	feminine
tall	**grand**	**grande**
intelligent	**intelligent**	**intelligente**

A4 TRANSLATION

1. I am French (masc.).
2. I am French (fem.).
3. You are nice.
4. You are intelligent (masc.).
5. You are intelligent (fem.).
6. Nicolas is not English.
7. He is Irish.
8. He is tall and fair.
9. He is very nice.
10. Anne is English.
11. She is very pretty.
12. She isn't very tall.

6 Ils sont tristes.

B1 PRESENTATION

■ Grammar

Être		To be
nous	**sommes**	*we are*
vous	**êtes**	*you are*
ils, elles	**sont**	*they are*

- Adjectives also agree in number with the noun or pronoun they refer to.
- The plural of adjectives is usually formed by adding an **s** to the singular form:

		singular	plural
intelligent	masc.	**intelligent**	**intelligents**
	fem.	**intelligente**	**intelligentes**

■ Vocabulary

allemand(e) *German*
jeune *young*
content(e) *glad, happy*
triste *sad*
gentil/gentille *kind*

B2 EXAMPLES *(People)* CD

1. **Nous sommes allemands.**
2. **Nous sommes allemandes.**
3. **Vous êtes trop jeunes.**
4. **Vous êtes contentes ?**
5. **Elles ne sont pas contentes.**
6. **Elles sont tristes.**
7. **Ils sont tristes.**
8. **Philippe est gentil.**
9. **Anne aussi est gentille.**
10. **Anne et Philippe sont gentils.**
11. **Ils ne sont pas contents.**
12. **Elles ne sont pas gentilles.**

B3 COMMENTS

Grammar

- When an adjective refers to several nouns, and at least one of them is masculine, the form of the adjective is masculine plural:

  Pierre et Marie sont gentils.
  Peter and Mary are kind.

- In French, adjectives referring to nationality are not capitalized (see lesson 3, A3), but nouns referring to nationality are.

  Adj.: **Nous sommes allemands.** *We are German.*
  Noun: **Un Allemand.** *A German.*

Pronunciation

- **g + e** or **i** is pronounced like **j** (ex.: **gentil**); otherwise it is pronounced like *g* in *good* (ex.: **anglais**).
- **ill** + vowel is pronounced like *y* in *yes* (ex.: **gentille**).

B4 TRANSLATION

1. We are German (masc.).
2. We are German (fem.).
3. You are too young.
4. Are you happy?
5. They are not happy (fem.).
6. They are sad (fem.).
7. They are sad (masc.).
8. Philippe is kind.
9. Anne is kind too.
10. Anne and Philippe are kind.
11. They are not happy (masc.).
12. They are not nice (fem.).

C1 EXERCISES

A. **Fill in the blanks :**

1.... sont blondes.
2. Je... près de Frédéric.
3. Elle... petite.
4. Vous... très sympathique.
5.... sommes à Paris.
6. Ils... devant Notre-Dame.

B. Make 8 sentences with one element of each column :

je	sommes	sympathique
tu	sont	tristes
il	es	jeune
elle	suis	jolies
nous	êtes	contents
vous	est	contents
ils		

C2 ANSWERS

A. 1. Elles sont blondes.
2. Je suis près de Frédéric.
3. Elle est petite.
4. Vous êtes très sympathique.
5. Nous sommes à Paris.
6. Ils sont devant Notre-Dame.

B. **Here are some possibilities :**

1. Je suis sympathique.
2. Tu es sympathique.
3. Il est jeune.
4. Elle est jeune.
5. Nous sommes contents.
6. Vous êtes tristes.
7. Ils sont contents.
8. Elles sont jolies.

C3 NOMBRES/*NUMBERS* (see lesson 4, C2) CD

20	**vingt**	60	**soixante**
30	**trente**	70	**soixante-dix** *(sixty ten)*
40	**quarante**	80	**quatre-vingts** *(four twenty)*
50	**cinquante**	90	**quatre-vingt-dix** *(four twenty ten)*

→ Notice the odd way of saying **70, 80, 90.**

100	**cent**
1000	**mille***

* Here **ill** is pronounced **il.**

C4 THE MONUMENTS OF PARIS

■ Political powers have always sought to leave their imprint on Paris urbanism. Most areas of Paris consequently bear the mark of the architectural ambition of passing governments.

■ During the Renaissance, the **Louvre** was built on the foundations of a fort built by **Philippe Auguste. Louis XIII** gave Paris the Place Royale, today called the **Place des Vosges, Luxembourg,** and the **Palais Royal.** The monuments built during the reign of Louis XIV, the church of the **Sorbonne,** the **Val-de-Grace,** the **Invalides,** beautify numerous neighborhoods of the city.

■ But the veritable rupture in Parisian urbanism dates from the **Second Empire. Haussmann,** the Prefect, had new wide roads built through the center of Paris, improved the squares, and began the vast construction around the train stations. **Napoléon III** inaugurated the **Opéra,** the Halles, etc. Under the Third Republic, for the World Fairs of 1889, 1900 and 1937, **Paris** modernized with the Eiffel Tower, the **Grand** and the **Petit Palais,** Trocadéro and the Sacré-Cœur Basilica.

■ Under the Fifth Republic, vertical urbanism gave Paris its first sky-scrapers : the **Défense** and the Montparnasse Tower. Georges Pompidou, a lover of modernism, gave his name to the new museum of modern art, the **Centre National d'Art Contemporain Georges Pompidou** in the neighborhood where the old Parisian wholesale food market, les Halles, was once located. Major construction projects at the end of the century have also contributed to the transformation of the Parisian landscape (see page 89).

D1 VACANCES (CD)

(*Nicolas et Anne sont au téléphone*)

Anne : Allô 1, ?
Nicolas : Anne ? Ici Nicolas.
Anne : Bonjour, tu es à Paris ?
Nicolas : Non, je ne suis pas à Paris, je suis en Savoie.
Anne : Marc est là aussi ?
Nicolas : Oui. Nous sommes en vacances, mais malheureusement on va partir demain.
On arrive à neuf heures.
Anne : Neuf heures du matin ou neuf heures du soir ?
Nicolas : Neuf heures du soir.
Anne : Et vous arrivez où ?
Nicolas : On arrive Gare de Lyon.
Anne : Très bien, venez dîner, je vous invite.
Nicolas : Tu es très gentille, merci. A demain.

1. The French use *Allô* when answering the telephone.

D2 WRITTEN ACCENTS

■ ´ ` ^ are written accents which are placed on vowels.

- ´ is the acute accent. It is only used over e.
  é has the sound of the English letter *A* in *A B C*.
- ` is the grave accent. It is mainly used over e.
  è has the sound of *e* in *pet*.
  – is also used over a and u without affecting their pronunciation.
- ^ is the circumflex accent. It is used over any vowel. It generally lengthens the sound.

➔ Look back at A2 and B2 ans note the following words :
plaît, où, Hélène, à côté.

D3 VACATION (GB : HOLIDAY)

(*Nicolas and Anne are talking on the telephone.*)

Anne : Hello ?
Nicolas : Anne ? This is Nicolas.
Anne : Hello. Are you in Paris ?
Nicolas : No, I'm not in Paris, I'm in Savoie.
Anne : Is Marc there, too ?
Nicolas : Yes, he is. We're on vacation (GB : on holiday), but unfortunately we're leaving tomorrow. We're arriving at nine o'clock.
Anne : Nine o'clock in the morning or nine o'clock in the evening ?
Nicolas : Nine o'clock in the evening.
Anne : Where are you arriving ?
Nicolas : We're arriving at the Lyon Station.
Anne : Very good. You're invited to dinner.
Nicolas : That's very nice of you, thank you. See you tomorrow.

D4 DIRE L'HEURE/ *TELLING TIME*

- **heure** is used both for *o'clock* and *hour.*
- The expressions : **du matin** *(a.m.)*, **de l'après-midi** *(p.m. up to six o'clock)*, **du soir** *(p.m.)* are used to tell the time more precisely.
  Ex. : **six heures du matin**
  quatre heures de l'après-midi
  dix heures du soir
- **qu** in **quatre** is pronounced like *ck* in *back.*
- Note the unusual liaison : **neuf heures.**
  v

7 Nous préparons un repas froid.

A1 PRESENTATION

Grammar

- All French nouns are masculine (masc.) or feminine (fem.).
  Ex.: **restaurant** (masc.) *restaurant*
  salade (fem.) *salad*
- The singular indefinite article has a masculine and a feminine form:

singular	
masculine	feminine
un	**une**
a, an	*a, an*

Vocabulary

manger	*to eat*	**chaud(e)**	*warm, hot*
préparer	*to prepare*	**froid(e)**	*cold*
acheter	*to buy*	**baguette** (fem.)	*long French loaf*
demander	*to ask for*		
repas (masc.)	*meal*	**croissant** (masc.)	*croissant*
bouteille (fem.)	*bottle*	(You can buy a **croissant** and a **baguette** at the baker's.)	
vin (masc.)	*wine*		
samedi (masc.)	*Saturday*	**de**	*of*

A2 EXAMPLES *(Bread and wine)* (CD)

1. **Elle mange un croissant.**
2. **Il mange un croissant chaud.**
3. **Il mange souvent un croissant chaud à neuf heures.**
4. **Vous préparez un repas froid ?**
5. **Oui, nous préparons un repas froid.**
6. **Ils vont acheter une baguette.**
7. **Achète une salade et une bouteille de vin pour demain !**
8. **Nous allons dans un restaurant grec samedi ?**
9. **Non, nous allons dans un restaurant italien.**
10. **Un croissant s'il vous plaît !**
11. **Elle demande un croissant.**
12. **Elle demande un croissant et une baguette.**

7 We are preparing a cold meal.

A3 COMMENTS

Grammar

- The articles and adjectives agree in gender with the noun they accompany.

Ex.:	**un restaurant** (masc.)	*a restaurant*
	une salade (fem.)	*a salad*

- In French, most adjectives come after the noun they accompany.

Ex.:	**un croissant chaud**	*a hot 'croissant'*
	un repas froid	*a cold meal*
	un restaurant grec	*a Greek restaurant*

Pronunciation

- **un**: this nasal vowel is pronounced like the vowel sound in *earn*.
- **une**: here the **u** is pronounced like in **tu** (see p. 23) followed by **n**. The final **e** is silent.
- **eille** in **bouteille** is pronounced like *ay* in *gay* + *y* in *yes*.

A4 TRANSLATION

1. She is eating a 'croissant'.
2. He is eating a warm 'croissant'.
3. He often eats a warm 'croissant' at nine.
4. Are you preparing a cold meal?
5. Yes, we are preparing a cold meal.
6. They are going to buy a 'baguette'.
7. Buy a salad and a bottle of wine for tomorrow!
8. Are we going to a Greek restaurant on Saturday?
9. No, we are going to an Italian restaurant.
10. A 'croissant' please!
11. She is asking for a 'croissant'.
12. She is asking for a 'croissant' and a 'baguette'.

7 Elle habite avec des amis.

B1 PRESENTATION

Grammar

- In French the indefinite article has a plural form:

plural	
masculine	feminine
des	

- The plural of nouns is usually formed by adding an **s** to the singular form.

  Ex.: **des étudiants / des étudiantes** *students.*

Vocabulary

rencontrer	*to meet*	**livre** (masc.)	*book*
voici	*here is, here are*	**magazine** (masc.)	*magazine*
photo (fem.)	*photo*	**journaliste** (masc., fem.)	*journalist*
étudiant (masc.)	*student*	**artiste** (masc., fem.)	*artist*
ami (masc.)	*friend*	**écrivain** (masc.)	*writer*
examen (masc.)	*exam*	**étranger**	*foreign*
		célèbre	*famous*

B2 EXAMPLES *(Studying abroad)* CD

1. **Voici des photos d'Anne, une étudiante anglaise.**
2. **Ici, elle parle avec des étudiants étrangers.**
3. **Là, elle visite une cathédrale avec des amis français.**
4. **Elle habite avec des amis.**
5. **Elle prépare des examens.**
6. **Elle va acheter des livres et des magazines français.**
7. **Peter et John sont des journalistes anglais.**
8. **Ils parlent avec des artistes.**
9. **Ils rencontrent des journalistes français.**
10. **Ils rencontrent aussi des écrivains célèbres.**
11. **Nous rencontrons souvent des amis ici.**
12. **Nous allons souvent dans des restaurants étrangers.**

B3 COMMENTS

Grammar

- In the plural, don't forget to use the indefinite article **des**, even if there is no such article in English.
  In French, it is practically impossible to use a noun alone. An article is almost always necessary.
  Ex.: **des photos** *photos*
  des examens *exams*
- The nouns which end with an **s** in the singular do not change in the plural.
  Ex.: **un repas - des repas** *meals*
  un pays - des pays *countries*

Pronunciation

- **es** in **des** is pronounced like *A* in *A B C.*
- Note that in **cathédrale : th** is pronounced **t.**
- Don't forget the liaison:
  des amis, des artistes, des étudiants, des écrivains.
  (z) (z) (z) (z)

B4 TRANSLATION

1. Here are photos of Anne, an English student.
2. Here, she is speaking with foreign students.
3. There, she is visiting a cathedral with French friends.
4. She lives with friends.
5. She is preparing exams.
6. She is going to buy French books and magazines.
7. Peter and John are English journalists.
8. They speak with artists.
9. They meet French journalists.
10. They meet famous writers too.
11. We often meet friends here.
12. We often go to foreign restaurants.

7 Exercises and *FRIENDS*

C1 EXERCISES

A. **Match the articles, nouns and adjectives :**

pays	un	française
amie	une	intelligents
photo	des	français
portrait		sympathiques
étudiants		étranger
livres		célèbre
écrivain		étrangers
restaurants		chaud
repas		froids
amis		italienne
journaliste		

C2 ANSWERS

A. **Some possibilities :**

Un pays étranger.
Une amie française.
Une amie italienne.
Une photo célèbre.
Un portrait célèbre.
Des étudiants intelligents.
Des livres français.
Des écrivrains étrangers.
Des restaurants sympathiques.
Des repas froids.
Un ami français.
Une journaliste italienne.
Un journaliste étranger.

C3 UN AMI/UNE AMIE - *A FRIEND*

- Nouns denoting masculine persons are masculine and nouns denoting feminine persons are feminine.
  The usual way to form a feminine noun is by adding an e to the masculine.
  Ex. : **ami** **amie**
  étudiant **étudiante**
- However, some nouns can be used either for the masculine or for the feminine.
  Ex. : **journaliste**
  artiste
- In a word with a final **e**, the **e** is not pronounced as such but the preceding consonant is : **un étudiant - une étudiante.**

C2 FRUIT AND VEGETABLES

SOME COLLOQUIAL EXPRESSIONS

- **mi-figue, mi-raisin** *(half fig, half grape)* : it's like the curate's egg, good in parts : mixed feelings (a mixture of satisfaction and displeasure ; or half serious, half in jest).
- **entre la poire et le fromage** *(between the pear and the cheese)* : over the walnuts and wine ; over coffee : at the end of a meal, when conversation becomes less serious.
- **une poire** *(a pear)* : a sucker, a person who is easily fooled
- **couper la poire en deux** *(cut the pear in half)* : to meet half-way : come to a compromise.
- **garder une poire pour la soif** *(keep a pear for thirst)* : keep something in hand for a rainy day ; keep something up one's sleeve.
- **haut comme trois pommes** *(as tall as three apples)* : pint-sized, knee-high to a grasshopper.
- **tomber dans les pommes** *(fall into the apples)* : pass out, faint.
- **un pépin** *(pip, seed)* : a hitch, a snag ; a problem.
- **pour des prunes** *(for plums)* : for nothing, to no avail.
- **bête comme chou** *(as silly as cabbage)* : child's play, easy as pie.
- **feuille de chou** *(cabbage-leaf)* : rag : poor-quality newspaper or piece of writing.
- **ménager la chèvre et le chou** *(spare the goat and the cabbage)* : run with the hare and hunt with the hounds ; sit on the fence : not take sides ; put off deciding until one of the sides wins.
- **pas un radis** *(not a radish)* : not a bean : (have) no money
- **un navet** *(a turnip)* : third-rate play or film.

7 DIALOGUES AND EXPRESSIONS

D1 UN RESTAURANT SYMPATHIQUE (CD)

Garçon [1] : Bonsoir Madame, bonsoir Monsieur, une table pour deux ?
Jean [2] : Oui, près d'une fenêtre s'il vous plaît.
Garçon : Par ici… Voici un menu.
Marie : Euh… Je vais prendre une salade en hors d'œuvre et une entrecôte, saignante avec des haricots verts.
Garçon : Et pour Monsieur ?
Jean : Des poireaux vinaigrette et une escalope panée bien cuite.
Garçon : Avec des frites ?
Jean : Non, je préfère des pâtes. Et comme vin, on va prendre un Bordeaux.
Marie : Bonne idée !
Garçon : Et comme dessert ? Une crème caramel ? Un gâteau ?
Marie : Je préfère une glace.

1. **Garçon** means *waiter* in cafés and restaurants
2. **Jean** is a masculine name in French.

D2 EXPRESSIONS

Bonjour - Bonsoir - Au revoir

- The *day* **(jour)** is divided into :
  matin *(morning)* **après-midi** *(afternoon)* **soir** *(evening).*
- When you meet a person during the day, say : **bonjour** *(good morning or good afternoon).* At the end of the day, use : **bonsoir** *(good evening).*
- When you leave somebody, say : **au revoir** *(good bye).* You can also say : **bonsoir** when leaving someone in the evening.
- **Bonne nuit** is used to wish somebody a good night.
  Ex. : **Bonjour Louis.** *Good morning Louis.*
  Au revoir Anne. *Good bye Anne.*
  Bonne nuit Antoine. *Good night Antoine.*
- In **jour, au revoir, soir**, the final **r** is pronounced.

D3 A PLEASANT RESTAURANT

Waiter: Good evening Madam, good evening Sir. A table for two ?

Jean : Yes, near a window, please.

Waiter: This way. Here's a menu.

Marie: Um… I'm going to have a salad first, and then a steak, rare, with green beans.

Waiter: And for you, Sir ?

Jean : Leeks with oil and vinegar dressing and breaded veal, well done.

Waiter: With French fries ? (GB : chips)

Jean : No, I'd rather have pasta. And for wine, we'll have a Bordeaux.

Marie: Good idea !

Waiter: And for dessert ? A caramel custard ? A piece of cake ?

Marie: I'd rather have ice cream.

D4 PREPOSITIONS AND EXPRESSIONS TO INDICATE THE PLACE

→ remember	où = where ?
par ici	*this way*
par là	*that way*
dans	*in*
devant	*in front of*
derrière	*behind*
entre	*between*
sous	*under*
dessous	*below*
près	*near*
près <u>de</u> Louis	*near Louis* (notice the **de** when the preposition is followed by a noun).

8 C'est une maison confortable.

A1 PRESENTATION

Grammar

- **c'est** can be the equivalent of: *he is, she is, it is* or *this is*, when followed by a noun in the singular.

Ex. :	**C'est un ami.**	*He is a friend.*
	C'est une amie.	*She is a friend.*
	C'est un studio.	*It is a studio.*

- **c'est** can be followed by an adjective or adverb alone. It is then the equivalent of: *it is* or *that is*.

Ex.:	**C'est gentil.**	*It is nice.*

- The negative form is: **ce n'est pas,** *it is not* ; (in colloquial French: **c'est pas**).

Vocabulary

à louer	*to let (*US: *to rent, for rent)*
voisin (masc.)	*neighbour*
appartement (masc.)	*flat (*US: *apartment)*
immeuble (masc.)	*building*
maison (fem.)	*house*
petit(e)	*small*
grand(e)	*big, large*
confortable	*comfortable*
moderne	*modern*
pas cher	*not expensive, cheap*
vraiment	*really*

A2 EXAMPLES *(Looking for a flat)* CD

1. **C'est Anne.**
2. **C'est une amie.**
3. **C'est Pierre.**
4. **C'est un voisin.**
5. **C'est un appartement à louer.**
6. **C'est un petit appartement dans un grand immeuble.**
7. **C'est une maison confortable.**
8. **Ce n'est pas une maison très moderne.**
9. **C'est loin ?**
10. **Non, ce n'est pas loin.**
11. **Ce n'est pas cher.**
12. **Ce n'est vraiment pas cher !**

A3 COMMENTS

Grammar

- As we have seen, in French most adjectives come after the noun they accompany (see lesson 7, A3).
  However, some short, commonly used adjectives are placed before the noun (see list in C2).
  Ex.: **C'est un petit appartement.** *It is a small flat.*
- Note that in colloquial French, you may hear **c'est pas** instead of **ce n'est pas.**
  Ex.: **C'est pas grand (ce n'est pas grand).**
  It's not big.

Pronunciation

- **c'est** is pronounced like *set* without the *t*.
- **ce** is pronounced like *ce* in *certain*.
- **im** in **immeuble** is pronounced like *im* in *important*.

A4 TRANSLATION

1. This is Anne.
2. She is a friend.
3. This is Pierre.
4. He is a neighbour.
5. It is a flat for rent.
6. It is a small flat in a big building.
7. It is a comfortable house.
8. It isn't a very modern house.
9. Is it far?
10. No, it isn't far.
11. It isn't expensive.
12. It's really cheap!

8 Ce sont des immeubles modernes.

B1 PRESENTATION

Grammar

- When followed by a noun in the plural, **c'est** becomes **ce sont**.
  Ex.: **Ce sont des appartements très chers.**
  They are very expensive flats.
- The negative form is: **ce ne sont pas**.
- Note that: **ce sont**, contrary to **c'est**, is never used with an adjective alone.

Vocabulary

pièce (fem.) — *room*
chambre (fem.) — *bedroom*
chaise (fem.) — *chair*
lampe (fem.) — *lamp*
fenêtre (fem.) — *window*
rideau (masc.) — *curtain*
tapis (masc.) — *carpet (*US: *rug)*
cher — *expensive*
sombre — *dark*
beau (masc.) / **belle** (fem.) — *beautiful*
bon marché — *cheap*

B2 EXAMPLES *(Furnishing a flat)* (CD)

1. **Ce sont des immeubles chers.**
2. **Ce sont des appartements très confortables.**
3. **Ce sont des pièces sombres.**
4. **Ce ne sont pas de grandes pièces.**
5. **Ce sont de petites chambres.**
6. **Ce ne sont pas des chaises confortables.**
7. **Ce sont de jolies lampes.**
8. **Ce sont de grandes fenêtres.**
9. **Ce sont de beaux rideaux.**
10. **Ce ne sont pas des tapis bon marché !**
11. **Ce ne sont pas de beaux tapis.**
12. **Ce sont des immeubles modernes.**

B3 COMMENTS

Grammar

- Note that **des** becomes **de** when there is an adjective before the noun.

  Ce sont des lampes.
  They are lamps.
  Ce sont de jolies lampes.
  They are pretty lamps.

- Words ending in **eau** add an **x**, instead of an **s**, to make the plural.
  Ex.: **De beaux rideaux.** *Beautiful curtains.*

- Remember: adjectives agree in gender and number with the noun (or the nouns) they refer to (see lesson 6, A1, B1).

  Un appartement confortable.
  A comfortable flat.
  Des appartements confortables.
  Comfortable flats.
  Un petit appartement.
  A small flat.
  De petits appartements.
  Small flats.

Pronunciation

- **o, au, eau:** three spellings for the sound of *o* in *note.*
  Ex.: **Sophie, restaurant, beau, rideau.**

B4 TRANSLATION

1. They are expensive buildings.
2. They are very comfortable flats.
3. They are dark rooms.
4. They are not big rooms.
5. They are small bedrooms.
6. They are not comfortable chairs.
7. They are pretty lamps.
8. They are big windows.
9. They are beautiful curtains.
10. They are not cheap carpets!
11. They are not beautiful carpets.
12. They are modern buildings.

8 Exercises and adjectives before nouns

C1 EXERCISES

A. Put the adjectives in the right place, and mind the gender and number :

1. moderne :	c'est une lampe.
2. joli :	c'est une chambre.
3. mauvais :	c'est un restaurant.
4. froid :	c'est un repas.
5. petit :	c'est une maison.
6. bon :	ce sont des bouteilles.
7. confortable :	ce sont des appartements.
8. jeune :	ce sont des étudiants.

C2 ANSWERS

A. 1. C'est une lampe moderne.
2. C'est une jolie chambre.
3. C'est un mauvais restaurant.
4. C'est un repas froid.
5. C'est une petite maison.
6. Ce sont de bonnes bouteilles.
7. Ce sont des appartements confortables.
8. Ce sont de jeunes étudiants.

C3 COMMONLY USED ADJECTIVES GENERALLY PLACED BEFORE THE NOUN

Masculine	Féminine	
bon	**bonne**	*good*
cher	**chère**	*dear, expensive*
grand	**grande**	*tall, big, great*
jeune	**jeune**	*young*
joli	**jolie**	*pretty*
long	**longue**	*long*
mauvais	**mauvaise**	*bad*
petit	**petite**	*little, small*
beau*	**belle**	*beautiful*
vieux*	**vieille**	*old*
nouveau*	**nouvelle**	*new*

* Note some adjectives whose feminine form is not made the usual way.

C4 AROUND THE TABLE

■ French meals

The French have a reputation for being lovers of wine and good food ; that may be why meals - particularly the evening meal, which they have about 8 p.m. - are regarded as special moments for getting together ; they are occasions of great importance. They provide an opportunity for members of the family, as well as any guests present, to have animated conversations, to talk about the day's events, to take stocks of things, to "set the world to rights", even to argue…

However, it is not unusual for people to arrange to meet in a café or pub to have a drink, have an aperitif and chat with their

Un repas sans fromage est un jour sans soleil.
A meal without cheese is a day without sunshine.

Un repas sans fromage est comme une belle à qui il manque un œil.
A meal without cheese is like a beautiful woman with an eye missing.

■ French Cheese

France produces around 350 varieties of cheese, some of which are famous the world over. General de Gaulle, when he was the President of the Republic, is reputed to have remarked, "How do you expect to govern a country which makes more than 300 cheeses ?"

8 DIALOGUES AND LIAISON

D1 UNE COLLEGUE DE TRAVAIL (CD)

Frédéric : Bastien, regarde là-bas près des escaliers, c'est une nouvelle collègue. Elle est italienne, elle s'appelle Silvia.

Bastien : C'est une fille superbe !

Frédéric : C'est une fille très bien. Elle est vraiment sympa.

Bastien : Elle habite où ?

Frédéric : Dans un petit appartement dans un immeuble ancien du centre-ville. C'est un quartier très vivant mais ce n'est pas très bruyant.

Bastien : Pierre et Marc habitent aussi le centre-ville.

Frédéric : Pierre et Marc ?

Bastien : Oui, ce sont de vieux copains. Ils travaillent dans une boîte d'informatique.

1. **Boîte** is colloquial for *firm* or *company*.

D2 "LIAISON" (CD)

- The final consonant of a word is pronounced when the following word starts with a vowel or **h**. The words run together, this is called a **liaison** in French.
  Ex. : **restez ici** (z) **parlons ensemble** (z)
  pas ici (z) **pas encore** (z) **avec Anne** (k)

- When a word ends with an **e**, the **e** being silent, there is a liaison with the following vowel.
  Ex. : **reste à côté** (t) **reste ici** (t)
  Anne et Louis (n) **Anne ou Louis** (n)

D3 A COLLEAGUE AT WORK

Frédéric : Bastien ? Look over there near the stairs, it's our new colleague. She's Italian ; her name is Silvia.
Bastien : She's a good looking girl !
Frédéric : She's a very nice woman. She's really friendly.
Bastien : Where does she live ?
Frédéric : In a little apartment (GB : flat) in an old building in the center of town. It's a very busy neighborhood, but it's not very noisy.
Bastien : Pierre and Marc live in the center of town, too.
Frédéric : Pierre and Marc ?
Bastien : Yes, they're old buddies. They work for a computer company.

D4 Monsieur (M.), Madame (Mme), Mademoiselle (Mlle)

- They can be used with a name.
  Ex. : **monsieur Lenoir** **madame Lenoir**
  mademoiselle Lemercier
- They can also be used alone as equivalent of : *Sir, Madam, Miss.*
- **on** in **monsieur** is pronounced like *ur* in *hurt.*
- In the plural : **messieurs, mesdames, mesdemoiselles, mes** is pronounced like **mé**.

■ To introduce oneself or somebody else, the commonly used expression is :

je m'appelle *...	*my name ** is...* (literally : *I call myself...*)
tu t'appelles *...	*your name is...*
il, elle s'appelle *...	*his, her, its name is...*
nous nous appelons...	*our names are...*
vous vous appelez...	*your names are...*
ils, elles s'appellent *...	*their names are...*

* Notice the double l, in that case, the first e is pronounced like *e* in *pet.* In appelons and appelez, there is only one l and the e is glided over.
** **Nom, prénom/***Name, first name.*

9 Tu as des enfants aussi ?

A1 PRESENTATION

■ Grammar

Avoir	*To have*
j'ai **tu as** **il, elle a**	*I have* *you have* *he, she, it has*

→ Note that **avoir** is the French equivalent of: *to have got.*

Ex.: *I have got a car.* **J'ai une voiture.**
He's got two children. **Il a deux enfants.**
You've got a nice house. **Tu as une belle maison.**

■ Vocabulary

rue (fem.) *street*
enfant (masc. fem.) *child*
fils (masc.) *son*
fille (fem.) *daughter, girl*
docteur (masc.) *doctor*
métier (masc.) *job*
chat (masc.) *cat*
en (avion) *by (plane)*
intéressant *interesting*

Évry is a town near **Paris.**
Nantes is a town on the **Loire** river.

A2 EXAMPLES *(Talking about the family)* CD

1. **J'ai un appartement rue Monge à Paris.**
2. **J'ai une maison près de Nantes.**
3. **Il a une maison à Nice, il y va en avion.**
4. **J'ai deux enfants.**
5. **Tu as des enfants aussi ?**
6. **Oui, un fils et une fille.**
7. **Agnès a un métier intéressant.**
8. **Elle travaille à Évry, elle y va en train.**
9. **Guy est docteur, il a une grande maison.**
10. **Il a des enfants.**
11. **Il a un chat.**
12. **Il a une petite voiture.**

9 Have you got children too?

A3 COMMENTS

Grammar

- Remember:
  — **à** is a preposition: **à Nice, à Évry** (The accent doesn't affect the pronunciation);
  — **a** is the 3rd person singular of the verb **avoir.**
- **rue Monge:** note that most of the time, no preposition is used before the expression: **rue...**
- **y,** there refers to a place which has already been mentionned. It is placed just before the verb.
  Ex.: **Il y va en avion** (**y** refers to Nice).
  He goes there by plane.
  Elle y va en train (**y** refers to Évry).
  She goes there by train.

Pronunciation

- **gu + i**
  gu + e → is pronounced like *g* in *good* (ex.: **Guy).**
  gu + y
- **ion** in **avion** is pronounced like *y* in *yes* followed by the nasal vowel **on.**
- In **fils**, the **s** is pronounced like *s* in *set*, but the **l** is not heard.
- **y** (there) is pronounced like *ee* in *see.*

A4 TRANSLATION

1. I have got a flat on rue Monge, in Paris.
2. I have got a house near Nantes.
3. He has got a house in Nice, he goes there by plane.
4. I have got two children.
5. Have you got children too?
6. Yes, a son and a daughter.
7. Agnès has an interesting job.
8. She works in Évry, she goes there by train.
9. Guy is a doctor, he has got a big house.
10. He has got children.
11. He has got a cat.
12. He has got a small car.

9 Nous avons une vieille voiture.

B1 PRESENTATION

■ Grammar

Avoir		To have	
nous	**avons**	*we*	*have*
vous	**avez**	*you*	*have*
ils, elles	**ont**	*they*	*have*

- In French, **avoir** is used in a series of expressions where *to be* is used in English (see C2).
  Ex. : **avoir faim** *to be hungry*
  avoir soif *to be thirsty*

■ Vocabulary

semaine (fem.) *week*
vacances (fem. plural) *holidays*
valise (fem.) *suitcase*
sac (masc.) *bag*
parent (masc.) *relative*
hôtel (masc.) *hotel*
avenue (fem.) *avenue*
neuf/neuve *new*

B2 EXAMPLES *(To have and have not)* (CD)

1. **Nous avons une vieille voiture.**
2. **Ils ont une voiture neuve.**
3. **Ils ont de longues vacances.**
4. **Nous avons trois semaines de vacances.**
5. **Vous avez des valises ?**
6. **Oui, nous avons deux valises et un sac.**
7. **Elles ont des sacs neufs.**
8. **Agnès et Guy ont des parents à Nice.**
9. **Nous avons des voisins sympathiques.**
10. **Ils ont un hôtel avenue Masséna.**
11. **Vous avez faim ?**
12. **Non, mais nous avons soif.**

B3 COMMENTS

Vocabulary

- Note that:

  — **neuf, neuve** means: which has not yet been used.

  — **nouveau** or **nouvelle** is closer to the meaning of *recent*.
  Ex.: **un nouveau livre** *a new book*
  une voiture neuve *a new car*

- Remember that **parents** in French means both *parents* and *relatives*.

Grammar

- *three weeks' holidays*, **trois semaines de vacances** (= literally *three weeks of holidays*).

→ Note that there is no equivalent of **'** or **'s** in French.

Pronunciation

- **aim** in **faim** is pronounced like **ain** in **maintenant** (see lesson 4, B3).
- Final consonants are silent except **c, f, l, q, r** which are usually sounded.
  Ex.: **neuf, soif, sac, hôtel, cinq, Marc.**

B4 TRANSLATION

1. We have an old car.
2. They have a new car.
3. They have long holidays.
4. We have three weeks' holidays.
5. Have you got suitcases?
6. Yes, we have two suitcases and a bag.
7. They have new bags.
8. Agnès and Guy have relatives in Nice.
9. We have nice neighbours.
10. They have a hotel on avenue Masséna.
11. Are you hungry?
12. No, but we are thirsty.

9 Exercises and "AVOIR"

C1 EXERCISES

A. Put the verb <u>avoir</u> in the correct form :

1. Je… trois photos de Guy.
2. Tu… des voisins sympathiques.
3. Il… deux fils et une fille.
4. Ils… une vieille voiture.
5. Nous… des amis en Espagne.
6. Vous… des enfants ?

C2 ANSWERS

A. 1. J'ai trois photos de Guy.
2. Tu as des voisins sympathiques.
3. Il a deux fils et une fille.
4. Ils ont une vieille voiture.
5. Nous avons des amis en Espagne.
6. Vous avez des enfants ?

C3 EXPRESSION (CD)

- **avoir** is used in the following expressions :

avoir chaud	*to be warm*
avoir froid	*to be cold*
avoir soif	*to be thirsty*
avoir faim	*to be hungry*
avoir peur *	*to be afraid*
avoir raison	*to be right*
avoir tort	*to be wrong*
avoir de la chance	*to be lucky*
avoir l'habitude de	*to be used to*

- You also use **avoir** to express age in French. The equivalent of *How old are you ?* is **Quel âge as-tu ? Quel âge avez-vous ?** (literally : *what age have you ?*).

Ex. :	**J'ai vingt ans.**	*I am twenty.*
	Elle a cinquante ans.	*She is fifty.*
	Quel âge a-t-il ?	*How old is he ?*
	Il a trente ans	*He is thirty.*

- Remember : **ans** *(years)* can't be omitted (as it is in English).

C4 TOURISM IN FRANCE

■ For the last ten years, France has broken all the records for international tourism with some 50 million foreign tourists per year. The Germans visit in the greatest numbers, followed by the Spanish, the Japanese and the Italians, who appreciate the diversity of France's scenery, its climate, its gastronomy and its exceptional cultural heritage which includes more than 12,000 listed monuments and 1,300 museums.
■ Examples of France's cultural heritage are spread out over the country and span several millennia, from the prehistoric relics of the southwest to modern achievements such as the Pyramid of the Louvre and the Very Big Library (**Très Grande Bibliothèque**). ■ The overseas territories such as the French West Indies and French Polynesia also attract vast numbers of tourists from the United States, Australia and Japan.
■ Seaside tourism, already popular on the Riviera in the 18th century, draws people to the coasts of the North Sea, the Channel, Brittany, the Basque country, etc. Corsica receives each year more than a million and a half vacationers, more than five times the resident population of the island. Furthermore, the interest in ecology and the desire for peace and quiet and fresh air have given new popularity in the summertime to the mountain ranges of the **Massif Central**, the **Pyrénées** and the **Jura**, threatened by an exodus from the land and the fact that many traditional activities have been abandoned. Thus « green tourism » is growing by leaps and bounds with the development of self-catering country cottages, camping on the farm, and accommodations in the homes of local inhabitants.
■ The various French regions offer an infinite wealth of attractions : prehistoric relics in **Périgord**, castles in the Loire country, Romanesque architecture in **Bourgogne**, among others. Some cities such as **Aix-en-Provence, Avignon** or **Cannes** have become internationally known for their music, theater or film festivals. Other cities such as **Rouen, Dijon** or **Nîmes** prefer to showcase their historical centers and have treasures that are often not well known in their museums. The world soccer cup in 1998 drew an additional several hundred thousand tourists to Paris, which remains the top world capital for business tourism and congresses.

D1 DEVANT UNE MACHINE A CAFÉ (CD)

Marc: Vous avez des pièces s'il vous plaît? J'ai seulement un billet de cinq euros.

Paul: Vous avez de la chance! J'ai trois pièces de un euro. Vous êtes nouveau ici?

Marc: Oui, je suis en stage pour deux mois; je m'appelle Marc Van Beer, je suis hollandais.

Paul: Enchanté! Je m'appelle Paul Robin, j'ai vingt sept ans.

Marc: Tiens[1], nous avons le même âge!

Paul: Vous êtes marié ?

Marc: Oui, et j'ai deux enfants.

Paul: Quel âge ont-ils?

Marc: J'ai une fille de deux ans et un fils de trois mois. Et vous?

Paul: Je suis marié, mais nous n'avons pas d'enfants... Vous avez envie d'un autre café?

Marc: Non merci, j'y vais, j'ai du travail.

1. **Tiens!** A colloquial exclamation of surprise.

D2 NOUS HABITONS EN EUROPE
WE LIVE IN EUROPE

Pays	*Country*
Allemagne*	*Germany*
Angleterre	*England*
Belgique	*Belgium*
Danemark	*Denmark*
Espagne	*Spain*
France	*France*
Grèce	*Greece*
Italie	*Italy*
Irlande	*Ireland*
Pays-Bas	*the Netherlands*
Portugal**	*Portugal*

* **gn** is pronounced like *ni* in *onion* (**Allemagne**).

** Note that the final **l** in **Portugal** is heard.

D3 IN FRONT OF A COFFEE MACHINE

Marc: Do you happen to have change? I only have a five-euro bill (GB: note).

Paul: You're in luck! I have three one-euro coins. Are you new here?

Marc: Yes, I'm doing an internship for two months. My name is Marc Van Beer; I'm Dutch.

Paul: Pleased to meet you! My name is Paul Robin; I'm twenty-seven.

Marc: Hey, we're the same age!

Paul: Are you married?

Marc: Yes, and I have two children.

Paul: How old are they?

Marc: I have a daughter who's two and a son who's three months. What about you?

Paul: I'm married, but we don't have any children. Would you like more coffee?

Marc: No thank you, I'd better go. I've got work to do.

D2 NOUS SOMMES EUROPÉENS (CD)
WE ARE EUROPEAN

Adjectives (nationality)

Masc.	Fem.	
allemand	**allemande**	*German*
anglais	**anglaise**	*English*
belge	**belge**	*Belgian*
danois	**danoise**	*Danish*
espagnol	**espagnole**	*Spanish*
français	**française**	*French*
grec	**grecque**	*Greek*
italien	**italienne**	*Italian*
irlandais	**irlandaise**	*Irish*
portugais	**portugaise**	*Portuguese*

10 Est-ce que c'est facile ?

A1 PRESENTATION

Grammar

- **Est-ce que... ?**
  The most commonly used way of turning a statement into a question is to start with: **est-ce que... ?**

Tu chantes	→ **Est-ce que tu chantes ?**
You sing	*Do you sing?*
Il est jeune	→ **Est-ce qu'il est jeune ?**
He is young	*Is he young?*
C'est une voiture neuve	→ **Est-ce que c'est une voiture neuve ?**
It's a new car	*Is it a new car?*

⟶ The intonation is a rising one.

Vocabulary

utiliser	*to use*
commencer	*to start*
bureau (masc.)	*office*
secrétaire (masc., fem.)	*secretary* (for a person)
ordinateur (masc.)	*computer*
directeur (masc.)	*manager*
facile	*easy*
tard	*late*
tôt	*early*
en panne	*out of order*

A2 EXAMPLES *(Jobs)* (CD)

1. **Est-ce que Bruno a un bon métier ?**
2. **Est-ce qu'il travaille dans un bureau ?**
3. **Est-ce que tu commences à huit heures ?**
4. **Est-ce que vous commencez tôt ?**
5. **Est-ce que vous avez des secrétaires ?**
6. **Est-ce qu'elles utilisent des ordinateurs ?**
7. **Est-ce que c'est facile ?**
8. **Est-ce qu'ils sont souvent en panne ?**
9. **Est-ce que c'est un nouveau directeur ?**
10. **Est-ce qu'il est sympathique ?**
11. **Est-ce que c'est trop tard ?**
12. **Est-ce que nous travaillons aujourd'hui ?**

10 Is it easy?

A3 COMMENTS

■ Pronunciation

- **est-ce** is pronounced like *S* in *R,S,T.*
- **que** becomes **qu'** before a vowel.
  Ex.: **Est-ce qu'il travaille ?**
  Est-ce qu'elles utilisent des ordinateurs ?
- **Bruno, bureau, restaurant, beaucoup : o, eau, au,** three spellings for one sound: **o** like *o* in *go.*
- In **eur (ordinateur, directeur)** the final **r** is heard.
- **anne** in **panne** is pronounced like *ann* in *anniversary.*

■ Grammar

- Note that there is no change in the order of the words in the statement after **est-ce que... ?**
- Remember that **est-ce que** is invariable.

Est-ce que tu chantes ?	*Do you*		*Are you*	
Est-ce que vous chantez ?	*Do you*	*sing?*	*Are you*	*singing?*
Est-ce qu'elles chantent ?	*Do they*		*Are they*	

A4 TRANSLATION

1. Does Bruno have a good job? / *or* Has Bruno got...
2. Does he work in an office?
3. Do you start at eight?
4. Do you start early?
5. Do you have secretaries? / *or* Have you got...
6. Do they use computers?
7. Is it easy?
8. Are they often out of order?
9. Is he a new manager?
10. Is he nice?
11. Is it too late?
12. Do we work today?

10 Avez-vous de longues vacances ?

B1 PRESENTATION

Grammar

- **Voyages-tu seul ?** *Do you travel alone?*

So far we have seen two ways of turning a statement into a question (see B3). There is also a 3rd way when the subject is a pronoun. Subject and verb can be inverted (mostly with **vous, il, elle, ils, elles**):

Aimez-vous Brahms ? *Do you like Brahms?*

Vocabulary

inviter	*to invite*
jouer	*to play*
comprendre	*to understand*
concert (masc.)	*concert*
musée (masc.)	*museum*
théâtre (masc.)	*theatre*
pièce (fem.)	*play*
libre	*free*
récent(e)	*recent*
seul(e)	*alone*
quelquefois	*sometimes*

B2 EXAMPLES *(Entertainment)* CD

1. **Avez-vous de longues vacances ?**
2. **Voyages-tu seul ?**
3. **Sont-ils libres le samedi ?**
4. **Invitent-elles des amis mercredi ?**
5. **Vont-ils écouter un concert ?**
6. **Aimez-vous Brahms ?**
7. **Rencontrez-vous souvent des artistes ?**
8. **Est-ce qu'il visite quelquefois des musées ?**
9. **Joue-t-elle dans un nouveau théâtre ?**
10. **Est-ce une pièce récente ?**
11. **Est-elle facile à comprendre ?**
12. **Parlez-vous français ?**

10 Do you have long holidays?

B3 COMMENTS

Grammar

- Remember: two ways of turning a statement into a question:
  1. The speaker may simply use rising intonation at the end of the sentence (see lesson 3, A3).
     Ex.: **Tu chantes ?** *Do you sing? / Are you singing?*
  2. **est-ce que** can be used at the beginning of the sentence.
     Ex.: **Est-ce que tu chantes ?**
- When the verb is inverted:
  — it is joined to the pronoun by a hyphen.
     Ex.: **Parlez-vous ?** *Do you speak? / Are you speaking.*
  — if the verb ends with a vowel, **t** is introduced between the vert and **il** or **elle.**
     Ex.: **A-t-il... ?** *Has he got...?*
     Commence-t-elle... ? *Is she beginning...?*
     Visite-t-il...? *Is he visiting...?*

Pronunciation

- Note that in **théâtre**, **th** is pronounced **t**.

B4 TRANSLATION

1. Do you have long holidays?
2. Do you travel alone?
3. Are they free on Saturdays?
4. Are they inviting friends on Wednesday?
5. Are they going to listen to a concert?
6. Do you like Brahms?
7. Do you often meet artists?
8. Does he sometimes visit museums?
9. Is she playing in a new theatre?
10. Is it a recent play?
11. Is it easy to understand?
12. Do you speak French?

10 Exercises and "HOW ARE YOU"

C1 EXERCISES

A. Turn these statements into questions (three ways) :
1. Elles voyagent souvent.
2. Ils ont une voiture neuve.
3. Vous commencez tôt.
4. Elle a un bon métier.
5. Vous allez très vite.
6. C'est un nouveau théâtre.

C2 ANSWERS

A. 1. Elles voyagent souvent ?/Est-ce qu'elles voyagent souvent ?/Voyagent-elles souvent ?
2. Ils ont une voiture neuve ?/Est-ce qu'ils ont une voiture neuve ?/Ont-ils une voiture neuve ?
3. Vous commencez tôt ?/Est-ce que vous commencez tôt ?/Commencez-vous tôt ?
4. Elle a un bon métier ?/Est-ce qu'elle a un bon métier ?/A-t-elle un bon métier ?
5. Vous allez très vite ?/Est-ce que vous allez très vite ?/Allez-vous très vite ?
6. C'est un nouveau théâtre ?/Est-ce que c'est un nouveau théâtre ?/Est-ce un nouveau théâtre ?

C3 COMMENT ALLEZ-VOUS ? (CD)
HOW ARE YOU ?

• aller, in questions where the verb is inverted, is commonly used in French to ask people how they are when you meet them :

Comment allez-vous ?/Comment vas-tu	*How are you ?*
Comment va-t-elle ?	*How is she ?*
Comment va-t-il ?	*How is he ?*
Comment vont-ils ?	*How are they ?*
Je vais bien.	*I'm fine.*
Je vais très bien.	*I'm very well.*
Je ne vais pas très bien.	*I'm not very well.*

• In colloquial French, **ça va ?** *(is everything all right ?)* and **ça va** *(everything is all right)* are very much used.

C4 PARIS, A POLE OF ATTRACTION

Paris was the focus of attention for artists, men of letters and science in the eighteenth and nineteenth centuries, and today still keeps up a tradition of hospitality. Paris is in the lead for business tourism and congresses. It is also France's foremost city for cultural tourism : its cultural heritage spanning millenia of history, its prestigious museums, its many theaters, its famous revues (**Folies Bergère, Paradis Latin…**) beat all the records for the number of tourists from all over the world. The capital'sappeal seems to withstand time and the economic crisis, and a great many people go to it to enjoy the "Parisian way of life" for a weekend.

■ The Major Construction Projects

Starting in 1981, there have been several major construction projects under the aegis of the President of the Republic. The first of these was the **Grand Louvre** under whose glass pyramid millions of visitors pass each year. Just west of Paris, the **Défense** quarter is enclosed by the Arch. To the east, the move of the Ministry of Economy and Finances to a new building built on the banks of the Seine, at **Bercy**, has accelerated the transformations of the area. To the north, the neighborhood of the **Villette** has been radically modified by the arrival of the **Géode**, the **Cité des Sciences et de l'Industrie**, the **Grande Halle** and the **Zénith**. To the south, the **Bibliothèque de France** (also known as the **TGB, Très Grande Bibliothèque** : Very Big Library) is now the repository of the volumes from the **Bibliothèque Nationale**.

D1 ON PREND RENDEZ-VOUS (CD)

Frédéric : Bonjour Sylvie, comment vas-tu ?
Sylvie : Ça va, ça va.
Frédéric : On déjeune ensemble ?
Sylvie : Pas aujourd'hui, je suis très en retard.
Frédéric : Est-ce que tu es libre demain à midi ?
Sylvie : Non j'ai un rendez-vous, je suis libre jeudi ou vendredi.
Frédéric : D'accord pour vendredi. As-tu une idée pour un restaurant ?
Sylvie : Est - ce que tu préfères « Chez Pierre » ou « Délices de Shangaï « ?
Frédéric : « Délices de Shangaï » ? Où est-ce ?
Sylvie : Ce n'est pas très loin. C'est rue[1] Gambetta.
Frédéric : Est-ce que je réserve une table ?
Sylvie : Bonne idée, mais pas avant une heure.
Frédéric : D'accord ! A vendredi !

1. Note that **rue, boulevard, avenue** is always placed before the name.

D2 AUJOURD'HUI… DEMAIN
TODAY *TOMORROW*

lundi	*Monday*
mardi	*Tuesday*
mercredi	*Wednesday*
jeudi	*Thursday*
vendredi	*Friday*
samedi	*Saturday*
dimanche	*Sunday*

- The days of the week are all masculine.
- Note that in French, the name of the day is used without any preposition.
  Ex. : **lundi** = *on Monday.*
  dimanche = *on Sunday.*

D3 MAKING A DATE

Frédéric : Hello, Sylvie. How are you ?
Sylvie : Fine, fine.
Frédéric : Can we have lunch together ?
Sylvie : Not today, I'm late.
Frédéric : Are you free tomorrow at noon ?
Sylvie : No, I have an appointment. I'm free Thursday or Friday.
Frédéric : Friday's good. What restaurant shall we go to ?
Sylvie : Do you prefer "Pierre's Place" or "Shangai Delights" ?
Frédéric : "Shangai Delights". Where is it ?
Sylvie : It's not very far away. It's on Gambetta Street.
Frédéric : Shall I reserve a table ?
Sylvie : Good idea, but not before one o'clock.
Frédéric : Okay. See you on Friday !

D4 MOIS/*MONTHS* (CD)

janvier	*January*
février	*February*
mars	*March*
avril	*April*
mai	*May*
juin *	*June*
juillet	*July*
août **	*August*
septembre	*September*
octobre	*October*
novembre	*November*
décembre	*December*

* **uin** in **juin** is pronounced **u** + the nasal vowel **in**.
** In **août**, **a** is not pronounced.

10 TESTS - LESSONS 1 TO 10

Complete with a, b, c or d : (There is only one correct answer for each item)

1. Tu ——— souvent ?
   a) danser
   b) danses
   c) dansez
   d) danse

2. Anne et Pierre ——— en Italie.
   a) aller
   b) va
   c) allons
   d) vont

3. Elle va venir ——— Paris ——— septembre.
   a) à en
   b) à à
   c) en à
   d) en en

4. Elles sont ———
   a) allemande
   b) allemandes
   c) allemands
   d) allemand

5. Vous ——— appelez Martin ?
   a) s'
   b) t'
   c) vous
   d) nous

6. Nous avons ——— amis étrangers.
   a) un
   b) des
   c) Ø
   d) une

7. ——— avons faim.
   a) Tu
   b) Ils
   c) Nous
   d) J'

8. Ils ——— anglais.
   a) es
   b) est
   c) sommes
   d) sont

9. Je ——— content.
   a) ne suis pas
   b) ne pas suis
   c) pas suis
   d) ne suis

10. Ils ——— près de Lyon.
   a) habite
   b) habitent
   c) habites
   d) habitez.

11 Le train n'est pas à l'heure.

A1 PRESENTATION

■ Grammar

- Definite articles

masculine	← singular →	feminine
le	← *the* →	**la**

- The article agrees in gender with the noun it accompanies:
  Le bureau. *The desk.* **Le train.** *The train.*
  La secrétaire. *The secretary.* **La valise.** *The suitcase.*
- **le, la** become **l'** before a vowel or **h**:
  L'étudiant. *The student.* **L'avion.** *The plane.* **L'heure.** *The hour.*

■ Vocabulary

partir — *to leave*
oublier — *to forget*
porter — *to carry*
métro (masc.) — *tube (*US: *subway)*
taxi (masc.) — *taxi*
autobus/bus (masc.) — *bus*
gare (fem.) — *station*
quai (masc.) — *platform*
rouge — *red*
beaucoup de monde — *a lot of people*
en grève — *on strike*
à l'heure — *on time*
sur — *on*

A2 EXAMPLES *(Means of transport)* (CD)

1. **Le métro est en grève mais il y a des taxis.**
2. **Il y a des bus près de la maison.**
3. **Le bus va partir dans cinq minutes.**
4. **Ce n'est pas le 20 (vingt), c'est le 30 (trente).**
5. **Est-ce que l'avion est à l'heure ?**
6. **La gare est loin ?**
7. **Non, la gare n'est pas loin.**
8. **Le train n'est pas à l'heure.**
9. **N'oublie pas la petite valise !**
10. **Il porte le sac rouge.**
11. **Il y a des gens sur le quai.**
12. **C'est l'heure ! Au revoir !**

11 The train isn't on time.

A3 COMMENTS

■ Grammar

• Remember: to make a sentence negative use **ne... pas**, or **n'... pas** on either side of the verb (see lesson 2, A1).

Le train n'est pas à l'heure. *The train isn't on time.*

• Note two ways of translating *people* in French:
— **monde (monde** (masc.) = *world***)** which is singular and practically never used as a subject.
Ex.: **Il y a du monde.** *There are (a lot of) people.*
— **gens (gens** (masc.) = *people***)** which is plural.
Ex.: **Il y a des gens.** *There are (a lot of) people.*

• Note that for bus numbers, the definite article is used in French.
Ex. : **le 20, le 30.**

■ Pronunciation

• In **bus**, the final **s** is heard.

A4 TRANSLATION

1. The tube is on strike, but there are taxis.
2. There are buses near the house.
3. The bus is leaving in five minutes.
4. It isn't a 20, it's a 30.
5. Is the plane on time?
6. Is the station far?
7. No, the station isn't far.
8. The train isn't on time.
9. Don't forget the little case!
10. He is carrying the red bag.
11. There are people on the platform.
12. It's time! Good bye!

11 Nous allons inviter les voisins.

B1 PRESENTATION

Grammar

- Definite articles.
  There is only one plural article:

les	*the*

  The article agrees in number with the noun it accompanies.
  Ex.: **les trains, les gares, les avions, les heures.**
- **es** in **les** is pronounced like *A* in *A, B, C.*

Vocabulary

apporter *to bring*
chercher *to fetch / to look for*
verre (masc.) *glass*
assiette (fem.) *plate*
table (fem.) *table*
serviette (fem.) *napkin*
invité (masc.) *guest*
pain (masc.) *bread*
boisson (fem.) *drink*
blanc/blanche *white*

B2 EXAMPLES *(Getting ready for a party)* CD

1. **Nous allons inviter les voisins.**
2. **Où sont les grands verres ?**
3. **Est-ce que les verres sont sur la table ?**
4. **Les verres sont dans la salle à manger.**
5. **Est-ce que Pierre apporte les vins ?**
6. **Allez chercher les bouteilles, s'il vous plaît.**
7. **Où sont les assiettes ?**
8. **Demande à Antoine.**
9. **Où sont les serviettes blanches ?**
10. **Les voisins vont apporter les boissons.**
11. **Va acheter le pain, s'il te plaît.**
12. **Les invités sont là, apportez les chaises !**

11 We are going to invite the neighbours.

B3 COMMENTS

Grammar

- We have seen that **aller** + infinitive may be equivalent of *to be going to*.

  Ex.: **Nous allons inviter.** *We are going to invite.*

  The French equivalent of *go and* + verb is also: **aller** + infinitive.

  Ex.: **Allez chercher.** *Go and fetch, go and get.*
  Va acheter. *Go and buy.*

- Note that the equivalent of *to ask somebody* is **demander à quelqu'un**.

  Ex.: **Demande à Antoine.** *Ask Antoine.*

Pronunciation

- Don't forget the liaison when **les** is followed by a vowel or **h**.

  Ex.: **les‿assiettes, les‿amis.**
  (z) (z)

B4 TRANSLATION

1. We are going to invite the neighbours.
2. Where are the big glasses?
3. Are the glasses on the table?
4. The glasses are in the dining-room.
5. Is Pierre bringing the wines?
6. Go and fetch the bottles, please.
7. Where are the plates?
8. Ask Antoine.
9. Where are the white napkins?
10. The neighbours are going to bring the drinks.
11. Go and buy the bread, please.
12. The guests are here, bring the chairs!

11 Exercises and MEASURES

C1 EXERCISES

A. Fill in the gaps with : <u>le, la, les, l':</u>
1. Elle regarde… photos.
2.… métro est devant… restaurant.
3.… enfant cherche… petite voiture.
4.… invités apportent… vins.

B. (CD) **Translate into French :**
1. Go and fetch the red case.
2. He is going to bring the photos.
3. They are going to visit the museum.
4. Go and speak with the guests.

C2 ANSWERS

A. 1. Elle regarde les photos.
2. Le métro est devant le restaurant.
3. L'enfant cherche la petite voiture.
4. Les invités apportent les vins.

B. 1. Va chercher la valise rouge./Allez chercher la valise rouge.
2. Il va apporter les photos.
3. Ils vont visiter le musée.
4. Va parler avec les invités./Allez parler avec les invités.

C3 MEASURES

Mesures	*Measures*
un centimètre	*a centimetre*
un mètre	*a metre*
un kilomètre	*a kilometre* (= 0.62 mile)

C4 THE TGV

■ Since the beginning of the 1980s, the network of TGVs (**trains à grande vitesse** : high speed trains) has led to a veritable revolution in mass transportation. Thanks to this train, which attains speeds of more than 300 kph (185 mph), the capital and the provinces have drawn closer together. Business and leisure trips have increased, and companies have developed new strategies for setting up factories. The possibilities offered by the southeast TGV, introduced in 1981, were extended by the Atlantic TGV that was finished in 1990 and the northern network leading to London and Brussels. To the original orange and blue cars were added those of the Eurostar in the middle of the 1990s and, since 1997, the red trains of the Thalys linking Paris to Brussels. In the near future, the east and south of France will also be equipped with high speed tracks. And soon afterwards the connections with the Rhineland and northern Italy will be operational, according to the project approved by the Commission in Brussels.

■ The Spaniards, the Texans and the Koreans have all chosen French know-how to modernize their railroads. It is true that the Germans have invented a magnetic levitation train, but the system conceived by Alsthom and French engineers allows trains to travel at slower speeds on normal tracks. The only drawback of the TGV is that it requires special tracks to attain speeds of more than 185 mph. Consequently, its real competitor is the pendular train whose cars are made with high tech jacks so that it can use ordinary tracks at speeds above 200 kph (125 mph).

■ The commercial success of the TGV has not yet made it possible for the **SNCF (Société nationale des chemins de fer français** : National Company for French Railroads) to get into the black. It is in competition with road transportation and with large trucks, which seem more adapted to modern economic imperatives. But growing interest in ecology in Europe will no doubt lead to the development of new solutions such as rail/road, the transportation of trucks on flat rail cars.

D1 A LA GARE (CD)

Nathalie : Dix heures, nous sommes juste à l'heure.
Serge : Où est le T.G.V. pour Bordeaux ?
Nathalie : Regarde, il y a un panneau des horaires de départ.
Serge : Bordeaux, c'est la voie trois.
Nathalie : Tu as les billets ?
Serge : Non, ils sont dans la poche de la petite valise.
Nathalie : Il y a une machine à composter là, mais il y a la queue, allons plus loin.
Serge : Eh, attention, tu oublies le sac noir.
Le T.G.V. pour Bordeaux entre en gare voie trois.
Serge : C'est la voiture douze, non ? Vérifie le numéro.
Nathalie : C'est bon, voiture douze. Montons.
Serge : Tu préfères la place près de la fenêtre, pour voir le paysage ?
Nathalie : Oui, merci. Ne range pas le sac il y a les magazines dedans.

D2 A VERY USEFUL EXPRESSION : IL Y A...

- **il y a** is the French equivalent of both *there* is and *there are.*
  Ex. : **Il y a un appartement à louer.**
  There is a flat to let.
  Il y a une jolie maison ici.
  There is a nice house here.
  Il y a des restaurants rue Monge.
  There are restaurants on Monge Street.
- Notice the pronunciation « eeleeya » (the three words run together).
- In spoken French, you very often hear **y a** (ya), instead of **il y a.**
- In the interrogative :

Il y a un concert aujourd'hui ?
Est-ce qu'il y a un concert aujourd'hui ?
Y a-t-il un concert aujourd'hui ?
] *Is there a concert today ?*

D3 AT THE TRAIN STATION

Nathalie : Ten o'clock. We're right on time.
Serge : Where is the High Speed Train for Bordeaux ?
Nathalie : Look, there's a board with the departure times.
Serge : Bordeaux, it's on Platform 3.
Nathalie : Do you have the tickets ?
Serge : No, they're in the pocket of the small suitcase.
Nathalie : There's a ticket stamping machine there, but there's a line (GB : a queue). Let's go farther.
Serge : Hey, watch it ! You almost forgot the black bag.
The High Speed Train for Bordeaux is arriving on Platform 3.
Serge : It's car 12, isn't it ? Check the number.
Nathalie : That's right, car 12. Let's get on.
Serge : Would you rather have the window seat, so you can see the scenery ?
Nathalie : Yes, thanks. Don't put the bag away, the magazines are in it.

C3 MOYENS DE TRANSPORT
MEANS OF TRANSPORTATION

- **RER (Réseau Express Régional) :**
  rapid transit to the suburbs from the centre of Paris.
- **SNCF (Société Nationale des Chemins de Fer Français) :**
  French Railways.
- **TGV (Train à Grande Vitesse) :**
  the fastest and one of the most comfortable trains in the world, runs at speeds of up to 500 **km/h (kilomètres à l'heure)**.

12 Quelle belle journée !

A1 PRESENTATION

Grammar

- **quel,** *what.*
  The exclamative **quel** *(= what)* agrees in gender and number with the noun it refers to:

quel	(masc. sg.)	**quels**	(masc. pl.)
quelle	(fem. sg.)	**quelles**	(fem. pl.)

The exclamation can be formed with: **quel** + noun

Quel homme !	*What a man!*	**Quels artistes !**	*What artists!*
Quelle femme !	*What a woman!*	**Quelles photos !**	*What photos!*

or: **quel** + adjective + noun

Quel grand bateau !	*What a big boat!*
Quels bons vins !	*What good wines!*
Quelle jolie fille !	*What a pretty girl!*
Quelles belles années !	*What beautiful years!*

Vocabulary

temps (masc.)	*weather*	**journée** (fem.)	*day*
orage (masc.), **tempête** (fem.)	*storm*	**année** (fem.)	*year*
		terrible	*terrible*
pluie (fem.)	*rain*	**splendide**	*splendid*
nuage (masc.)	*cloud*	**magnifique**	*magnificent*
coucher de soleil (masc.)	*sunset*	**drôle**	*funny*

A2 EXAMPLES *(Weather)* (CD)

1. **Quel temps !**
2. **Quel orage !**
3. **Quelle pluie !**
4. **Quelles tempêtes !**
5. **Quel froid terrible !**
6. **Quelle mauvaise année !**
7. **Quelle belle journée !**
8. **Quel temps splendide !**
9. **Quel magnifique coucher de soleil !**
10. **Quels drôles de nuages !**
11. **Quelles terribles tempêtes !**
12. **Quels vents violents !**

A3 COMMENTS

Grammar

- Note that there is no article before the noun in the exclamative.

  Quelle journée ! — **Quel orage !**
  What a day! — *What a storm!*

- **drôle** when placed before the noun it refers to is always followed by **de** and conveys the meaning of *strange*.

  Ex.: **C'est une drôle de fille.**
  She is a funny girl (meaning an *odd girl*).

  But **cette fille est drôle** can mean either *that girl is amusing* or *that girl is odd.*

- **journée** and **année** are generally used to insist on the length of time of a day or a year, otherwise **jour** and **an** are used.

Pronunciation

- Note that **el** in **quel** is pronounced **èl** like *e* in *pet*.
- Remember that **qu** in the final **que** (ex.: **magnifique**) is pronounced like *ck* in *back*.
- Note that in **temps**, neither **p** nor **s** are heard.
- Note that **er** in **coucher**, **ée** in **journée**, have the sound of *A (*in *A, B, C).*

A4 TRANSLATION

1. What weather!
2. What a storm!
3. What rain!
4. What storms!
5. What terrible cold!
6. What a bad year!
7. What a beautiful day!
8. What splendid weather!
9. What a magnificent sunset!
10. What funny clouds!
11. What terrible storms!
12. What violent winds!

12 Regardez les singes ! Comme ils sont drôles !

B1 PRESENTATION

■ Grammar

- **Que, comme,** *how.*
  Another exclamatory form is obtained by putting **que** or **comme** before a statement:

1 **que** or **comme** + subject + **être** + adjective

Que le ciel est bleu ! **Comme le ciel est bleu !**	*How blue the sky is!*
Qu'elle est belle !	*How beautiful she is!*
Comme c'est beau ! **Que c'est beau !**	*How beautiful it is!*

2 **que** or **comme** + subject + verb

Que cette voiture va vite !	*How fast this car is going!*
Comme il parle bien !	*How well he speaks!*

■ Vocabulary

avoir l'air	*to look, to sound*	**yeux** (masc. pl.)	*eyes*
		lion (masc.)	*lion*
détester	*to hate*	**éléphant** (masc.)	*elephant*
chien (masc.)	*dog*	**serpent** (masc.)	*snake*
oiseau (masc.)	*bird*	**joyeux**	*merry*
singe (masc.)	*monkey*	**fort**	*strong*

B2 EXAMPLES *(Animals)* (CD)

1. **Comme j'aime ce chat !**
2. **Que j'aime ce chat gris !**
3. **Que ce chien a l'air intelligent !**
4. **Comme les oiseaux chantent fort ce matin !**
5. **Qu'ils ont l'air joyeux !**
6. **Regardez les singes ! Comme ils sont drôles !**
7. **Qu'ils sont drôles !**
8. **Comme ce lion a l'air triste !**
9. **Qu'il a les yeux tristes !**
10. **Que l'éléphant est drôle !**
11. **Comme il est fort !**
12. **Que je déteste les serpents !**

B3 COMMENTS

Grammar

- Note that **fort** can be either an adjective meaning *strong*, or an adverb meaning *loud*.

  Ex.: **C'est un garçon très fort.** *He is a very strong boy.*
  Ne parle pas trop fort. *Don't speak too loud.*

- Note that when parts of the body are not the subject of the sentence, the definite article is used.

  Ex.: **Il a les yeux bleus.** *He has blue eyes.*
  Elle a les yeux tristes. *Her eyes are sad.*

- Note that with the exclamative **comme** *(how)* the construction remains the same as in a simple statement.

  Ils ont l'air joyeux. *They look merry.*
  Comme / **Qu'** → **ils ont l'air joyeux !** *How merry they look!*

Pronunciation

- Remember that **j** (in **je, bonjour, joli, jeune,** etc.) is pronounced like *su* in *pleasure*.
- Remember that **oy** in **joyeux** is pronounced like **oi** followed by the sound of *y* in *yes*.

B4 TRANSLATION

1. How I love this cat!
2. How I love this grey cat!
3. How intelligent this dog looks!
4. How loud the birds are singing this morning!
5. How merry they sound!
6. Look at the monkeys! How funny they are!
7. How funny they are!
8. How sad this lion looks!
9. How sad his eyes are!
10. How funny the elephant is!
11. How strong he is!
12. How I hate snakes!

12 Exercises and EMOTIONS

C1 EXERCISES

A. Match the words :

quelle	hôtel	bel	!
quelles	yeux	belles	!
quels	voiture	jolie	!
quel	vacances	splendides	!

B. (CD) Translate into French :

1. What a beautiful autumn !
2. How nice you are !
3. How slowly this bus is going !
4. How thirsty I am !

C2 ANSWERS

A. 1. Quelle jolie voiture !
2. Quelles belles vacances !
3. Quels yeux splendides !
4. Quel bel hôtel !

B. 1. Quel bel automne !
2. Que vous êtes (tu es) gentil !
3. Que cet autobus avance lentement !
4. Que j'ai soif !

C3 EMOTIONS (CD)

Quel bonheur !	*What a blessing !*
Quelle tristesse !	*How sad !*
Quelle horreur !	*How horrible !*
Quel dommage !	*What a shame !*
Quel malheur !	*What a pity !*

C4 THE PARIS METRO AND RER

■ The first **métro** (US : subway ; GB : underground) line in Paris was inaugurated for the World Fair in 1900. **Porte Dauphine** is the only métro station to have kept its original covered entrance, designed by **Hector Guimard**. Today the Paris métro includes fifteen lines that are used by more than five million commuters a day on week days. The tracks, above and below ground, follow the paths of the Paris streets, and the trains are all made up of five cars.

■ To respond to a growing need, the **RATP (Régie autonome des transports parisiens** : Autonomous Regime of Parisian Transportation) and the **SNCF (Société nationale des chemins de fer français** : National Company of French Railroads) put the **RER (Réseau Express Régional** : Regional Express Network) into service starting in 1969. Numerous interconnections with the métro network exist, notably in stations at **Auber, Charles-de-Gaulle-Etoile, Châtelet-les-Halles** and **Nation.** A system of season tickets with a unique fare according to the zones travelled outside of the city and more flexible schedules make it easier for Parisians, inhabitants of the **Ile de France,** and tourists to get around the city and its suburbs.

■ In the 1980s, around one hundred stations were decorated in shades of yellow and orange. Today, preference is given to a style that fits in with the surrounding area and to improving the running of the trains as well as the lighting and floor and wall coverings. For veritable creation, it will be necessary to wait for the future **Météor** stations. Theme stations, such as the **Louvre** or the **Hôtel de Ville,** have been frequently remodeled. So has the **Arts et Métiers** station, which has become a sort of underground Nautilus, and the National Assembly station, which houses a work in progress in which large posters featuring the silhouettes of the deputies are changed from one parliamentary session to another.

■ Since the métro has an important sociological impact, the **SNCF** has sought to improve its image by calling on specialists in communications. On their recommendation, the métro is also the stage for numerous artistic events (concerts and expositions) or for discussions, occasionally over a cup of coffee offered to commuters. These efforts have been completed by a policy of increased surveillance in an attempt to end underground insecurity and delinquency.

D1 CHIENS ET CHATS (CD)

Marie : Regarde le petit chien, là, près de l'arbre ! Comme il est drôle !
Anne : Tu aimes les animaux, Marie ? Quelle surprise !
Marie : J'adore les animaux. J'ai un chien. C'est un épagneul, il est brun mais il a une oreille blanche. Il est très marrant[1].
Anne : Une seule oreille blanche, c'est original !
Marie : Il a de grands yeux marron et un air parfois un peu triste. C'est le grand ami de Figaro, le chat de la maison.
Anne : Tu as aussi un chat ?
Marie : Oui, un gros chat jaune avec des yeux verts, superbes. Il a une tête de tigre mais il est vraiment gentil.
Anne : Un chien, un chat, quel travail ! Et pour partir en vacances, ce n'est pas trop difficile ?
Marie : Pas du tout, j'ai une maison de campagne et j'emmène aussi les poissons rouges.
Anne : Quel courage ! A vrai dire, je déteste les animaux.
Marie : C'est incroyable !

1. **Marrant** : colloquial for *funny*.

D2 COULEURS/*COLOURS*

Remain the same in the masculine or feminine	Add an e in the feminine	Are different in the feminine
rouge *red* **jaune** *yellow* **rose** *pink*	**vert (e)** *green* **bleu (e)** *blue* **noir (e)** *black* **gris (e)** *grey* **brun (e)** *brown*	**blanc/blanche** *white* **violet/violette** *purple*

- Some more colours : **rouge cerise** *cherry-red*
  bleu marine *navy-blue*
  vert émeraude *emerald-green*

D3 DOGS AND CATS

Marie : Look at the little dog there, near the tree. It's so funny !

Anne : You like animals, Marie ? What a surprise !

Marie : I adore animals. I have a dog. It's a spaniel ; he's brown but he has one white ear. He's very funny.

Anne : A single white ear, that's original !

Marie : He has big brown eyes and sometimes looks a little sad. He's a great friend of Figaro, the house cat.

Anne : You have a cat, too ?

Marie : Yes, a big yellow cat with magnificent green eyes ! He's got the head of a tiger, but he's really nice.

Anne : A dog, a cat ! What a lot of work ! And isn't it too difficult to go on vacation ?

Marie : Not at all. I have a house in the country, and I also take the goldfish.

Anne : You're so full of energy ! To tell the truth, I detest animals.

Marie : That's unbelievable !

D4 LE CORPS HUMAIN/ *THE HUMAN BODY*

tête (fem.)	*bead*	**joue** (fem.)	*cheek*
cheveux (masc., usually pl.)	*hair*	**menton** (masc.)	*chin*
visage (masc.)	*face*	**cou** (masc.)	*neck*
front (masc..)	*forebead*	**bras** (masc.)	*arm*
œil (masc. sg.)	*eye*	**main** (fem.)	*hand*
yeux (masc. pl.)	*eyes*	**doigt** (masc.)	*finger*
nez (masc.)	*nose*	**pouce** (masc.)	*thumb*
bouche (fem.)	*mouth*	**jambe** (fem.)	*leg*
oreille (fem.)	*ear*	**pied** (masc.)	*foot*

13 Cette chemise coûte trente euros

A1 PRESENTATION

■ Grammar

• **ce / cette** + nom

are the French equivalents of : *this/that* + noun.

– **ce** + a masculine singular.

Ex. : **Ce journaliste.** *This (that) journalist.*

– **cette** + a feminine singular.

Ex. : **Cette amie.** *This (that) friend.*

• **ces** + a noun in the plural

is the French equivalent of : *these/those* + noun.

Ex. : **Ces livres.** *These (those) books.*

Ces maisons. *These (those) houses.*

■ Vocabulary

coûter	*to cost*
poser	*to put*
manteau (masc.)	*coat*
robe (fem.)	*dress*
pantalon or **pantalons** (masc.)	*trousers*
chemise (fem.)	*shirt*
chaussure (fem.)	*shoe*
imperméable (masc.)	*raincoat*
vêtements (masc. pl.)	*clothes*

court *short*

The **euro** is the new French currency (has replaced the franc)

A2 EXEMPLES *(Buying clothes)* (CD)

1. **Tu aimes ce manteau ?**
2. **Cet imperméable est trop long.**
3. **Je vais acheter cette robe.**
4. **Cette robe est trop courte !**
5. **J'aime cette chemise.**
6. **Est-ce que cette chemise est chère ?**
7. **Cette chemise coûte trente euros (€ 30)**
8. **Je n'aime pas ces chaussures avec ce pantalon.**
9. **Est-ce que ces chaussures sont chères ?**
10. **Ces chaussures coûtent soixante euros (€ 60).**
11. **N'achète pas ces pantalons, ils sont trop courts.**
12. **Pose ces vêtements sur cette chaise, s'il te plaît.**

A3 COMMENTS

■ Pronunciation

- **cet / cette** are pronounced like *set.*
- **ces** is pronounced like **cé (é,** sound of *A* in *A, B, C+*).
- When the noun which follows starts with a vowel or h, **ce** becomes **cet**.

  Ex.: **Cet ami**. — *This (that) friend.*
  Cet imperméable. — *This (that) raincoat.*
- Don't forger the liaison:

  Ex.: **Cet enfant.** (∪ t) — **Ces enfants.** (∪ z)

■ Grammar

- Remember that in French the endings of the verbs vary according to the person and number of the subject:

J'aime cette chemise. — *I like this shirt.*
Tu aimes cette chemise. — *You like this shirt.*
Ils aiment cette chemise. — *They like ibis shirt.*

A4 TRANSLATION

1. Do you like this coat?
2. That raincoat is too long.
3. I'm going to buy that dress.
4. That dress is too short!
5. I like this shirt.
6. Is this shirt expensive?
7. This shirt costs thirty euros (€ 30).
8. I don't like these (those) shoes with those (these) trousers.
9. Are these shoes expensive?
10. These shoes cost sixty euros (€ 60).
11. Don't buy those trousters, they are too short.
12. Put these clothes on that chair, please.

13 Ne parlons plus de ça.

B1 PRESENTATION

■ Grammar

- *this*, when used alone is translated by **ceci** ;
  that, when used alone is translated by **cela**.

  Ex. : **Je n'aime pas cela.** / **Je n'aime pas ça.** } *I don't like that (it).*

  ça is very commonly used and can mean *this/that* or *it*, according to the context.
- **ceci, cela, ça** usually refer to an object or concept which has already been mentioned or can be clearly identified in the situation or context.
- **ne... plus, n'... plus**, *not... any more, no longer.*

■ Vocabulary

goûter	*to taste*
disque (masc.)	*record*
album (masc.)	*album*
mille (1 000)	*thousand (1,000)*
superbe	*superb*
délicieux	*delicious*
malade	*sick, ill*
armagnac (masc.)	*is a kind of brandy*

B2 EXAMPLES *(Likes and dislikes)* CD

1. **Voici un nouveau disque ; écoute ça, c'est superbe.**
2. **Tu trouves ? Je n'aime pas ça.**
3. **Regarde ça, c'est un nouvel album.**
4. **Je vais acheter ça pour Pierre.**
5. **Ça coûte cher ?**
6. **Ça coûte mille euros (€ 1 000)**
7. **Ne parlons plus de ça.**
8. **Voilà un vieil armagnac, tu aimes ca ?**
9. **Goûte ça, c'est délicieux.**
10. **Ne fume pas comme ça, tu vas être malade !**
11. **Ne parle pas comme ça, ce n'est pas gentil.**
12. **Je déteste ça.**

B3 COMMENTS

■ <u>Grammar</u>

- Notice that **ça** is used either as a subject or an object.
  Ex. : **Ça coûte cher.** *It costs a lot.*
  Je n'aima pas ça. *I don't like that.*

- **ne... plus, n'... plus**, like **ne... pas**, is placed on either side of the verb.
  Ex. : **Elle n'habite plus ici.** *Shoe doesn't live here any more.*

■ <u>Vocabulary</u>

- In the singuler :
  – **vieux** / – **nouveau** when preceding a vowel or **h** become **vieil** / **nouvel**
  Ex. : **Un vieil armagnac.**
  Un nouvel album.

- Remember :
  g + **e** or **i** is pronounced **j** (ex. : **gentil**) (see lesson 12, B3).
  g + other vowels is pronounced **g** like in *good* (ex. : **goûte**).

B4 TRANSLATION

1. Here is a new record ; listen to this, it's superb.
2. You think so ? I don't like it.
3. Look at that, it's a new album.
4. I'm going to buy it for Pierre.
5. Does it cost a lot ?
6. It costs one thousand euros.
7. Let's not speak about that any more.
8. Here is an old brandy, do you like it ?
9. Taste that, it's delicious.
10. Don't smoke like that, you are going to be sick.
11. Don't speak like that, it's not nice.
12. I hate that.

13 Exercises and EXPRESSIONS

C1 EXERCISES

A. (CD) **Transform as in the example :**
Un portrait célèbre. Ce portrait est célèbre.

1. Une pièce sombre.
2. Un mauvais restaurant.
3. Une jupe courte.
4. Des étudiants étrangers.
5. Des maisons modernes.

B. Translate into French :

1. They don't like that.
2. I hate that book.
3. She is going to buy these shoes.
4. Don't look at that.

C2 ANSWERS

A. 1. Cette pièce est sombre.
2. Ce restaurant est mauvais.
3. Cette jupe est courte.
4. Ces étudiants sont étrangers.
5. Ces maisons sont modernes.

B. 1. Ils n'aiment pas ça./Elles n'aiment pas ça.
2. Je déteste ce livre.
3. Elle va acheter ces chaussures.
4. Ne regarde pas ça./Ne regardez pas ça.

C3 EXPRESSIONS (CD)

Ça va ?	*Is everything all right ?*
Ça va/ça va bien !	*Everything's fine !*
Ça va mal	*Things are going badly.*
Ça va aller	*It is going to be all right.*
Ça dépend	*It depends.*
C'est ça	*That's right/that's correct.*
Ça suffit !	*That's enough !*

C4 THOSE WINES WE DREAM OF

■ French wines are universally renowned for their quality and variety. The cultivation of grapes, which in the past was present throughout most of the country, is today concentrated in specific regions. The exposure and lay-out (on hills or plains), the type of soil (chalky in the **Bordeaux** country, rocky in **Bourgogne**), and the type of vine are all essential factors in the quality of a vineyard. Of course, it's also necessary to add in the talent and the work of generations of wine-makers.

■ The biggest wine country in the world stretches over the plains of **Languedoc** and **Rousillon**. That of the west follows the rivers : the **Loire** valley, the **Garonne** Valley, **Dordogne**, etc. The vineyards in the north are mainly situated on hilly ground facing east. Those in the **Provence** and **vallée du Rhône** regions are either on the plains, or on the sides of valleys.

■ The production of certain vineyards has been commercialized since the Middle Ages. Wines from Bourgogne were at the time exported to Flanders, the Bordeaux wines to England, and **cognac** and **armagnac** to Holland. Champagne remains the crown jewel, and has been the finest example of French viticulture since the time of **Louis XV**.

■ Today, regional and table wines are rivals of **VDQS** (**vins de qualité supérieure** : superior quality wines) and AOC (**vins d'appelation d'origine contrôlée** : wines whose quality is guaranteed). The latter must meet strict criteria concerning the demarcation of the vineyards, the verification of the vines, the amount produced, the percentage of alcohol, etc. Where **Médoc** wines are concerned, for example, the five appellations of the finest vintages are among the most famous in the world : **Lafite-Rothschild, Latour, Margaux, Mouton-Rothschild** and **Haut-Brion.** These classifications are regularly reviewed by the **INAO** (**Institut national des appellations d'origine**) and the wine syndicates in order to ensure that the consumer receives an exceptional product.

13 DIALOGUES AND ADJECTIVES

D1 ACHAT ET VÊTEMENTS

Paul : Tu as des chaussures super[1] ! Elles ont l'air très confortables.

Nicolas : C'est vrai. Je vais toujours dans la même boutique. Il y a un choix extraordinaire.

Paul : C'est cher ?

Nicolas : Non, ça ne coûte pas les yeux de la tête. Le rapport « qualité/prix » est très bon.

Paul : J'ai justement besoin d'une paire de chaussures. Je suis invité à un mariage ce samedi.
Je vais noter l'adresse de cette boutique. Tu n'as pas une bonne adresse pour les chemises ?

….. (*Dans le magasin*)

Paul : Est-ce que tu aimes cette couleur ?

Nicolas : Oh, ce bleu pâle est très chic, ça va avec tout. Mais elle est un peu large. Essaye la taille quarante.

Paul : Tu as raison, ça va mieux comme ça. Je vais aussi prendre cette cravate et cette ceinture.

Nicolas : Eh ! ! Ça suffit, tu vas dépenser une fortune.

1. Super is used in colloquial French only.

D2 ADJECTIVES USED BOTH IN THE MASCULINE AND FEMININE

Superbe and **malade** like **jeune, sympathique, triste,** and **célèbre** are used both for the masculine and feminine. Here are some more adjectives of the same kind :

large	*broad, wide*
pauvre	*poor*
riche	*rich*
simple	*simple*
utile	*useful*
vide	*empty*

D3 BUYING CLOTHES

Paul : What great shoes you have ! They look very comfortable.
Nicolas : It's true, they are. I always go to the same store. It's got an extraordinary selection.
Paul : Is it expensive ?
Nicolas : No, it doesn't cost an arm and a leg. You get very good value for your money.
Paul : As it happens, I need a pair of shoes. I'm invited to a wedding this Saturday. Give me the address of the store. Do you have a good address for shirts, too ?
….. (*In the store*)
Paul : Do you like this color ?
Nicolas : Oh, that pale blue is very elegant ; it goes with everything. But it's a little big. Try on a size 15 1/2.
Paul : You're right. This is better. I'm also going to take this tie and this belt.
Nicolas : Hey ! That's enough, you're going to spend a fortune !

D4 SIZES

Men's suits							
France :	38	40	42	44	46	48	50
UK/US :	10	12	14	16	18	20	22
Trouser sizes (waist)							
France :	36	38	40	42	44	46	48
UK/US :	28	30	32	33	34	36	38
Collar sizes							
France :	36	37	38	39	41	42	43
UK/US :	14	14 1/2	15	15 1/2	16	16 1/2	17
Men's shoe sizes							
France :		41	42	43	44	45	46
UK :		7	8	9	10	10 1/2	11
US :		7 1/2	8 1/2	9 1/2	10 1/2	11	11 1/2

14 La femme qui habite à côté est une journaliste danoise.

A1 PRESENTATION

Grammar

- In French, the relative pronouns which are most often used are:

qui	*who, that, which*	used as subject
que	*whom, that, which*	used as direct object

Both may refer to persons or things.

Ex.: **Écoute l'homme qui parle à la radio.**
Listen to the man who is speaking on the radio.

L'homme que vous allez rencontrer est américain.
The man you're going to meet is American.

Apporte le livre qui est sur la table, s'il te plaît.
Bring the book which is on the table, please.

Où est le livre que tu utilises ?
Where is the book you use?

Vocabulary

montre (fem.)	*watch*
homme (masc.)	*man*
femme (fem.)	*woman*
chanson (fem.)	*song*
liberté (fem.)	*freedom*
en vitrine	*in the shopwindow*
à côté	*next door*

A2 EXAMPLES *(Specifying which one)* (CD)

1. **J'aime bien la montre qui est en vitrine.**
2. **J'aime bien la montre que tu as aujourd'hui.**
3. **Regarde l'homme qui est sur la photo.**
4. **Voici l'homme que j'aime !**
5. **La femme qui habite à côté est une journaliste danoise.**
6. **La femme que tu regardes est une artiste.**
7. **Les gens qui sont sur cette photo habitent en Espagne.**
8. **J'invite des gens que tu aimes bien.**
9. **Ils écoutent des chansons qui parlent de liberté.**
10. **Écoute la chanson qu'ils chantent.**
11. **Nous allons visiter l'appartement qui est à louer.**
12. **Nous allons visiter l'appartement que nous allons acheter.**

A3 COMMENTS

Grammar

- **qui** and **que** may refer to a masculine or feminine, singular or plural noun.
- **que** becomes **qu'** before a vowel or **h**, but **qui** does not change.
  Ex.: **L'ordinateur qu'elle utilise.**
  The computer she uses.
  L'ordinateur qui est sur le bureau.
  The computer that is on the desk.
- **que** as a relative pronoun used as direct object can never be omitted in French.
  Ex.: **L'homme que j'aime.** *The man I love.*
  Le repas que je prépare. *The meal I'm preparing.*
- Remember: **nous allons,** *we are going to.*
  Aller, *to go,* is an irregular verb (see lesson 5, A1). Followed by a verb in the infinitive, **aller** expresses either an intention or the immediate future. It is the French equivalent of *to be going to* (see lesson 5, B1).

Pronunciation

- **qu** is pronounced like *ck* in *back.*
- The first **e** in **femme** is pronounced like *a* in *Pat* (the second is mute).

A4 TRANSLATION

1. I like the watch that is in the shopwindow.
2. I like the watch you have on today.
3. Look at the man who is in the photograph.
4. Here is the man I love!
5. The woman who lives next door is a Danish journalist.
6. The woman you are looking at is an artist.
7. The people who are in this photograph live in Spain.
8. I am inviting some people that you like.
9. They are listening to songs that speak of freedom.
10. Listen to the song they are singing.
11. We are going to visit the flat that is to let.
12. We are going to visit the flat we are going to buy.

14 Écoute ce que le guide explique.

B1 PRESENTATION

Grammar

- **qui** and **que** are often used in the expressions: **c'est... qui, c'est... que.**

  Ex.: **Louis est ici.** ***C'est Louis qui est ici.***
  It is Louis who is here.
  Anne chante. ***C'est Anne qui chante.***
  It is Anne who is singing.
  J'utilise ce livre. ***C'est ce livre que j'utilise.***
  It is this book I use.

  In the sentences in italics, ***Louis, Anne, ce livre*** are emphasized.

- **ce qui, ce que** are compound relative pronouns which are equivalent to *what.*

ce qui is used as subject
ce que is used as object

Ex.: **Regarde ce qui est ici.** *Look what is here.*
Regarde ce que j'ai. *Look what I've got.*

Vocabulary

préférer	*to prefer*	**étage** (masc.)	*floor*
expliquer	*to explain*	**tableau** (masc.)	*painting*
guide (masc.)	*guide*	**premier**	*first*
salle (fem.)	*room*	**en ce moment**	*at the moment*

B2 EXAMPLES *(Visiting a museum)* CD

1. **C'est le musée que je préfère.**
2. **C'est un musée qui est à Amsterdam.**
3. **C'est un jeune guide qui parle.**
4. **Écoute ce que le guide explique.**
5. **Écoute ce qu'explique le guide.**
6. **Ce qu'il explique est intéressant.**
7. **Regarde ce qu'il y a dans cette salle.**
8. **C'est une salle qui est vide en ce moment.**
9. **Allons visiter ce qu'il y a au premier étage.**
10. **Ce sont des tableaux qui sont très modernes.**
11. **Je n'aime pas ce qui est dans la première salle.**
12. **Mais j'aime bien ce qui est dans la salle à côté.**

B3 COMMENTS

Grammar

- Remember that in the plural, **c'est... qui, c'est... que** become **ce sont... qui, ce sont... que**.
  Ex.: **Ce sont des amis qui sont drôles.**
  They are friends who are funny.
  Ce sont les amis que je préfère.
  They are the friends I prefer.

- Note that after **ce que**, the verb may be inverted if the subject is not a pronoun:

Écoute ce que les enfants chantent. **Écoute ce que chantent les enfants.**	*Listen to what the children are singing.*
Écoute ce que le guide explique. **Écoute ce qu'explique le guide.**	*Listen to what the guide is explaining.*

→ But:

Écoute ce qu'ils chantent. *Listen to what they are singing.*
Écoute ce qu'il explique. *Listen to what he is explaining.*

- **premier** in the feminine becomes **première**. Note the grave accent. Also note the grave accent in **préfère**.

B4 TRANSLATION

1. It is the museum I prefer.
2. It is a museum that is in Amsterdam.
3. It is a young guide who is speaking.
4. Listen to what the guide is explaining.
5. Listen to what the guide is explaining.
6. What he is explaining is interesting.
7. Look what there is in that room.
8. It is a room which is empty at the moment.
9. Let's go and visit what there is on the first floor.
10. They are paintings which are very modern.
11. I don't like what there is in the first room.
12. But I like what is in the room next door.

14 Exercises

C1 EXERCISES

A. Choose between <u>qui</u> and <u>que</u> :

1. J'ai une fille… travaille à Évry.
2. C'est un nouveau directeur… je n'aime pas.
3. Allez chercher les verres… sont sur la table.
4. Nous avons des amis… habitent Paris.
5. Voici un restaurant… est très sympathique.

B. Choose between <u>ce qui</u>, <u>ce que</u>, <u>ce qu'</u>:

1.… est dans ce musée est très moderne.
2. Elle prépare… nous allons manger.
3. Nous écoutons… explique le journaliste.
4. Apporte… il y a sur la table, s'il te plaît.

C. Translate into French

1. It is a wine I often buy.
2. Anne and Pierre are neighbours we sometimes meet.
3. They are friends Antoine does not like.
4. Listen to what this woman is explaining.

C2 ANSWERS

A. 1. J'ai une fille qui travaille à Évry.
2. C'est un nouveau directeur que je n'aime pas.
3. Allez chercher les verres qui sont sur la table.
4. Nous avons des amis qui habitent Paris.
5. Voici un restaurant qui est très sympathique.

B. 1. Ce qui est dans ce musée est très moderne.
2. Elle prépare ce que nous allons manger.
3. Nous écoutons ce qu'explique le journaliste.
4. Apporte ce qu'il y a sur la table, s'il te plaît.

C. 1. C'est un vin que j'achète souvent.
2. Anne et Pierre sont des voisins que nous rencontrons parfois.
3. Ce sont des amis qu'Antoine n'aime pas.
4. Écoutez ce qu'explique cette femme.

C4 FRENCH MUSEUMS

■ Around seventy million entrance tickets for all of the French museums are sold each year, and there is increasing interest in historical monuments. These data reflect the passion for the cultural heritage of the country, and an indication of how great the flow of tourists is.

■ There are in France some forty national museums (the **Orangerie des Tuileries**, the **Château d'Ecouen**, the **Fernand Léger** Museum in Biot, etc.), dozens of museums run by local authorities or private foundations (such as the **Maeght** Foundation in **Saint-Paul de Vence**, in the south), and more than a thousand public museums run mainly by the Ministry of Culture. Paris possesses one of the most important museums in the world, the **Louvre**, which has developed over a period of 800 years of history and houses thousands of works of art, the oldest of which go back more than 5,000 years.

■ Legislation on dations, complemented by that on donations, continues to enrich the national cultural heritage considerably. One of these made it possible to open the National **Picasso** Museum in the **Hôtel Salé**.

■ Reflecting on the place of the museum in the city, its architecture, the problems of museumology, the links and the complementarity of the various establishments is a question that concerns the French Museum Administration.

■ Local authorities devote enormous sums of money to cultural and artistic operations because the museums represent veritable poles of economic activity : the **Château de Versailles** receives more than five million visitors per year ; the **Parc de la Villette** in Paris or the **Futuroscope** of Poitiers are drawing larger and larger crowds.

■ In the capital and its surroundings, as is true in the diverse regions, whether it be the Castle-Museum of **Fontainebleau**, the Museum and National Domain of **Versailles**, the Ceramics Museum of **Sèvres**, or the Prehistory Museum of **Eyzies-de-Tayac**, museums have opted for a truly cultural project. This often includes the participation of the local population in showing off the local treasures of cultural history, as is the case in the eco-museums in **Auvergne**, in **Le Creusot, Monceau-les-Mines**, or in museums of art and popular tradition which appeal to those interested in folklore or the practice of ancient crafts.

14 DIALOGUES AND NUMBERS

D1 DANS UNE AGENCE DE VOYAGE (CD)

Sylvie :	Est-ce que vous avez des séjours organisés pour le week-end ?
Employé :	Bien sûr, nous avons une formule qui marche bien : voyage plus deux nuits d'hôtel.
Sylvie :	Est-ce que c'est une formule que vous proposez toute l'année ?
Employé :	Oui, sauf dans la période qui va de début juillet à fin août à cause des vacances.
Sylvie :	J'ai envie d'aller dans le sud de la France.
Employé :	Il y a plusieurs villes qui attirent un grand nombre de touristes. Regardez ce qu'il y a dans les catalogues que vous avez sur le comptoir. Prenez le temps de choisir.
Sylvie :	C'est Toulouse que je préfère.
Employé :	Vous avez raison, c'est une ville qui est intéressante.
Sylvie :	Est-ce que c'est un tarif qui est valable toute l'année ?
Employé :	Oui, il n'y a aucun supplément.
Sylvie :	Alors je réserve pour le deuxième week-end d'avril, du seize au dix-huit.
Employé :	Pour deux personnes ?
Sylvie :	Oui. Je verse un acompte ?
Employé :	Oui, le quart de la somme, s'il vous plaît.

D2 LES NOMBRES/*NUMBERS* (CD)

13 treize	**20 vingt** *
14 quatorze	**21 vingt et un** **
15 quinze	**31 trente et un** **
16 seize	**41 quarante et un** **
17 dix-sept	**51 cinquante et un** **
18 dix-huit	**61 soixante et un** **
19 dix-neuf	

* Note that in **vingt**, neigher the **g** nor the **t** is pronounced.

** Note that the et (literally *twenty and one*) is necessary only with **un**.

22 vingt-deux	**23 vingt-trois**	**24 vingt-quatre**	**25 vingt-cinq,**	etc.
32 trente-deux	**33 trente-trois**	**34 trente-quatre**	**35 trente-cinq,**	etc.

D3 IN A TRAVEL AGENCY

Sylvie: Do you have weekend vacation packages?
Employee: Of course. We have a package that's very popular: travel plus two nights in a hotel.
Sylvie: Is it a package that you offer all year?
Employee: Yes, except for the period from the beginning of July until the end of August, because of the vacation period.
Sylvie: I feel like going to the south of France.
Employee: There are several cities that attract large numbers of tourists. Look at what's available in the catalogs that you have there on the counter. Take your time to choose.
Sylvie: It's Toulouse that I prefer.
Employee: You're right; it's an interesting city.
Sylvie: Is this a rate that's valid all year long?
Employee: Yes, there's no supplement.
Sylvie: So, I'll reserve for the second weekend in April, from the 16th to the 18th.
Employee: For two people?
Sylvie: Yes. Is a deposit required?
Employee: Yes, a quarter of the amount, please.

D4 LES NOMBRES ORDINAUX
ORDINAL NUMBERS

premier (masc.) première (fem.)	1re	*first*
deuxième/second(e)	2e	*second*
troisième	3e	*third*
quatrième	4e	*fourth*
cinquième	5e	*fifth*
sixième	6e	*sixth*
septième	7e	*seventh*
huitième	8e	*eighth*
neuvième	9e	*ninth*
dixième	10e	*tenth*

and so on... But for *21st, 31st, 41st,* etc., the French equivalents are: vingt et unième, trente et unième, quarante et unième...
• Note that x in deuxième, sixième, dixième is pronounced.

15 Où est la rue de la Gare ? Est-ce que c'est celle-ci ?

A1 PRESENTATION

■ Grammar

- The demonstrative pronoun agrees in gender with the noun it refers to:

  masc. sg.: **celui** fem. sg.: **celle**

  With **ci** added to the pronoun, it is the equivalent of: *this one.*
  masc. sg.: **celui-ci** fem. sg.: **celle-ci** *this one.*

  With **là** added to the pronoun it is the equivalent of: *that one.*
  masc. sg.: **celui-là** fem. sg.: **celle-là** *that one.*

  Ex.: **Est-ce que tu utilises un ordinateur ? — Oui, celui-ci.**
  Are you using a computer? — Yes, this one.

  Est-ce que vous avez une voiture ? — Oui, c'est celle-ci.
  Have you got a car? — Yes, it is this one.

■ Vocabulary

traverser	*to cross*
tourner	*to turn*
bureau de poste (masc.), **poste** (fem.)	*post office*
aéroport (masc.)	*airport*
rapide	*fast*
juste	*just*
en face	*opposite*

A2 EXAMPLES *(This one or that one?)* (CD)

1. **Où est la rue de la Gare ? Est-ce que c'est celle-ci ?**
2. **Non, ce n'est pas celle-ci.**
3. **C'est celle qui traverse le boulevard.**
4. **C'est celle qui est juste après la poste.**
5. **Celle-là ?**
6. **Oui, celle-là. Tournez là.**
7. **Est-ce qu'il y a des bus qui vont à la gare ?**
   Est-ce que celui-ci y va ?
8. **Celui-ci, non. Celui-ci va à l'aéroport.**
9. **Celui qui est en face va à la gare.**
10. **Celui-là ?**
11. **Oui, celui-là.**
12. **Celui-là est très rapide.**

15 Where is Station Road? Is it this one?

A3 COMMENTS

Grammar

- The demonstrative pronoun can be followed by a relative (see lesson 14); in that case **ci** and **là** are omitted. Ex.:

Utilises-tu un ordinateur ? — Oui, celui qui est dans le bureau.
Are you using a computer? — Yes, the one that is in the office.

Avez-vous une voiture ? — Oui, celle qui est en face.
Have you got a car? — Yes, the one which is opposite.

- Note that in **celui-ci, non** *(this one doesn't)*, **non** is used to avoid repeating the complete negative form, here **n'y va pas**.

  In **celui-ci, oui** *(this one does)*, **oui** is used to avoid repeating the complete statement, here **y va**.

- Pay attention to the order of the words in:
  bureau de poste = *post office.*

  In French the noun which is determined by another noun comes first; they are linked by the preposition **de**:
  une station de métro = *a tube station.*
  une pièce de théâtre = *a theatre play.*

→ Don't forget the preposition **de**.

A4 TRANSLATION

1. Where is Station Road? Is it this one?
2. No, it isn't this one.
3. It is the one that crosses the boulevard.
4. It is the one that is just after the post office.
5. That one?
6. Yes, that one. Turn there.
7. Are there buses that go to the station?
   Does this one go there?
8. This one doesn't. This one goes to the airport.
9. The one opposite goes to the station.
10. That one?
11. Yes, that one.
12. That one is very fast.

15 Avez-vous des lunettes de soleil comme celles-ci ?

B1 PRESENTATION

■ Grammar

• The demonstrative pronoun agrees in number with the noun it refers to:

masc. pl. : **ceux** fem. pl. : **celles**

— With **ci** added to the pronoun, it is the equivalent of: *these (ones).*
masc. pl. : **ceux-ci** fem. pl. : **celles-ci** *these (ones).*

— With **là** added to the pronoun it is the equivalent of: *those (ones).*
masc. pl. : **ceux-là** fem. pl. : **celles-là** *those (ones).*

Ex. : **Est-ce que tu utilises des ordinateurs ? — Oui, ceux-ci.**
Are you using computers? — Yes, these (ones).
Est-ce que vous avez des cartes postales ? — Oui, celles-ci.
Have you got postcards? — Yes, these (ones).

■ Vocabulary

essayer	*to try / to try on*	**champion** (masc.)	*champion*
jeter un coup d'œil à	*to have a look at*	**short** (masc.)	*a pair of shorts*
lunettes (fem. pl.)	*glasses*	**tee-shirt** (masc.)	*tee-shirt*
sport (masc.)	*sport*	**léger**	*light*
rayure (fem.)	*stripe*	**autre**	*other*
		pas mal	*nice*
		comme	*like*

B2 EXAMPLES *(Sportswear)* CD

1. **Avez-vous des lunettes de soleil comme celles-ci ?**
2. **Non, mais essayez celles-là, elles sont très légères.**
3. **Elles sont trop petites, je vais essayer celles que vous avez en vitrine.**
4. **Avez-vous d'autres chaussures de sport ? Celles-là ne sont pas confortables.**
5. **Jetez un coup d'œil à celles qui sont là.**
6. **Celles-là ?**
7. **Oui, celles qui ont des rayures bleues.**
8. **Ce sont celles que les champions utilisent !**
9. **Ce short est trop court, je vais essayer un de ceux-là.**
10. **Je vais aussi essayer des tee-shirts ; ceux-ci ne sont pas mal.**
11. **Celui-là est trop cher !**
12. **Jetez un coup d'œil à ceux-là.**

B3 COMMENTS

Pronunciation

- The pronunciation of **ayer** in **essayer** : is **é** followed by the sound of *y* in *yes* followed by **é**.
- Note the grave accent in the feminine form of the adjectives:
  léger **légère**
  cher **chère**

Vocabulary

- Note that:
  sport
  champion
  tee-shirt
  are the same in French and English.
- *Shorts* is used in the singular in French
  More is said about this in C4.

B4 TRANSLATION

1. Have you got sunglasses like these?
2. No, but try those on, they are very light.
3. They are too small, I am going to try on those you have in the window.
4. Have you got any other sports shoes? Those aren't comfortable.
5. Have a look at those there.
6. Those?
7. Yes, those that have got blue stripes.
8. They are the ones the champions use!
9. These shorts are too short, I am going to try on a pair of those.
10. I am going to try on tee-shirts too; these are nice.
11. That one is too expensive!
12. Have a look at those.

C1 EXERCISES

A. (CD) **Replace the words in italics by <u>celui</u>, <u>celle</u>, <u>ceux</u> or <u>celles</u>:**

1. J'aime bien *la montre* qui est en vitrine.
2. Il emporte *le sac* qui est sur la chaise.
3. Allons regarder *les tableaux* qui sont au premier étage.
4. Combien coûte *l'ordinateur* que vous utilisez?
5. C'est *l'appartement* qui est à louer?
6. Écoute *les chansons* qu'elle chante.

B. Write the adjective in the correct form:

1. Une valise (léger).
2. Des étudiantes (étranger).
3. Des pays (étranger).
4. La (premier) chanson.
5. Des chaussures (cher).

C2 ANSWERS

A.
1. J'aime bien celle qui est en vitrine.
2. Il emporte celui qui est sur la chaise.
3. Allons regarder ceux qui sont au premier étage.
4. Combien coute celui que vous utilisez?
5. C'est celui qui est à louer?
6. Écoute celles qu'elle chante.

B.
1. Une valise légère.
2. Des étudiantes étrangères.
3. Des pays étrangers.
4. La première chanson.
5. Des chaussures chères.

C3 TEAM SPORTS

■ Soccer (Football association) is the most popular sport in France. More than two million people hold permits. Every year, the French Football Federation organises the National Championships, the League Cup and the French Cup whose final is held in the presence of the President of the Republic.
Until 1998, the Cup Final traditionally took place at **Parc des Princes** but supporters can now cheer their favourite team in the suburbs of Saint-Denis, north of Paris. Indeed, the **Stade de France**, which can accommodate 80,000 spectactors, was constructed here as the stadium of the 21st century. That's where the French team won its first World Cup ever in 1998. That victory brought about an explosion of mirth and elation throughout the country. Hundred of thousands of people went out and invaded the major thoroughfares to make meny together. The best clubs in the 1st Division Championships as well as the France Cup Winner, participate in the European competitions. Included among the most prestigious teams are **PSG (Paris Saint-Germain)**, **Monaco**, and **OM (Olympique de Marseille)** but, of course, the "glotious uncertainty of the sport" must always be taken into account !

■ Rugby (Rugby Football) is above all, practised in the Southwest and the **Languedoc** region where a genuine "rugby culture" exists but fans of the "oval ball" are numerous all around the country and they follow closely the results of the "15 French teams" during the Five Nation Tournament.

■ As for basketball, volleyball and especially handball, there are more and more followers.

TV broadcasts of these matches obtain huge audiences and specialised programmes are followed by a wide, mainly masculine, public.

D1 AU MATCH (CD)

Marc : Ça va être un sacré match !
Serge : Ces deux équipes sont très fortes. Est-ce que tu as un pronostic ?
Marc : Celle de Nantes est pas mal mais c'est Auxerre qui va gagner.
(*Le match commence*)
Marc : Joli coup de pied !
Serge : Oh la la, il y a hors-jeu, l'arbitre est aveugle ou quoi !
Marc : Regarde celui-là ? Il a l'air fatigué. Il n'arrive pas à courir après le ballon.
Serge : Ecoute les supporters ! C'est pas croyable[1] !
Marc : Ceux qui sont pour Nantes vont être déçus. Nantes va perdre !
Serge : Doucement, il y a encore une mi-temps pour égaliser.
Marc : Regarde celui qui a le ballon, il joue comme un dieu.
Serge : Il va marquer.
Marc : Tu plaisantes ! Avec le gardien qu'ils ont en face !

1. In informal spoken French the **ne** part of the negative is nearly always omitted.

D2 IN FRENCH MANY WORDS CONNECTED WITH SPORTS ARE BORROWED FROM ENGLISH

basketball
football
hockey
rugby
tennis
volleyball

D3 AT THE GAME

Marc : This is going to be one heck of a game !
Serge : Both these teams are very good. Do you have a forecast ?
Marc : Nantes'team isn't bad, but Auxerre's going to win.
(*The game begins.*)
Marc : Nice kick !
Serge : Oh oh ! Offside ! Is the referee blind, or what ?
Marc : Look at that one ! He looks tired. He can't even run after the ball.
Serge : Listen to the fans ! It's unbelievable !
Marc : The Nantes supporters are going to be disappointed. Nantes is going to lose !
Serge : Hold on, there's still a half time to equalize.
Marc : Look at the one with the ball ; he's playing like a god !
Serge : He's going to score.
Marc : You're joking ! With the goalkeeper they've got on the other side !

D4 COUP DE FOUDRE/ *LOVE AT FIRST SIGHT*

- The word **coup** is used in many expressions in French ; here are some :

coup de soleil	*sunburn*
coup de pied	*kick*
coup de poing	*blow (with the fist)*
coup de feu	*shot*
coup de vent	*gust of wind*
coup de fil (téléphone)	*telephone call*
tout à coup	*all of a sudden*
du premier coup	*on be first try*

- **Un dicton : « Faire d'une pierre deux coups. »** (literally : *"Hit twice with one stone."*)
A saying : "To kill two birds with one stone."

16 Quelle valise emportons-nous ?

A1 PRESENTATION

Grammar

- The French interrogative adjective is **quel** *(which, what)*.
Its form depends on the gender and number of the noun concerned:

masc. sg.	**quel**	fem. sg.	**quelle**
masc. pl.	**quels**	fem. pl.	**quelles**

Quel livre regardes-tu ? *Which book are you looking at?*
Quels livres regardes-tu ? *Which books are you looking at?*
Quelle photo préfères-tu ? *Which photo do you prefer?*
Quelles photos préfères-tu ? *Which photos do you prefer?*

Vocabulary

emporter *to take (away)*
porter *to wear*
voyage (masc.) *journey, trip*
or (masc.) *gold*
livre de poche (masc.) *paperback*
étagère (fem.) *shelf*
quart (masc.) *quarter*
marron *brown*

A2 EXAMPLES *(Packing)* (CD)

1. **Quelle valise emportons-nous ?**
2. **La grande valise noire.**
3. **Quel manteau est-ce que tu vas emporter ?**
4. **Le neuf.**
5. **Quelle montre ?**
6. **La montre en or.**
7. **Quelles chaussures vas-tu porter pour le voyage ?**
8. **Les marron ; elles sont très confortables.**
9. **Quels livres préfères-tu emporter ?**
10. **Les livres de poche qui sont sur l'étagère.**
11. **À quelle heure va-t-on arriver ?**
12. **À neuf heures moins le quart.**

A3 COMMENTS

■ Grammar

- One of the most frequent ways of answering a question with **quel** is to use the definite article **le, la** or **les** plus a noun and adjective(s); note that, very often, the noun is understood.

  Ex.: **Le neuf.** *The new one.*
  Les marron. *The brown ones.*

- Remember that **marron** (literally: *chestnut*), though it is used as an adjective, is invariable.
- Remember the two meanings of **porter**:

  to carry:
  Il porte les valises. *He is carrying the suitcases.*

  to wear:
  Il porte un manteau gris. *He is wearing a grey coat.*

- Note that in a question where the verb is inverted, **t** is introduced between the verb and the pronouns: **il, elle** or **on**, if the verb ends with a vowel.

→ **À quelle heure** [**va-t-on arriver ?** / **va-t-il arriver ?** / **va-t-elle arriver ?**

A4 TRANSLATION

1. Which suitcase shall we take?
2. The big black suitcase.
3. Which coat are you going to take?
4. The new one.
5. Which watch?
6. The gold watch.
7. Which shoes are you going to wear for the journey?
8. The brown ones; they are very comfortable.
9. Which books do you prefer to take?
10. The paperbacks that are on the shelf.
11. What time will we arrive?
12. At quarter to nine.

16 Avez-vous de nouveaux livres ? Lesquels ?

B1 PRESENTATION

■ Grammar

- The interrogative pronoun corresponding to **quel** is **lequel**, it also agrees in gender and number with the noun it refers to:

masc. sg.	**lequel**	fem. sg.	**laquelle**	*which one*
masc. pl.	**lesquels**	fem. pl.	**lesquelles**	*which ones*

(Note the resemblance with the definite articles. See lesson 11.)

Regarde ces livres ! Lequel/lesquels préfères-tu ?
Look at these books! Which one/ones do you prefer?

Voici les photos ! Laquelle/lesquelles préfères-tu ?
Here are the photos! Which one/ones do you prefer?

■ Vocabulary

désirer	*to want, to desire*
représenter	*to represent*
dictionnaire (masc.)	*dictionary*
couverture (fem.)	*cover*
carte de vœux (fem.)	*greeting card*
à gauche	*on the left*
à gauche de	*to the left of*
à droite	*on the right*
à droite de	*to the right of*

B2 EXAMPLES *(At the bookshop)* (CD)

1. **Avez-vous de nouveaux livres ? Lesquels ?**
2. **Ceux qui sont dans la vitrine.**
3. **Lequel désirez-vous regarder ?**
4. **Celui qui est à gauche sur l'étagère.**
5. **Lequel ? Celui-ci ou celui-là ?**
6. **Celui qui est à droite des dictionnaires.**
7. **Celui qui a une couverture rouge.**
8. **Laquelle ? Celle qui représente un coucher de soleil ?**
9. **Oui, celle-là.**
10. **J'ai de nouvelles cartes de vœux. Lesquelles préférez-vous ?**
11. **Celles que vous avez dans la main.**
12. **Ce sont celles que je préfère.**

B3 COMMENTS

Pronunciation

- The nearest equivalent to **œu** in **vœux** is *e* in *open* with lips slightly rounded. The same sound is found in:

	nœud (masc.)	*knot*
	œufs (masc. pl.)	*eggs*
But in	**œuf** (masc. sg.)	*egg*
	bœuf (masc.)	*beef*
	sœur (fem.)	*sister*

it is pronounced like *ur* in *hurt*.

Grammar

- **la main:** note that in French, nouns referring to parts of the body or clothes are generally preceded by a definite article and not a possessive adjective.

Ex.: **Il a un livre à la main.**
He's got a book in his hand.
Il a une baguette sous le bras.
He's got a 'baguette' under his arm.
Il a les mains dans les poches.
He's got his hands in his pockets.

B4 TRANSLATION

1. Have you got any new books? Which ones?
2. Those that are in the shopwindow.
3. Which one do you want to look at?
4. The one that is on the left, on the shelf.
5. Which one? This one or that one?
6. The one that is to the right of the dictionaries.
7. The one that has got a red cover.
8. Which one? The one with a sunset on it?
9. Yes, that one.
10. I have got new greeting cards. Which ones do you prefer?
11. Those you have in your hand.
12. They are the ones I prefer.

16 Exercises

C1 EXERCISES

A. Choose between quel, quelle, quels, quelles :

1.... magazine est-ce que tu emportes ?
2.... écrivains français préférez-vous ?
3.... amies allons-nous inviter lundi ?
4.... examen prépares-tu ?
5.... carte allez-vous utiliser ?
6.... chaussures aime-t-elle ?

B. In the preceding exercise replace the interrogative adjective and noun by the corresponding pronoun.

Ex. : Quel magazine... ? Lequel... ?

C2 ANSWERS

A. 1. Quel magazine est-ce que tu emportes ?
2. Quels écrivains français préférez-vous ?
3. Quelles amies allons-nous inviter lundi ?
4. Quel examen prépares-tu ?
5. Quelle carte allez-vous utiliser ?
6. Quelles chaussures aime-t-elle ?

B. 1. Lequel est-ce que tu emportes ?
2. Lesquels préférez-vous ?
3. Lesquelles allons-nous inviter lundi ?
4. Lequel prépares-tu ?
5. Laquelle allez-vous utiliser ?
6. Lesquelles aime-t-elle ?
7. Lesquels est-ce que tu vas acheter ?
8. Laquelle préfère-t-il ?

C3 CYCLING RACES

■ The Tour de France

The Tour de France, first launched by **Henri Desgranges** in 1903, is held every year in July. This cycling competition is made up of about twenty stages (**étapes**), among which there are several "classic" ones through the Alps and the Pyrénées, leading up to the final finish on the Champs-Elysées in Paris. All the participants dream of being able to put on the **maillot jaune**, the yellow jersey of the winner, or the **maillot vert** of the best sprinter, or the white jersey with red polka dots of the best climber (which **Richard Virenque** has worn several times these past years). There are French cyclists who have won the Tour de France several times : **Jacques Anquetil**, **Louison Bobet** and, more recently, **Bernard Hinault** and **Laurent Fignon**. Television broadcasts of the race often include news stories on the regions the Tour goes through, and they attract a huge audience. The Tour remains the most famous international cycling competition.
Among foreign winners, the American competitor Greg Le Mond won three times, Irishman Stephen Roche once, but is also known for having convinced the Tour organizers in 1998 to start it in Dublin and have two more stages in Ireland before going back to France.

■ The great « classics »

Whether they are run in stages like the **Paris-Nice** or in one day like the **Paris-Roubaix**, these first two races of the year (they take place in the spring) are extremely popular. The Paris-Roubaix is particularly famous and has won the nickname of « Hell of the North » because of its cobblestoned sections.

COLLOQUIAL EXPRESSIONS

la Grande Boucle = the Tour de France
la petite reine = *le vélo* (bicycle)
le nez dans le guidon = (literally) the nose in the handlebar

D1 CADEAU D'ANNIVERSAIRE (CD)

Paul : Quel cadeau offrir à Bastien ? Tu as une idée ?
Agnès : Pas vraiment, un jouet ? un livre ?..
Paul : Peut-être un baladeur ?
Agnès : Très bien. Où est la hi-fi dans ce magasin ? A quel étage ?
Paul : Au premier, je pense.
Vendeur : Bonjour. Vous cherchez quelque chose de particulier ?
Agnès : Oui, un baladeur, c'est pour un cadeau d'anniversaire, pour un enfant qui a onze ans.
Vendeur : Voici les derniers modèles.
Paul : Lesquels conseillez-vous ?
Vendeur : Ils sont tous très bien.
Paul : Lequel préfères-tu, Agnès ?
Agnès : Le rouge, c'est marrant pour un enfant.
Paul : Est-ce que les piles sont à l'intérieur ?
Vendeur : Non, mais voici deux piles de un volt cinq. Allez payer à la caisse, je vais faire un paquet-cadeau.

D2 EN.../*MADE OF*...

en or	*gold*
en argent	*silver*
en fer	*iron*
en bois	*wood*
en plastique	*plastic*
en verre	*glass*
en laine	*wool*
en coton	*cotton*
en cuir	*leather*

→ Remember that **en** can sometimes be replaced by **de.**
Ex. : **une robe en coton/une robe de coton**, a *cotton dress.*
But the preposition cannot be omitted.

D3 BIRTHDAY PRESENT

Paul : What shall we give Bastien for a present ? Do you have an idea ?
Agnès : Not really. A toy, a book ?
Paul : Maybe a walkman ?
Agnès : Very good. Which floor is the hi-fi on in this store ?
Paul : On the first floor, I think.
Salesperson : Hello. Are you looking for something in particular ?
Agnès : Yes, a walkman. It's for a birthday present for an eleven-year-old child.
Salesperson : Here are the latest models.
Paul : Which ones would you recommend ?
Salesperson : They're all very good.
Paul : Which one do you prefer, Agnès ?
Agnès : The red one ; it's amusing for a child.
Paul : Are the batteries inside ?
Salesperson : No, but here are two 1.5 volt batteries. You pay for it at the cash register ; I'll gift wrap it.

D4 QUELLE HEURE EST-IL ?
WHAT TIME IS IT ?

7 o'clock *It's seven (o'clock).*
Il est sept heures.
(Note : **heures** can't be omitted.)

7.30 *It's half past seven.*
Il est sept heures et demie.
(Literally : *it is seven hours and half.*)

8.10 *It's ten past eight.*
Il est huit heures dix.
(Literally : it is eight hours ten.)

7.15 *It is (a) quarter past seven..*
Il est sept heures et quart.
(Literally : *it is seven hours and quarter.*)

7.45 *It's (a) quarter to eight.*
Il est huit heures moins le quart.
(Literally : *it is eight hours less the quarter.*)

8.40 *It's twenty to nine.*
Il est neuf heures moins vingt.
(Literally : *it is nine hours less twenty*.)

Note : hours first, then minutes.

17 Achète du pain et du fromage.

A1 PRESENTATION

■ Grammar

- The partitive construction.
  It requires **de** + the appropriate singular definite article:
  — before a feminine noun: **de la, de l'**
  — before a masculine noun: **du** (which is a contracted form of: **de le**); **de l'** (if the noun starts with a vowel or **h**)
  — In the plural, there is only one possibility for both masculine and feminine nouns: **des**

■ Vocabulary

faire	*to make, to do*
beurre (masc.)	*butter*
légume (masc.)	*vegetable*
viande (fem.)	*meat*
fromage (masc.)	*cheese*
cigarette (fem.)	*cigarette*
argent (masc.)	*money*
fruit (masc.)	*fruit*
lait (masc.)	*milk*
crème (fem.)	*custard*
sucre (masc.)	*sugar*
eau (fem.) **(minérale)**	*(mineral) water*

A2 EXAMPLES *(Making a shopping list)* (CD)

1. **Il y a du beurre ?**
2. **Est-ce qu'il y a de la salade ?**
3. **Y a-t-il des légumes ?**
4. **Je vais acheter de la viande.**
5. **Achète du pain et du fromage.**
6. **Achète des cigarettes aussi.**
7. **N'oublie pas d'acheter des cigarettes.**
8. **Est-ce que tu as de l'argent ?**
9. **Est-ce que nous avons des fruits ?**
10. **Achète du lait, je vais faire de la crème anglaise.**
11. **Je vais aussi acheter du sucre.**
12. **Est-ce qu'on a de l'eau minérale ?**

17 Buy some bread and some cheese.

A3 COMMENTS

■ Grammar

- Whether as the equivalents of *some* or *any*, or without any English equivalent, **du, de la, des** can't be omitted in a French partitive construction.
  Ex.: **Est-ce que j'achète aussi du sucre ?** *Do I buy sugar too?*
- In French, **fruit** can be singular or plural: **un fruit, des fruits**.

■ Pronunciation

- **acheter / achète,** *to buy / buy*
  Notice the **è** in: **j'achète**
  tu achètes
  il/elle achète
  ils/elles achètent
  achète !

  Remember: **è** is pronounced like *e* in *pet*.

  But in: **(nous) achetons**
  (vous) achetez

  the **e** is glided over.

A4 TRANSLATION

1. Is there any butter?
2. Is there any salad?
3. Are there any vegetables?
4. I'm going to buy some meat.
5. Buy some bread and some cheese.
6. Buy some cigarettes too.
7. Don't forget to buy cigarettes.
8. Have you got some money?
9. Do we have any fruit?
10. Buy some milk, I'm going to make custard.
11. I'm going to buy sugar too.
12. Have we got any mineral water?

17 Il n'y a pas de nuages, il va faire beau.

B1 PRESENTATION

Grammar

- In the negative, the partitive construction changes:

  — **du, de la, des** become **de.**
  Ex.: **Il n'y a pas de salade / il n'y a pas de lait / il n'y a pas de légumes.**
  There is no salad / there is no milk / there are no vegetables.

  — **de l', des** (when followed by a vowel or **h**) become **d'.**
  Ex.: **Il n'y a pas d'eau minérale / ils n'ont pas d'enfants.**
  There is no mineral water / they have no children.

Vocabulary

changer — *to change*
faire beau — *to be fine*
autoroute (fem.) — *motorway* (US: *freeway*)
neige (fem.) — *snow*
brouillard (masc.) — *fog*
soleil (masc.) — *sun*
parapluie (masc.) — *umbrella*
ciel (masc.) — *sky*
vent (masc.) — *wind*
étoile (fem.) — *star*
ruisseau (masc.) — *brook*

B2 EXAMPLES *(The weather)* (CD)

1. **Il y a de la neige sur l'autoroute.**
2. **Il n'y a pas de neige en ville.**
3. **Elle est sous la pluie et elle n'a pas d'imperméable !**
4. **Il n'y a pas de brouillard en ville.**
5. **On a de la chance, il n'y a pas de brouillard aujourd'hui.**
6. **Est-ce qu'on va avoir du soleil ou de la pluie dimanche ?**
7. **Il n'y a pas de nuages, il va faire beau.**
8. **On n'a pas de chance : le temps va changer.**
9. **Il n'y a pas d'étoiles.**
10. **Nous n'avons pas de parapluie.**
11. **Il n'y a pas d'eau dans le ruisseau ; il est sec.**
12. **Le ciel est rouge ; il n'y a pas de vent ; il va faire beau demain.**

B3 COMMENTS

Grammar

- **faire,** *to do, to make*, is an irregular verb.

Present tense:

je	**fais**	*I*	*do*	*make*
tu	**fais**	*you*	*do*	*make*
il, elle, on	**fait**	*he, she, it*	*does*	*makes*
nous	**faisons***	*we*	*do*	*make*
vous	**faites**	*you*	*do*	*make*
ils, elles	**font**	*they*	*do*	*make*

Pronunciation

- * Note that **faisons** is pronounced **fesons**.
- Remember:
  — **ei (neige)** has the sound of **è**.
  — **ui (fruit, pluie, ruisseau, parapluie)** is the sound of **u** quickly followed by the sound of **i**.

→ Note that **faire** conveys both the meaning of *to do* and *to make*.

B4 TRANSLATION

1. There is snow on the motorway.
2. There isn't any snow in town.
3. She is out in the rain and she hasn't got a raincoat!
4. There is no fog in town.
5. We are lucky, there is no fog today.
6. Are we going to have sun or rain on Sunday?
7. There aren't any clouds, it's going to be fine.
8. We are unlucky: the weather is going to change.
9. There aren't any stars.
10. We haven't got an umbrella.
11. There is no water in the brook; it is dry.
12. The sky is red; there's no wind; it will be fine tomorrow.

C1 EXERCISES

A. Swap the word in brackets with the word given at the end.
Make the necessary changes :

1. Nous n'avons pas d'(ordinateur) – secrétaire.
2. Vous mangez de la (salade) – fruits.
3. Il n'y a pas de (vent) – neige.
4. Ils achètent du vin) – viande.
5. On n'a pas de (chance) – argent.
6. Est-ce que tu as du (sucre) – lait ?

B. (CD) **Turn into the negative :**

1. J'ai du sucre
2. Nous avons des enfants.
3. Ils achètent des livres.
4. Il y a de l'eau sur la table.
5. Il a de la chance.

C2 ANSWERS

A. 1. Nous n'avons pas de secrétaire.
2. Vous mangez des fruits.
3. Il n'y a pas de neige.
4. Ils achètent de la viande.
5. On n'a pas d'argent.
6. Est-ce que tu as du lait ?

B. 1. Je n'ai pas de sucre.
2. Nous n'avons pas d'enfants.
3. Ils n'achètent pas de livres.
4. Il n'y a pas d'eau sur la table.
5. Il n'a pas de chance.

C3 NATIONAL AND PUBLIC HOLIDAYS

■ Bastille Day * is the main national holiday. It was first celebrated one year after the taking of the **Bastille**, on July 14th, 1790. On that day, an imposing demonstration took place on the **Champ-de-Mars** in Paris with King Louis XVI at its center, surrounded by federal troops from all over France : the festival of the Federation. After Louis XVI was beheaded with the recently invented **Guillotine**, the **Convention** declared the Festival of the Supreme Being (**La Fête de l'Être Suprême**) on June 9th, 1794. Under the **Empire**, August 15th became the national holiday and later, in 1879, the Chamber of Deputies and the Senate definitively adopted the date of July 14th.
Shortly after World War I, November 11th became a public holiday as an expression of the joy felt by French people when the Armistice was signed between Germany and the French Republic.
Following World War II, May 8th became a public holiday celebrating the unconditional surrender of Hitler's Reich.
The following dates are also public holidays in France : May 1st (Labor Day), August 15th (Assumption), November 1st (All Saints'Day), December 25th (Christmas), January 1st (New Year's Day). As well as Easter Monday, Whitsun Monday, and the Thursday of the Ascension.

---

* BASTILLE DAY

To resolve a serious, primarily budgetary crisis, Louis XVI summoned the States General. In June, 1789, the nobility, the clergy and the third estate (representatives of the common people) declared themselves to represent the National Constituent Assembly. The king ordered the people to leave and gathered troops around Paris. Insurrection broke out on July 14th, 1789 : the crowd stormed the Bastille prison where people could be imprisoned merely upon an order under the king's private seal. The Bastille was a symbol of royal absolutism and disdain for individual rights.

17 DIALOGUES AND THE WEATHER

D1 PLUIE ET LE BEAU TEMPS (CD)

Bruno :	Qu'il fait chaud aujourd'hui !
Nicole :	Il fait au moins trente cinq.
Bruno :	Oui, on étouffe, il n'y a pas un souffle d'air.
Nicole :	Avec une chaleur pareille il va certainement y avoir de l'orage.
Bruno :	Ce n'est pas le moment de faire une promenade.
Nicole :	Oh non, regarde ces gros nuages, le ciel est presque violet. Il va pleuvoir d'une minute à l'autre.
Nicole :	Ça va faire du bien au jardin. La terre est très sèche et les plantes ont besoin d 'eau.
Bruno :	Tiens, un éclair !
Nicole :	Et voici les premières gouttes !
Bruno.	Rentrons vite le parasol et les chaises du jardin. Il n'y a pas de temps à perdre.

D2 LE TEMPS/ *THE WEATHER*

- **faire** is used in many impersonal expressions to speak of the weather : **il fait**, here, is the equivalent of *it is* :

il fait froid	*it is cold*
il fait chaud	*it is hot*
il fait bon	*it is warm*
il fait beau	*it is fine*
il fait mauvais	*the weather is bad*
il fait soleil	*it is sunny*
il fait sec	*it is dry*
il fait jour	*it is daylight*
il fait nuit	*it is dark*

- Some common expressions about the weather refer to animals.

  Ex. : **Un temps de chien** *(dog)*, **un froid de canard** *(duck)*.

  But : *it's raining cats and dogs*, **il tombe des cordes** (literally : *ropes are falling*).

D3 RAIN AND SHINE

Bruno : It's so hot today !
Nicole : It's at least 35. (NB : Body temperature in Celsius is 37.)
Bruno : Yes, it's suffocating. There's not a breath of air.
Nicole : With heat like this, there's sure to be a thunderstorm.
Bruno : This is no time to go for a walk.
Nicole : Oh no, look at those big clouds. The sky is almost purple. It's going to rain any minute now.
Nicole : It'll be good for the garden. The earth is dry, and the plants need water.
Bruno : Look ! A flash of lightening !
Nicole : And here come the first drops !
Bruno : Quick, let's take in the umbrella and the garden chairs. There's no time to lose.

D2 SAISONS ET FÊTES
SEASONS AND FEAST DAYS

•	**printemps** (masc.)	*spring*
	été (masc.)	*summer*
	automne (masc.)	*autumn*
	hiver (masc.)	*winter*
	Pâques	*Easter*
	Noël	*Christmas*
	Jour de l'An	*New Year's Day*
• Note :	**en été**	*in summer*
	en automne	*in autumn*
	en hiver	*in winter*
But :	**<u>au</u> printemps**	*in spring*

• Remember that when the names of the seasons are used as subject or direct object the article <u>cannot</u> be omitted.

Ex. : **L'automne est parfois sec.** *Autumn is sometimes dry.*
J'aime l'été *I like summer.*

18 Combien de joueurs y a-t-il... ?

A1 PRESENTATION

Grammar

- To ask a question about either a number or a quantity, the interrogative word is the same in French: **Combien de/d',** *How many/How much.*

  Ex.: **Combien de chats avez-vous ?**
  How many cats have you got?
  Combien d'argent avez-vous ?
  How much money have you got?

— For a large number **beaucoup de/d'** followed by a plural is the equivalent of *a lot of, many.*

— For a small number **peu de/d'** followed by a plural is the equivalent of *few.*

— For a small number **quelques** followed by a plural is the èquivalent of *a few.*

Vocabulary

entrer	*to go in, to enter*	**billet** (masc.)	*ticket*
crier	*to shout*	**millier** (masc.)	*thousand*
joueur (masc.)	*player*	**quelqu'un**	*somebody/ anybody*
équipe (fem.)	*team*		
stade (masc.)	*stadium*	**personne**	*nobody*
personne (fem.)	*person*	**plusieurs**	*several*
match (masc.)	*match* (US: *game*)	**déjà**	*already*

A2 EXAMPLES *(Before a football match)* (CD)

1. **Combien y a-t-il de joueurs dans une équipe de football ?**
2. **Combien de joueurs y a-t-il dans une équipe de football ? Onze.**
3. **Y a-t-il quelqu'un dans le stade ?**
4. **Non, il n'y a personne.**
5. **Combien de personnes vont regarder le match ?**
6. **Beaucoup de gens vont regarder le match.**
7. **Combien de personnes vont aller à ce match ?**
8. **Plusieurs milliers de personnes vont aller à ce match.**
9. **Peu de gens ont déjà des billets.**
10. **Il y a pas mal de personnes qui chantent.**
11. **Quelques personnes crient.**
12. **Il y a beaucoup de voitures près du stade.**

A3 COMMENTS

Grammar

- **Combien y a-t-il de joueurs ? / Combien de joueurs y a-t-il ?**
  How many players are there?
  Note that the question can be asked in two different ways.
- Remember that **personne** is a feminine noun but can also be an invariable indefinite word meaning *nobody*.
  Ex.: **Quelques personnes regardent le match.**
  A few people are watching the match.
  Personne ne regarde le match.
  Nobody is watching the match.

→ Note that **personne** *(nobody)* is always used with **ne**.

- Note that **déjà** is placed after the verb.
  Ex.: **Ils préparent déjà le repas.**
  They are already preparing the meal.
  Nous avons déjà un chat, un chien et des oiseaux, ça suffit !
  We already have a cat, a dog and birds, that's enough!

A4 TRANSLATION

1. How many players are there on a football team?
2. How many players are there on a football team? Eleven.
3. Is there anybody in the stadium?
4. No, there's nobody.
5. How many people are going to watch the match?
6. A lot of people are going to watch the match.
7. How many people are going to go to this match?
8. Several thousand people are going to go to this match.
9. Few people already have tickets.
10. There are quite a lot of people who are singing.
11. A few people are shouting.
12. There are many cars near the stadium.

18 Vous avez beaucoup d'humour.

B1 PRESENTATION

Grammar

- To express the notion of quantity with non-countable nouns:

— For a large quantity: **beaucoup de/d'** followed by a singular is the equivalent of *a lot of, much.*

— For a small quantity: **peu de/d', un peu de/d'** followed by a singular are the equivalents of *little, a little.*

— For a small quantity: **quelque** followed by a singular is the equivalent of *some.*

- A subjective judgment about a number or a quantity will be expressed by:

trop de/d'	*too many, too much*
assez de/d'	*enough*
pas assez de/d'	*not enough*

Vocabulary

sembler	*to seem*
imagination (fem.)	*imagination*
humour (masc.)	*humour*
talent (masc.)	*talent*
travail (masc.)	*work*
patience (fem.)	*patience*
bizarre	*odd*
assez	*enough*
pas mal	*quite a lot*

B2 EXAMPLES *(At the fortune-teller's)* (CD)

1. **Vous semblez avoir assez d'imagination.**
2. **Vous avez beaucoup d'humour.**
3. **Mais vous semblez un peu triste.**
4. **Dans peu de temps vous allez rencontrer quelqu'un.**
5. **Cette personne a beaucoup de talent.**
6. **Elle a peu d'argent.**
7. **Elle semble être un peu bizarre.**
8. **Vous allez rester quelque temps ensemble.**
9. **Combien de temps ? Peu de temps.**
10. **Vous allez avoir pas mal de travail et beaucoup d'argent.**
11. **Vous allez avoir beaucoup de chance.**
12. **Ayez un peu de patience !**

18 You have a good sense of humour.

B3 COMMENTS

■ Grammar

- Note that **sembler** can be followed by:

  — an infinitive

  Ex.: **Cet étudiant semble avoir beaucoup de travail.**
  This student seems to have a lot of work.

  — an adjective

  Ex.: **Cet étudiant semble très sympathique.**
  This student seems very nice.

- **pas mal** is a colloquial expression meaning *quite a lot, quite enough.*

  Ex.: **Il y a pas mal de gens ce soir.**
  There are quite a lot of people tonight.

  J'ai pas mal de travail à faire aujourd'hui.
  I have quite a lot of work to do today.

- Remember that **combien de temps ?** is the equivalent of *how long?*

  Ex.: **Combien de temps est-ce que le match va durer* ?**
  How long is the match going to last?

* **durer :** *to last.*

B4 TRANSLATION

1. You seem to have enough imagination.
2. You have a good sense of humour.
3. But you seem a little sad.
4. In a short while you are going to meet someone.
5. This person has a lot of talent.
6. He/she has little money.
7. He/she seems a bit odd.
8. You are going to stay together for a while.
9. How long? A short while.
10. You are going to have quite a lot of work and a lot of money.
11. You are going to be very lucky.
12. Have a little patience!

C1 EXERCISES

A. Ask the question in another way :

1. Combien y a-t-il d'appartements dans cet immeuble ?
2. Combien y a-t-il d'ordinateurs dans ce bureau ?
3. Combien d'aéroports y a-t-il à Paris ?
4. Combien y a-t-il de livres sur l'étagère ?

B. (CD) Translate into French :

1. How long is he going to stay here ? He is going to stay here a few days.
2. A lot of children play here on Wednesdays.
3. Many people are on strike today.
4. How long is the film going to last,
5. This person seems to have little work.

C2 ANSWERS

A. 1. Combien d'appartements y a-t-il dans cet immeuble ?
2. Combien d'ordinateurs y a-t-il dans ce bureau ?
3. Combien y a-t-il d'aéroports à Paris ?
4. Combien de livres y a-t-il sur l'étagère ?

B. 1. Combien de temps va-t-il rester ici ? Il va rester ici quelques jours.
2. Beaucoup d'enfants jouent ici le mercredi.
3. Beaucoup de gens sont en grève aujourd'hui.
4. Combien de temps va durer le film ?
5. Cette personne semble avoir peu de travail.

C3 THE DEVIL AND THE GOOD LORD *
* (title of a play by Jean Paul Sartre)

■ French abounds in colorful colloquial expressions whose origin is often unknown. The devil, like God, has left his mark on the history of the language.
You can tell someone "*to go to the devil,*" (**aller au diable**) or talk of those who "*live in the devil's place*" (**au diable vauvert,** *miles from nowhere*), or who "*pull the devil's tail*" (**tirer le diable par la queue,** *live from hand to mouth*). The latter phrase is thought to go back to the 17th century, when it referred to working hard to earn one's living.
It's just the next step to go on to assume that the poor wretch ended up turning to the devil for help.
According to tradition, the devil would force his way into the empty purses of the impoverished. The « devil's tail » might thus be a reference to the purse strings of some poor penniless individual. And in France hell itself, rather than merely the road to hell, is *paved with good intentions* (**l'enfer est pavé de bonnes intentions**).

The word "*God*" is also used in many expressions, from the simple **Mon Dieu** ("*My goodness*" or "*Good heavens*") to the more elaborate si Dieu le veut « God willing » and including **Dieu merci** "*Thank God,*" **grâce à Dieu** "*Thanks be to God,*" **Dieu soit loué** "*Praise be to God,*" and **Dieu m'en garde** or **Dieu m'en préserve** "*God forbid*".

There's also the threat that "*You can't take it with you !*"
Tu ne l'emporteras pas au paradis.

D1 AU MARCHE (CD)

Marie : Il ne reste pas beaucoup de choses dans le frigo… Peu de légumes, pas assez de fruits.. Je vais faire quelques courses.
Jean : Tu vas au marché maintenant ?
Marie : Oui, je préfère, il y a trop de monde en fin de matinée.
Jean : N'oublie pas de prendre un peu de fromage !
Vendeur : Haricots verts, laitues bien fraîches, champignons pas chers !.. Et pour Madame
Marie : Une livre de haricots verts, s'il vous plaît.
Vendeur : Et avec ça ?
Marie : Un kilo de pommes de terre et quelques tomates.
Vendeur : Combien de tomates ?
Marie : Un kilo et ajoutez quelques carottes…. et… un peu de persil.
Vendeur : Ça suffit comme ça ?
Marie : Oui merci, au -revoir.

D2 10, 12, 15, 20… 1 000 000 000

dizaine (fem.)	*ten*
douzaine (fem.)	*dozen*
quinzaine (fem.)	*fifteen*
vingtaine (fem.)	*a score*
cinquantaine (fem.)	*hundred*
millier (masc.)	*thousand*
million (masc.)	*million*
milliard (masc.)	*milliard* (US : *billion*)

D3 AT THE MARKET

Marie : There's not much left in the fridge… Not very many vegetables, not enough fruit… I'm going to do some shopping.
Jean : Are you going to the market now ?
Marie : Yes, I'd rather. There are too many people near noon.
Jean : Don't forget to get a little cheese !
Salesperson : Green beans, fresh lettuce, inexpensive mushrooms. And for you, Madam ?
Marie : A pound of green beans, please.
Salesperson : And with that ?
Marie : A kilo (= 2.2 pounds) of potatoes and some tomatoes.
Salesperson : How many tomatoes ?
Marie : A kilo, and add some carrots and, um, a bit of parsley.
Salesperson : Is that enough ?
Marie : Yes, thank you. Goodbye.

D4 LE 1er MAI/LE 8 MAI
MAY 1st/MAY 8th

- To express the date in French, the ordinal number is used for the first day of the month, the cardinal for the other days.
  Ex. : **le 1er janvier, le 1er mai, le 1er août.**
  le premier janvier, le premier mai, le premier août.
  le 14 juillet, le 11 novembre, le 25 décembre.
  le quatorze juillet, le onze novembre, le vingt-cinq décembre.

- Note that : **Nous sommes le…** is the usual way to say the date.
  In colloquial French ; **On est le…** is the usual form.
  Ex. : **Nous sommes le mardi 30 juin.**
  On est le mardi 30 juin.
  Today is Tuesday, June 30th.

19 Une grosse moto est aussi chère qu'une voiture.

A1 PRESENTATION

Grammar

- The comparative is formed by adding:

  + **plus... que** *-er... than, more... than*
  = **aussi... que** *as... as*
  – **moins... que** *less... than*

  on either side of the adjective (whatever the length of the adjective).

  Ex.: **Pierre est plus jeune que Louis.**
  Pierre is younger than Louis.
  Louis est plus sympathique que Pierre.
  Louis is nicer than Pierre.

- The superlative is formed by placing:

  le, la, les plus... *the most*
  le, la, les moins... *the least*

  before the adjective.

  The article agrees in gender and number with the noun:

  Ex.: **Ces voitures sont les moins chères.**
  These cars are the least expensive.

Vocabulary

groupe (masc.)	*group*	**journal** (masc.)	*newspaper*
train (masc.)	*train*	**monde** (masc.)	*world*
moto (fem.)	*motorcycle*	**ville** (fem.)	*town*
église (fem.)	*church*		

A2 EXAMPLES *(Comparing)* (CD)

1. **Je suis plus jeune que Mme Lenoir.**
2. **Tu es le plus sympathique du groupe.**
3. **Un avion est plus rapide qu'un train.**
4. **Un livre est plus cher qu'un journal.**
5. **Il est aussi grand qu'Antoine.**
6. **Une grosse moto est aussi chère qu'une voiture.**
7. **M. Martin n'est pas aussi intelligent que Mme Martin.**
8. **Une église est plus petite qu'une cathédrale.**
9. **Une rue est moins large qu'un boulevard.**
10. **C'est la rue la plus large de la ville.**
11. **Paris n'est pas aussi grand que Londres.**
12. **Paris n'est pas la plus grande ville du monde.**

19 A big motorcycle is as expensive as a car.

A3 COMMENTS

Grammar

- Note that **que** becomes **qu'** before a vowel or **h**.

  Ex.: **Anne est plus jolie qu'Hélène.**
  Anne is prettier than Hélène.
  Hélène est plus grande qu'Anne.
  Hélène is taller than Anne.

- Note that after a superlative, the complement is introduced by **de** or the contracted form **du**.

  Ex.: **Le plus grand immeuble de la ville.**
  The tallest building in town.
  La plus belle fille du monde.
  The most beautiful girl in the world.

- The names of towns and cities are either masculine or feminine. Here are some feminine ones:

  Athènes *(Athens)*, **Marseille, Rome, Venise** *(Venice).*

- Remember that adjectives agree in gender and number with the noun they refer to.

  Ex.: **La plus belle maison. Les plus belles maisons.**
  The most beautiful house. The most beautiful houses.

Pronunciation

- Note the **è** in **chère**, feminine of **cher**.
- Note that in **ville**, **-ille** is pronounced **il**.

A4 TRANSLATION

1. I'm younger than Mrs. Lenoir.
2. You are the nicest of the group.
3. A plane is faster than a train.
4. A book is more expensive than a newspaper.
5. He is as tall as Antoine.
6. A big motorcycle is as expensive as a car.
7. Mr. Martin isn't as intelligent as Mrs. Martin.
8. A church is smaller than a cathedral.
9. A street is less broad than a boulevard.
10. It is the widest street in town.
11. Paris is not as large as London.
12. Paris is not the largest city in the world.

19 Elle parle doucement.

B1 PRESENTATION

Grammar

- Most adverbs are also used in comparisons.
Most adverbs are formed by adding **ment** to the feminine adjective. They are invariable. Ex.:

masculine singular	feminine singular	adverb
lent *(slow)*	**lente**	**lentement** *(slowly)*
rapide *(quick)*	**rapide**	**rapidement** *(quickly)*

- They are usually placed after the verb they modify.
Ex.: **Elle parle bizarrement.**
She speaks strangely.
Vous ne marchez pas rapidement.
You don't walk quickly.

Vocabulary

vélo (masc.)	*bike*
bateau (masc.)	*boat*
doucement	*softly*
rapidement	*quickly*
rarement	*rarely*
lentement	*slowly*

B2 EXAMPLES *(More comparisons)* (CD)

1. **Elle parle doucement.**
2. **Parle plus lentement, s'il te plaît.**
3. **Il marche rapidement.**
4. **Tu marches plus rapidement qu'Anne.**
5. **Vous voyagez plus rarement que Pierre.**
6. **Vous n'habitez pas aussi loin que Pierre.**
7. **Un bateau ne va pas aussi vite qu'un avion.**
8. **Il danse aussi bien que Philippe.**
9. **Un vélo ne va pas aussi vite qu'une moto.**
10. **Tu vas en Angleterre moins souvent qu'en Italie.**
11. **Nous allons au théâtre aussi souvent que possible.**
12. **Nous allons au théâtre le plus souvent possible.**

19 She speaks softly.

B3 COMMENTS

Grammar

- Not all adverbs end in **ment**, especially adverbs of:

— time:	**souvent**	*often*
	maintenant	*now*
	parfois	*sometimes*
— place:	**ici**	*here*
	loin	*far*
and of course:	**bien**	*well*

Vocabulary

- **doucement / lentement:** when referring to motion, you can often use one or the other without changing the meaning. In that case, **doucement** means *slowly*.
  Ex.: **Elle avance doucement** (or **lentement).**
  She's walking slowly.

- In colloquial French, words of three syllables or more which are often used in everyday life are shortened to their first two syllables.
  Ex.: **photo(graphie), moto(cyclette), vélo(cipède), auto(mobile).**

Pronunciation

- Note that in **rapid(e)ment, rar(e)ment, lent(e)ment, douc(e)ment**, the **e** is glided over.

B4 TRANSLATION

1. She speaks softly.
2. Speak more slowly, please.
3. He walks quickly.
4. You walk more quickly than Anne.
5. You travel more rarely than Pierre.
6. You don't live as far away as Pierre.
7. A boat doesn't go as fast as a plane.
8. He dances as well as Philippe.
9. A bike doesn't go as fast as a motorcycle.
10. You go to England less often than to Italy.
11. We go to the theatre as often as possible.
12. We go to the theatre as often as possible.

C1 EXERCISES

A. Compare using the adjective in brackets :

1. un avion	(rapide)	un vélo
2. Pierre	(intelligent)	Louis
3. Anne	(gentille)	Hélène
4. M. Martin	(célèbre)	Picasso
5. Des magazines	(chers)	des livres
6. Paris	(grand)	Londres

B. Put the adverb in the comparative (mind the sign in brackets) :

1. Il voyage (souvent) Pierre. (–)
2. Tu danses (bien) Louis ! (–)
3. Vous habitez (loin) Mme Martin. (=)
4. Une voiture va (lentement) un avion. (+)
5. Nous n'allons pas (vite) Anne. (=)

C2 ANSWERS

A. 1. Un avion est plus rapide qu'un vélo.
2. Pierre est plus intelligent que Louis.
3. Anne est aussi gentille qu'Hélène.
4. M. Martin est moins célèbre que Picasso.
5. Des magazines sont moins chers que des livres.
6. Paris et moins grand que Londres.

B. Il voyage moins souvent que Pierre.
2. Tu danses moins bien que Louis !
3. Vous habitez aussi loin que Mme Martin.
4. Une voiture va plus lentement qu'un avion.
5. Nous n'allons pas aussi vite qu'Anne.

C3 EDUCATION

■ France is a country where a large percentage of children and young people are in school (57.7 % of those from 5 to 29 years of age), with nearly 800,000 teachers. The educational system is constantly undergoing review, for what is taught and the way it is taught as well as for the organization of the increasingly decentralized system. The public school system, "National Education," receives more than 80 % of the students. It co-exists with a « free » system made up of private schools, most of which have contracts linking them to the national education system.
■ There is great demand for nursery school education (99.3 % of three year olds), but it is not compulsory. Schooling for children from 6 to 16 years of age is mandatory and takes place for five years in primary school, then for four years in middle school. Students subsequently go either to a *high school* (**lycée**) or to a professional high school. High school studies end with an examination called the **baccalauréat**. The "bac" is taken after three years of study.

■ After the « bac », some students continue their studies in the lycée for a two-year degree called the **BTS** (**Brevet de Technicien Supérieur**). Some go on to the university or to classes that prepare them for the nation-wide competitive entrance examinations to what are called the **grandes écoles**. The **grandes écoles** are part of a national tradition and specific to France. They prepare students for future careers as high-ranking civil servants (**ENA**), for the scientific and engineering fields (**Polytechnique, Centrale, Mines, Arts et Métiers, Ponts et Chaussées, Supélec** etc.), for business (**HEC, ESSEC, Sup de Co.**), or for high-level research or teaching positions in literary or scientific fields (the **Ecoles Normales Supérieures**).

19 DIALOGUES AND COMPARISON

D1 LE BAC (CD)

Agnès : Salut Nathalie, ça va ?
Nathalie : Je suis morte ! Deux heures de math cette après-midi
Agnès : Quel prof [1] tu as ?
Nathalie : M. Blanchet, le pire du lycée !
Agnès : Le pire, vraiment ?.
Nathalie : Ah oui, il note trop sévèrement, nous avons la moyenne la plus faible de l'établissement et pourtant nous ne sommes pas moins bons que les autres.
Agnès : Est - ce qu'il donne plus de devoirs que le prof de l'an dernier ?
Nathalie : Malheureusement oui. Nous avons énormément de travail et en plus nous commençons à réviser. C'est le moment le plus fatiguant de l'année
Agnès : Tu passes le bac [2] bientôt ?
Nathalie : Dans moins de deux mois.
Agnès : Bonne chance !

1. **Prof** short for **professeur** = *teacher.*
2. **Bac,** short for **baccalauréat,** the exam taken at the end of secondary school.

D2 IRREGULAR COMPARATIVES AND SUPERLATIVES

- **bon** *(good)* :
  meilleur (masc. sg.) / **meilleurs** (masc. pl.)] **que** — **meilleure** (fem. sg.) / **meilleures** (fem. pl.)] **que** = *better than…*
  le, la, les meilleur (e) (s) = *the best…*
- **bien** *(well)* : **mieux que** = *better… than*
  le mieux = *the best*
- **mauvais** *(bad)* : **pire que** = *worse than* (both masc. and fem.)
  le pire = *the worst…*
- **mal** *(badly)* : **pire que** = *worse than.*
  le pire = *the worst*

D3 THE EXAM

Agnès : Hi, Nathalie, how are you ?
Nathalie : I'm dead ! Two hours of math this afternoon.
Agnès : Which teacher do you have ?
Nathalie : Mr. Blanchet, the worst one in the high school !
Agnès : The worst, really ?
Nathalie : Oh, yes ; he grades really hard ; we have the lowest grade average in the school and yet we're not that far below the others.
Agnès : Does he give more homework than last year's teacher ?
Nathalie : Unfortunately, yes. We have an enormous amount of work, and on top of that we've started reviewing. It's the most tiring time of the year.
Agnès : Are you taking the exam soon ?
Nathalie : In less than two months.
Agnès : Good luck !

D4 GOOD GRADES AND BAD GRADES

• In French both **note** and **point** refer to *grades* (GB : *marks*) : **une note** is the total and **les points** are the units added or subtracted to make up the total.
• The verb **noter** means to give grades or marks (good, bad, etc.) or *to mark* (strictly, leniently, etc.) while **corriger** (*to correct*) means to mark in the sense of find and comment on right and wrong answers.
• Note too that French doesn't distinguish between *degree* and *diploma* : **un diplôme** is used for both.

20 Qu'est-ce qu'il y a à la télévision aujourd'hui ?

A1 PRESENTATION

Grammar

- Remember the two interrogative forms:
  — Manges-tu ?
  — Est-ce que tu manges ?
- To ask a question about the object, use **que** or **qu'** placed just before the interrogative form.

  Ex.: **Que manges-tu ? / Qu'est-ce que tu manges ?**
  What are your eating?
  Qu'apportez-vous ? / Qu'est-ce que vous apportez ?
  What are you bringing?

Vocabulary

regarder *to watch*
penser *to think*
télévision (fem.) *television*
feuilleton (masc.) *serial, series*
chaîne (fem.) *channel*
émission (fem.) *broadcast* (US: *show*)

A2 EXAMPLES *(Television)* CD

1. **Qu'est-ce qu'il y a à la télévision aujourd'hui ?**
2. **Qu'est-ce que tu regardes d'habitude ?**
3. **Que préférez-vous ?**
4. **Que regardez-vous l'après-midi ?**
5. **Qu'est-ce que vous pensez des feuilletons américains ?**
6. **Que pensez-vous de l'émission ?**
7. **Qu'est-ce qu'il y a sur la première chaîne ?**
8. **Qu'allons-nous regarder maintenant ?**
9. **Qu'est-ce que nous allons regarder ?**
10. **Qu'est-ce que vous aimez ?**
11. **Qu'est-ce que vous aimez le mieux ?**
12. **Que vont-ils faire après l'émission ?**

20 What's on television today?

A3 COMMENTS

■ Grammar

- Though both forms are equivalent, **qu'est-ce que** is more often used in colloquial French.
  Notice that the words run together: **qu'est-ce que tu manges ?**
- Note that **la première chaîne** *(channel 1)* literally means *the first channel* (it is the same for channel 2, 3, 4...).

  premier agrees with the noun it accompanies.

  Ex.: **Le premier jour ; les premiers jours.**
  The first day ; the first days.
  La première heure ; les premières heures.
  The first hour ; the first hours.

→ Don't forget the grave accent in the feminine.

■ Pronunciation

- **ion** (in **télévision, émission)** is pronounced like *ee* + *y* + the nasal vowel **on**.
- Remember the liaison between the final consonant of a word and the initial vowel of the following word:

  Qu'est-ce que nous allons regarder ? (z)

  Qu'est-ce que vous aimez ? (z) **Que vont-ils faire ?** (t)

A4 TRANSLATION

1. What's on television today?
2. What do you usually watch?
3. What do you prefer?
4. What do you watch in the afternoon?
5. What do you think of American serials?
6. What do you think of the broadcast?
7. What's on channel 1?
8. What are we going to watch now?
9. What are we going to watch?
10. What do you like?
11. What do you like most?
12. What are they going to do after the show?

20 Pourquoi préférez-vous la campagne ?

B1 PRESENTATION

Grammar

- When used with a preposition, **que** becomes **quoi**.
  The preposition always precedes **quoi**.
  Ex.: **Avec quoi travailles-tu ?** *What are you working with?*
  À quoi penses-tu ? *What are you thinking about?*
  Pour quoi faire ? *What for?*
- **quoi** is also found in **pourquoi**, the French equivalent of *why*. The answer to a question with **pourquoi** usually starts with **parce que**.
  Ex.: **Pourquoi manges-tu ?** — **Parce que j'ai faim.**
  Why do you eat? *Because I am hungry.*

Vocabulary

rêver	*to dream*
marcher	*to walk*
faire une promenade	*to go for a walk, a ride*
campagne (fem.)	*country, countryside*
nature (fem.)	*nature*
animal (masc.), pl. : **animaux**	*animal*
promenade (fem.)	*walk, ride*
marche (fem.)	*walking*
politique (fem.)	*politics*
musique (fem.)	*music*
n'importe quoi	*anything*
par exemple	*for instance*

B2 EXAMPLES *(Why and why not...)* CD

1. **À quoi pensez-vous ?**
2. **De quoi rêvez-vous ?**
3. **De quoi ? D'une maison à la campagne.**
4. **Pourquoi préférez-vous la campagne ?**
5. **Parce que j'aime la nature.**
6. **Pourquoi a-t-elle un chien ?**
7. **Parce qu'elle aime les animaux.**
8. **Pourquoi n'allez-vous pas faire une promenade après manger ?**
9. **Pourquoi n'allez-vous pas faire une promenade à vélo ?**
10. **Parce que nous aimons la marche.**
11. **De quoi parlez-vous quand vous marchez ?**
12. **De n'importe quoi, de sport, de politique, de musique par exemple.**

B3 COMMENTS

Grammar

- In a negative question with the verb inverted, **ne... pas** is placed on either side of the group verb-pronoun.
  Ex.: **N'allez-vous pas faire une promenade ?**
  Aren't you going for a walk?

  In a negative question with **est-ce que, ne... pas** is on either side of the verb.
  Ex.: **Est-ce que vous n'allez pas faire une promenade ?**
  Aren't you going for a walk?

- Note that the French equivalent of a gerund is often either a substantive:
  Ex.: **la marche** *walking*
  la peinture *painting*
  or an infinitive (after a preposition).
  Ex.: **après manger** *after eating*
  sans parler *without speaking*

- With **parler de**, when the complement is a general concept, the article is omitted. Ex.:
  parler de musique, parler de cinéma, parler de théâtre, parler de sport : *to talk about music, ... films, ... theatre, ... sports.*

Pronunciation

- Note that the nearest English equivalent sound to **quoi** is *qua* in *quality*.

B4 TRANSLATION

1. What are you thinking about?
2. What are you dreaming of?
3. Of what? Of a house in the country.
4. Why do you prefer the country?
5. Because I love nature.
6. Why has she got a dog?
7. Because she loves animals.
8. Why don't you go for a walk after eating?
9. Why don't you go for a bike ride?
10. Because we like walking.
11. What do you talk about while walking?
12. Anything, sports, politics, music for instance.

C1 EXERCISES

A. (CD) Use <u>que</u> and <u>qu'est-ce que</u> to form questions as in the example :
Il mange une tarte : Qu'est-ce qu'il mange ?/Que mange-t-il ?

1. Elles achètent des livres.
2. Il utilise un ordinateur.
3. Elle regarde un film.
4. Elle porte une grosse valise.
5. Ils vont apporter le vin.
6. Il va faire une photo.

B. Match the questions and answers :

Q. 1. Pourquoi invites-tu les voisins ?
2. Pourquoi habitez-vous ici ?
3. Pourquoi est-ce que tu achètes un croissant ?
4. Pourquoi va-t-elle souvent à Nice ?
5. Pourquoi a-t-il beaucoup de travail ?

A. 7. Parce qu'il est médecin.
8. Parce qu'ils sont sympathiques.
9. Parce que c'est près de la gare.
10. Parce que j'ai faim.
11. Parce qu'elle a des parents à Nice.

D2 VIE PRATIQUE

A. 1. Qu'est-ce qu'elles achètent ?/Qu'achètent-elles ?
2. Qu'est-ce qu'il utilise ?/Qu'utilise-t-il ?
3. Qu'est-ce qu'elle regarde ?/Que regarde-t-elle ?
4. Qu'est-ce qu'elle porte ?/Que porte-t-elle ?
5. Qu'est-ce qu'ils vont apporter ?/Que vont-ils apporter ?
6. Qu'est-ce qu'il va faire ?/Que va-t-il faire ?

B. 1. Pourquoi invites-tu les voisins ? - 8. Parce qu'ils sont sympathiques.
2. Pourquoi habitez-vous ici ? - 9. Parce que c'est près de la gare.
3. Pourquoi est-ce que tu achètes un croissant, - 10. Parce que j'ai faim.
4. Pourquoi va-t-elle souvent à Nice ? - 11. Parce qu'elle a des parents à Nice.
5. Pourquoi a-t-il beaucoup de travail ? - 7. Parce qu'il est médecin.

C3 THE POST OFFICE

■ Mail as it was then and as it is now

Up to the last century, horses were used as the main means of transporting mail. Halts were set up every eight kilometers or so to change horses. The numerous hotels and restaurants called "The Post Relay" and "The Post Inn" bear witness to those times.

Today **La Poste** is the equivalent of the the PO (USA) or the GPO (UK). This public service makes use of commercial flights and trains to carry letters and parcels. It offers various services which guarantee delivery within 24 or 48 hours all over the country. **La Poste** has entered into a partnership with **Air France** for the management and operation of **l'Aéropostale**, en airline exclusively devoted to the transportation of mail and parcels.

The vans, letter boxes, etc., of **La Poste** are yellow, and its symbol is a stylized dark blue bird. The zip code - **le code postal** - begins with the number of the **département**, the administrative district in which it is located (see pages 25 and 27). For Paris, for instance, the post code is 750 + the number of the **arrondissement** : 75005 (Paris 5e), 75013 (Paris 13e), etc.

But La Poste does more than transport and distribute mail ; it has become a banking institution. In addition to the post office savings banks, there are various financial services : money orders, currency exchange, life insurance, housing savings schemes, and stocks and bonds.

■ A useful expression :

« Le cachet de la poste faisant foi »

The postmark will be accepted as proof.

The postmark indicates the date and the place from which something is sent. It can be used as proof in case of dispute.

20 DIALOGUES AND "ANYTHING"

D1 A LA POSTE (CD)

Serge : Qu'est-ce que tu fais là Nathalie ?
Nathalie : Oh salut Serge, j'achète des timbres.
Serge : Pourquoi est-ce que tu n'utilises pas le distributeur automatique au lieu de faire la queue devant le guichet ?
Nathalie : Parce que j'ai aussi un paquet à envoyer…
Employé : Qu'est-ce que vous préférez : paquet ordinaire ou recommandé ?
Nathalie : En recommandé.
Employé : Alors remplissez cette fiche s'il vous plaît. N'oubliez pas le nom de l'expéditeur.
Nathalie : Voilà. Le code postal de Toulouse c'est bien 31000 ?
Employé : Oui. Voilà votre reçu.
Nathalie : Merci. Le colis va arriver dans combien de temps ?
Employé : Pour Toulouse ? Dans deux jours, trois au maximum.
Nathalie : Ah, j'oublie les timbres, un carnet s'il vous plaît.
Employé : Je n'ai plus de carnet. Dix timbres ça va ?
Nathalie : Oui, merci.

D2 N'IMPORTE QUOI
ANYTHING

The meaning of *any* can be conveyed by the expression **n'importe…**

n'importe où	*anywhere*
n'importe comment *	*anyhow*
n'importe qui	*anybody/anyone*
n'importe quoi	*anything*
n'importe quand	*any time*

* Note that **n'importe comment** often means *carelessly.*

D3 AT THE POST OFFICE

Serge : What are you doing here, Nathalie ?
Nathalie : Oh hi, Serge. I'm buying stamps.
Serge : Why don't you just use the stamp machine instead of standing in line at the counter ?
Nathalie : Because I've also got a package to send.....
Employee Which do you prefer, regular or registered mail ?
Nathalie : Registered.
Employee : Then fill out this form, please. Don't forget the name of sender.
Nathalie : Here you are. The postal code of Toulouse is 31000, isn't it ?
Employee : Yes. Here's your receipt.
Nathalie : Thank you. How long will it take the package to get there ?
Employee : To Toulouse ? Two days, three maximum.
Nathalie : Oh, I'm forgetting the stamps. A book of stamps, please.
Employee : I'm out of stamp books. Will ten stamps do ?
Nathalie : Yes, thank you.

D4 USEFUL EXPRESSIONS

affranchir : *to put stamps on*
chez... : *in care of...*
destinataire (m, f) : *addressee*
expédier : *to send*
faire suivre : *to forward (mail)*
ne pas plier : *do not bend*
carte postale (f) : *postcard*
courrier (m) : *mail* (US), *post* (GB)
distribution (f) : *delivery*
facteur (m) : *mailman, postman*
levée (f) : *collection*
par avion : *by air mail*
vente par correspondance : *mail order*

20 TESTS - LESSONS 11 TO 20

Complete with a, b, c or d : (There is only one correct answer for each item)

1. ——— gare n'est pas loin.
   a) La
   b) L'
   c) Les
   d) Le

2. Elle va à ——— aéroport.
   a) la
   b) l'
   c) les
   d) le

3. Pose ——— livres sur ——— table, s'il te plaît.
   a) ce ces
   b) cette cette
   c) ces cette
   d) cet cette

4. J'aime bien les chaussures ——— sont en vitrine.
   a) que
   b) qui
   c) quelles
   d) où

5. Je n'écoute pas ——— elle dit.
   a) que
   b) qu'
   c) ce que
   d) ce qu'

6. ——— chanson préférez-vous ?
   a) quelle
   b) quels
   c) quel
   d) quelles

7. Est-ce qu'il y a ——— eau ?
   a) du
   b) de l'
   c) de la
   d) Ø

8. Je n'ai pas ——— argent.
   a) de la
   b) de l'
   c) d'
   d) de

9. Personne ——— prépare le repas.
   a) Ø
   b) pas
   c) ne
   d) ne pas

10. ——— attention à ce qu'ils ———

a) Faire	fait
b) Font	font
c) Fais	font
d) Fais	faites

21 Qui est le président de la République ?

A1 PRESENTATION

■ Grammar

- To ask a question about a person, **qui** is the word to use. It is used as subject.

  Ex.: **Qui est là ?** *Who is there?*
  Qui est-ce ? *Who is it?*
  Qui est-ce qui commence ? *Who starts?*

- Here note **qui est-ce qui...** when the question is asked with **est-ce**.

■ Vocabulary

gouverner	*to govern*
nommer	*to name*
faire un discours	*to make a speech*
voter	*to vote*
président (masc.)	*president*
république (fem.)	*republic*
ministre (masc.)	*minister*
candidat (masc.)	*candidate*
élection (fem.)	*election*
affiche (fem.)	*poster*
prochain	*next*

A2 EXAMPLES *(Government)* CD

1. **Qui gouverne ce pays ?**
2. **Qui est le président de la République ?**
3. **Qui va nommer les ministres ?**
4. **Qui est-ce qui va nommer les ministres ?**
5. **Qui va être Premier ministre ?**
6. **Qui est-ce qui va voter pour le président ?**
7. **Qui est-ce qui est candidat ?**
8. **Qui est candidat aux prochaines élections ?**
9. **Qui parle aux journalistes ?**
10. **Qui va faire un discours ce soir ?**
11. **Qui est sur l'affiche ?**
12. **Qui vote pour ce candidat ?**

21 Who is the President of the Republic?

A3 COMMENTS

Grammar

- Note that **qui** remains the same even when preceding a vowel or **h**.
  Ex.: **Qui est là ?**
  Qui apporte les affiches ?
- **élection** is generally used in the plural **(les élections)** unless it is followed by a complement.
  Ex.: **L'élection de l'Assemblée.**
  The election of the Assembly.
- Remember that **aller** followed by a verb in the infinitive conveys either an intention or the immediate future.
  Ex.: **Qui va nommer les ministres ?**
  Who is going to name the ministers?
  Qui va être le Premier ministre ?
  Who is going to be Prime Minister?

Pronunciation

- **tion** (ex.: **élection)** is pronounced **sion** unless it is preceded by **s** as in **question** *(question)*, in which case the **t** is pronounced **t.**

A4 TRANSLATION

1. Who governs this country?
2. Who is the President of the Republic?
3. Who is going to name the ministers?
4. Who is going to name the ministers?
5. Who is going to be Prime Minister?
6. Who is going to vote for the President?
7. Who is a candidate?
8. Who is a candidate for the next election?
9. Who is speaking to the journalists?
10. Who is going to make a speech tonight?
11. Who is on the poster?
12. Who votes for this candidate?

21 À qui fais-tu confiance ?

B1 PRESENTATION

Grammar

- **qui** may also be used as a direct object. Ex.:
  Qui cherchent-ils ? *Who are they looking for?*
  Qui est-ce <u>que</u> tu préfères ? *Who(m) do you prefer?*
  Here, note the **que**.
- Or with a preposition. Ex.:
  Avec qui parlez-vous ? *Who are you talking with?*
  Pour qui travaille-t-il ? *Who does he work for?*
  À qui apporte-t-elle les photos ? *Who(m) is she bringing the photos to?*

Vocabulary

donner	*to give*
discuter	*to discuss*
avoir confiance / **faire confiance**	*to trust*
compter sur	*to rely on*
régler	*to settle*
document (masc.)	*document*
affaire (fem.)	*case, matter*
mission (fem.)	*mission*
actuellement	*presently*
d'autre	*else*

B2 EXAMPLES *(A special mission)* (CD)

1. **À qui téléphones-tu ?**
2. **À qui vas-tu donner ce document ?**
3. **Pour qui fais-tu ça ?**
4. **Pour qui est-ce que tu travailles actuellement ?**
5. **Pour qui travaille cet homme ?**
6. **Avec qui discutez-vous de cette affaire ?**
7. **Avec qui est-ce que vous discutez de cette affaire ?**
8. **En qui ont-ils confiance ?**
9. **À qui fais-tu confiance ?**
10. **À qui penses-tu pour la prochaine mission ?**
11. **À qui d'autre est-ce que tu penses ?**
12. **Sur qui comptez-vous pour régler cette affaire ?**

B3 COMMENTS

Grammar

- Note that in questions about the indirect object, the preposition must be placed at the beginning. Ex.:

À qui penses-tu ?	*Who are you thinking of?*
Avec qui déjeunez-vous ?	*Who are you having lunch with?*
Pour qui travaille-t-il ?	*Who does he work for?*
Sur qui comptez-vous ?	*Who do you rely on?*

- Note that **compter** and **compter sur** have very different meanings:

compter	*to count*
compter sur	*to rely on*

- Note two expressions whose meanings are close:

  faire confiance à

  avoir confiance en

  Ex.: **Il fait confiance à M. Lenoir.**
  Il a confiance en M. Lenoir. → *He trusts Mr. Lenoir.*

B4 TRANSLATION

1. Who are you phoning?
2. Who are you going to give this document to?
3. Who are you doing that for?
4. Who are you working for now?
5. Who is this man working for?
6. Who do you discuss this matter with?
7. Who do you discuss this matter with?
8. Who do they trust?
9. Who do you trust?
10. Who are you thinking of for the next mission?
11. Who else are you thinking of?
12. Who do you rely on to settle this matter?

C1 EXERCISES

A. Change the question as in the example :
Qui chante ?/Qui est-ce qui chante ?

1. Qui habite ici ?
2. Qui écoute l'émission ?
3. Qui regarde la télévision ?
4. Qui apporte le vin ?

B. Find the questions about the words in capital letters.
Ex. : Elle va parler AUX ÉTUDIANTS. À qui va-t-elle parler ?

1. Ils vont parler AUX ÉLECTEURS.
2. Il prépare ce repas pour LES ENFANTS.
3. Nous voyageons avec NOS AMIS.
4. C'est la voiture de MA FILLE.

C. Choose between qui and que :

1. Qui est-ce… sonne ?
2. Qui est-ce… les journalistes regardent ?
3. Qui est-ce… tu écoutes ?

C2 ANSWERS

A. 1. Qui est-ce qui habite ici ?
2. Qui est-ce qui écoute l'émission ?
3. Qui est-ce qui regarde la télévision ?
4. Qui est-ce qui apporte le vin ?

B. 1. À qui vont-ils parler ?
2. Pour qui prépare-t-il ce repas ?
3. Avec qui voyagez-vous ?/Avec qui voyageons-nous ?
4. À qui est la voiture ?

C. 1. Qui est-ce qui sonne ?
2. Qui est-ce que les journalistes regardent ?
3. Qui est-ce que tu écoutes ?

C3 THE RIGHT AND THE LEFT IN FRENCH POLITICS

■ The distinction between the *right* (**la droite**) and *the left* (**la gauche**) in France dates from the French Revolution. Up until the Fifth Republic, the leftist parties sat to the left of the president of the National Assembly in the Bourbon Place hemicycle.

■ Since the beginning of the 19th century, the left has called for political, social and economic modifications symbolized by the motto "liberty, equality, fraternity". To the dilemma "liberal or authoritarian regime?" has been added the question of secularism, the separation of church and state, and, with **Jaurès**, the demand for economic and social democracy.

■ International affairs came to the forefront in the period between the two wars. The left, while divided between Communists and Socialists, defined itself in relation to the Bolshevik Revolution. The fascist menace led it to form a Popular Front government in 1936.

■ The compromises of the right, which rallied massively to the **Pétain** government during World War II, the colonial wars, the diplomatic stakes, would all lead to further sharper divisions between right and left.

■ Gaullism, starting in 1958, would attempt to transcend this opposition: the Communists approved the policy of national independence opposed to the American and Soviet "block"s; the Christian Democrats were in favor of transatlantic solidarity. The opposition between the hard-core Gaullists and the more **laissez-faire** right represented by **Jacques Chirac** and **Valéry Giscard d'Estaing**, gained ground at the end of the 60s.

■ With the government of **François Mitterand** (1981-1996), no doubt because of economic constraints and of its firm ties to Europe, the traditional lines separating right from left tended to become somewhat blurred. The left and the right drew closer together on some questions of domestic and international politics. This drift, accompanied by the incapacity to resolve the main problems facing society linked notably to immigration, integration, and violence may be at the origin of the rise of the far right.

■ Today the left is represented essentially by the **PS** (Socialist Party). The **LCR** (Revolutionary Communist League) is a party of the extreme left.

The right is mainly represented by the **UMP** (Union for the Presidential Majority). It became the governing party after the election to Presidency of its leader, **Nicolas Sarkozy**, in May 2007.

The **FN** (National Front) is a party of the extreme right.

21 DIALOGUES AND VOTERS

D1 ELECTIONS (CD)

Sylvie : Allume la télé s'il te plaît, c'est l'heure du journal.
Nicolas : Quelle chaîne ?
Sylvie : La deux.... Tiens c'est Durieux qui fait un discours.
Nicolas : Durieux ? Qui est-ce ?
Sylvie : C'est le candidat du Parti Républicain aux élections législatives de mars prochain. Il a des chances de gagner.
Nicolas : Et qui sont les autres ?
Sylvie : Je n'ai pas les noms en tête.... Il y a dix ou douze candidats
Nicolas : Pour qui vas-tu voter ?
Sylvie : Oh, j'ai le temps de décider, je vais regarder de près les différents programmes.
Nicolas : Qui est-ce qui est en tête dans les sondages ?
Sylvie : Le candidat de la majorité et le principal candidat de l'opposition sont à égalité.
Nicolas :. Qui va être le nouveau député ? La lutte est serrée !

D2 ÉLECTEUR (masc.), ÉLECTRICE (fem.)/ *VOTER*

• For some nouns denoting masculine persons, the ending **-teur** (**directeur, électeur**) changes into trice in the feminine (**directrice, électrice**). Here are some examples :

masculine	féminine	
acteur	**actrice**	*actor, actress*
admirateur	**admiratrice**	*admirer*
auditeur	**auditrice**	*listener*
(les auditeurs, *the audience*)		
collaborateur	**collaboratrice**	*colleague*
conducteur	**conductrice**	*driver*
instituteur	**institutrice**	*teacher (primary school)*
spectateur	**spectatrice**	*spectator*

But :

chanteur	**chanteuse**	*singer*

D3 ELECTIONS

Sylvie : Turn the TV on, please ; it's time for the news.
Nicolas : Which channel ?
Sylvie : Channel 2. Hey, that's Durieux making a speech.
Nicolas : Durieux ? Who's he ?
Sylvie : He's the Republican Party candidate for the legislative elections next March. He's got a good chance to win.
Nicolas : And who are the others ?
Sylvie : I can't remember their names right now. There are ten or twelve candidates.
Nicolas : Who are you going to vote for ?
Sylvie : Oh, I've got time to make up my mind. I'm going to look closely at the different programs.
Nicolas : Who's ahead in the polls ?
Sylvie : The majority candidate and the opposition candidate are running neck to neck.
Nicolas :. Who's going to be the new deputy ? It's a close race !

D4 LA VIE POLITIQUE/ *POLITICAL LIFE*

campagne électorale (fem.)	*election campaign*
droit de vote (masc.)	*right to vote*
voix (fem.)	*vote*
majorité (fem.)	*majority*
parti politique (masc.)	*political party*
syndicat (masc.)	*trade union*
gouvernement (masc.)	*government*
député (masc.)	*member of Parliament* (US : *Congress)*
roi (masc.)	*king*
reins (fem.)	*queen*
monarchie (fem.)	*monarchy*
démocratie (fem.)	*democracy*

22 Voici la salle de conférences, ...

A1 PRESENTATION

■ Grammar: Possession.

- There is no form corresponding to *'s* in French.
  Ex.: **La voiture de Pierre.** *Peter's car.*
  Le sac de la secrétaire. *The secretary's bag.*
  The form used is comparable to « *the car of Peter* », « *the bag of the secretary* ».

- **à qui** is the equivalent of *whose* as well as *to whom.*
  Note the construction when asking about the possessor:
  À qui est la voiture ? *Whose car is it?*
  (literally: *to whom is the car?)*
  À qui sont ces vêtements ? *Whose clothes are they?*

■ Vocabulary

P.-D.G. (Président-Directeur général) (masc.)
President and Managing Director (US: *CEO, Chief Executive Officer)*

employé (masc.), **employée** (fem.)	*employee*
parking (masc.)	*car park* (US: *parking lot)*
stylo (masc.)	*pen*
calculatrice (fem.)	*calculator*
bureau (masc.)	*desk*
dossier (masc.)	*file*
comptable (masc. and fem.)	*accountant*
salle de conférences (fem.)	*conference room*

A2 EXAMPLES *(At the office)* CD

1. **À qui est cette grosse voiture ? C'est la voiture du P.-D.G.**
2. **Les voitures des employés sont sur le parking.**
3. **À qui est ce stylo ? C'est le stylo de M. Lenoir.**
4. **Il est à M. Lenoir.**
5. **À qui sont ces lunettes ? Elles sont à M. Lenoir.**
6. **Ce sont les lunettes de M. Lenoir.**
7. **Est-ce que c'est la calculatrice de la secrétaire, là, sur le bureau ?**
8. **Non, c'est la calculatrice de Pierre.**
9. **Elle est à Pierre.**
10. **Le dossier « Martin » est sur le bureau de la secrétaire.**
11. **Regarde le nouvel ordinateur du comptable.**
12. **Voici la salle de conférences, elle est à côté du bureau du P.-D.G.**

A3 COMMENTS

■ Grammar

- **être à** is commonly used to answer a question starting with **à qui**.
  Ex. : **À qui est ce livre ?** *Whose book is it?*
  Il est à Pierre. *It is Peter's.*
- **du** is the contracted form of: **de le** *(of the).*
  la voiture du directeur *the manager's car*
  le bureau du président *the president's office*
  la fille du patron *the boss's daughter*
- **des** is the contracted form of **de les**
  les livres des enfants *the children's books*
  le travail des secrétaires *the secretaries' work*
- Similarly, **à le** is contracted in **au**
  à les **aux**
  Je vais au cinéma. *I'm going to the pictures/the movies.*
  Il est au bureau. *He's at the office.*
  Elle parle aux étudiants. *She's talking to the students.*
- Remember that **nouvel** is a form of the adjective **nouveau** whèn it precedes a masculine noun starting with a vowel or **h**.
  un nouvel ordinateur, un nouvel album, le Nouvel An.
  a new computer, a new album, the New Year.

A4 TRANSLATION

1. Who does this big car belong to? It is the Managing Director's car.
2. The employees' cars are in the car park.
3. Whose pen is this? It is Mr. Lenoir's pen.
4. It is Mr. Lenoir's. (It belongs to Mr. Lenoir.)
5. Whose glasses are these? They are Mr. Lenoir's.
6. They are Mr. Lenoir's glasses.
7. Is that the secretary's calculator there, on the desk?
8. No, it is Peter's calculator.
9. It is Peter's.
10. The « Martin » file is on the secretary's desk.
11. Look at the accountant's new computer.
12. Here is the conference room, it is next to the Managing Director's office.

22 Mon père et ma mère...

B1 PRESENTATION

■ Grammar

- Possessive adjectives.

The French possessive adjectives agree in gender and number with the nouns they accompany:

masc. sg.	fem. sg.	masc. & fem. pl.	
mon	**ma**	**mes**	*my*
ton	**ta**	**tes**	*your*
son	**sa**	**ses**	*his, her, its*
notre	**notre**	**nos**	*our*
votre	**votre**	**vos**	*your*
leur	**leur**	**leurs**	*their*

■ Vocabulary

posséder *to own*
venir *to come*
passer *to spend*
famille (fem.) *family*
père (masc.) *father*
mère (fem.) *mother*
sud (masc.) *south*
oncle (masc.) *uncle*
cousin (masc.) *cousin*
entreprise (fem.) *firm*
affaires (fem. pl.) *business*
à l'étranger *abroad*

B2 EXAMPLES *(Family)* CD

1. **Est-ce que vos parents habitent ici ?**
2. **Est-ce que votre famille habite près de Paris ?**
3. **Non, notre famille vient du sud de la France.**
4. **Mon père et ma mère possèdent une grande maison dans le Midi.**
5. **Mon oncle Pierre travaille à l'étranger, en Italie.**
6. **Il ne vient pas souvent voir ses enfants.**
7. **Mes cousins vont parfois voir leur père.**
8. **Sa maison est près de Rome.**
9. **Son entreprise est dans le centre ville.**
10. **Ses affaires marchent bien.**
11. **Ses fils vont aller travailler là-bas.**
12. **Nos enfants vont passer les vacances avec leur oncle à Rome cet été.**

B3 COMMENTS

Grammar

- Note that the feminine singular possessives **ma, ta, sa** when preceding a vowel or **h** change into **mon, ton, son**.
  Ex.: **mon amie, ton élection, son affiche, son histoire** *his/her story.* **(amie, élection, affiche, histoire** are feminine nouns.)
- **Venir** *(to come)* is an irregular verb:

Present tense			
je	**viens***	*I*	*come*
tu	**viens**	*you*	*come*
il, elle	**vient**	*he, she, it*	*comes*
nous	**venons**	*we*	*come*
vous	**venez**	*you*	*come*
ils, elles	**viennent**	*they*	*come*

- Note the change of accent in **posséder.**
  Je possède, tu possèdes, il/elle possède
  nous possédons, vous possédez, ils/elles possèdent.
- Note the particular meaning of **marcher,** *to walk* and *to be successful:* **Ça ne marche pas.** *It doesn't work.*

Pronunciation

* Note that **ien** in **viens, vient** or **viennent** is pronounced like *y* in *yes* followed by the sound of *an* in *bang* (see lesson 3, B3).

B4 TRANSLATION

1. Do your parents live here?
2. Does your family live near Paris?
3. No, our family comes from the south of France.
4. My father and mother own a big house in the south.
5. My uncle Pierre works abroad, in Italy.
6. He does not often come to see his children.
7. My cousins sometimes go and see their father.
8. His house is near Rome.
9. His firm is in the centre of town.
10. His business is very successful.
11. His sons are going to work there.
12. Our children are going to spend the holidays with their uncle in Rome this summer.

C1 EXERCICES

A. (CD) **Modify as in the example :**
Cette voiture est à Pierre ; C'est sa voiture.

1. Ce stylo est à Anne.
2. Ces lunettes sont à Marc.
3. Cette maison est à oncle Louis.
4. Ce chien est aux voisins.
5. Ces vêtements sont à Marie.

B. (CD) **Translate into French :**

1. My son is working with his manager today.
2. His two children are students.
3. This is her house, it is near her office.
4. Her daughter lives in our flat.
5. My shirt and my shoes are new.
6. They are going to prepare their cases.
7. Our friends are going to travel with their dog.
8. Your friend isn't ready.

C2 ANSWERS

A. 1. Ce stylo est à Anne. C'est son stylo.
2. Ces lunettes sont à Marc. Ce sont ses lunettes.
3. Cette maison est à oncle Louis. C'est sa maison.
4. Ce chien est aux voisins. C'est leur chien.
5. Ces vêtements sont à Marie. Ce sont ses vêtements.

B. 1. Mon fils travaille avec son directeur aujourd'hui.
2. Ses deux enfants sont étudiants.
3. C'est sa maison, elle est près de son bureau.
4. Sa fille habite dans notre appartement.
5. Ma chemise et mes chaussures sont neuves.
6. Ils/elles vont préparer leurs valises.
7. Nos ami(e)s vont voyager avec leur chien.
8. Ton/votre ami(e) n'est pas prêt(e).

C3 AGRICULTURE

■ Although it was for a long time hampered by out-dated methods, French agriculture has undergone, in the space of a generation, a spectacular mutation. It has become efficient and productive, ranking first in the European Union and second in the world for the production of sugar beets and wine. France is also the second exporter in the world of food products. Large subsidies, paid through the European Union, are intended to ensure revenue to farmers and to make exportation possible. In spite of this, the number of farmers has decreased continuously : today there are fewer than one million. At the same time, farms that were not profitable have disappeared and the others have grown larger and use costly, improved techniques. Cultivated land is being reduced because of urbanism and industry, but also due to the Common Agricultural Policy which endeavors to limit overproduction. The overproduction of milk and butter, in fact, requires that some land be left to lie fallow.

■ There are three different concepts of agricultural production : The first, on the vast farms of the Parisian Basin, for example, relies on growing cereals, complemented by industrial cultures such as sugar beets (**betterave à sucre**), rape (**colza**) and flax (**lin**). In relation with the large food industry, well educated heads of agricultural businesses can count on enormous financial and technical support.

■ Another type of agriculture specializes rather in the search for non-standardized food products and emphasizes quality, even if this leads to higher prices. It is based on a policy of labels : free range "farmer's" chicken, **Guérande** salt, **Beaufort** cheese, **Camembert**, wines whose label guarantees the quality, etc.

■ Lastly, for highly-subsidized farmers in mountainous regions that receive large numbers of tourists from urban areas : maintaining farming for reasons of tourism and ecology (e.g. conservation of the soil to avalanches).

■ Whichever perspective is chosen, these farmers with different situations are all grouped in the powerful **FNSEA** (Farming Federation) whose aim is to obtain more advantages from the government, occasionally through spectacular demonstrations.

D1 UN VIEIL AMI (CD)

Marie : Qui est-ce là, sur la photo ?
Frédéric : Une amie de ma mère avec son fils.
Marie : Et ce garçon roux, qui est-ce ?
Frédéric : C'est mon copain Yann.
Marie : Il fait ses études à Paris ?
Frédéric : Oui, mais il vient de Bretagne. Nos parents sont de vieux amis. Nous passons toujours nos vacances ensemble.
Marie : Où ça ?
Frédéric : Ses parents ont une grande maison dans le sud du Finistère.
Marie : Tu as des photos de la maison ?
Frédéric : Oui. Là, c'est l'année dernière au mois de septembre, il n'y a presque personne. Là c'est en été. Son frère, sa soeur et ses cousins viennent en vacances au mois d'août. On fait de grandes parties de pêche dans leur bateau.

D2 NOTE THE USE OF GRAND AND GROS IN FRENCH

une grande église	*a big church*
une grande rue	*a wide street*
un grand écrivain	*a great writer*
une grande fille	*a tall girl, a big girl*

But :

une grosse voiture	*a big car*
un gros repas	*a big metal*
un gros gâteau	*a big cake*
un gros livre	*a big book*

D3 AN OLD FRIEND

Marie : Who's that in the photo ?
Frédéric : A friend of my mother's, with her son.
Marie : And who's this red-headed boy ?
Frédéric : That's my friend Yann.
Marie : Is he studying in Paris ?
Frédéric : Yes, but he comes from Brittany. Our parents are old friends. We always spend our vacations together.
Marie : Where ?
Frédéric : His parents have a big house in the south of Finistere.
Marie : Do you have any photos of the house ?
Frédéric : Yes, this one is last year in September. There's almost nobody around. This one is in the summer. His brother, his sister, and his cousins come for a vacation in August. We have big fishing parties on their boat.

D4 DIRECTIONS/ *DIRECTIONS*

nord/ *north*

ouest/ *west* **est/** *east*

sud/ *south*

- In **est**, **ouest**, and **sud**, the final consonants are heard.
- Notice the prepositions in some common expressions referring to places :

dans le Nord	*in the north*
dans l'Est	*in the east*
dans l'Ouest	*in the west*
dans le Sud	*int he south*
dans le Midi	*in the south (of France)*

à la mer	*at the seaside*	**en province**	*outside Paris*
à la campagne	*in the country*	**en banlieue**	*in the suburbs*
à la montagne	*in the mountains*	**en ville**	*in town*

23 On appelle M. ou Mme Lenoir !

A1 PRESENTATION

Grammar

- We have seen that the pronoun **on** often means *we*. It is also used to replace an indefinite subject.

Ex.:	**On sonne à la porte.**	*Someone is ringing the doorbell.*
	On n'entend rien.	*One can't hear anything.*
	On vient.	*Someone is coming.*

Vocabulary

sonner	*to ring (the doorbell)*
ouvrir	*to open*
appeler	*to call*
répondre	*to answer*
entendre	*to hear*
finir	*to finish*
fermer	*to close / to shut*
porte (fem.)	*door*
bruit (masc.)	*noise*
avant	*before*
ne... rien	*not anything*
ne... jamais	*never*

A2 EXAMPLES *(Calling)* CD

1. **On sonne ! Va ouvrir la porte, s'il te plaît !**
2. **On appelle M. ou Mme Lenoir !**
3. **On appelle Mlle Lemercier !**
4. **On appelle ; allez répondre, s'il vous plaît.**
5. **On va téléphoner.**
6. **On n'entend rien, il y a trop de bruit !**
7. **On arrive !**
8. **On arrive le 20 mars à cinq heures.**
9. **Trop tard, on ferme !**
10. **On n'a pas assez de temps.**
11. **Téléphonez après neuf heures ; on ne finit jamais avant neuf heures.**
12. **Est-ce qu'on commence bientôt ?**

23 Someone is calling Mr. or Mrs. Lenoir!

A3 COMMENTS

Grammar

- Remember:
  on impersonal pronoun.
  ont 3rd person plural of **avoir** in the present tense.
  (The pronunciation is the same.)
- Remember that in the negative form, **ne** or **n'** is placed before the verb. Ex.: **On ne regarde pas.**
  On n'appelle pas.
  On n'arrive pas.
- Regular French verbs belong to:
  — the 1st group ending in **er: chanter** (see lesson 4, A3).
  — the 2nd group ending in **ir: finir**.
  — the 3rd group, others: **répondre, voir, ouvrir...**
  Verbs of the same group have the same conjugation.
- Note that **rien** can be used as a subject: then **ne** is placed between **rien** and the verb.
  Ex.: **Rien ne marche.** *Nothing works.*

Pronunciation

- Don't forget the liaison when **on** is followed by a vowel or **h**.
  Ex.: **on‿appelle, on‿arrive, on‿habite.**
  n n n

A4 TRANSLATION

1. Someone is ringing the doorbell! Go and open the door, please!
2. Someone is calling Mr. or Mrs. Lenoir!
3. Someone is calling Miss Lemercier!
4. The phone is ringing; go and answer it, please.
5. We are going to phone.
6. We can't hear anything*, there is too much noise!
7. We are coming!
8. We are coming on March 20th, at five o'clock.
9. Too late, we are closing!
10. We haven't got enough time.
11. Call after nine; we never finish before nine.
12. Are we going to start soon?

* Note that there is no equivalent of *can* in the French sentence.

23 On signale un accident.

B1 PRESENTATION

Grammar

- **on** is also used to express an indefinite idea.
  Ex.: **on pense que** meaning:
  people think / one thinks / they think / it is thought.
- *That* when linking two sentence units is translated by: **que** or **qu'**.
  Ex.: *I think that the computer is out of order.*
  Je pense que l'ordinateur est en panne.

que or **qu'** can't be omitted in French.

Vocabulary

signaler — *to report*
conduire — *to drive*
améliorer — *to improve*
avoir le droit de — *to be allowed to*
accident (masc.) — *accident*
permis de conduire (masc.) — *driving licence*
embouteillage (masc.) — *traffic jam*
périphérique (masc.) — *ring road*
circulation (fem.) — *traffic*
travaux (masc. pl.) — *road works*
sans — *without*

B2 EXAMPLES *(Road conditions)* (CD)

1. **On signale un accident.**
2. **On signale un accident sur l'autoroute.**
3. **On a le droit de conduire à dix-huit ans.**
4. **On n'a pas le droit de conduire avant dix-huit ans.**
5. **On n'a pas le droit de conduire sans permis de conduire.**
6. **On signale des embouteillages sur le périphérique.**
7. **On signale des embouteillages en ville.**
8. **On n'aime pas rester dans les embouteillages.**
9. **On pense que les travaux vont finir bientôt.**
10. **On pense qu'on va améliorer la circulation en ville.**
11. **Est-ce qu'on va utiliser des ordinateurs ?**
12. **Oui, on pense que les ordinateurs vont améliorer la circulation.**

B3 COMMENTS

Grammar

- Present tense of the verbs:

2nd group, ex.: **finir**				3rd group, ex.: **entendre**			
je	**finis**	*I*	*finish*	**j'**	**entends**	*I*	*hear*
tu	**finis**	*you*	*finish*	**tu**	**entends**	*you*	*hear*
il, elle	**finit**	*he, she, it*	*finishes*	**il, elle**	**entend**	*he, she, it*	*hears*
nous	**finissons**	*we*	*finish*	**nous**	**entendons**	*we*	*hear*
vous	**finissez**	*you*	*finish*	**vous**	**entendez**	*you*	*hear*
ils, elles	**finissent**	*they*	*finish*	**ils, elles**	**entendent**	*they*	*hear*

- Note that in French there is no article before the noun which follows **sans**.
  Ex.: **sans permis de conduire** *without a driving licence*
- **on** can mean *we* (see lesson 4, B1).
- **on** often corresponds to the passive voice in English.
  Ex.: **On signale un accident.**
  An accident has been reported.

Pronunciation

- **ss** between two vowels is pronounced like *s* in *sun*.
  Ex.: **finissez, finissons, finissent.**

B4 TRANSLATION

1. An accident has been reported.
2. An accident on the motorway has been reported.
3. You are allowed to drive at eighteen.
4. You are not allowed to drive before eighteen.
5. People are not allowed to drive without a licence.
6. Traffic jams are reported on the ring road.
7. Traffic jams are reported in town.
8. People don't like staying in traffic jams.
9. They think the road works are going to be finished soon.
10. They think they are going to improve the traffic in town.
11. Are they going to use computers?
12. Yes, it is thought that the computers will improve the traffic.

23 Exercises

C1 EXERCISES

A. <u>on/ont</u> : choose the right one :

1. Ici,… parle anglais.
2. Ils… deux enfants.
3. Pierre et Marie… un appartement près d'ici.
4.… appelle la secrétaire.
5. Elles… des valises neuves.
6.… ne travaille pas le dimanche.

B. Use the correct form of the verb finir :

1. Elles… la bouteille de vin.
2. On… à neuf heures.
3.… vous la tarte ?
4. Nous… le repas.

C. (CD) Translate into French :

1. People think Europe is very important.
2. We think the museum is going to open at three.
3. Someone is calling in the street.
4. We are going to leave together on Thursday.

C2 ANSWERS

A. 1. Ici, on parle anglais.
2. Ils ont deux enfants.
3. Pierre et Marie ont un appartement près d'ici.
4. On appelle la secrétaire.
5. Elles ont des valises neuves.
6. On ne travaille pas le dimanche.

B. 1. Elles finissent la bouteille de vin.
2. On finit à neuf heures.
3. Finissez-vous la tarte ?
4. Nous finissons le repas.

C. 1. On pense que l'Europe est très importante.
2. On pense que le musée va ouvrir à trois heures.
3. On appelle dans la rue.
4. On va partir ensemble jeudi.

C3 TELECOM

■ The French telecommunications market was opened in January 1998, one year after the government set up the **ART, l'Autorité de régulation des télécommunications.** The consumer has since benefited from a drop in prices and increased service.

■ Formerly a part of the Ministry of the Post, Tele-communications, and Space, **France Télécom** has shown that France is at the forefront of new technologies. This private limited company is the world's fourth largest in telecommunications and counts over 170,000 employees. It is now present on the French stock market, with the state keeping a 50 % share and the rest belonging to its employees and private investors.

■ **France Télécom** is primarily a telephone company since this activity represents 75 % of its turnover and includes the **Audiotel**, telecopy, **Numeris**, and **Minitel** services.

■ The Minitel is the most widespread of its telematics operations, and allows access to all sorts of services, home banking, reservations, news and weather reports, communications services.

Facing increasing demand for instantaneous news and services, the company wants to respond not only to basic needs in the realm of telecopy-fax and information exchange, but also to new demands such as mobility, visuals, and virtual networks.

■ Digital technology has torn down borders between data, sound and image, progress in microelectronics has lead to powerful cell telephones and computers. Hence the recent explosion in the market for these products, and today the client may choose from several suppliers such as **ITINERIS, SFR**, or **Bouygues Télécom**. The **RTC (Réseau téléphonique commuté**, *CTN, commuted telephone network*) despatches written and oral information and electronic data..

■ Within this context of industrial and commercial transformation, **France Télécom** has therefore intensified its international presence and strenghtened its competitiveness, and today holds over half of the telephone market in France.

23 DIALOGUES AND MEASURES

D1 AU TELEPHONE (CD)

Agnès : On signale des embouteillages sur l'autoroute. Je vais appeler Inter-service-route pour avoir plus de précisions.

Paul : Tu as le numéro ?

Agnès : Je pense qu'il est dans mon agenda, regarde s'il te plaît

Paul : C'est le[1]… 01 48 99 33 33.
(elle compose le numéro)

Agnès : Zut[2], il y a un message, on demande de patienter. Je vais rappeler dans un moment.

……

Agnès : …33 33. On n'entend rien.

Paul : Pas étonnant, avec les portables ça arrive souvent.

Agnès : Maintenant ça sonne occupé, pas de chance ! Je recommence.

Paul : Ah non arrête, tu vas finir par avoir un accident. Je prends l'appareil… Voilà : on signale un bouchon de quatre kilomètres à l'entrée du prochain tunnel.

---

1. The word **numéro** is often understood.
2. **Zut** ! is an informal but not vulgar exclamation expressing annoyance or disappointment.

D2 VIE PRATIQUE : MESURES/*MEASURES*

- Here are some commonly used measures of weight :
  gramme (g) (masc.)
  kilogramme (kg) (masc.)
  tonne (t) (fem.)

→ Note that for half a kilo, the word **livre** (fem.) is used. Ex. :

Combien pèse ce paquet ? *How much does this parcel weigh ?*
Ce paquet pèse trois kilos. *This parcel weighs three kilos.*
Achète une livre de cerises. *Buy a pound of cherries.*

- For liquids, **litre (l)** (masc.) and **demi-litre** (masc.) are the most commonly used expressions.
  Ex. : **Il y a deux litres de lait sur l'étagère.**
  There are two litres of milk on the shelf.

D3 ON THE TELEPHONE

Agnès : They're reporting traffic jams on the freeway (GB : motorway). I'm going to call Highway Information for more details.
Paul : Do you have the number ?
Agnès : I think it's in my diary. Would you look, please ?
Paul : It's 01 48 99 33 33.
(She dials the number.)
Agnès : Darn, there's a recorded message asking me to wait. I'll call back in a little while.

....

Agnès : ...33 33... You can't hear anything.
Paul : That's not surprising ; that often happens with cell phones (mobile phones).
Agnès : Now it's busy, bum luck ! I'll try again.
Paul : Oh no, stop calling ! You're going to end up having an accident. I'll take the phone. Here we go : they're reporting a traffic jam four kilometers long at the entry to the next tunnel.

D4 NUMÉROS DE TÉLÉPHONE *PHONE NUMBERS*

- In France, phone numbers are said as follows :

42	17	19	30
quarante-deux	**dix-sept**	**dix-neuf**	**trente**
(forty two)	*(seventeen)*	*(ninteen)*	*(thirty)*
45	04	26	08
quarante-cinq	**zéro quatre**	**vingt-six**	**zéro huit**
(forty five)	*(o four)*	*(twenty six)*	*(o eight)*

(CD) A few words and expressions about phone calls :

une cabine	*a phone box* (US : *booth*)
décrocher	*to lift the receiver*
raccrocher	*to hang up*
composer le numéro	*to dial the number*
c'est occupé !	*the line is engaged !* (US : *busy*)
ne quittez pas !	*hold on !*

24 Nous avons acheté des cadeaux pour...

A1 PRESENTATION

Grammar

- To refer to a past event, the most commonly used tense is the **passé composé**. It is formed with the present tense of **avoir** and the past participle of the verb (like the present perfect).
  The endings of the past participles are:

é	for all the verbs in	**er**
i	for most verbs in	**ir**
u	for most verbs in	**oir** and **re**

→ But some verbs are irregular.
Ex.: **prendre - pris** *(to take - taken).*

Vocabulary

prendre	*to take*
louer	*to rent*
vie (fem.)	*life*
plage (fem.)	*beach*
village (masc.)	*village*
cadeau (masc.)	*present*
au bord de la mer	*at the seaside*
dernier	*last*
tout	*all, the whole*
pour	*for*

A2 EXAMPLES *(Touring)* CD

1. **J'ai beaucoup voyagé avec Guy.**
2. **Nous avons visité l'Espagne et le Portugal.**
3. **Nous avons pris le train l'été dernier.**
4. **Vous avez aimé la vie à Lisbonne ?**
5. **Nous avons loué une maison au bord de la mer.**
6. **Les enfants ont joué sur la plage toute la journée.**
7. **Nous avons parlé avec tous les gens du village.**
8. **Le dernier jour, on a chanté et dansé toute la nuit.**
9. **Vous avez pris beaucoup de photos ?**
10. **Oui, et nous avons acheté des cadeaux pour toute la famille.**
11. **Nous avons fini les vacances dans un hôtel dans le Sud.**
12. **Mais Guy a oublié une valise à l'hôtel, avec toutes les photos !**

24 We bought presents for...

A3 COMMENTS

Grammar

- The **passé composé** corresponds to the English simple past (preterit) as well as to the English present perfect.
  Ex.: **Il a pris le train à huit heures.**
  He took the train at eight o'clock.
  Il n'a jamais pris le train.
  He has never taken a train.

- **tout** agrees in gender and number with the noun(s) it accompanies :

singular :	**tout / toute**	*all, the whole*
plural :	**tous / toutes**	*all*

Ex.: **tout le village** *the whole village*
toute la ville *the whole city*
tous les villages *all the villages*
toutes les villes *all the cities*

Pronunciation

- In **mer**, **er** is pronounced as in **merci**.
- **village, famille**
  Remember : **ill** is normally pronounced like *y* in *yes*, but in **village** the double **l** is pronounced like an **l**.

A4 TRANSLATION

1. I have travelled a lot with Guy.
2. We have visited Spain and Portugal.
3. We took the train last summer.
4. Did you like life in Lisbon?
5. We rented a house at the seaside.
6. The children played on the beach all day.
7. We talked to all the people in the village.
8. On the last day, we sang and danced all night.
9. Did you take many photos?
10. Yes, and we bought presents for the whole family.
11. We finished the holidays in a hotel in the south.
12. But Guy forgot a case at the hotel, with all the photos!

24 Nous avons cherché partout mais...

B1 PRESENTATION

Grammar

- The three usual ways of asking a question can be used with the **passé composé**:

1. Vous avez acheté des cadeaux ?
2. Est-ce que vous avez acheté des cadeaux ? → *Did you buy any gifts?*
3. Avez-vous acheté des cadeaux ?

Note that in 3, the auxiliary is inverted, not the verb.

Vocabulary

perdre	*to lose*
dire	*to say, to tell*
coin (masc.)	*corner*
objets trouvés (masc. pl.)	*lost property* (literally « found things »)
quelque chose	*something, anything*
autre chose	*something, anything else*
hier	*yesterday*
partout	*everywhere*
à propos de	*about*

B2 EXAMPLES *(Lost property)* CD

1. **J'ai perdu quelque chose dans le train hier.**
2. **Avez-vous regardé dans tous les coins ?**
3. **Nous avons cherché partout mais nous n'avons rien trouvé.**
4. **Quand avez-vous pris le train ?**
5. **J'ai pris le train lundi soir tard, mais j'ai oublié l'heure exacte.**
6. **Avez-vous téléphoné à la gare ?**
7. **Qu'avez-vous dit ?**
8. **Ils n'ont pas très bien compris.**
9. **Ils ont dit quelque chose à propos des objets trouvés.**
10. **Je n'ai pas bien entendu.**
11. **Est-ce que vous avez dit autre chose ?**
12. **Non, je n'ai pas eu le temps.**

B3 COMMENTS

Grammar

- Note the following past participles, they are irregular:
  avoir - eu *(to have - had)* (pronounced like **u** in **tu**)
  dire - dit *(to say - said)*

  Ex.: **J'ai eu dix-huit ans hier.** *I was eighteen yesterday.*
  Il a dit au revoir. *He said good bye.*

- In the negative **ne pas** or **ne rien** are on either side of the auxiliary.
  Ex.: **Nous n'avons pas acheté de cadeaux.**
  We didn't buy any gifts.
  Nous n'avons rien trouvé.
  We didn't find anything.
  Nous n'avons rien acheté.
  We didn't buy anything.
  Ils n'ont rien eu.
  They didn't get anything.

- Note that *every* + singular is usually translated by:
  tous/toutes + **les** + plural

  Ex.: **tous les coins** *every corner*
  tous les jours *every day*
  toutes les semaines *every week*

B4 TRANSLATION

1. I lost something on the train yesterday.
2. Did you look in every corner?
3. We looked everywhere, but we didn't find anything.
4. When did you take the train?
5. I took the train late on Monday night, but I've forgotten the exact time.
6. Have you phoned the station?
7. What did you say?
8. They didn't understand very well.
9. They said something about lost property.
10. I couldn't hear well.
11. Did you say anything else?
12. No, I hadn't time.

C1 EXERCISES

A. Put the verbs in the passé composé :

1. Elle (manger) dans un restaurant grec hier soir.
2. Nous (oublier) les parapluies.
3. Ils (finir) les travaux l'hiver dernier.
4. Les voisins (inviter) des amis.
5. Tu (avoir) peur ?

B. Put in negative, use the negation in brackets :

1. J'ai pris la voiture hier.	(ne… pas)
2. Il a répondu à Pierre.	(ne… rien)
3. Elles ont préparé le repas.	(ne… pas)
4. Nous avons eu le temps.	(ne… pas)
5. Vous avez trouvé.	(ne… rien)

C2 ANSWERS

A. 1. Elle a mangé dans un restaurant grec hier soir.
2. Nous avons oublié les parapluies.
3. Ils ont fini les travaux l'hiver dernier.
4. Les voisins ont invité des amis.
5. Tu as eu peur ?

B. 1. Je n'ai pas pris la voiture hier.
2. Il n'a rien répondu à Pierre.
3. Elles n'ont pas préparé le repas.
4. Nous n'avons pas eu le temps.
5. Vous n'avez rien trouvé.

C3 TELEVISION

■ In 1982, a law established the principle of free and pluralistic access to audiovisual communication. This began a new era, since private individuals may now, with the authorization of the state, enter broadcasting. Several years later, the **CSA** (Superior Council of Audiovisual Affairs), an independent body, guarantees the freedom of communication, defends competition, ensures the quality and diversity of the programs, and sees that the rules concerning French language and culture in broadcasting are respected. Television, it is true, plays an important role in the life of the French, and they spend on the average two and a half hours per day in front of the box.

■ The **PAF** (the French audio-visual landscape) has undergone profound changes, and television viewers today have a choice between the public channels - **France 2, France 3** and **la Cinq** - and the private ones : **TF1, M6** and **Canal Plus**, the latter a paying encrypted channel. To watch the Canal Plus programs, one must have a decoder although some of them are shown "clearly" (not encrypted).

■ The role of the general channels is to inform, entertain and educate : they combine cultural programs and shows for the general public. Regional news is broadcast daily on France 3. Canal Plus and **Arte** – a French-German joint-venture – are more thematic, the first specializing in movies and sports, the second in cultural creation. The dictatorship of the ratings (**les sondages**) makes it possible to calculate the daily audience of the programs and thus the cost of the advertising that finances them.

■ The progress of cable TV illustrates the increasing popularity of several thematic channels such as Eurosport or Planète. It is also possible in France to get channels throughout Europe on cable or with a satellite dish. **Canal France International** (CFI), which was created in 1989 by the Ministry of Cooperation and Development, is a channel promoting French audiovisual programs throughout the world, e.g. **TV5** : it offers a specific program in more than 80 countries and can reach 600 million potential television viewers through agreements with national channels.

D1 UN FILM A LA TELEVISION (CD)

Hadrien : Qu'est ce que tu as fait hier soir ? Tu as dîné au restaurant ?
Isabelle : Non, j'ai passé toute la soirée à la maison.
Hadrien : Ne dis pas que tu as travaillé !
Isabelle : Non, bien sûr. J'ai regardé la télé.
Hadrien : Tu as suivi le débat sur l'Euro ?
Isabelle : J'ai écouté le début mais j'ai vite abandonné et j'ai regardé un film américain qui a eu du succès à sa sortie et qui n'a pas tellement vieilli : « *Ecrit sur du vent* ».
Hadrien : Tu as aimé ?
Isabelle : Oui assez, j'ai trouvé le scénario un peu mélodramatique mais ça passe.
Hadrien : Il y a longtemps que j'ai renoncé à voir les films à la télévision, je suis toujours déçu. Je préfère le grand écran.
Isabelle : Dis donc tu exagères !
Hadrien : Non, j'ai toujours aimé l'atmosphère des salles de cinéma.

D2 VERBS WITH IRREGULAR PAST PARTICIPLES

avoir	*to have*	**eu**	*had*
boire	*to drink*	**bu**	*drunk*
connaître	*to know*	**connu**	*known*
croire	*to believe*	**cru**	*believed*
dire	*to say, to tell*	**dit**	*said, told*
écrire	*to write*	**écrit**	*written*
être	*to be*	**été**	*been*
faire	*to do, to make*	**fait**	*done, made*
lire	*to read*	**lu**	*read*
mettre	*to put*	**mis**	*put*
ouvrir	*to open*	**ouvert**	*opened*
savoir	*to know*	**su**	*known*
venir	*to come*	**venu**	*come*

D3 A MOVIE ON TELEVISION

Hadrien : What did you do last night ? Did you eat out ?
Isabelle : No, I spent the whole evening at home.
Hadrien : Don't tell me you were working !
Isabelle : No, of course not. I was watching TV.
Hadrien : Did you follow the debate on the Euro ?
Isabelle : I listened to the beginning, but gave up fast and watched an American movie that was a hit when it came out and hasn't aged much : *Written on the Wind.*
Hadrien : Did you like it ?
Isabelle : Yes, quite a bit. I found the scenario a little melodramatic, but it was okay.
Hadrien : I gave up watching movies on TV a long time ago ; I'm always disappointed. I prefer the big screen.
Isabelle : Oh come on, aren't you exaggerating a bit ?
Hadrien : No, I've always liked the atmosphere in movie theaters.

D4 COMMON EXPRESSIONS WITH DIRE

c'est-à-dire	*that is to say*
à vrai dire	*to tell the truth*
dis donc !/dites donc !	*I say !*
j'ai deux mots à vous dire	*I'd like a word with you*
dire que (qu')...	*to think that...*
autrement dit	*in other words*
ça vous dit de + infinitive ?	*do you feel like... ?*
ça ne me dit rien	*I don't feel like it* *it doesn't remind me of anything*
qu'est-ce que ça veut dire ?	*what does it mean ?*

25 Il est resté trois semaines à l'hôpital.

A1 PRESENTATION

Grammar

- For some verbs, the **passé composé** is formed with **être** (see list in C2).

  Il est resté deux heures. *He stayed for two hours.*
  Il est allé à la campagne. *He has gone to the country.*
  Il est parti samedi matin. *He left saturday morning.*

Vocabulary

skier, faire du ski	*to ski*
tomber	*to fall*
devenir	*to become*
repartir	*to go back*
retourner	*to return*
descendre	*to go down*
hôpital (masc.)	*hospital*
piste (fem.)	*trail*
endroit (masc.)	*place*
dangereux	*dangerous*
prudent	*prudent, careful*
tout de suite	*straight away, immediately*

A2 EXAMPLES *(Winter holidays)* (CD)

1. **Louis est parti en vacances le mois dernier.**
2. **Il est allé à la montagne.**
3. **Il est arrivé un dimanche.**
4. **Il a fait du ski tout de suite, mais il est allé trop vite et il est tombé.**
5. **Il n'a pas eu de chance, il est resté trois semaines à l'hôpital.**
6. **Il est sorti il y a huit jours, il va très bien.**
7. **Est-ce qu'il est reparti à la montagne ?**
8. **Oui, il est reparti il y a deux jours.**
9. **Est-il allé sur les pistes noires ?**
10. **Non, il n'est pas retourné dans les endroits dangereux.**
11. **Il est descendu lentement.**
12. **Il est devenu prudent.**

25 He stayed three weeks in hospital.

A3 COMMENTS

Grammar

- **il y a,** can be the French equivalent of *ago*.
  It is placed before the expression of time.

Ex.:	**Il y a huit jours.**	*A week ago.*
	Il y a un mois.	*A month ago.*

- Note that **huit jours** is often used to mean *a week*. In the same way, **quinze jours** is often used for *two weeks*.
- Adjectives ending in **eux** change into **euse** in the feminine form.

Ex.:	**dangereux / dangereuse**	*dangerous*
	joyeux / joyeuse	*merry*
	heureux / heureuse	*happy*
	délicieux / délicieuse	*delicious*

→ But remember: **vieux / vieille** *old*

- **vieil** is used instead of **vieux** in the singular before a vowel or **h**.

	un vieil ami (y)	**un vieil hôtel** (y)
	an old friend	*an old hotel*
→ But	**de vieux amis** (z)	**de vieux hôtels** (z)
	old friends	*old hotels*

Don't forget the liaison.

A4 TRANSLATION

1. Louis went on holiday last month.
2. He went to the mountains.
3. He arrived on a Sunday.
4. He went skiing straight away, but he went too fast and he fell.
5. He was unlucky, he stayed three weeks in hospital.
6. He got out a week ago, he is fine.
7. Did he go back to the mountains?
8. Yes, he went back two days ago.
9. Has he been on the black trails?
10. No, he hasn't returned to the dangerous places.
11. He went down slowly.
12. He has become prudent.

25 Marie est née en 1932

B1 PRESENTATION

Grammar

- With **être** in the **passé composé**, the past participle agrees in gender and number with the subject.

  Ex.: **Elle est partie.** *She left.*
  Ils sont tombés. *They fell.*
  Elles sont arrivées. *They arrived.*

Vocabulary

naître *to be born*
guerre (fem.) *war*
bébé (masc.) *baby*
grands-parents (masc. pl.) *grandparents*
petite-fille (fem.) *grand-daughter*
le lendemain (masc.) *the next day*
juste à temps *just in time*
longtemps *a long time*

B2 EXAMPLES *(Birth)* CD

1. **Marie est née en 1932 ; Philippe est né en 1931.**
2. **Ils sont nés avant la guerre.**
3. **Hélène est née la semaine dernière.**
4. **La mère est partie seule à l'hôpital.**
5. **Le père est arrivé juste à temps.**
6. **Elles sont sorties huit jours après.**
7. **Nous sommes allés voir le bébé hier, il va bien.**
8. **Nous ne sommes pas restés longtemps.**
9. **Des amies sont venues avec des cadeaux.**
10. **Les grands-parents sont venus voir leur petite-fille.**
11. **Ils sont repartis le lendemain matin.**
12. **Ils sont retournés dans le Midi.**

B3 COMMENTS

Grammar

- Remember:
  the **passé composé** of **être** is formed with **avoir** and the past participle **été**.
  Ex.: **J'ai été malade.** *I have been sick.*
  Tu as été malade. *You have been sick.*
  Il, elle a été malade. *He, she, it has been sick.*

- Dates:
  in French dates are said like ordinary numbers.
  Ex.: 1931 : **mille neuf cent trente et un** (literally: « thousand nine hundred thirty and one »).
  1789 : **mille sept cent quatre-vingt-neuf.**
  1900 : **mille neuf cent.**

Pronunciation

- In **longtemps**, **g** is not heard.
- Remember:
  — **ô** in **hôpital** and **eau** in **cadeaux** are pronounced the same. They are nearly pronounced like *o* in *note.*
  — **o** in **sorties** is pronounced like *o* in *not.*

B4 TRANSLATION

1. Marie was born in 1932; Philippe was born in 1931.
2. They were born before the war.
3. Hélène was born last week.
4. The mother left for the hospital alone.
5. The father arrived just in time.
6. They came out a week later.
7. We went to see the baby yesterday; she is fine.
8. We didn't stay long.
9. Friends came with presents.
10. The grandparents came to see their grand-daughter.
11. They went back the next day in the morning.
12. They returned to the south of France.

25 Exercises

C1 EXERCISES

A. Match beginnings and ends :

	parties trop tard.
Elles sont	parti hier.
Il est	arrivées la semaine dernière.
Nous sommes	née en 1954.
Elle est	partis tôt.
Ils sont	nés après la guerre.

B. Put the verb in the passé composé :

1. M. Lenoir (repartir) à cinq heures.
2. Est-ce que Mme Lenoir (rester) à Paris ?
3. Ils (aller) sur la plage.
4. Elles (devenir) prudentes.

C. Write these dates in full :

1. 1666	3. 1914
2. 1818	4. 1991

C2 ANSWERS

A. Elles sont parties trop tard.
Elles sont arrivées la semaine dernière.
Il est parti hier.
Nous sommes parits tôt.
Nous sommes nés après la guerre.
Nous sommes arrivées la semaine dernière.
Nous sommes parties trop tard.
Elle est née en 1954.
Ils sont nés après la guerre.
Ils sont partis tôt.

B. 1. M. Lenoir est reparti à cinq heures.
2. Est-ce que Mme Lenoir est restée à Paris ?
3. Ils sont allées sur la plage.
4. Elles sont devenues prudentes.

C. 1. 1666 : mille six cent soixante-six.
2. 1818 : mille huit cent dix-huit.
3. 1914 : mille neuf cent quatorze.
4. 1991 : mille neuf cent quatre-vingt-onze.

C3 SOCIAL SECURITY/*SÉCURITÉ SOCIALE*

■ Since the end of World War II, the French have had social insurance covering medical expenses : doctors'visits, medicine, laboratory tests and hospital fees are all paid out for, for a large part, out of Social Security funds. All wage-earners are covered by Social Security, which also insures other forms of "risk" : family benefits, pensions and unemployment.
The system works on a sharing-out principle, i.e., health expenses are financed by contributions paid in by employers and employees.
■ Enormous amounts of money, more than the state budget, are at stake. The system was founded during the "baby boom," at a time of economic growth and prosperity, when medical techniques were less sophisticated and expensive, and it is presently running into increasing difficulties. It has come under fire today because it weighs heavily on companies and households faced with larger and larger health insurance payments.

■ How are the pensions of generations that now live longer and longer to be paid ? How are the health costs that are growing at a rate of more than 10 % per year to be met ?

■ These days it is becoming harder and harder to stay in the black, for expenses are soaring and revenue is stagnating. Given the Social Security deficit, the government is forced to devise reforms to encourage those benefiting from coverage to open retirement savings schemes and thus be better prepared for the future.

D1 CHEZ LE MEDECIN (CD)

Docteur : Bonjour Madame, qu'est-ce qui est arrivé à ce petit garçon ?
Catherine : Mon fils est tombé dans le square. J'ai eu très peur. Je suis d'abord allée à la pharmacie, mais le pharmacien a préféré ne pas intervenir.
Docteur : Il a eu raison.....Votre fils est tombé il y a combien de temps ?
Catherine : Il y a une demi-heure à peu près. Je suis venue aussi vite que possible.
Docteur : Où a-t-il mal ?
Catherine : Au bras et au dos.
Docteur : Est-ce qu'il a perdu connaissance ?
Catherine : Pas vraiment, mais il est resté un moment étourdi.
Docteur : Est-ce qu'il a eu des nausées ?
Catherine : Non mais il a eu un peu mal à la tête.
Docteur : Cela n'a pas l'air très grave mais je préfère être sûr. Voici une ordonnance, vous allez faire faire des radios.

D2 VERBS WHOSE PASSÉ COMPOSÉ IS FORMED WITH *ÊTRE*

aller	*to go*
arriver	*to arrive*
descendre	*to go down*
devenir	*to become*
entrer	*to enter*
monter	*to go up*
mourir	*to die*
naître	*to be born*
partir	*to leave*
rentrer	*to go home, to come back*
rester	*to stay, to remain*
retourner	*to return*
revenir	*to come back*
sortir	*to go out*
tomber	*to fall*
venir	*to come*

D3 IN THE DOCTOR'S OFFICE

Doctor : Good morning, Madam. What happened to the little boy ?

Catherine : My son fell in the playground. He gave me quite a scare. First I went to the drugstore *(GB* : chemist's), but the pharmacist preferred not to do anything.

Doctor : He's right. How long ago did your son fall ?

Catherine : About half an hour ago. I came as quickly as possible.

Doctor : Where does it hurt ?

Catherine : His arm and his back.

Doctor : Did he lose consciousness ?

Catherine : Not really, but he was dizzy for a little while.

Doctor : Has he been nauseated ?

Catherine : No, but he had a bit of a headache.

Doctor : It doesn't look very serious, but I would rather be sure. Here's a prescription ; you should go have some X-rays taken.

D4 (CD) THE WORD TEMPS
APPEARS IN MANY COMMON EXPRESSIONS

à temps	*in time*
de temps en temps	*from time to time*
dans le temps	*formerly*
en un rien de temps	*in no time*
prendre du bon temps	*to enjoy oneself/to have fun*
c'était le bon temps	*those were the days*
le bon vieux temps	*the good old days*
en temps voulu	*in due time*
perdre du temps	*to waste time*
gagner du temps	*to save time*

26 Il y a longtemps que je suis commerçant.

A1 PRESENTATION

■ Grammar

- The idea of duration of an action which started in the past is expressed with the **present tense** when the action is still going on. The expression of time is introduced by:

depuis = il y a... que, cela fait... que.

Ex.:	**J'habite ici depuis 20 ans.**	*I have lived here for 20 years.*
=	**Il y a 20 ans que j'habite ici.**	
=	**Cela fait 20 ans que j'habite ici.**	

- When the action is finished the **passé composé** is used. The expression of time is introduced by:

pendant or **durant**

Ex.:	**J'ai habité ici pendant 20 ans.**	*I lived here for 20 years.*
	J'ai habité ici durant 20 ans.	

■ Vocabulary

connaître	*to know*
vendre	*to sell*
commerçant (masc.)	*shopkeeper*
client (masc.)	*customer*
appareil ménager (masc.)	*domestic appliance*
téléviseur (masc.)	*television set*

A2 EXAMPLES *(How long...?)* (CD)

1. **Depuis combien de temps êtes-vous commerçant ?**
2. **Je suis commerçant depuis longtemps.**
3. **Je connais mes clients depuis longtemps.**
4. **Il y a longtemps que je suis commerçant.**
5. **Il y a des années que je suis commerçant.**
6. **Cela fait des années que je connais mes clients.**
7. **Je vends des appareils ménagers depuis dix-huit ans.**
8. **Il y a dix-huit ans que je vends des appareils ménagers.**
9. **Cela fait dix-huit ans que je vends des appareils ménagers.**
10. **Ça fait trois ans que je ne vends plus de téléviseurs noir et blanc.**
11. **J'ai vendu des téléviseurs noir et blanc pendant quinze ans.**
12. **Il y a trois ans que je ne vends plus de téléviseurs noir et blanc.**

26 I have been a shopkeeper for a long time.

A3 COMMENTS

■ Grammar

- Remember that in colloquial French **cela** often becomes **ça**.
  Ex.: **Ça fait 20 ans que j'habite ici.**
  I have lived here for 20 years.
- Note that with the **passé composé pendant** or **durant** can be omitted.
  Ex.: **J'ai habité ici 20 ans.** *I lived here for 20 years.*

⟶ Note that **durant** is less frequently used than **pendant**.

- To ask how long the action has lasted, the expression is:
  Depuis combien de temps...?
  Ex.: **Depuis combien de temps habites-tu ici ?**
  How long have you lived here?

or **Il y a combien de temps que... ?**
  Ex.: **Il y a combien de temps que tu habites ici ?**
  How long have you lived here?

- When the action is finished the question will be:
  Pendant combien de temps... ?
  Ex.: **Pendant combien de temps as-tu habité ici ?**
  How long did you live here?

A4 TRANSLATION

1. How long have you been a shopkeeper?
2. I have been a shopkeeper for a long time.
3. I have known my customers for a long time.
4. I have been a shopkeeper for a long time.
5. I have been a shopkeeper for years.
6. I have known my customers for years.
7. I have sold domestic appliances for eighteen years.
8. I have sold domestic appliances for eighteen years.
9. I have sold domestic appliances for eighteen years.
10. It's been three years since I sold any black and white TV sets.
11. I sold black and white TV sets for fifteen years.
12. I haven't sold any black and white TV sets for three years.

26 Depuis que je connais ces musiciens...

B1 PRESENTATION

Grammar

- To indicate the moment when the action began, **depuis** is used followed by the expression of time.
  Ex.: **J'habite ici depuis 1945 / depuis la fin de la guerre.**
  I have lived here since 1945 / since the end of the war.
- When the expression of time is a subordinate clause, **depuis que** is used:
  - if the action is still going on, the verb is in the **present tense**.
    Ex.: **Nous sommes amis depuis que je le connais.**
    We have been friends since I have known him.
  - if the action is finished, the verb is in the **passé composé**.
    Ex.: **Nous sommes amis depuis le jour où je l'ai rencontré.**
    We have been friends since the day I met him.

Vocabulary

réserver	*to reserve, to book*	**fois** (fem.)	*time*
manquer	*to miss*	**chaîne stéréo** (fem.)	*stereo equipment*
musicien (masc.)	*musician*	**régal** (masc.)	*treat*
place (fem.)	*seat*	**enthousiaste**	*enthusiastic*
public (masc.)	*audience*	**extraordinaire**	*extraordinary*
		chaque	*each*

B2 EXAMPLES *(Music lovers)* (CD)

1. **Depuis quand connaissez-vous les musiciens qui jouent ce soir ?**
2. **Depuis décembre.**
3. **Depuis Noël dernier.**
4. **Depuis que nous habitons Paris.**
5. **Depuis que je connais ces musiciens, je ne manque jamais un concert.**
6. **Chaque fois qu'ils donnent un concert, je réserve des places.**
7. **Toutes les fois qu'ils donnent un concert, j'y vais.**
8. **Ils jouent à Paris depuis 1984.**
9. **Chaque fois qu'ils jouent, le public est enthousiaste.**
10. **Ils sont chaque fois extraordinaires !**
11. **J'écoute leurs disques du matin au soir depuis que je suis devenue une de leurs admiratrices.**
12. **Depuis que nous avons acheté une nouvelle chaîne stéréo, c'est un vrai régal !**

B3 COMMENTS

■ Grammar

- To ask a question about the beginning of the action the expression is **depuis quand ?** *(since when?)*
  Ex.: **Depuis quand connais-tu Pierre ?**
  Since when have you known Peter?
- Note that the idea of repetition can be expressed with:
  chaque*..., tous/toutes les..., le/l'/les...
  Ex.: **Il va au cinéma chaque lundi.**
  He goes to the pictures each Monday.
  Il va au cinéma tous les lundis.
  He goes to the pictures every Monday.
  Il va au cinéma le lundi.
  *He goes to the pictures on Mondays***.*
  * **Chaque** is invariable.
  ** Note the singular in French.
- **Chaque fois que...** *(each time)*, **toutes les fois que...** *(every time)* are followed:
  - by a verb in the **present tense** when the action will be repeated.
    Ex.: **Chaque fois que je vais en Espagne, je vais dans le Sud.** *Each time I go to Spain, I go to the south.*
  - by a verb in the **passé composé** when repetition in the past is referred to.
    Ex.: **Chaque fois que je suis allé en Espagne je suis allé dans le Sud.** *Each time I went to Spain, I went to the south.*

B4 TRANSLATION

1. How long have you known the musicians who are playing tonight?
2. Since December.
3. Since last Christmas.
4. Since we've lived in Paris.
5. Since I met these musicians, I never miss a concert.
6. Each time they give a concert, I book seats.
7. Everytime they give a concert, I go to it.
8. They have been playing in Paris since 1984.
9. Each time they play, the public is enthusiastic.
10. They are extraordinary each time!
11. I listen to their records from morning till night since I became an admirer of theirs.
12. Since we bought some new stereo equipment, it's a real treat!

26 Exercises

C1 EXERCISES

A. Change as in the example :
La secrétaire utilise cet ordinateur depuis deux ans./Il y a deux ans que la secrétaire utilise cet ordinateur./Ça fait deux ans qu'elle utilise cet ordinateur.
1. Nous travaillons dans cette entreprise depuis des années. – 2. Je ne fume plus depuis six mois. – 3. Il ne pleut pas depuix dix jours.

B. Put the verb in the correct tense :
1. Depuis que louis (être) directeur, ses affaires (marcher) bien. – 2. Depuis qu'ils (avoir) une maison à la campagne, ils y (aller) souvent. – 3. Hélène ne (pratiquer) aucun sport depuis qu'elle (tomber) l'an dernier. – 4. Depuis que je (rencontrer) cette musicienne, je (devenir) un de ses admirateurs.

C. Change the sentences to show these things happen each time ; use <u>chaque fois que</u> :
1. Il va à Nice - il fait beau. – 2. Nous avons voyagé en Espagne - nous avons pris le train. – 3. Je rencontre Pierre - nous parlons de politique. – 4. On téléphone - elle va répondre.

C2 ANSWERS

A. 1. Il y a des années que nous travaillons dans cette entreprise. Ça fait des années que nous travaillons dans cette entreprise.
2. Il y a six mois que je ne fume plus. Ça fait six mois que je ne fume plus.
3. Il y a dix jours qu'il ne pleut pas. Ça fait dix jours qu'il ne pleut pas.

B. 1. Depuis que Louis est directeur, ses affaires marchent bien.
2. Depuis qu'ils ont une maison à la campagne, ils y vont souvent.
3. Hélène ne pratique aucun sport depuis qu'elle est tombée l'an dernier.
4. Depuis que j'ai rencontré cette musicienne, je suis devenu un de ses admirateurs.

C. 1. Chaque fois qu'il va à Nice, il fait beau.
2. Chaque fois que nous avons voyagé en Espagne, nous avons pris le train.
3. Chaque fois que je rencontre Pierre, nous parlons de politique.
4. Chaque fois qu'on téléphone, elle va répondre.

C3 LAW AND ORDER

■ The police force

The municipal police is run locally, and its role is one of prevention. As for the national police, which is under the authority of the Ministry of the Interior, it is made up of :
– the **PJ (Police judiciaire)** (akin to the criminal investi gation department) which finds and questions people who commit crimes and criminal offenses in urban areas, and brings them before the courts ;
– the **CRS (Compagnie républicaine de sécurité)** (state security police force), mobile units which participate in enforcing law and order, act as life guards on beaches and provide rescue teams in the mountains ;
– the **RG (les Renseignements généraux)** (intelligence service) which collects local information needed by the government ;
– the **DST (Direction de la surveillance du territoire)** (counter espionage services) which detects and attempts to neutralize espionage operations and interference controlled from outside the country ;
– the **IGS, (Inspection générale des services)** (*Internal affairs division*) nicknamed "the police's police".

■ The Gendarmerie

The **Gendarmerie** is part of the armed forces and is under the authority of the Ministry of Defense. It performs several functions. It is at one and the same time a criminal investigation force that deals with infringements of criminal law (criminal, civil and petty offenses), an administrative force whose duty it is to maintain law and order, a military police force and a highway police force that acts to prevent accidents and punish road violations. The Gendarmerie also includes the **Garde Républicaine**, which was formed in 1813 and provides escorts, protection in official functions, and sees to the security of the Élysée (residence of the French President) and the Palais-Bourbon (Parliament).

In the view of the Nancy magistrate's court, calling policemen **"clowns"** *or* **"flics"** *(cops) does not constitute behavior insulting to the forces of law and order !*

D1 DEVANT LA BOUTIQUE (CD)

(*Les deux commerçants sont sortis de leur boutique*)

Libraire : Quelle circulation aujourd'hui !

Boulanger : Vous avez raison. Il n'y a jamais eu autant de voitures.

Libraire : Ça fait dix ans que je suis ici, je n'ai jamais vu ça.

Boulanger : Vous êtes ici depuis dix ans ! ? Comme le temps passe.

Libraire : Et vous, Depuis quand avez-vous la boulangerie ?

Boulanger : Depuis 85. J'ai d'abord été ouvrier pendant huit ans. Puis, après mon mariage, j'ai acheté cette boutique.

Libraire : Vous ne regrettez pas ?

Boulanger : Pas du tout, j'aime beaucoup ce quartier et je connais mes clients. Certains viennent tous les jours acheter leur pain depuis des années.

Libraire : C'est vrai que le quartier est sympathique. En peu de temps j'ai fait la connaissance de beaucoup de monde et j'ai de fidèles clients qui sont presque devenus des amis.

D2 CONNAÎTRE/CONNAISSANCE *TO KNOW*

- **Connaissance** (fem.) from the verb **connaître** is used in a few set expressions :
  faire connaissance avec…, faire la connaissance de…
  to meet, to make the acquaintance of…
  Ex. : **J'ai fait connaissance avec Mme Martin.**
  J'ai fait la connaissance de Mme Martin l'an dernier.
  I met Mrs. Martin last year.
  Enchanté de faire votre connaissance.
  I'm delighted to meet you.
  prendre connaissance de… *to take not of…*
  perdre connaissance *to faint*
  sans connaissance *unconscious*

D3 IN FRONT OF THE SHOP

(*Two shopkeepers have come out of their shop.*)

Bookseller: What a lot of traffic today!

Baker: You're right. There've never been so many cars!

Bookseller: I've been here for ten years, and I've never seen anything like it.

Baker: You've been here for ten years? How time flies!

Bookseller: What about you? How long have you had the bakery?

Baker: Since 85. First I was an employee for eight years. Then, after I got married, I bought the shop.

Bookseller: You don't regret it?

Baker: Not at all. I like this neighborhood a lot, and I know my customers. Some of them have been coming every day for years to buy their bread.

Bookseller: It's true that it's a nice neighborhood. In just a short time, I've met a lot of people, and I have faithful customers who've practically become friends.

D4 MAGASINS/COMMERÇANTS
SHOPS/SHOPKEEPERS

épicerie (fem.), alimentation	*grocer's*	**épicier**
boucherie (fem.)	*butcher's*	**boucher**
boulangerie (fem.)	*baker's*	**boulanger**
librairie (fem.)	*bookshop*	**libraire**
pharmacie (fem.)	*chemist's* (US: *druggist's*)	**pharmacien**
poissonnerie (fem.)	*fishmonger's*	**poissonnier**
teinturerie (fem.)	*cleaner's*	**teinturier**

27 Le facteur a apporté un colis pour toi.

A1 PRESENTATION

Grammar

moi	toi	lui	elle	nous	vous	eux, elles
me	*you*	*him*	*her*	*us*	*you*	*them*

- Strong personal pronouns can be used:
  - to emphasize the subject.
    Ex.: **Moi, j'aime ce film.** *I like this film.*
    Toi, tu travailles trop ! *You work too much!*
  - as indirect object pronouns (with a preposition).
    Ex.: **Il est avec moi.** *He is with me.*
    Elle parle de toi. *She is talking about you.*

Vocabulary

poster — *to post (US: to mail)*
nouvelles (fem. pl.) — *news*
lettre (fem.) — *letter*
ligne (fem.) — *line*
télégramme (masc.) — *telegram*
facteur (masc.) — *postman (US: mailman)*
colis (masc.) — *parcel*
carte postale (fem.) — *postcard*
timbre (masc.) — *stamp*
paquet (masc.) — *packet*
courrier (masc.) — *mail*

A2 EXAMPLES *(Mail)* CD

1. **J'ai eu des nouvelles de lui hier.**
2. **Il parle de vous dans sa lettre.**
3. **Est-ce qu'il dit quelque chose de moi ?**
4. **Oui, il y a quelques lignes sur vous.**
5. **Où est Anne ? Il y a un télégramme pour elle.**
6. **Le facteur a apporté un colis pour toi.**
7. **À qui sont ces cartes postales ? — À eux.**
8. **Qui a écrit cette lettre ? — Moi.**
9. **Donne-moi des timbres, s'il te plaît.**
10. **Va poster ces lettres pour moi, s'il te plaît.**
11. **Ils ont pris le paquet avec eux.**
12. **Il n'y a pas de courrier pour nous aujourd'hui.**

A3 COMMENTS

■ Grammar

- **à moi, à toi,** etc., are commonly used to express the idea that something belongs *to me, to you,* etc.

  Ex.: **C'est à moi.** *It is mine.*
  Ils sont à vous. *They are yours.*
  La voiture est à lui. *The car is his.*
  Ces livres sont à nous. *These books are ours.*

- The same pronouns are used when standing alone without a verb.

  Ex.: **Qui a dit cela ? — Moi.**
  Who said that? — I did.
  Qui est le patron ici ? — Lui.
  Who is the boss here? — He is.

  You could also say: **C'est moi.** *It's me.*
  C'est lui. *It's him.*

- In the first and second person, even without a preposition, strong pronouns must be used after a command form.

  Ex.: **Donne-moi.** *Give me.*
  Dis-moi, dites-moi. *Tell me.*

A4 TRANSLATION

1. I had some news from him yesterday.
2. He mentions you in his letter.
3. Does he say anything about me?
4. Yes, there are a few lines about you.
5. Where is Anne? There's a telegram for her.
6. The postman has brought a parcel for you.
7. Whose postcards are these? — Theirs.
8. Who wrote this letter? — I did.
9. Give me some stamps, please.
10. Go and post these letters for me, please.
11. They have taken the packet with them.
12. There's no mail for us today.

27 Sa femme n'aime pas la natation. Lui non plus.

B1 PRESENTATION

Grammar

- Strong personal pronouns are also used to express agreement or disagreement with what has been said:

the initial statement is	agreement	disagreement
affirmative	moi aussi	pas moi moi non
negative	moi non plus	moi si

Of course, the pronoun changes according to the person who agrees or disagrees.

Vocabulary

aimer beaucoup *to be very fond of*
pratiquer *to practise*
femme (fem.) *wife*
natation (fem.) *swimming*
mari (masc.) *husband*
chez moi *at home*
vrai *real, true*
aucun(e) *not... any*

B2 EXAMPLES *(Opinions about sports)* (CD)

1. **J'aime beaucoup le sport, et toi ?**
2. **Moi aussi, je joue au volley tous les jours.**
3. **Je vais au match de football dimanche prochain.**
4. **Moi non, je reste chez moi.**
5. **Sa femme n'aime pas la natation.**
6. **Lui non plus.**
7. **Mon mari ne joue pas au tennis.**
8. **Nous si !**
9. **Je ne pratique aucun sport.**
10. **Moi si, je joue au basket.**
11. **J'ai été un vrai champion.**
12. **Pas moi !**

B3 COMMENTS

Grammar

- The complement of **jouer** is generally introduced by a preposition.

  If it is the name of a sport or a game, the preposition used is **à**, often contracted with the article into **au**.

Ex.:	**jouer au tennis**	*to play tennis*
	jouer au football	*to play football*
	jouer à la balle	*to play ball*

  If it is followed by the name of an instrument the preposition used is **de**, often contracted with the article into **du**.

Ex.:	**jouer du piano**	*to play the piano*
	jouer de la flûte	*to play the flute*
	jouer du saxophone	*to play the saxophone*

Pronunciation

- **Champion:** even if the word is the same in English and French, the pronunciation is different: **ch** like *sh* in *shoe* followed by the nasal vowel **an**.

  Remember that **ion** is pronounced like *y* in *yes* followed by the nasal vowel **on**.

B4 TRANSLATION

1. I am very fond of sports, what about you?
2. Me too, I play volleyball every day.
3. I'm going to the football match next Sunday.
4. I'm not, I'm staying at home.
5. His wife doesn't like swimming.
6. Neither does he.
7. My husband doesn't play tennis.
8. We do!
9. I don't practise any sport.
10. I do, I play basketball.
11. I was a real champion.
12. I wasn't!

27 Exercises and POSSESSIVE PRONOUNS

C1 EXERCISES

A. Fill the blanks with the appropriate personal pronoun :
1…., je ne parle pas très bien français.
2…., tu as tort.
3…., nous allons au cinéma, et vous ?
4…., elle est trop jeune.

B. 1. There is a telegram for you.
2.He played tennis with us.
3. Here is the teacher, I am going to speak with her.

C2 ANSWERS

A. 1. Moi, je ne parle pas très bien français.
2. Toi, tu as tort.
3. Nous, nous allons au cinéma, et vous ?
4. Elle, elle est tro pjeune.

B. 1. Il y a un télégramm epour toi/vous.
2. Il a joué au tennis avec nous.
3. Voici l'institutrice, je vais parler ave celle.

C3 PRONOMS POSSESSIFS
POSSESSIVE PRONOUNS

à moi	*mine*	**le mien, la mienne** **les miens, les miennes**
à toi	*yours*	**le tien, la tienne** **les tiens, les tiennes**
à lui, à elle	*his, hers, its*	**le sien, la sienne** **les siens, les siennes** **les nôtres ***
à nous	*ours*	**le nôtre *, la nôtre *** **les nôtres ***
à vous	*yours*	**le vôtre *, la vôtre *** **les vôtres ***
à eux, à elles	*theirs*	**le leur, la leur, les leurs**

* The ô is pronounced like *o* in note.

C3 GAMES OF CHANCE

■ Tens of billions of francs are gambled on games of chance each year in France, three fourths of which go to the state in the form of taxes. With thirty million people who gamble and hundreds of employees, games of chance and betting represent both a genuine economic sector unto themselves and the expression of a socio-cultural phenomenon.

■ The **Française des Jeux** is the organization which manages the lotteries. It is a semi-public corporation with the main part of its capital held by the state, which authorizes the games, and by the issuers, private shareholders who represent the traditions of the lottery, originally associated with great humanitarian causes. The instant games, which consist of uncovering numbers by scratching a card (like **Le Millionnaire, Astro, Morpion** or **France 98,** the latter directly linked to the Football World Cup), are very successful. They can be purchased in almost all tobacco shops.

■ But the passion for gambling is now linked to technology : the **Française des Jeux** constitutes the second network of computerized lottery games in the world. **Loto**, which calls for guessing six winning numbers, is played by six million players. The drawings are broadcast by several television channels.

The **PMU (Paris mutuel urbain**), which controls betting on horse racing, is the oldest and takes in the largest amount of money. This "Group of Economic Interests" under the Ministry of Agriculture and a State Controller is made up of several Parisian and provincial horse racing companies which develop stud farms and horseback riding stables. France is, furthermore, one of the major suppliers of the pure blooded yearlings sold in the **Deauville** auctions. Famous horse races, such as the Arc of Triumph Prize, and thousands of races in the hippodromes of **Saint Cloud, Vincennes, Longchamp, Chantilly,** and **Cagnes-sur-Mer**, draw more than eight million players. A specialized press is constantly growing to give tips on how to win, place, or win on the tiercé, the quarté or the quinté.

■ As to the French casinos like the well-known ones in **Divonne-les-Bains, Deauville, Cannes, Enghien** and **Nice**, they attract a national and a foreign clientele.

D1 FUITE D'EAU (CD)

Florent : Allô L'entreprise de plomberie Girard ? Ici Florent Mercier.
Plombier : Encore vous, Quel est le problème ?
Florent : J'ai besoin de vous d'urgence : il y a de nouveau une fuite d'eau chez moi.
Plombier : Ça vient d'où ?
Florent : Du robinet du lavabo, j'ai de l'eau partout dans la salle de bain.
Plombier : J'envoie un ouvrier dès que possible. Rappelez-moi votre étage.
Florent : Cinquième droite.
(*Florent appelle son amie Fabienne*)
Florent : Impossible de déjeuner avec toi, j'attends le plombier d'une minute à l'autre. Il y a une inondation dans mon appartement, c'est la deuxième fois cette semaine.
Fabienne : Décidément, tu n'as pas de chance.
Florent : Excuse-moi Fabienne la moquette est trempée je vais éponger sinon il va y avoir des dégâts.
Fabienne : Tant pis, bon courage, je vais chez Paul, je mange avec lui.

D2 CHEZ MOI/*AT HOME*

- Chez + a strong pronoun (ex. : **chez lui, chez toi, chez nous**)
  + the name of a person (ex. : **chez Pierre, chez Mme Lenoir**)
  + article or possessive or demonstrative + noun (ex. : **chez le dentiste, chez mon docteur, chez ce ministre**)

means *at* or *to somebody's place.*

Ex. : **Il est chez nous.** *He is at our place.*
Elle rentre chez elle. *She is going back home.*
Ils vont chez vous. *They are going to your house.*
Nous avons dîné chez nos amis.
We had dinner at our friends.

D3 THE LEAK

Florent : Hello ? Girard Plumbers ? This is Florent Mercier.
Plumber : You again. What's the problem ?
Florent : This is an emergency. I've got another leak.
Plumber : Where's it coming from ?
Florent : The tap in the washbasin. I've got water all over the bathroom.
Plumber : I'll send a worker as soon as possible. Tell me again which floor you're on.
Florent : Fifth floor, door on the right.
(*Florent calls his friend Fabienne.*)
Florent : It's impossible for me to have lunch with you ; I'm waiting for the plumber from one minute to the next. I've got a flood in my apartment. It's the second time this week.
Fabienne : You certainly are unlucky.
Florent : Excuse me, Fabienne, the carpet is soaking wet and I've got to go mop it up, otherwise there'll be permanent damage.
Fabienne : Never mind. Keep your chin up ! I'm going to Paul's ; I'll have lunch with him.

D4 LOGEMENT/*HOUSING*

séjour (masc.)	*living room*
salon (masc.)	*drawing room (US : living room)*
salle à manger (fem.)	*dining room*
cuisine (fem.)	*kitchen*
salle de bains (fem.)	*bathroom*
jardin (masc.)	*garden*
garage (masc.)	*garage*

28 Le moniteur nous appelle.

A1 PRESENTATION

Grammar

- Personal pronouns object.
  In the 1st and 2nd persons, the object pronouns are the same whether direct or indirect.

	subject		object	
singular	**je**	*I*	**me (m')**	*me*
	tu	*you*	**te (t')**	*you*
plural	**nous**	*we*	**nous**	*us*
	vous	*you*	**vous**	*you*

- With a preposition: **moi** is used instead of **me**
  toi is used instead of **te**

Vocabulary

voir* *to see*
apprendre *to learn / to teach*
suivre *to follow*
attendre *to wait*
moniteur (masc.) *instructor*
tout le monde *everybody*
vers *to, towards*
attentivement *carefully*

* Irregular verb (see Grammar Summary).

A2 EXAMPLES *(Skiing lesson)* CD

1. **Le moniteur nous appelle.**
2. **Écoutez-moi attentivement.**
3. **Pierre, tu ne m'écoutes pas !**
4. **Regarde-moi ! Nous allons apprendre à tourner.**
5. **Suivez-moi.**
6. **Est-ce que tout le monde me voit bien ?**
7. **Nous vous attendons. Venez avec nous !**
8. **Regardez devant vous.**
9. **Ne regarde pas derrière toi !**
10. **Pierre, je ne te vois pas, viens vers moi.**
11. **Eh, attendez-moi !**
12. **Tout le monde m'a vu ? Allez-y maintenant !**

28 The instructor is calling us.

A3 COMMENTS

■ Grammar

- **me, te, nous, vous** (object) always immediately precede the verb (or auxiliary).
  Ex.: **Tu ne m'écoutes pas.**
  You aren't listening to me.
  Tout le monde m'a vu ?
  Did everybody see me?
- In the imperative affirmative, **moi** is used instead of **me**.
  Ex.: **Regarde-moi !**
- In the imperative affirmative, the object follows the verb and is linked to it by a hyphen.
  Ex.: **Attendez-moi !**
  Look at me!
- Note that **apprendre à** + an infinitive is the French equivalent of
  to learn how to
  Ex.: **Nous apprenons à skier.** *We are learning how to ski.*
  or
  to teach how to
  Ex.: **Elle nous apprend à skier.** *She's teaching us how to ski.*

A4 TRANSLATION

1. The instructor is calling us.
2. Listen to me carefully!
3. Pierre, you aren't listening to me!
4. Look at me! We are going to learn how to turn.
5. Follow me.
6. Can everybody see me all right* ?
7. We are waiting for you. Come with us!
8. Look in front of you.
9. Don't look behind you!
10. Pierre, I can't see you, come towards me*.
11. Hey, wait for me!
12. Did everybody see me? Go ahead now!

* Note that there is no equivalent of *can* in the French sentence.

28 Elle lui fait signe.

B1 PRESENTATION

■ Grammar

- Personal pronoun object
  In the 3rd person, the object pronouns are:

	direct	indirect
sing.	**le (l')** to replace a masculine noun *(= him, it)* **la (l')** to replace a feminine noun *(= her, it)*	**lui** to replace any person or animal *(= her, him, it)*
pl.	**les** to replace any noun or group of nouns *(= them)*	**leur** to replace any persons or animals *(= them)*

■ Vocabulary

commander	*to order*	**café** (masc.)	*pub*
faire signe	*to wave*	**café** (masc.)	*coffee*
sourire	*to smile*	**garçon (de café)** (masc.)	*waiter*
arrêter	*to arrest.* / *to stop*	**agent de police** (masc.)	*policeman*
		soudain	*suddenly*

B2 EXAMPLES *(Detective story)* (CD)

1. **Un homme entre dans un café, prend un journal et l'ouvre.**
2. **Il commande une boisson ; le garçon l'apporte.**
3. **Il y a une femme près de lui, elle le regarde.**
4. **Il ne la voit pas.**
5. **Elle appelle le garçon ; il ne l'entend pas.**
6. **Elle lui fait signe.**
7. **Des musiciens entrent. Elle leur sourit.**
8. **L'homme vient vers elle.**
9. **Il lui demande quelque chose.**
10. **Elle l'écoute attentivement.**
11. **Soudain deux agents de police vont vers eux et les arrêtent.**
12. **Tout le monde les regarde.**

B3 COMMENTS

■ Grammar

- Personal pronouns object.
  When the indirect object is introduced by a preposition (**à, avec, devant, derrière, pour, près de, vers**...):

— **lui** *(him)*	is used for a	masculine singular
— **elle** *(her)*	" " "	feminine singular
— **eux** *(them)*	" " "	masculine plural
— **elles** *(them)*	" " "	feminine plural

Je marche devant elle.	*I'm walking in front of her.*
Parlons avec elles.	*Let's speak with them.*
Nous allons vers eux.	*We're going towards them.*
Va derrière lui.	*Go behind him.*

- Note that the personal pronoun **leur** is invariable.

B4 TRANSLATION

1. A man enters a pub, takes a newspaper and opens it.
2. He orders a drink; the waiter brings it.
3. There is a woman near him; she is looking at him.
4. He doesn't see her.
5. She calls the waiter; he doesn't hear her.
6. She waves to him.
7. Some musicians are coming in. She smiles at them.
8. The man is coming towards her.
9. He asks her something.
10. She listens to him carefully.
11. Suddenly two policemen go towards them and arrest them.
12. Everybody looks at them.

C1 EXERCISES

A. (CD) **Put in pronouns instead, of names or nouns :**

1. On ne voit pas la mer.
2. Marc appelle Marie.
3. Les enfants parlent à la voisine.
4. M. et Mme Martin ont apporté le vin.
5. Nous écoutons les musiciens.

B. (CD) **Translate into French :**

1. He is looking at me.
2. Look at me.
3. I'm speaking to you.
4. I spoke to him.
5. They spoke to her.
6. They are waiting for it.
7. Don't wait for them.

C2 ANSWERS

A. 1. On ne la voit pas.
2. Il l'appelle.
3. Ils lui parlent.
4. Ils l'ont apporté.
5. Nous les écoutons.

B. 1. Il me regarde.
2. Regarde-moi./Regardez-moi.
3. Je te parle./Je vous parle.
4. Je lui ai parlé.
5. Ils lui ont parlé./Elles lui ont parlé.
6. Ils l'attendent./Elles l'attendent.
7. Ne les attends pas./Ne les attendez pas.

C3 ROADS AND MOTORWAYS

■ France possesses the longest road network in Europe. It is made up of turnpikes (GB : toll motorways) and highways for fast traffic that have been increasing in number especially since the country joined the European Community. After linking the north to the south, the public works authorities are now concentrating on east-west cross-country connections. The network of trunk roads (**routes nationales**), the most famous of which is the N7 which links Paris to the Riviera, runs along the old route of the royal highways. The hundred-year-old plane trees alongside them remind one of the times when carriages sought shelter from the sun during their travels. These roads radiate outwards from the capital. At local level, smaller roadways called **départementales** (running across **départements**), **communales** (administered by municipalities) and sometimes untarred byways make up the rest of the network.

"The French love cars." (Georges Pompidou)

■ The former president of the Republic was not wrong, since today three households out of four own a car ; but the French are taking more and more to… foreign cars. To hold out against competition, the manufacturers have formed a group, since there are only two companies : **Renault** (nationalized in 1945 and privatized in the mid-nineties), and **Peugeot Société Anonyme**, which manufactures **Peugeots** and **Citroëns**. The lozenge is Renault's trade mark, the lion is Peugeot's, and Citroën's is the double chevron. Car sales throughout the common market formerly, now in the European Union, have made up somewhat for the losses on the home market to foreign – mosthy European – manufacturers. The best-selling cars are in the 5 to 7-horsepower range, i.e., medium-engined cars. Imitating their foreign rivals, French industrialists are implementing a "zero defect" policy to improve the quality/price ratio.

D1 EN VOITURE (CD)

Hadrien : Est-ce qu'on est loin de l'entrée de l'autoroute ?
Nadine : Où est la carte ?
Hadrien : Prends-la dans la boîte à gants.
Nadine : On vient de passer le pont... il y a une entrée à six kilomètres, juste après un carrefour.
Hadrien : Bien on va la prendre tout de suite !
Nadine : On a assez d'essence ?
Hadrien : Oui je viens de faire le plein, je suis passé à la station service avant de partir, j'ai aussi vérifié l'huile et la pression des pneus. Rassure-toi.
(*sur l'autoroute*)
Nadine : Je te rappelle que la vitesse est limitée à 130 (km/h).
Hadrien : Laisse-moi conduire ! Je respecte les limitations.
Nadine : On approche du péage, je te donne le ticket.
Hadrien : Tu me passes aussi la carte bleue[1] s'il te plaît.

1. Most people say **carte bleue** instead of **carte bancaire** which is the normal expression.

D2 VERBES ENDING WITH VENIR

- Here are some werbs with the same conjugation as **venir** :
  - **convenir** *(to be convenient)*
    Ex. : **Est-ce que cela vous convient ?**
    Is that convenient for you ?
  - **devenir** *(to become)*
    Ex. : **Elle est devenue institutrice il y a un an.**
    She became a primary school teacher a year ago.
  - **parvenir à** *(to reach/to succeed)*
    Ex. : **Nous ne sommes pas parvenus à un accord.**
    We couldn't reach an agreement.

➔Remember that there is no equivalent of *can* in the French sentence.
  - **prévenir** *(to warn/to let know)*
    Ex. : **Prévenez-moi avant de partir.**
    Let me know before you leave.
  - **revenir** *(to come back)*
    Ex. : **Ils sont revenus en train.** *They came back by train.*

D3 IN THE CAR

Hadrien : Are we far from the entrance to the freeway ? (GB : motorway)

Nadine : Where's the map ?

Hadrien : Get it out of the glove compartment.

Nadine : We've just crossed the bridge. There's an entrance in six kilometers, just after the intersection.

Hadrien : Good, we'll take it right away.

Nadine : Do we have enough gas (GB : petrol) ?

Hadrien : I just filled up the tank. I stopped by the service station before we left ; I also checked the oil and the tire pressure. Don't worry.

(*On the freeway*)

Nadine : May I remind you that the speed limit is 130 (kilometers/hour).

Hadrien : Let me drive ! I'm not going over the speed limit.

Nadine : We're coming to the tollgate ; I'll give you the ticket.

Hadrien : Would you also hand me my credit card, please.

D4 PASSÉ RÉCENT/*RECENT PAST*

- **Venir de** + infinitive is used to refer to what has just happened or been done :

  Il vient de partir.
  He has just left.
  Ils viennent d'arriver.
  They have just arrived.
  Nous venons de le voir.
  We have just seen him.

- But : **venir de** + the name of a place is the French equivalent of *to come from* :

  Il vient de Londres.
  He comes from London.
  Elle vient de la campagne.
  She comes from the country.
  Je viens d'Allemagne.
  I come from Germany.

29 Quand la cérémonie a-t-elle lieu ?

A1 PRESENTATION

Grammar

- In addition to the three interrogative forms already seen, there is a fourth one, which is used in more elegant French.

  Ex.: **Les enfants sont-ils dans le jardin ?**
  Are the children in the garden?
  Pierre va-t-il acheter une voiture ?
  Is Pierre going to buy a car?
  Ta mère vient-elle demain ?
  Is your mother coming tomorrow?
  Vos amies repartent-elles bientôt ?
  Are your friends going back soon?
  Pierre et toi connaissez-vous Rome ?
  Do Pierre and you know Rome?

  In this form you can find both a subject and a pronoun which recalls it, following the verbal form:

  Subject + Verbal Form + Pronoun + ...

Vocabulary

avoir lieu — *to take place*
cérémonie (fem.) — *ceremony*
sœur (fem.) — *sister*
frère (masc.) — *brother*
fleur (fem.) — *flower*
couple (masc.) — *couple*
voyage de noces (masc.) — *honeymoon (trip)*

A2 EXAMPLES *(A wedding ceremony)* (CD)

1. **À quelle heure les gens arrivent-ils ?**
2. **Quand la cérémonie a-t-elle lieu ?**
3. **Les parents vont-ils venir ensemble ?**
5. **Anne va-t-elle venir seule ?**
6. **Antoine vient-il avec elle ?**
7. **Ton frère arrive-t-il par le train ?**
8. **Quelqu'un va-t-il le chercher à la gare ?**
9. **Ta sœur a-t-elle commandé les fleurs ?**
10. **Où les invités vont-ils danser ?**
11. **Quelqu'un a-t-il pensé à la musique ?**
12. **Où le jeune couple part-il en voyage de noces ?**

A3 COMMENTS

Grammar

- Remember that when the verb is inverted in this interrogative form it is joined to the pronoun by a hyphen.
  Ex.: **Les invités arrivent-ils ?** *Are the guests arriving?*
  If the verb ends with a vowel, **t** is introduced between the verb and the pronoun.
  Ex.: **Pierre va-t-il venir ?** *Is Peter going to come?*
  Antoine arrive-t-il ? *Is Antoine arriving?*
- If the verb is in the **passé composé**, the pronoun is placed between the auxiliary and the past participle.
  Ex.: **Quelqu'un a-t-il pensé à la musique ?**
  Has someone thought about the music?
  Ta sœur est-elle arrivée ?
  Has your sister arrived?

Pronunciation

- Remember:
  — **g** followed by **e**, **i** or **y** is pronounced like *su* in *pleasure*: **gens, voyage**.
  — **g** followed by another vowel is pronounced like *g* in *good*: **gare**.

A4 TRANSLATION

1. What time are the people coming?
2. When is the ceremony taking place?
3. Are the relatives coming together?
5. Is Anne coming alone?
6. Is Antoine coming with her?
7. Is your brother coming by train?
8. Is someone going to meet him at the station?
9. Did your sister order the flowers?
10. Where are the guests going to dance?
11. Has someone thought about the music?
12. Where are the young couple going on their honeymoon?

29 Une femme demande si la banque ferme à midi.

B1 PRESENTATION

Grammar

- A reported question is generally introduced by the verb **demander**.

  Ex. : **Pierre : « Est-ce qu'il fait froid ? »**
  Pierre demande s'il fait froid.
  Pierre : « Anne va-t-elle venir ? »
  Pierre demande si Anne va venir.

- As the reported question is a statement, **est-ce que** or the inverted form disappear. The intonation, of course, is not rising.
- When the expected answer is yes or no, the reported question is introduced by : **si** = *if*.

Vocabulary

changer	*to exchange*	**banque** (fem.)	*bank*
recevoir	*to receive*	**chéquier** (m.)	*cheque book*
devoir	*must, to have to*	**carte de crédit** (f.)	*credit card*
remplir	*to fill in, to fill*	**compte (en banque)** (m.)	*account*
touriste (m., f.)	*tourist*	**formulaire** (m.)	*form*
bureau de change (m.)	*foreign exchange office*		

B2 EXAMPLES *(At the bank)* (CD)

1. **Une femme : « Est-ce que la banque ferme à midi ? »**
2. **Une femme demande si la banque ferme à midi.**
3. **Un touriste : « Est-ce qu'il y a un bureau de change ? »**
4. **Un touriste demande s'il y a un bureau de change.**
5. **Un client : « Est-ce qu'il y a un chéquier pour moi ? »**
6. **Un client demande s'il y a un chéquier pour lui.**
7. **Une cliente : « Pourquoi est-ce que je n'ai pas reçu ma carte de crédit ? »**
8. **Une cliente demande pourquoi elle n'a pas reçu sa carte de crédit.**
9. **Un jeune homme : « Que dois-je faire pour ouvrir un compte ? »**
10. **Un jeune homme demande ce qu'il doit faire pour ouvrir un compte.**
11. **Un commerçant : « Dois-je remplir un formulaire ? »**
12. **Un commerçant demande s'il doit remplir un formulaire.**

B3 COMMENTS

Grammar

- To convey the idea of obligation, it is possible to use the verb **devoir** followed by an infinitive.
  Ex.: **Je dois aller à la gare.**
  I must go to the station. / I have to go to the station.

Present tense											
je	**dois**	*I*	*must*	**nous**	**devons**	*we*	*must*
tu	**dois**	*you*	*must*	**vous**	**devez**	*you*	*must*
il, elle	**doit**	*he, she, it*	*must*	**ils, elles**	**doivent**	*they*	*must*
Past participle : **dû**							

- Note that most interrogative words or expressions remain the same in a reported question except : **que** which becomes **ce que.**
  Ex.: **Anne : « Que fait Pierre ? »**
  Anne: "What is Pierre doing?"
  Anne demande ce que fait Pierre.
  Anne asks what Pierre is doing.

- If the direct question starts with **qu'est-ce qui** or **qu'est-ce que,** only **ce qui** or **ce que** remain in the reported question.
  Ex.: **Qu'est-ce qui manque ?**
  What is missing?
  On demande ce qui manque.
  Someone asks what is missing.

B4 TRANSLATION

1. A woman: "Does the bank close at twelve?"
2. A woman asks if the bank closes at twelve.
3. A tourist: "Is there a foreign exchange office?"
4. A tourist asks if there is a foreign exchange office.
5. A customer: "Is there a cheque book for me?"
6. A customer asks if there is a cheque book for him.
7. A customer: "Why haven't I received my credit card?"
8. A customer asks why she hasn't received her credit card.
9. A young man: "What must I do to open an account?"
10. A young man asks what he must do to open an account.
11. A shopkeeper: "Do I have to fill in a form?"
12. A shopkeeper asks if he has to fill in a form.

Exercises

C1 EXERCISES

A. Use the verb <u>devoir</u> in the correct form :

1. Je… repartir demain.
2. Pourquoi…-tu aller à la banque ?
3. Que… -nous dire ?
4. Elle… prendre l'avion.
5. Vous… téléphoner au directeur.
6. Combien de temps…-on attendre ?
7. Quand…-ils commencer ?

B. Turn into reported questions :

1. L'étudiant : « Est-ce qu'on doit écrire l'adresse sur le formulaire ?
2. La secrétaire : « Depuis combien d'années cet employé travaille-t-il ? »
3. Le moniteur : « Quel sport préférez-vous ?
4. Une étudiante : « Que dois-je faire pour avoir une carte de crédit ? »
5. Un touriste : « À quelle heure ouvrent les bureaux de change ? »
6. Le directeur : « Y a-t-il des télégrammes pour moi ? »

C2 ANSWERS

A.
1. Je dois repartir demain.
2. Pourquoi dois-tu aller à la banque ?
3. Que devons-nous dire ?
4. Elle doit prendre l'avion.
5. Vous devez téléphoner au directeur.
6. Combien de temps doit-on attendre ?
7. Quand doivent-ils commencer ?

B.
1. L'étudiant demande si on doit écrire l'adresse sur le formulaire.
2. La secrétaire demande depuis combien d'années cet employé travaille.
3. Le moniteur demande quel sport je préfère (*or* nous préférons, vous préférez).
4. Une étudiante demande ce qu'elle doit faire pour avoir une carte de crédit.
5. Un touriste demande à quelle heure ouvrent les bureaux de change.
6. Le directeur demande s'il y a des télégrammes pour lui.

C3 FROM THE *FRANC* TO THE *EURO*

■ The origin of the word **franc** is said to come from the motto "**Francorum rex,**" king of the **Francs,** on the first coins called by that name. In olden times, they were made of gold and were worth one pound. From 1800 to 1914, the Bank of France was given the task of issuing and guaranteeing the "germinal franc" defined by a certain weight of gold and silver.

■ Beginning with the First World War, the franc entered the era of devaluations : in 1928 it lost four fifths of its value and became the "four penny franc ;" thirty years later, it was worth 150 times less than when it was created.

■ Two "saviors of the franc," **Raymond Poincaré** in 1928 and **Antoine Pinay** in 1958, managed to reestablish the faith of the French in their currency. Seeking to break with the governments who let themselves be drawn into a spiral of inflation/devaluation, the Fifth Republic attempted to follow a strong franc policy and struggled against slipping prices since free exchange with the partners of the European Economic Community implied more and more an adaptation to a competitive environment. **De Gaulle,** as President of the Republic, created the "new franc" which was worth one hundred old francs and came into effect in January, 1960.

■ Twenty years later, in the context of the **SME (système monétaire européen** : European monetary system), France lost part of its sovereignty to be in accordance with European Community rules. Today, with economic and monetary union, the franc will bow out to leave the scene to the Euro, and the Bank of France will be a subsidiary of the CEB (*Central European Bank*).

■ Nevertheless, the roots of language are such that one still finds in colloquial speech a goodly number of expressions referring to the **sou** (a coin long gone) or to the franc. (see also p. 246).

Un sou est un sou = *A penny saved is a penny earned.* (*Waste not, want not.*)
Economiser sou à sou = *to save penny by penny*
Etre près de ses sous = *to be tight fisted*
Parler de gros sous/Question de gros sous = *a matter of pounds, shillings and pence*
N'avoir pas cent francs en poche = *To not have a penny to one's name.*
Acheter quelque chose pour trois francs six sous = *to get something for practically nothing*
Etre propre comme un sou neuf = *to be as clean as a new penny*
S'embêter à cent sous de l'heure = *to be bored to death/to tears*
Ce n'est pas compliqué pour un sou = *it's really easy*

29 DIALOGUES AND MUST/TO OWE

D1 A LA BANQUE (CD)

Nicolas : Je n'ai plus un sou[1] sur moi. Je dois absolument prendre du liquide. Sylvie : Il y a un distributeur là au coin.
Nicolas : Oh, zut ! J'ai oublié ma carte. Tu as la tienne ?
Sylvie : Inutile, regarde ce distributeur est hors service. Passons à la banque.
(*à la banque*)
Nicolas : Bonjour, c'est pour un retrait. Combien y a-t-il sur mon compte ?
Employé : Votre numéro s'il vous plaît… Voici votre solde.
Nicolas : Quand le prochain relevé va-t-il arriver ?
Employé : Vous l'avez normalement à la fin du mois.
Sylvie : Demande s'il y a un chéquier pour moi, je n'ai presque plus de chèque.
Employé : Oui voilà Madame. Datez et signez ici s'il vous plaît.
Sylvie : Que dois-je faire pour commander des chèques de voyage.
Employé : Vous devez remplir ce formulaire.

1. **Sou** was the lowest-value coin, like the English farthing. **Sou** is often found in colloquial expressions **être sans le sou** = *to be penniless*, **une machine à sous** = *a slot machine.*

D2 DEVOIR = *MUST*/DEVOIR = *TO OWE*

- The word **devoir** has several meanings and is used in many expressions :

Combien je vous dois ?	*How much do I owe you ?*
Nous devons de l'argent à quelqu'un.	*We owe someone money.*
Avec tout le repsect qui lui/leur est dû.	*With due respect.*
Comme il se doit.	*As it should be.*
Ce doit être vrai.	*It must be true.*
Il a fait son devoir.	*He has done his duty.*
Il a fait ses devoirs.	*He has done his homework.*

D 3 AT THE BANK

Nicolas : I don't have a penny on me. I absolutely must get some cash.
Sylvie : There's an ATM there on the corner.
Nicolas : Oh darn ! I've forgotten my card. Do you have yours ?
Sylvie : There's no point because the ATM is out of order. Let's go to the bank.
(*At the bank*)
Nicolas : Hello, I'd like to make a withdrawal. How much is there in my account ?
Employé : Your account number, please. Here's your balance.
Nicolas : When will the next statement come ?
Employé : Normally you'll have it at the end of the month.
Sylvie : Ask if there's a checkbook for me ; I have almost no checks left.
Employé : Yes, here you are, Madam. Date and sign it here, please.
Sylvie : What do I have to do to order traveller's checks ?
Employé : Fill out this form.

D4 C'EST LE MOMENT DE PAYER
IT'S TIME TO PAY

• Here are useful expressions to ask how much you have to pay :

Quel est le prix de… ?	*What's the price of… ?*
Combien coûte (nt)… ?	*How much is/are… ?*
Combien vaut/valent… ?	*How much is/are… worth ?*
Combien fait/font… ?	*How much is/are… ?*

In colloquial French you will often hear :

Combien ça coûte ?
Combien ça vaut ?
Combien ça fait ?
C'est combien ?
] *How much is it ?*

30 Désolé, je ne peux pas venir, je suis occupé.

A1 PRESENTATION

Grammar

- In French, the idea of possibility is expressed by: **pouvoir**. Here is its conjugation:

Present			
je	**peux**	*I*	*can*
tu	**peux**	*you*	*can*
il, elle	**peut**	*he, she, it*	*can*
nous	**pouvons**	*we*	*can*
vous	**pouvez**	*you*	*can*
ils, elles	**peuvent**	*they*	*can*
Past participle: **pu**			

- **pouvoir** is followed by an infinitive.

Ex.: **Vous pouvez venir.** *You can come.*
Ils peuvent rester. *They can stay.*

Vocabulary

épeler	*to spell*	**occupé**	*busy*
rappeler	*to call back*	**désolé**	*sorry*
rendez-vous (masc.)	*appointment*	**possible**	*possible*
problème (masc.)	*problem*	**tout à fait**	*quite*
répondeur (masc.)	*answering machine*	**à partir de**	*from*
		d'accord	*all right*

A2 EXAMPLES *(Making an appointment)* (CD)

1. **Est-ce que le docteur peut me voir demain ?**
2. **Pouvez-vous venir l'après-midi ? À quatorze heures par exemple ?**
3. **Désolé, je ne peux pas venir, je suis occupé.**
4. **Il ne pourra pas vous voir plus tard, il est occupé.**
5. **Est-ce possible mardi soir ?**
6. **Oui, c'est tout à fait possible, vous pouvez avoir un rendez-vous à partir de dix-sept heures.**
7. **D'accord, je peux venir à dix-sept heures trente.**
8. **Pouvez-vous me donner votre nom ?**
9. **Je ne vous entends pas très bien. Pouvez-vous l'épeler ?**
10. **Vous m'entendez mieux ?**
11. **Puis-je vous rappeler s'il y a un problème ?**
12. **On peut rappeler n'importe quand : il y a un répondeur.**

30 Sorry, I can't come, I'm busy.

A3 COMMENTS

■ Grammar

- Note that with verbs like: **entendre** *to hear*
  voir *to see*
  sentir *to smell, to feel*

  the idea of possibility is never expressed in French.
  Ex.: **J'entends.** *I can hear.*
  Je vois. *I can see.*

- Note that in a question in the 1st person singular where the verb is inverted, **puis** is used instead of **peux**.
  Ex.: **Puis-je vous aider ?**
  Can I help you?
  Que puis-je faire pour vous ?
  What can I do for you?

- **Pouvoir** is often used to make an order more polite.
  Ex.: **Pouvez-vous me donner votre nom ?**
  Can you give me your name?
  Peux-tu m'aider ?
  Can you help me?
  Pouvez-vous venir ?
  Can you come?

A4 TRANSLATION

1. Can the doctor see me tomorrow?
2. Can you come in the afternoon? At two p.m. for instance?
3. Sorry, I can't come, I'm busy.
4. He won't be able to see you later, he's busy.
5. Is Tuesday evening possible?
6. Yes, it's quite possible, you can have an appointment from five onward.
7. All right, I can come at five thirty.
8. Can you give me your name?
9. I can't hear you very well. Can you spell it?
10. Can you hear me better?
11. Can I call back if there's a problem?
12. You can call back any time, there's an answering machine.

30 Savez-vous parler plusieurs langues ?

B1 PRESENTATION

Grammar

- A possibility which is the result of capacity + training is expressed in French by **savoir**, *to know*. Here is its conjugation:

Present			
je	sais	*I*	*know*
tu	sais	*you*	*know*
il, elle	sait	*he, she, it*	*knows*
nous	savons	*we*	*know*
vous	savez	*you*	*know*
ils, elles	savent	*they*	*know*

- **savoir** is followed by an infinitive.

Ex.: **Je sais conduire.** *I know how to drive.*
Ils savent lire et écrire. *They can read and write.*

Vocabulary

taper à la machine	*to type*	**message** (masc.)	*message*
se servir de	*to use*	**langue** (fem.)	*language*
quitter	*to leave*	**salaire** (masc.)	*salary*
gagner	*to earn*	**idée** (fem.)	*idea*
traitement de texte (masc.)	*word processor*	**moyen**	*average*
		exactement	*exactly*

B2 EXAMPLES *(Questions when applying for a job)* CD

1. **Quand pouvez-vous commencer à travailler ?**
2. **Je peux commencer tout de suite.**
3. **Savez-vous taper à la machine ?**
4. **Oui, et je sais me servir d'un traitement de texte.**
5. **Comprenez-vous bien le français, pouvez-vous prendre des messages au téléphone ?**
6. **Pouvez-vous quitter la France facilement ?**
7. **Savez-vous conduire ?**
8. **Non, je ne sais pas.**
9. **Savez-vous parler plusieurs langues ?**
10. **Pouvons-nous parler du salaire ?**
11. **Je ne peux pas vous dire exactement combien vous allez gagner.**
12. **Je peux vous donner une idée du salaire moyen pour ce travail.**

30 Can you speak several languages?

B3 COMMENTS

Grammar

- Verbs indicating the beginning, the continuation, or the end of an action are followed by a preposition and an infinitive:

  commencer
  continuer + **à** + infinitive

  Ex.: **Il a commencé à lire il y a une heure.**
  He started reading an hour ago.
  Il a commencé à pleuvoir.
  It's started to rain.

  arrêter
  finir + **de** + infinitive

  Ex.: **Il a arrêté de fumer il y a un mois.**
  He stopped smoking a month ago.
  J'ai fini d'écrire mon livre.
  I've finished writing my book.

- **Pouvez-vous quitter la France ?**
  Note that when the name of a country is subject or object, it is necessary to use the article.

  Ex.: **La Grèce a rejoint l'Europe en 1981.**
  Greece joined Europe in 1981.
  Je ne connais pas le Danemark.
  I don't know Denmark.
  Je connais bien les États-Unis.
  I know the United States well.

B4 TRANSLATION

1. When can you start work?
2. I can start straight away.
3. Do you know how to type?
4. Yes, and I can use a word processor.
5. Do you understand French well, can you take messages on the phone?
6. Are you free to travel? (Literally: Can you leave France easily?)
7. Can you drive?
8. No, I can't.
9. Can you speak several languages?
10. Can we talk about the salary?
11. I can't tell you exactly how much you are going to earn.
12. I can give you an idea of the average salary for this job.

30 Exercises

C1 EXERCISES

A. (CD) **Translate into French :**

1. This student can speak several languages.
2. Pierre can't drive.
3. Can you help me ?
4. Our manager can make superb speeches.
5. Can you see him ?
6. I can play the piano.

B. Write the article before the name of the country when necessary :

1. J'ai visité... France il y a trois ans.
2. Tu fais tes études en... Italie ?
3. L'avion quittera... Belgique à six heures.
4. ... Danemark est plus petit que... Angleterre.
5. Nous revenons de... France.

C2 ANSWERS

A. 1. Cet étudiant sait parler plusieurs langues. – 2. Pierre ne sait pas conduire. – 3. Est-ce que vous pouvez m'aider ? – 4. Notre directeur sait faire de superbes discours. – 5. Est-ce que vous le voyez ? – 6. Je sais jouer du piano.

B. 1. J'ai visité la France il y a trois ans. – 2. Tu fais tes études en Italie ? – 3. L'avion quittera la Belgique à six heures. – 4. Le Danemark est plus petit que l'Angleterre. – 5. Nous revenons de France.

C3 PROBABILITÉ - PERMISSION
PROBABILITY- PERMISSION

• **pouvoir** can also express an idea of probability ; it is then an equivalent of *may.* Ex. :

Un accident peut toujours arriver. *An accident can always happen.*
Il peut y avoir une grève. *There may be a strike.*
Il peut arriver n'importe quoi. *Anything may happen.*
Le train peut arriver en retard. *The train may arrive late.*

• **pouvoir** is used to express permission. Ex. :

Vous pouvez sortir. *You may go.*
Puis-je emprunter votre stylo ? *May I borrow your pen ?*

C3 THE PRESS

■ The daily news

• One Frenchman out of two reads a daily paper regularly but fewer than 200 copies for 1,000 inhabitants are sold each day. Seven nationwide papers and 20 regional ones have a daily circulation of more than 100,000 copies. Among the big national newspapers, the reader can choose between the morning papers **Le Figaro, Libération** and **Le Parisien,** etc., and the evening ones, **Le Monde, France-Soir, La Croix**, etc. Newspaper kiosks also sell dailies from outside Paris. **Ouest-France** has the largest circulation : it brings out 30 local editions.

• Today, the press is going through a serious crisis : fewer readers and a drop in advertising revenue. All the dailies have attempted to resolve their problems by adopting new layout, printing and distribution techniques. Some press magnates had built up real empires, such as the late Robert Hersant with **France-Soir, Le Figaro** and many provincial newspapers, but the difficulties of the Press have made then more fragile today..

■ Weekly magazines

The magazines, on the other hand, are thriving. With 1354 sold for 1,000 inhabitants, the French are the greatest readers of magazines in the world. This is due to general information weeklies (such as **Paris Match, l'Express, le Point, le Nouvel Observateur** or **l'Evénement du Jeudi**) and the satirical weekly, **Le Canard Enchainé** (without advertising) and the economic press, women's magazines, radio and television weeklies and a rich and varied specialized press.

■ Press agencies

France has a world famous press agency (**Agence France Press,** developed from **Agence Havas** founded in 1835) and various press agencies in the field of photography (**Sygma, Gamma and Sipa**).

D1 LA PRESSE (CD)

Marc : Je vais au kiosque acheter le journal. Tu veux que je te rapporte quelque chose ?
Florence : Oui, achète-moi deux ou trois magazines.
Marc : Quel genre de magazines
Florence : Je ne sais pas… tu peux me prendre quelque chose sur la mode et une revue sur le jardinage. Ce weekend je reste tranquille, je vais lire, faire des mots croisés…
Marc : Quel programme !
(*au kiosque*)
Marc : Le numéro d'avril de « *Mon jardin* » est sorti ?
Employé : Je ne connais pas ce titre. Ce n'est pas plutôt « *Votre jardin* » ?
Marc : Ah oui, c'est ça. Je ne l'achète pas souvent, excusez-moi.
Employé : C'est un bon magazine on le demande beaucoup.
Marc : Avez-vous des journaux étrangers ?
Employé : Bien sûr et je peux vous commander ceux que vous voulez.

D2 SAVOIR/CONNAÎTRE *TO KNOW*

- **savoir** and **connaître** have close meanings but can't always be used one for the other.

– **savoir** means to have information about facts, to *know how to* ; it is generally followed by an infinitive or a subordinate clause.
Ex. : **Il sait tout faire.** *He can do anything.*
Il sait lire. *He can read.*
Savez-vous quand elle arrive ?
Do you know when she is coming ?
Savent-ils où nous sommes ?
Do they know where we are ?
On ne sait pas ce qu'il a dit.
We don't know what he said.

– **connaître** means to *have knowledge of things, to be acquainted with* persons, places.
Ex. : **Je connais cette chanson.** *I know that song.*
Est-ce qu'elle connaît le président ?
Does she know the president ?
Je ne connais pas l'Italie. *I don't know Italy.*

D3 THE PRESS

Marc : I'm going to the newsstand to buy the newspaper. Do you want me to bring you back something ?
Florence : Yes, buy me two or three magazines.
Marc : What kind of magazines ?
Florence : I don't know, get me something about fashion and a gardening magazine. This weekend I'm going to relax, read, and do crossword puzzles.
Marc : What a program !
(*At the newsstand*)
Marc : Is the April issue of "My Garden" out yet ?
Employé : I'm not familiar with that name. Don't you mean "Your Garden" ?
Marc : Oh yes, that's it. I don't buy it often, sorry.
Employé : It's a good magazine, and very popular.
Marc : Do you have any foreign newspapers ?
Employé : Of course, and I can order any you like.

D4 LA PRESSE/ *THE PRESS*

quotidien (masc.)	*daily*
hebdomadaire (masc.)	*weekly*
revue (fem.)	*review, magazine*
nouvelles (fem. pl.)	*news*
faits divers (masc. pl.)	*news in brief*
titre (masc.)	*headline*
petites annonces (fem. pl.)	*classified ads*
dessin humoristique (masc.)]	*cartoon*
caricature (fem.)]	

30 TESTS - LESSONS 20 TO 30

Complete with a, b, c or d : (There is only one correct answer for each item)

1. ——— va acheter le pain,
   a) Qui est-ce qui
   b) Qui est-ce que
   c) Qui est-ce
   d) Qu'est-ce

2. Le candidat parle ——— électeurs.
   a) au
   b) à les
   c) aux
   d) à l'

3. N'oublie pas ——— sac, ——— clefs, ——— radio.

a)	tates	ta	
b)	ton	tes	ton
c)	ton	tes	ta
d)	tata	ta	

4. C'est la voiture de mon oncle, c'est ——— nouvelle voiture.
   a) son
   b) sa
   c) ses
   d) ma

5. À quelle heure ——— - tu ?
   a) vient
   b) venons
   c) viennent
   d) viens

6. Je pense ——— la machine à laver ne marche pas.
   a) Ø
   b) que
   c) qu'
   d) qui

7. ——— votre travail avant de partir.
   a) Finis
   b) Finissons
   c) Finir
   d) F inissez

8. Qui a pris ——— ces photos ?
   a) tous
   b) toute
   c) toutes
   d) tout

9. Est-ce que vous ———à Jean ?
   a) êtes téléphoné
   b) avez téléphoné
   c) a téléphoné
   d) ont téléphoné.

10. Je ne ——— pas lui dire ce qu'elle ——— faire

a)	peut	doit
b)	peux	doivent
c)	peux	devoir
d	peux	doit

31 Nous discutions politique pendant des heures.

A1 PRESENTATION

Grammar

- The **imparfait** is a past tense used to express what was taking place or what used to happen.
  It is formed by dropping the ending **ons** of the 1st person plural of the present tense and adding the following endings to the stem.
  Ex.: **marcher,** *to walk*

sing.	-ais	je	marchais
	-ais	tu	marchais
	-ait	il, elle	marchait
plur.	-ions	nous	marchions
	-iez	vous	marchiez
	-aient	ils, elles	marchaient

I was walking or *I used to walk,* etc.

→ It is the same for all verbs, except **être**.

Vocabulary

faire ses études	*to study*	**manifestation** (fem.)	*demonstration*
défiler	*to march*	**réunion** (fem.)	*meeting*
éclater	*to break out*	**bagarre** (fem.)	*fight*
brûler	*to burn*	**transistor** (masc.)	*transistor*
faculté (fem.)	*college*	**pendant**	*for*
		pendant que	*while*

A2 EXAMPLES *(Those were the days)* CD

1. **En 68, je faisais mes études à Paris.**
2. **J'avais les cheveux longs.**
3. **J'allais à la « fac » tous les jours.**
4. **Nous parlions beaucoup.**
5. **En mai, pendant les manifestations, il y avait beaucoup de réunions.**
6. **Nous discutions politique pendant des heures.**
7. **Dans les rues, les étudiants défilaient.**
8. **On les entendait de loin.**
9. **La police essayait de les arrêter.**
10. **Un soir, pendant qu'ils défilaient, une bagarre a éclaté.**
11. **Des voitures brûlaient au quartier Latin.**
12. **Les gens écoutaient les nouvelles sur leurs transistors.**

31 We used to discuss politics for hours.

A3 COMMENTS

■ Pronunciation

- **ais, ait** and **aient** are pronounced like **è**.

■ Grammar

- The **imparfait** is often used in past description to describe a state of affairs
  Ex.: **Il faisait chaud.** *It was hot.*
  or an action taking place when something else happened. The action taking place is in the **imparfait**, what happened is in the **passé composé**.
  Ex.: **J'écoutais les nouvelles quand il est entré.**
  I was listening to the news when he came in.
  Il travaillait quand elle a appelé.
  He was working when she called.
- In colloquial French, some long words are shortened to one or two syllables.
  Ex.: **fac** for **faculté**
  manif for **manifestation**
  métro for **métropolitain**
  pub for **publicité** *(advert* or *advertising)*
- **police** is followed by a verb in the singular, as is **gouvernement**.
- When the stem of the verb ends with **t**, note that in the 1st person plural of the imperfect **tions** is pronounced **tion** with the sound **t**.
  Ex.: **arrêtions, quittions, partions.**

A4 TRANSLATION

1. In 68, I was studying in Paris.
2. I had long hair.
3. I used to go to college every day.
4. We talked a lot.
5. In May, during the demonstrations, there were a lot of meetings.
6. We used to discuss politics for hours.
7. In the streets the students were marching.
8. You could hear them from far away.
9. The police were trying to stop them.
10. One evening, while they were marching, a fight broke out.
11. Cars were burning in the Latin Quarter.
12. People were listening to the news on their transistor radios.

31 C'était un petit garçon aux yeux noirs et aux...

B1 PRESENTATION

■ Grammar

• **Être** *(to be)*

Imparfait			
j'	**étais**	*I*	*was*
tu	**étais**	*you*	*were*
il, elle	**était**	*he, she, it*	*was*
nous	**étions**	*we*	*were*
vous	**étiez**	*you*	*were*
ils, elles	**étaient**	*they*	*were*

■ Vocabulary

s'échapper *to get away, to escape*
aider *to help*
enfance (fem.) *childhood*
ferme (fem.) *farm*
champ (masc.) *field*
forêt (fem.) *forest*
devoirs (masc. pl.) *homework*
tracteur (masc.) *tractor*
cheval (masc.) *horse*
écurie (fem.) *stable*
brun *dark-haired*
différent *different*
autrefois *in the past*

B2 EXAMPLES *(Childhood)* (CD)

1. **Quand j'étais jeune, mon père me parlait de son enfance.**
2. **C'était un petit garçon aux yeux noirs et aux cheveux bruns.**
3. **Il avait deux frères, ils vivaient dans une ferme.**
4. **Ils étaient souvent dans les champs.**
5. **Ils n'étaient pas très riches.**
6. **Leur ferme n'était pas très grande.**
7. **La forêt était tout près.**
8. **Leur mère était toujours occupée.**
9. **Autrefois, la vie à la campagne était très différente.**
10. **Quand il avait fait ses devoirs, il aidait ses parents.**
11. **Il n'y avait pas de tracteur, ils avaient des chevaux.**
12. **Un jour, pendant qu'il était en train de jouer dans l'écurie, les chevaux s'étaient échappés.**

31 He was a dark-eyed, dark-haired little boy.

B3 COMMENTS

Grammar

- To insist on the action taking place, the expression:
  être en train de + infinitive is sometimes used.

  Ex.: **Il jouait.**
  Il était en train de jouer. → *He was playing.*

  J'écoutais les nouvelles.
  J'étais en train d'écouter les nouvelles.
  I was listening to the news.

NB: the same expression can be used in the present.

  Ex.: **Il joue.**
  Il est en train de jouer. → *He is playing.*

- The **imparfait** of **être** or **avoir** + the past participle of a verb form the **plus-que-parfait**.
  The **plus-que-parfait** is the same in usage as the pluperfect in English.

  Ex.: **Il avait fini quand elle a appelé.**
  He had finished when she called.
  Nous étions partis quand vous êtes arrivés.
  We had left when you arrived.

- As for the **passé composé**, the past participle agrees with the subject when the auxiliary is **être**.

B4 TRANSLATION

1. When I was young, my father used to tell me about his childhood.
2. He was a dark-eyed, dark-haired little boy.
3. He had two brothers, they used to live on a farm.
4. They were often in the fields.
5. They were not very rich.
6. Their farm was not very big.
7. The forest was near by.
8. Their mother was always busy.
9. In the past, life in the country was very different.
10. When he had finished his homework, he used to help his parents.
11. There were no tractors, they had horses.
12. One day, while he was playing in the stable, the horses escaped.

31 Exercises

C1 EXERCISES

A. Put the verb in the correct form of the <u>imparfait</u> :

1. Où (être) tu ?
2. Que (faire) vous ?
3. Il ne (travailler) pas à Paris.
4. Autrefois, les femmes (porter) des jupes longues.
5. Les vacances (finir) en octobre quand j'(être) jeune.

B. Use the <u>imparfait</u> or <u>passé composé</u> :

1. Pendant que je (faire) une promenade, je (rencontrer) Pierre.
2. Pendant qu'ils (regarder) la télévision, le téléphone (sonner).
3. Quand vous (arriver), nous (discuter).

C. (CD) Insist on the action taking place :

1. Je parlais.
2. Tu travaillais.
3. Il faisait un discours.
4. Nous jouions.

C2 ANSWERS

A. 1. Où étais-tu ?
2. Que faisiez-vous ?
3. Il ne travaillait pas à Paris.
4. Autrefois, les femmes portaient des jupes longues.
5. Les vacances finissaient en octobre quand j'étais jeune.

B. 1. Pendant que je faisais une promenade, j'ai rencontré Pierre.
2. Pendant qu'ils regardaient la télévision, le téléphone a sonné.
3. Quand vous êtes arrivé (arrivée, arrivés, arrivées), nous discutions.

C. 1. J'étais en train de parler.
2. Tu étais en train de travailler.
3. Il était en train de faire un discours.
4. Nous étions en train de jouer.

C3 FASHION

■ France ranks fourth in the world for the exportation of consumer goods, in large part due to its perfume industry (l'**Oréal** is the first cosmetic group in the world) and to textiles, clothing (faced with low-cost imports) and, of course, haute couture. Its luxury goods industry is in fact first in the world and makes 77 % of its sales abroad.
■ At the beginning of every season, Parisian society's smart set attends the show of collections given by models from **Chanel, Dior, Yves Saint Laurent, Sonia Rykiel, Christian Lacroix, Jean-Paul Gauthier, Paco Rabanne**, etc. Trends in town suits, sportswear, afternoon or evening dresses seem to be set, but only for a time.
■ Whether haute couture or ready-to-wear, the fashion is for cotton, velvet, silk, natural or synthetic fibers by turns ; hems are long or short, cuts go traditional or wild, colors are soft or garish, accessories are discreet or weird. ■ Whatever the fashions are, a very close watch is kept on them by women's magazines like **Elle, Marie-Claire and Femme Actuelle**, which spark off the desire to buy or make people "fall" for things, and teem with advice of all kinds (make-up, hair styles, jewelry) to make women attractive, "in" or to give them the right

WOMEN'S DRESSES

France	38	40	42	44	46	48	50
UK	10	12	14	16	18	20	22
US	8	10	12	14	16	18	20

WOMEN'S SHOE SIZES

France	36	37	38	39	40	41
UK	3 1/2	4 1/2	5	5 1/2	6 1/2	7
US	5	6	6 1/2	7	8	8 1/2

D1 SOUVENIRS DE VACANCES A LA MER (CD)

Marie : Comme tu es bronzé ! Où étais-tu en vacances ?
Paul : J'étais en Corse, j'ai passé deux semaines au bord de la mer dans le sud de l'île.
Marie : Qu'est-ce que vous faisiez ?
Paul : On allait de plage en plage en bateau, il faisait un temps idéal pour la croisière.
Marie : Tu faisais aussi de la planche à voile ?
Paul : Oui, c'était l'endroit de rêve pour ça. Et toi tu es partie ?
Marie : Oui, j'étais en Irlande, sur la côte ouest. On ne pouvait pas rester longtemps dans l'eau elle était glacée.
Paul : Et ça te plaisait ?
Marie : Oh, c'était magnifique ! Il y avait des vagues énormes qui frappaient les rochers c'était spectaculaire.
Paul : Je ne savais pas que tu aimais ce genre de paysage.
Marie : Déjà, enfant, en Bretagne, j'adorais ça

C2 SOME WORDS ARE USUALLY IN THE PLURAL IN FRENCH

cheveux (masc. pl.) *hair*

Others have different meanings in the singular and in the plural :

devoir (masc.)	*duty*	**devoirs**	*homework*
lunette (masc.)	*telescope*	**lunettes**	*glasses*
course (fem.)	*race*	**courses**	*shopping*
vêtement (masc.)	*garment*	**vêtements**	*clothes* .

D3 MEMORIES OF A VACATION BY THE SEA

Marie : You're so tan ! Where were you on vacation ?
Paul : I was in Corsica. I spent two weeks at the seaside in the south of the island.
Marie : What did you do ?
Paul : We went from beach to beach by boat ; it was ideal weather for cruising.
Marie : Did you windsurf, too ?
Paul : Yes, it was the perfect place for it. What about you ? Did you go away ?
Marie : Yes, I was in Ireland, on the west coast. We couldn't stay in the water long ; it was ice cold.
Paul : And did you like it ?
Marie : Oh, it was magnificent ! There were enormous waves that lashed against the rocks : it was spectacular !
Paul : I didn't know you liked that kind of scenery.
Marie : I adored it even as a child while growing up in Brittany.

D4 PHYSICAL OR MORAL DESCRIPTIONS

- The equivalents of the compound adjectives : *fair-haired, blue-eyed*, etc., are expressions with :

à la, au, aux + noun + adjective

un garçon aux yeux noirs	*a dark-eyed boy*
une fille aux cheveux blonds	*a fair-haired girl*
un bébé à la peau douce	*a soft-skinned baby*
un garçon au nez pointu	*a sharp-nosed boy*
un homme à l'œil brillant	*a bright-eyed man*
une personne à l'esprit étroit	*a narrow-minded person*

32 Je me lève tous les jours à sept heures.

A1 PRESENTATION

■ Grammar

- When the same person is both the subject and the object of the action, the verb is called a reflexive verb.
  Reflexive verbs must be used with special reflexive pronouns:

  me, m'
  te, t'
  se, s'
  nous
  vous
  se, s'

- The reflexive pronoun precedes the verb or auxiliary except in the imperative.
  Ex.: **Je me dépêche / Dépêchez-vous.**
  I'm hurrying! / Hurry up!

- **s'appeler**, the equivalent of *his, her, its name is...*, is a reflexive verb.

■ Vocabulary

se lever	*to get up*	**se faire mal**	*to hurt oneself*
se raser	*to shave*	**se dépêcher**	*to hurry*
s'habiller	*to dress, to dress up*	**se disputer**	*to quarrel*
		se tromper	*to be mistaken*
se laver	*to wash*	**d'habitude**	*usually*
se préparer	*to get ready*		

A2 EXAMPLES *(Everyday life)* (CD)

1. **Je m'appelle Pierre Lebon.**
2. **Je me lève tous les jours à sept heures.**
3. **Je me rase avant de partir.**
4. **D'habitude, il s'habille pour le dîner.**
5. **Les enfants se lavent.**
6. **Elle se prépare pour le dîner.**
7. **On se prépare pour sortir.**
8. **Nous nous levons tard le dimanche.**
9. **Tu t'es fait mal ?**
10. **Ils se dépêchent pour prendre le bus.**
11. **Les enfants se disputent beaucoup, mais ils s'entendent bien.**
12. **Tu te trompes !**

32 I get up at seven every day.

A3 COMMENTS

■ Grammar

me	French equivalent of	*myself*
te		*yourself*
se		*himself, herself, itself, themselves*
nous		*ourselves*
vous		*yourselves*

Ex.: **Je me regarde.** *I'm looking at myself.*
Il s'est fait mal. *He hurt himself.*

- **nous, vous, se, s'** are the equivalents of *each other* or *one another*.
  Ex.: **Ils se regardent.**
  They are looking at each other.
  Nous nous comprenons.
  We understand one another.

- Note the different uses of the singular and plural in French and English:
  tous les jours *every day*
  le dimanche *on Sundays*

A4 TRANSLATION

1. My name is Pierre Lebon.
2. I get up at seven every day.
3. I shave before leaving.
4. He usually dresses up for dinner.
5. The children are washing.
6. She is getting ready for dinner.
7. We're getting ready to go out.
8. We get up late on Sundays.
9. Did you hurt yourself?
10. They're hurrying to take the bus.
11. The children quarrel a lot, but they get on well.
12. You are mistaken!

32 Asseyez-vous, je vous en prie.

B1 PRESENTATION

Grammar

- In the imperative, the reflexive pronoun is a « strong » one:

  moi
  toi
  nous
  vous

  Ex.: **Habillez-vous !** *Get dressed!*
  Lève-toi ! *Get up!*

- For all reflexive verbs, the **passé composé** is formed with **être**, and the past participle agrees with the subject.

  Ex.: **Ils ne se sont pas reposés.**
  They didn't rest.

Vocabulary

s'asseoir	*to sit down*	**petit déjeuner** (masc.)	*breakfast*
s'amuser	*to have fun*		
se coucher	*to go to bed*	**chemin** (masc.)	*way*
se réveiller	*to wake up*	**demi-heure** (fem.)	*half an hour*
se promener	*to go for a walk*		
s'occuper de	*to look after*	**de bonne heure**	*early*
se reposer	*to rest*	**prêt**	*ready*

B2 EXAMPLES *(Sleeping late)* (CD)

1. **Levez-vous, il est sept heures !**
2. **Dépêche-toi, le petit déjeuner est prêt.**
3. **Dépêchez-vous, il est huit heures et demie !**
4. **Asseyez-vous, je vous en prie.**
5. **Vous vous êtes bien amusés hier soir ?**
6. **Oui, on s'est couché à minuit moins le quart.**
7. **On s'est trompé de chemin pour revenir.**
8. **Tu t'es réveillé de bonne heure ?**
9. **Oui, je me suis promené dans le jardin une demi-heure.**
10. **Je me suis occupé des fleurs.**
11. **Nous nous sommes reposés une heure.**
12. **Habillez-vous, nous allons nous promener.**

B3 COMMENTS

Grammar

- For a negative command, the reflexive pronoun precedes the verb.
  Ne vous dépêchez pas. *Don't hurry.*
  Ne te trompe pas. *Don't make a mistake.*
  Ne t'occupe pas des fleurs. *Don't take care of the flowers.*
- **Se tromper de** + noun is the French equivalent of:
  to take / *to have* / *to get* → *the wrong* + noun
  Ex.: **se tromper de bus** *to take the wrong bus*
  se tromper de numéro *to get a wrong number*
- Note the difference between:
  une demi-heure *half an hour*
  une heure et demie *an hour and a half*
  un quart d'heure *a quarter of an hour*
  une heure et quart *an hour and a quarter*

Pronunciation

- In **asseyez**, the first **e** is pronounced **é**.

B4 TRANSLATION

1. Get up, it is seven o'clock!
2. Hurry up, breakfast is ready.
3. Hurry up, it is half past eight!
4. Do sit down (literally: Sit down I pray you).
5. Did you have fun last night?
6. Yes, we went to bed at a quarter to twelve.
7. We took the wrong way back.
8. Did you wake up early?
9. Yes, I went for a walk in the garden for half an hour.
10. I looked after the flowers.
11. We rested for an hour.
12. Get dressed, we are going for a walk.

C1 EXERCISES

A. Match :

te		asseyons
je	me	regardes
tu	se, s'	assoit
il, elle	vous	disputent
nous	nous	promenez
vous		dépêchez
ils, elles		rase

B. (CD) Put in the imperative form :

1. Tu te lèves.
2. Tu t'occupes des enfants.
3. Nous nous reposons.
4. Vous vous habillez.
5. Vous vous amusez bien.

C. (CD) Translate into French :

1. I get up at nine o'clock.
2. She is hurrying
3. I'm getting ready.
4. We are taking the wrong car.
5. Did you hurt yourselves ?

C2 ANSWERS

A. je me rase – il se rase – tu te regardes – il, elle s'assoit
nous nous asseyons – vous vous promenez
vous vous dépêchez – ils, elles se disputent

B. 1. Lève-toi !
2. Occupe-toi des enfants.
3. Reposons-nous.
4. Habillez-vous.
5. Amusez-vous bien !

C. 1. Je me lève à neuf heures.
2. Elle se dépêche.
3. Je me prépare.
4. Nous nous trompons de voiture.
5. Vous vous êtes fait mal ?/Est-ce que vous vous êtes fait mal ?/ Vous êtes-vous fait - mal ?

C3 THE MOUNTAINS

■ About one-fifth of French territory is covered by mountains. The integration of the mountainous regions into the national economy occurred belatedly and with difficulty : livestock breeding was the main occupation, and there was an exodus from the land. Then new functions for these regions appeared : hydroelectricity, industry, and summer and winter tourism. Today the population and the prosperity of mountain communities depends mainly on their geographical proximity to organized economic and social activity and consequently on the impact of the region. Thus the major part of the **Massif Central**, the **Pyrénées**, Corsica and the Southern Alps, located outside of the major thoroughfares of activity where there are only small towns (with the exception of **Limoges** and **Clermont Ferrand**) depend mainly on raising livestock and are losing their populations. To the contrary, the Jura, the Northern Alps, the **Vosges** and the eastern part of the **Massif Central** are surrounded by dynamic urbanized zones and are themselves developing : electroindustry and tourism in the big ski resorts in the Alps, industry and "green" tourism in the Jura, textiles in the **Vosges**.

■ Given the economic importance of " white gold," recent policies have mostly contributed to the promotion of the Northern Alps, which have excellent snow cover, and to those parts of other mountainous zones which are most like it : the region around Briançon, the back country above **Nice**, and the central Pyrenees. The choice of **Albertville** for the Olympic Games in 1992 had already reinforced the public image of the Northern Alps, which profited economically. However, the popularity of winter sports is not limited to downhill skiing, and some rural districts have opted for cross country skiing, which requires less expensive investments. The mountains have also become a summer resort area.

■ There are three different models of regional development : one is based on the diversification of activities and the development of facilities for tourists. **Valmorel** in **Savoie**, for example, combines industrial activity, mid-altitude milk production, and tourism in the resort. In mid-altitude areas, there is a model of auto development that has come out of local experience : around **Grenoble**, the districts help young farmers get started, and local handicrafts and rural tourism are developing, along with socio-cultural activities in the resorts. Lastly, the model that emphasizes local culture, such as that of the **Parc National des Cévennes**, is centered on a respect for the environment and the discovery of nature.

D1 VALISE VOLEE (CD)

Serge : Excusez-moi Monsieur. Pouvez-vous m'indiquer où je peux déclarer un vol de bagages, s'il vous plaît.
Homme : Je suis désolé, je ne sais pas, je ne connais pas cet aéroport. Renseignez-vous à ce guichet.
Employée : Pour les objets volés c'est au premier étage juste en face de l'ascenseur. Vous ne pouvez pas vous tromper.
Serge : Merci beaucoup.
Employée : Je vous en prie. Mais dépêchez-vous parce que ça ferme dans un quart d'heure.
(*dans le bureau*)
Serge : Bonjour Madame On m'a volé ma valise, qu'est-ce que je dois faire ?
Employée : Asseyez - vous Monsieur, comment cela s'est-il passé ?
Serge : J'étais en train de téléphoner d'une cabine, et quand je me suis retourné ma valise n'était plus là.
Employée : Vous souvenez-vous de l'heure et de l'endroit exact. ?
Serge : Oui je me suis arrêté pour téléphoner juste à côté du kiosque à journaux dans le hall 4.

D2 SOYONS POLIS/ *LET'S BE POLITE*

Here are some useful expressions :

- *to apologize* :
  pardon, excusez-moi, je suis désolé (e), je suis navré (e).
- to say : *it doesn't matter*
  de rien, je vous en prie, ce n'est rien.
- to insist politely on an order :
  je vous en prie.

Ex. : a.	**Je suis désolée d'être en retard !**	*I'm sorry, I'm late !*
b.	**Je vous en prie !**	*It's all right !*
a.	**Asseyez-vous, je vous en prie !**	*Do sit down !*
b.	**Merci beaucoup !**	*Thanks a lot !*
a.	**De rien !**	*Don't mention it !*

D3 A STOLEN SUITCASE

Serge : Excuse me[1], can you tell me where to go to make a declaration about stolen luggage, please ?

Man : I'm sorry, I don't know. I'm not familiar with this airport. Ask at that counter.

Employee : To report stolen property, it's on the first floor, right across from the elevator (GB : lift). You can't miss it.

Serge : Thank you very much.

Employee : You're welcome. But hurry, because it closes in a quarter of an hour.

(*In the office*)

Serge : Hello. My suitcase has been stolen. What should I do ?

Employee : Take a seat. How did it happen ?

Serge : I was making a call from a telephone booth, and when I turned around, my suitcase wasn't there any more.

Employee : Do you remember the exact time and place ?

Serge : Yes, I stopped to telephone right next to the newsstand in Concourse 4.

1 **Madame** is used much more frequently in French than *Madam* is used in English.

D4 PRACTICAL LIFE : POLITENESS

It's the least one can do.

C'est le moins que l'on puisse faire.

Too polite to be honest.

Trop poli pour être honnête.

To make a courtesy call/visit (on someone)

Faire une visite de politesse

Punctuality is the politeness of kings.

L'exactitude est la politesse des rois.

33 Quand vous sortirez de l'aéroport...

A1 PRESENTATION

Grammar

- Remember we have seen: **aller** + infinitive to express a future action. Here is the future tense as such. Its construction is:

(sing.) infinitive +	**-ai**	(pl.) infinitive +	**-ons**
	-as		**-ez**
	-a		**-ont**

Ex.: **je sortirai, tu parleras, il jouera, nous finirons, vous partirez, ils donneront.**

- When the infinitive ends in **-re**, the **e** is dropped.

Ex.: **je conduirai, tu prendras, il rira.**

Vocabulary

décoller	*to take off*	**directeur commercial** (masc.)	*marketing manager*
se poser	*to land*	**renseignement** (masc.)	*information*
emmener à	*to take to*	**contrat** (masc.)	*contract*
prendre contact	*to contact*	**de toute façon**	*anyway*
signer	*to sign*		
accepter	*to accept*		

A2 EXAMPLES *(Business trip)* (CD)

1. **À quelle heure décollera l'avion ?**
2. **Il décollera à neuf heures et se posera à Tokyo seize heures plus tard.**
3. **Quand vous sortirez de l'aéroport, une voiture vous attendra.**
4. **Elle vous emmènera à votre hôtel dans le centre ville.**
5. **Notre directeur commercial prendra contact avec vous.**
6. **Quand vous connaîtrez votre planning, vous nous appellerez.**
7. **S'il y a un problème, nous vous donnerons des renseignements.**
8. **Quand vous rencontrerez nos clients, vous leur direz que le contrat est prêt.**
9. **Quand le patron arrivera, il le signera.**
10. **J'espère qu'ils accepteront nos conditions.**
11. **Vous n'aurez sûrement pas le temps de visiter la ville.**
12. **De toute façon, nous y retournerons ensemble l'an prochain.**

33 When you come out of the airport...

A3 COMMENTS

Grammar

- Note that to indicate the idea of future action, a sentence starting with **quand** must be in the future.
  Ex.: **Quand vous sortirez de l'aéroport, vous trouverez une voiture.**
  When you come out of the airport, you'll find a car.
- Other conjunctions of time follow the same rule:

dès que	*as soon as*
aussitôt que	*as soon as*
au moment où	*the moment when*

- Note that the English word *planning* is commonly used in French meaning *schedule* or *programme* or *calendar*.
- Note that **renseignement** is often used in the plural.

Pronunciation

- In A2, you see many words with a circumflex accent: **hôtel, connaîtrez, prêt, sûrement**.
  Remember it doesn't alter the pronunciation of the vowel.

A4 TRANSLATION

1. What time will the plane take off?
2. It'll take off at nine, and land in Tokyo sixteen hours later.
3. When you come out of the airport, a car will be waiting for you.
4. It'll take you to your hotel in the centre of town.
5. Our marketing manager will contact you.
6. You'll call us when you know your schedule.
7. If there's a problem, we'll give you information.
8. When you meet our customers, you'll tell them the contract is ready.
9. When the boss arrives, he'll sign it.
10. I hope they'll accept our conditions.
11. You surely won't have time to visit the city.
12. We'll go back there together next year anyway.

33 Nous découvrirons d'autres mondes.

B1 PRESENTATION

Grammar

- Irregular verbs in the future (see also B3)

	être *to be*	**avoir** *to have*
je	**serai**	**aurai**
tu	**seras**	**auras**
il/elle	**sera**	**aura**
nous	**serons**	**aurons**
vous	**serez**	**aurez**
ils/elles	**seront**	**auront**

Vocabulary

découvrir *to discover*
espérer *to hope*
éviter *to avoid*
espace (masc.) *space*
navette (fem.) *shuttle*
lune (fem.) *moon*
planète (fem.) *planet*
génération (f.) *generation*
médicament (masc.) *medicine*
maladie (fem.) *disease*
technologie (fem.) *technology*
pollution (fem.) *pollution*
paix (fem.) *peace*
peut-être *perhaps*
grâce à *thanks to*
jusqu'à quand *until when*

B2 EXAMPLES *(In 2010)* (CD)

1. **Un jour viendra où nous irons très loin dans l'espace.**
2. **Il y aura des navettes entre les planètes.**
3. **Nous ferons des voyages extraordinaires.**
4. **On se promènera sur la Lune.**
5. **Nous voyagerons de plus en plus loin.**
6. **Nous découvrirons d'autres mondes.**
7. **On découvrira de nouveaux médicaments, mais il y aura peut-être plus de maladies.**
8. **Grâce aux technologies nouvelles, on sera en contact avec le monde entier à tout moment.**
9. **On trouvera peut-être des solutions au problème de la pollution.**
10. **L'homme vivra peut-être de plus en plus longtemps.**
11. **Jusqu'à quand évitera-t-on la guerre ?**
12. **Espérons que les générations futures vivront en paix.**

B3 COMMENTS

Grammar

- Note that in such expressions of time as **un jour viendra où** *(a day will come when)*, **le jour où** *(the day when)*, **au moment où** *(the moment when)*, the word **où** is used meaning *WHEN* and not *WHERE*.
- Before nouns *more* is translated by **plus de**.
  Ex.: **Il y a plus de pollution à Paris que dans les Alpes.**
  There's more pollution in Paris than in the Alps.
- Remember that in an interrogative form with an inverted verb, if it ends with a vowel, **t** must be placed before **il, elle** or **on**:
  Ex.: **Évitera-t-on ?** **Viendra-t-elle ?** **Partira-t-il ?**
- Irregular verbs in the future:

	aller *to go*	**faire** *to do / to make*	**venir** *to come*
je/j'	**irai**	**ferai**	**viendrai**
tu	**iras**	**feras**	**viendras**
il/elle	**ira**	**fera**	**viendra**
nous	**irons**	**ferons**	**viendrons**
vous	**irez**	**ferez**	**viendrez**
ils/elles	**iront**	**feront**	**viendront**

B4 TRANSLATION

1. A day will come when we go very far into space.
2. There'll be shuttles between the planets.
3. We'll take extraordinary trips.
4. We'll walk on the moon.
5. We'll travel farther and farther.
6. We'll discover other worlds.
7. New medicines will be discovered, but there will perhaps be more diseases.
8. Thanks to new technologies, we'll be in contact with the whole world at all times.
9. Maybe solutions to the problem of pollution will be found.
10. Man will perhaps live longer and longer.
11. Until when will we avoid war?
12. Let's hope future generations will live in peace.

33 Exercises and NEAR FUTURE

C1 EXERCISES

A. Take the odd one out :

1. irons - prendrons - avons - viendrons -découvririons.
2. seront - font - sortiront - traverseront - entendront.
3. pleurez - claquerez - traverserez - possèderez - connaîtrez.

B. Translate into French :

1. Please call me as soon as you arrive.
2. When the boss sees her, he'll give her the contract.
3. When I'm eighty five, I'll write the story of my life.

C2 ANSWERS

A. 1. avons.
2. font.
3. pleurez.

B. 1. S'il vous plaît, appelez-moi dès que vous arriverez.
2. Quand le patron la verra, il lui donnera le contrat.
3. Quand j'aurai quate-vingt-cinq ans, j'écrirai l'histoire de ma vie.

C3 HOW TO EXPRESS THE NEAR FUTURE

bientôt	*soon*
demain	*tomorrow*
après-demain	*the day after tomorrow*
tout à l'heure	*in a moment*
plus tard	*later*
sous peu	*before long*
d'ici...	*within...*

C3 THE ENVIRONMENT

Industrialists and politicians as well as the average French citizen are ever more aware of the fact that only a respectful and responsible approach to the environment can save the natural resources of our planet.
Since 1996, the French Federation of Societies for Environmental Protection, several political parties like the Greens, Generation Ecology, and the Independent Ecological Movement have founded their programs upon environmental problems such as air and water pollution, and the disposal of toxic waste.

■ THE SEAS

The ecosystems of both the Atlantic ocean and the Mediterranean sea are being seriously damaged by industrial and agricultural pollution (nitrates, phosphates, etc.). On top of this, intensive fishing has now threatened the survival of several species.
In effect since 1994, the International Convention on Sea Rights is a step in the right direction as it imposes upon all the signatories the principle of protection and preservation of the marine environment. The International Court for the Laws of the Sea is based in Germany and, since 1997, has been responsible for enforcing the Convention.

■ THE PROBLEM OF WASTE

There has been an explosion in the use of plastics which seems irreversible, as these materials are very cheap and convenient for short-term use. Although burning them provides energy and heat, it also presents the major problem of toxic gases which must somehow be removed from the atmosphere. What about recycling ? The main problems this creates is in the collection and sorting of different types of material and the meagre profitability of recycled matter.
Regarding the treatment of nuclear waste, there is ever increasing concern and controversy as it becomes apparent that nobody can agree what to do about it.

■ THE AIR

The new laws concerning air quality require public authorities to measure and forecast atmospheric pollution. To this end, for example, the Airparif network is responsible for monitoring the air quality in the Ile de France. It brings together representatives of the State, the regions, and business, as well as associations for the protection of the environment. A variety of measures have been taken for urban centres, such as alternates traffic laws.

D1 L'AVENIR DE LA PLANETE (CD)

(*Agnès et Anne prépare un article sur l'avenir de la planète*)

Agnès : Quel titre va-t-on mettre ?

Anne : On choisira un titre à la fin.

Agnès : Je parlerai d'abord des animaux en voie de disparition : le tigre, la baleine bleue…ça fera, à peu près un tiers de l'article. j'aurai les chiffres demain soir.

Anne : Quand auras-tu les photos ?

Agnès : Je ne sais pas exactement mais dès que nous les aurons nous pourrons sélectionner celles qui nous sembleront les meilleures.

Anne : Tu n'oublieras de parler de l'ours des Pyrénées !

Agnès : Mais non, bien sûr. Est-ce que c'est toi qui écriras le passage sur l'effet de serre et la couche d'ozone.

Anne : Oui, je m'occuperai des interviews des spécialistes.

Agnès : Parfait ! Penses-tu qu'il y aura assez de place pour parler du recyclage des déchets ?

Anne : Oui, nous finirons là-dessus.

D2 COMPARATIVE EXPRESSIONS

- Double comparisons like *faster and faster or more and more comfortable* are translated by
  de plus en plus rapide/confortable.
  The equivalent of *less and less* is **de moins en moins.**
- Useful expressions :

The sooner the better.	**Le plus tôt sera le mieux.**
The more the merrier.	**Plus on est de fous plus on rit.** (Literally : *the more madmen there are the more they laugh.*)

But : *Sooner* or *later.* **Tôt ou tard.**

D3 THE FUTURE OF THE PLANET

(*Agnès and Anne are preparing an article on the future of the planet.*)

Agnès : What are we going to put as a title ?

Anne : We'll choose a title at the end.

Agnès : First, I'll talk about disappearing species : the tiger, the blue whale ; that will make about a third of the article. I'll have the figures tomorrow evening.

Anne : When will you have the photos ?

Agnès : I don't know exactly, but as soon as we get them, we can select the ones we think are the best.

Anne : You won't forget to talk about the Pyrenees bear, will you ?

Agnès : No, of course not. Are you the one who's going to write the part about the greenhouse effect and the ozone layer ?

Anne : Yes, I'll take care of the interviews with the specialists.

Agnès : Perfect ! Do you think there'll be enough room to talk about recycling waste ?

Anne : Yes, we'll end with that.

D4 PRACTICAL LIFE : FLOW WITH THE CURRENT

eau douce : *fresh water*
eau salée : *salt water*
eaux usées : *waste water*
eau potable : *drinking water*
eau non potable : *water unfit for drinking*
la propreté de l'eau : *clean water*

Se noyer dans un verre d'eau : *To make a mountain out of a molehole* (literally : *to drown oneself in a glass of water*).
Cela me fait venir l'eau à la bouche : *It makes my mouth water.*
Il n'est pire que l'eau qui dort : *Still waters run deep.*

34 Quand y es-tu allé ?

A1 PRESENTATION

Grammar

- **en** and **y** are pronouns used to avoid repeating the name of a place introduced by a preposition.
  Ex.: **Est-ce que tu vas à la gare ? — Oui, j'y vais.**
  On va au cinéma ? — Oui, on y va.
  Est-ce que tu viens de la campagne ? — Oui, j'en viens.

  Note that **à** (or the contracted forms **au, aux**) + noun = **y**
  de (or the contracted forms **du, des**) + noun = **en**

- **y** is also used to replace a complement (whether a noun or an infinitive) introduced by the preposition **à**. Ex.:
  Tu penses à ton travail ? — Oui, j'y pense.
  Est-ce que tu as pensé à prendre les livres ? — Oui, j'y ai pensé.

Vocabulary

sortir	*to go out, to come out*	**agence de voyages** (fem.)	*travel agency*
passer par	*to go via*	**liste** (fem.)	*list*
s'arrêter	*to stop*	**piscine** (fem.)	*swimming pool*
se renseigner	*to ask for information*	**ce soir**	*tonight*
choisir	*to choose*		

A2 EXAMPLES *(Booking)* CD

1. **Est-ce que tu es allé à l'agence de voyages pour prendre les billets ?**
2. **Oui, j'en viens.**
3. **Quand y es-tu allé ?**
4. **J'y suis allé à l'heure du déjeuner.**
5. **Il n'y avait personne, et j'en suis sorti cinq minutes plus tard.**
6. **On passe par Athènes ; est-ce que tu sais si l'avion s'y arrête ?**
7. **Non, je n'en sais rien, mais je peux me renseigner.**
8. **As-tu pensé à réserver l'hôtel ?**
9. **J'y ai pensé mais j'ai préféré attendre pour choisir avec toi.**
10. **L'agence m'a donné des listes d'hôtels, on en choisira un ce soir.**
11. **On en prendra un avec piscine ?**
12. **Pourquoi pas ? J'y pense depuis longtemps !**

34 When did you go?

A3 COMMENTS

Grammar

- Note that **y** can never be used for a person.

Je pense à mon examen.	**J'y pense.**
I'm thinking about my exam.	*I'm thinking about it.*
Je pense à mon oncle.	**Je pense à lui.**
I'm thinking about my uncle.	*I'm thinking about him.*

- On the contrary, **en** can be used for a person.

Je rêve de mes vacances.	**J'en rêve.**
I'm dreaming about my holidays.	*I'm dreaming about there.*
J'ai rêvé de mes enfants.	**J'en ai rêvé.**
I dreamed about my children.	*I dreamed about them.*

- **un** and **une** are not only indefinite articles. They are also pronouns. They are the French equivalent of *one*, but they are always used with **en**. Ex.:
  Tu prends un sac ? — Oui, j'en prends un.
  Are you taking a bag? — Yes, I'm taking one.
  Tu as réservé une chambre ? — Oui, j'en ai réservé une.
  Did you reserve a room? — Yes, I reserved one.
- Note a few set expressions where a noun is used without any article:

avec piscine	*with a swimming pool*
avec vue	*with a view*
avec salle de bains	*with a bathroom*

A4 TRANSLATION

1. Did you go to the travel agency to get the tickets?
2. Yes, I've just been there.
3. When did you go*?
4. I went at lunch time*.
5. There was nobody, and I came out five minutes later*.
6. We go via Athens; do you know whether the plane stops there?
7. No, I have no idea, but I can ask.
8. Did you think of reserving the hotel?
9. I thought of it, but I prefered to wait to choose with you.
10. The agency gave me lists of hotels, we'll choose one tonight.
11. Shall we take one with a swimming pool?
12. Why not? I've been thinking about it for a long time!

* Note that **y** or **en** can't be omitted in French whereas *there* can be in English.

34 Non, il n'en parlait jamais.

B1 PRESENTATION

Grammar

- **en** as a pronoun is used to avoid repeating a partitive construction with **de, du, de la, de l', des.**
  Ex.: **Avez-vous acheté du vin ? — Oui, j'en ai acheté.**
  Did you buy any wine? — Yes, I bought some.
  A-t-elle lu des livres de science-fiction ?
  Has she read science fiction books?
  Non, elle n'en a jamais lu.
  No, she has never read any.
- It is also used to avoid repeating the complement of an expression of quantity: **beaucoup de** *(a lot of)*, **un peu de** *(a little)*, **trop de** *(too much/many).*
  Ex.: **Il a beaucoup d'amis. — Oui, il en a beaucoup.**
  He has a lot of friends. — Yes, he has many.
  Ils ont trop de travail. — Oui, ils en ont trop.
  They have too much work. — Yes, they have too much.

Vocabulary

château (masc.)	*castle*
usine (fem.)	*factory*
fortune (fem.)	*fortune*
milliardaire (masc.)	*multimillionaire*
héritier (masc.)	*heir*
projet (masc.)	*plan*
immense	*huge*

B2 EXAMPLES *(After a rich man's death)* CD

1. **Est-ce qu'il avait beaucoup d'argent ?**
2. **Oui, il en avait beaucoup.**
3. **Possédait-il des châteaux ?**
4. **Oui, il en avait trois.**
5. **Avait-il aussi des usines ?**
6. **Oui, il en possédait en France et à l'étranger.**
7. **Parlait-il souvent de sa fortune ?**
8. **Non, il n'en parlait jamais.**
9. **Connaissait-il d'autres milliardaires ?**
10. **Il en connaissait, mais il ne les aimait pas.**
11. **Ses héritiers font-ils des projets ?**
12. **Oui, ils en font beaucoup : leur fortune est immense !**

B3 COMMENTS

Grammar

- Note that **en** and **y** precede the verbal form, except in the imperative. Ex.:

Est-ce qu'il prend du thé le matin ? — Oui, il en prend.
Does he have tea in the morning? — Yes, he does.

Prends du thé !	**Prends-en !**
Have some tea!	*Have some!*
J'y vais.	*I am going there.*
Vas-y !	*Go there!*

- In the negative, **en** and **y** always precede the verbal form.

Il n'en parle pas.	*He doesn't speak about it.*
Il n'en a pas parlé.	*He didn't speak about it.*
N'en parle pas.	*Don't speak about it.*
Elle n'y pense pas.	*She doesn't think about it.*
N'y pense pas.	*Don't think about it.*
Je n'en sais rien.	*I know nothing about it.*

Pronunciation

- Remember that **im** is pronounced **in**, at the beginning of a word.
  Ex.: **imperméable, impossible, important**,
  but when the **m** is doubled, **im** is pronounced **i + m**.
  Ex.: **immeuble, immense**.

B4 TRANSLATION

1. Did he have much money?
2. Yes, he had a lot.
3. Did he own castles?
4. Yes, he had three.
5. Did he also have factories?
6. Yes, he owned some, in France and abroad.
7. Did he often speak about his fortune?
8. No, he never spoke about it.
9. Did he know other multimillionnaires?
10. He knew a few but he did not like them.
11. Are his heirs making plans?
12. Yes, they are making many, they have a huge fortune!

34 Exercises

C1 EXERCISES

A. Choose between y or en :

1. Je pense souvent à ce film. J'… pense souvent.
2. Anne ne parle pas beaucoup de ses amis. Elle n'… parle pas beaucoup.
3. Elle rêve d'habiter Athènes. Elle… rêve.
4. Ne faisons pas attention à la pluie ! N'… faisons pas attention !
5. Ils discutent de leur contrat. Ils… discutent.
6. Pensez à réserver votre hôtel ! Pensez-… !

B. (CD) Translate into French :

1. Haye you got magazines ? – I have got one.
2. Did you write postcards ? – I wrote one.
3. Can I have a glass of whisky ? – Of course, have one.
4. Where are the plates ? Bring me one please.
5. Will you buy presents ? – Yes, I'll buy one for our friends.

C2 ANSWERS

A. 1. Je pense souvent à ce film. J'y pense souvent. – 2. Anne ne parle pas beaucoup de ses amis. Elle n'en parle pas beaucoup. – 3. Elle rêve d'habiter Athènes. Elle en rêve. – 4. Ne faisons pas attention à la pluie ! N'y faisons pas attention ! – 5. Ils discutent de leur contrat. Ils en discutent. – 6. Pensez à réserver votre hôtel ! Pensez-y !

B. 1. Avez-vous/As-tu des magazines ? – J'en ai un.
2. Avez-vous/As-tu écrit des cartes postales ? – J'en ai écrit une. – 3. Puis-je avoir un verre de whisky ? – Bien sûr, prenez-en un. ? – 4. Où sont les assiettes ? Apporte-m'en une s'il te plaît./Apportez-m'en… 5. Achèterez-vous/achèteras-tu des cadeaux ? – Oui, j'en achèterai un pour nos amis.

C3 THE ARIANE ROCKET

■ An experimental French rocket launching base has been operating between the mouths of the Kourou and Simmanary Rivers in the DOM (Overseas Department) of Guyana since 1966. The site is ideal : near the Atlantic Ocean in a sparsely populated area, it offers excellent security. Moreover, its position very close to the equator is well adapted to launching satellites into geostationary orbit. Kourou has grown continuously, and today makes possible the use of the **Ariane V** rocket launcher which increases the competitiveness of the Ariane family through improved performance, reduced launching costs, improved reliability, and an increase in the diameter of the satellites. Several big projects have been carried out there : the space glider **Hermès**, a rival of the American and Russian shuttles, the orbital station **Columbus**, and the reinforcement of the launch pad on the Kourou base. Hermès made it possible to improve the techniques of hypersonic flight and, above all, the return to the atmosphere.

■ As to the European launcher Ariane V, it is already able to place one or two satellites with a load of nearly 7,000 kg. (15,400 lbs.) into geostationary orbit. In addition, it makes it possible for Europe to accede to lower orbits to service installations such as the international space station. It is capable of carrying automatic loads, station parts and manned spacecraft.

■ The development program of Ariane V, which has already made some experimental flights, is controlled by the ESA (European Space Agency) which delegated its prime contractorship to the **CNES** (National Center for Space Studies). The Europe of Space has become a reality : several European countries are members of ESA, the production programs are shared among several countries, and NASA no longer has a monopoly : **Arianespace** has signed contracts with American clients. All this research in aerospace of course makes it possible to better manage the commercial use of space for telecommunications, remote sensing, and weather forecasting. Expeditions to Mars are planned for 2020-2025.

D1 UN ACCIDENT DE LA CIRCULATION (CD)

Agent de police : Qu'est-ce qui s'est passé ? Y a-t-il des blessés ?
Motocycliste : Non, rien de grave. Juste un coup à l'épale.
Agent de police : Dites-moi ce qui est arrivé.
Motocycliste : J'ai heurté la roue arrière d'une voiture qui m'a fait une queue de poisson. Mais heureusement le choc n'a pas été violent.
Agent de police : A quelle vitesse rouliez-vous ?
Motocycliste : Pas au-dessus de cinquante, j'en suis sûr, je venais de démarrer.
Agent de police : Est-ce qu'il y a des témoins ?
Motocycliste : Non, il n'y en a pas, il n'y avait personne dans la rue.
Agent de police : Vous faites une déclaration d'accident pour votre assurance ?
Motocycliste : Non, je n'en fais pas. Ma moto a l'air intact et je n'ai rien.
Agent de police : Je vous conseille quand même d'en faire une, on ne sait jamais. Passez aussi à l'hôpital pour votre épaule. c'est plus prudent.
Motocycliste : D'accord, j'y vais tout de suite.

D2 SOME VERBAL EXPRESSIONS ARE FOLLOWED BY A COMPLEMENT INTRODUCED BY *DE*

avoir envie de	*to feel like*
avoir besoin de	*to need*
avoir peur de	*to be afraid of*
avoir honte de	*to be ashamed of*

- en makes it possible to avoid repeating the complement with these expressions :
  As-tu envie de jouer au tennis ? – Oui, j'en ai envie.
  Do you feel like playing tennis ? – Yes, I do.
- Remember : **J'en ai assez.** *I'm fed up.*
  J'en ai assez de… *I'm fed up with…*

D3 A TRAFFIC ACCIDENT

Policeman : What happened ? Is anyone injured ?
Motocyclist : No, nothing serious. Just banged my shoulder.
Policeman : Tell me what happened.
Motocyclist : I bumped into the back wheel of a car that cut in front of me. But luckily it wasn't a very violent shock.
Policeman : How fast were you driving ?
Motocyclist : Not more than 50, I'm sure about that ; I had just moved off.
Policeman : Are there any witnesses ?
Motocyclist : No, there aren't any. There wasn't anyone in the street.
Policeman : Are you going to make an accident declaration to your insurance company ?
Motocyclist : No, I'm not going to make one. My motorcycle looks undamaged, and I'm not hurt.
Policeman : Still, I would advise you to make one ; you never know. And also go to the hospital for your shoulder, just to be on the safe side.
Motocyclist : Okay, I'll go right away.

D4 ROAD SIGNS / *PANNEAUX ROUTIERS*

No parking	*Stationnement interdit*
Parking allowed	*Stationnement autorisé*
Road works ahead (menat work)	*Attention travaux*
Toll	*Péage*
Bend	*Virage*
Caution, School	*Attention, École !*
Curves	*Virages*
Falling rocks	*Chute de pierres*
Give way / yield	*Cédez le passage*
Icy road	*Verglas*
Keep right	*Serrez à droite*
Level / rairoad crossing	*Passage à niveau*

35 En traversant le carrefour...

A1 PRESENTATION

Grammar

- **Je lis en écoutant la radio.**
  I'm reading and listening to the radio.

  To express the idea that two (or more) actions with the same subject are taking place simultaneously, the construction is:

action A (conjugated verb)	+ en +	action B (verb in the participe présent)
Je lis	**en**	**écoutant**

- The **participe présent** *(present participle)* is formed by adding **ant** or **issant** to the stem of the verb (see p. 266).

Vocabulary

traverser	*to cross*	**carrefour** (masc.)	*intersection*
renverser	*to run over*	**piéton** (masc.)	*pedestrian*
remonter la rue	*to go up the street*	**ambulance** (fem.)	*ambulance*
		infirmière (fem.)	*nurse*
courir	*to run*	**témoin** (masc.)	*witness*
poser des questions	*to ask questions*	**inquiet**	*anxious, worried*
soigner	*to take care of, to treat*	**avec inquiétude**	*anxiously*

A2 EXAMPLES *(An accident)* (CD)

1. **Mon mari et moi avons vu un accident en nous promenant dans la rue.**
2. **En traversant le carrefour, une voiture a renversé un piéton.**
3. **Le conducteur avait l'air inquiet en sortant de sa voiture.**
4. **Il a traversé la rue en courant.**
5. **Il était très inquiet en appelant l'ambulance.**
6. **L'ambulance allait très vite en remontant la rue.**
7. **Tout en soignant le piéton, le médecin lui posait des questions.**
8. **Il répondait en le regardant avec inquiétude.**
9. **Une infirmière lui parlait doucement en le soignant.**
10. **Un agent de police allait d'un témoin à l'autre en posant des questions.**
11. **Un témoin répondait en donnant des précisions.**
12. **Nous sommes rentrés chez nous en discutant de l'accident.**

A3 COMMENTS

Grammar

- To emphasize the idea of simultaneity **tout** can be placed before **en**.
  Ex.: **Je lis tout en écoutant la radio.**
  I'm reading while listening to the radio.
- Note irregular **participes présents:**

être	**étant**	*being*
avoir	**ayant**	*having*
savoir	**sachant**	*knowing*

- The construction **en + participe présent** often conveys the idea expressed in English by a prepositional verb.

Ex.:	**Il est parti en courant.**	*He ran away.*
	Il est monté en courant.	*He ran up.*
	Il est descendu en courant.	*He ran down.*
	Il est sorti en courant.	*He ran out.*

- Note that **moi, toi, lui, elle, nous, vous, eux, elles** are also used as unemphasized subjects when linked to other subjects by **et**.
  Ex.: **Pierre et moi sommes amis.**
  Peter and I are friends.
  Lui et moi sommes amis.
  He and I are friends.
  Ton frère et toi viendrez demain.
  You brother and you will come tomorrow.
- **Avec inquiétude:** note that the article is omitted (see C4).

A4 TRANSLATION

1. My husband and I saw an accident as we were walking in the street.
2. As it was crossing the intersection, a car ran over a pedestrian.
3. The driver seemed worried as he got out of his car.
4. He ran across the street.
5. He was very worried when he was calling the ambulance.
6. The ambulance went up the street very fast.
7. While treating the pedestrian, the doctor asked him some questions.
8. He answered, looking at him anxiously.
9. A nurse was talking to him quietly as she was taking care of him.
10. A policeman was going from one witness to the other, asking questions.
11. A witness was answering, giving details.
12. We went home talking about the accident.

35 En écoutant la radio...

B1 PRESENTATION

■ Grammar

- **En + participe présent** does not only express simultaneity:
  Ex.: **Elle est sortie en riant.** *She went out laughing.*
  Il a ouvert la porte en tournant la poignée.
  He opened the door by turning the knob.
- The **participe présent** is invariable, but the **ant** form can also be used as an adjective; it then agrees in gender and number with the noun it refers to.

Ex.:	**un livre intéressant**	*an interesting book*
	des livres intéressants	*interesting books*
	une femme charmante	*a charming woman*
	des amies charmantes	*charming friends*

■ Vocabulary

(se) perfectionner	*to improve*	**expression** (fem.)	*expression*
se distraire	*to have fun*	**régulièrement**	*regularly*
cassette (fem.)	*cassette*	**couramment**	*fluently*
		sans peine	*easily*

B2 EXAMPLES *(Learning languages)* (CD)

1. **On apprend une langue en utilisant des livres, des cassettes, etc.**
2. **Mais on apprend aussi une langue en la pratiquant.**
3. **En la pratiquant régulièrement, on oublie moins.**
4. **Que faire pour parler couramment ?**
5. **Bien sûr, en allant dans le pays, vous parlerez de mieux en mieux.**
6. **En écoutant la radio, vous améliorerez votre français.**
7. **Comment apprendre une langue sans dire un mot ?**
8. **En discutant avec vos voisins, vous vous perfectionnerez sans peine.**
9. **Vous apprendrez des expressions utiles en lisant les journaux.**
10. **Regarder la télévision vous aidera à mieux comprendre.**
11. **Voir des films en français peut vous aider.**
12. **C'est une façon d'apprendre une langue en se distrayant.**

35 By listening to the radio...

B3 COMMENTS

Grammar

- Note that **en** is the only preposition which is followed by a **participe présent**; all the others are followed by an infinitive.

  Ex.: **sans parler** *without speaking*
  pour oublier *in order to forget*
  après manger *after eating*

- Remember the spelling of:

  voir : **voyant**
  se distraire : **se distrayant**
  avoir : **ayant**
  s'asseoir : **s'asseyant**

Pronunciation

- Remember **an, en, em, am** are pronounced the same: nasal vowel **an** except for **am** when it is followed by a vowel.

  Ex.: **ami, améliorer, s'amuser, américain** *(American).*
  couramment is pronounced **coura/ment.**

B4 TRANSLATION

1. You learn a language using books, cassettes, etc.
2. But you also learn a language by practising it.
3. By practising regularly you forget less.
4. What can you do to speak fluently?
5. Of course, by going to the country, you'll speak better and better.
6. By listening to the radio, you'll improve your French.
7. How can you learn a language without saying a word?
8. By talking with your neighbours, you will improve easily.
9. You will learn useful expressions by reading the newspapers.
10. Watching television will help you to understand better.
11. Seeing films in French can help you.
12. It is a way to learn a language and have fun at the same time.

35 Exercises

C1 EXERCISES

A. Change as in the example : Il mange et il regarde la télévision./Il mange en regardant la télévision.

1. Je lis mon journal et j'attends le bus.
2. Les enfants marchent et ils s'amusent.
3. Nous discutons et nous préparons le repas.
4. La secrétaire répond au téléphone et elle écrit.
5. Ils regardent le château et ils font des projets.
6. Mon fils traverse la rue et il se dépêche.

B. Choose the infinitive or present participle :

1. Il est parti sans (perdre/perdant) une minute.
2. Il est parti en oublier/oubliant) son dossier.
3. Nous avons acheté une carte postale pour l'(envoyer / envoyant) à Louis.
4. La secrétaire travaille en (utiliser/utilisant) un ordinateur.
5. Venez me voir avant de (partir/partant).

C2 ANSWERS

A. 1. Je lis mon journal en attendant le bus.
2. Les enfants marchent en s'amusant.
3. Nous discutons en préparant le repas.
4. La secrétaire répond au téléphone en écrivant.
5. Ils regardent le château en faisant des projets.
6. Mon fils traverse la rue en se dépêchant.

B. 1. Il est parti sans perdre une minute.
2. Il est parti en oubliant son dossier.
3. Nous avons acheté une carte postale pour l'envoyer à Louis.
4. La secrétaire travaille en utilisant un ordinateur.
5. Venez me voir avant de partir.

C3 PARIS CAFES

■ Cafés appeared in France during the second half of the 17th century and their number grew during the reign of **Louis XV** (1723-1774). It was fashionable, especially in Paris, to leave the court and go have a discussion in the **Procope Café**, or the **Gradot**, or the **Laurent**, which became meeting places for writers. **Voltaire**, **Diderot** and the Encyclopaedists met there. The philosophers of the Enlightenment went to cafés to exchange the latest news and to participate in debates. Opposed to the political and social order, they talked about the defense of freedom, about tolerance or the search for happiness. Thus the Procope, still located today at number 13 on the rue de l'**Ancienne Comédie**, was a meeting spot for **Rousseau** and **Beaumarchais**, among others.

■ During the Revolution, **Marat**, **Danton** and **Robespierre** would come to have a fashionable drink.

■ In the 20th century, it would be the turn of artists of the Fauvist and Cubist schools. In the 1920s, Surrealists like **Breton** and **Aragon** met at the **Coupole.** And the **Café des Deux Magots** and the **Café Flore**, in the past meeting places for Sartre and other Existentialists, continue to attract writers and artists.

■ The café, which is now in competition with the bar and a French version of the English pub, still plays an important role as a convivial place in urban life. People go there to have a drink, especially before dinner, or after the theater. Some, in the neighborhoods of **Montparnasse** or the **Bastille** have disc jockeys. Others have reverted to their origins and are on certain days meeting places for philosophical discussions. As to the cyber cafés, which offer surfing on the net for the cost of a drink, they attract mainly a younger clientele.

D1 AU CAFE (CD)

Florence : Frédéric ne va pas tarder. On commande en attendant ?

Jean : Garçon, s'il vous plaît !

Garçon : Tout de suite Monsieur, j'arrive... Qu'est-ce que ce sera ?

Jean : Pour moi une bière pression et pour toi Flo ?

Florence : Une menthe à l'eau.... Tiens, tu sais j'ai rencontré Hadrien en allant au bureau ce matin.

Jean : Hadrien, ton copain musicien ? Il est toujours en forme ?

Florence : Oui et non, il s'est tordu la cheville en jouant au tennis, et il a du mal à se déplacer. Il est parti en boitant. Je le plains, c'est vraiment pas marrant pour lui de travailler dans ces conditions.

Jean : A propos de vieux amis, que devient la charmante Françoise ?

Florence : Justement, je l'ai croisée par hasard la semaine dernière en sortant du métro, elle est resplendissante ! Elle a perdu six kilos en faisant un régime !

D2 PARTICIPE PRÉSENT AND PAST PARTICIPLE

- One might expect the **participe présent** to be used to express physical attitudes, but in that case, that past participle is used in French :

assis	*sitting*
allongé	*lying down*
couché	*lying down*
penché	*leaning*
accroupi	*squatting*
agenouillé	*kneeling*

D3 IN THE CAFE

Florence : Frederic should be here any minute now. Shall we order while we're waiting ?
Jean : Waiter, please !
Garçon : Right away, Sir. I'll be right there. What will it be ?
Jean : A draft beer for me, and what about you, Flo ?
Florence : A peppermint cordial. Hey, you know what, I met Hadrien on my way to the office this morning.
Jean : Hadrien, your musician friend ? Is he as fit as ever ?
Florence : Yes and no. He twisted his ankle playing tennis, and he has trouble getting around. He was limping when he left. I feel sorry for him ; it's really not fun for him to be working under those conditions.
Jean : Speaking of old friends, how's your charming friend Françoise doing ?
Florence : As a matter of fact, I ran into her last week coming out of the subway (GB : underground). She looks gorgeous ! She went on a diet and lost six kilos !

D4 SANS RANCUNE.../*NO HARD FEELINGS...*

- In prepositional expressions, the article is omitted, which is unusual in French :

avec plaisir	*with pleasure*
avec joie	*with pleasure*
avec peine	*with difficulty*
sans arrêt	*endlessly*
sans crainte	*without fear*
sur place	*on the spot*
sur mesure	*tailored*
au fur et à mesure	*as, progressively*
par exemple	*for example*
par hasard	*by chance*

36 S'il fait beau, nous resterons une semaine...

A1 PRESENTATION

■ Grammar

- The idea of a condition is most often conveyed by: **si**

si + subordinate clause + main clause
présent future

with a high degree of certainty about the result.

Ex.: **Si vous venez à midi, nous déjeunerons ensemble.**
If you come at noon, we'll have lunch together.
S'il fait beau, nous irons à la campagne.
If the weather is nice, we'll go to the country.
S'il ne pleut pas, ils feront une promenade.
If it doesn't rain, they'll go for a walk.

■ Vocabulary

permettre *to allow*
être pressé *to be in a hurry*
se baigner *to go swimming*
se régaler *to have a real treat*
arriver à *to manage*
se libérer *to free oneself*
être le/la bienvenu(e) *to be welcome*
villa (fem.) *house, cottage*
clef (fem.) *key*
carte (fem.) *card*
poisson (masc.) *fish*
absent *absent, not at home*

A2 EXAMPLES *(Summer plans)* CD

1. **Si nous achetons une maison, nous irons chaque été au bord de la mer.**
2. **Si tu viens, tu seras le bienvenu.**
3. **Si nous sommes absents, tu pourras prendre la clef chez la voisine.**
4. **Si tu as le temps, tu passeras quelques jours avec nous.**
5. **Si tu n'es pas trop pressé, tu pourras prendre le train.**
6. **Si tu prends le TGV, le voyage te prendra six heures.**
7. **Si le temps le permet, nous ferons du bateau.**
8. **Nous nous baignerons s'il ne pleut pas.**
9. **S'il pleut, nous lirons ou nous jouerons aux cartes.**
10. **Si tu aimes le poisson, tu te régaleras.**
11. **S'il fait beau, nous resterons une semaine de plus.**
12. **Si tu n'arrives pas à te libérer en août, tu pourras venir en septembre.**

A3 COMMENTS

Grammar

- Note that **si** becomes **s'** before **il** or **ils**, but doesn't change before **elle** or **elles**.

  Ex.: **s'il vient...** **s'ils viennent...**
  si elle vient... **si elles viennent...**

- The subordinate clause introduced by **si** can be placed either before or after the main clause.

  Ex.: **Nous ferons du bateau si le temps le permet. / Si le temps le permet, nous ferons du bateau.**

- **faire** is used in many expressions where it has no equivalent in English:

faire du vélo	*to ride (a bike)*
faire du cheval	*to ride (a horse)*
faire du ski	*to ski*
faire du surf	*to windsurf*
faire de la voile	*to sail*
faire de la voiture	*to drive*
faire de l'auto-stop / **faire du stop**	*to hitchhike*

A4 TRANSLATION

1. If we buy a house, we'll go to the seaside every summer.
2. If you come, you'll be welcome.
3. If we're not at home, you can get the key from the neighbour.
4. If you have the time, you can spend a few days with us.
5. If you're not in too big a hurry, you can take the train.
6. If you take the high speed train, the trip will take you six hours.
7. Weather permitting, we'll go sailing.
8. We'll go swimming if it doesn't rain.
9. If it rains, we'll read or play cards.
10. If you like fish, you're in for a real treat.
11. If the weather is nice, we'll stay a week longer.
12. If you can't manage to be free in August, you could come in September.

36 Que ferais-tu si tu étais riche ?

B1 PRESENTATION

Grammar

- The present tense of the conditional is used when the condition is expressed in the **imparfait**:

si + subordinate clause	+ main clause
imparfait	conditional

The conditional is formed with the infinitive + **-ais** **-ions**
-ais **-iez**
-ait **-aient**

Ex.: **Si vous veniez à midi, nous déjeunerions ensemble.**
If you came at noon, we would have lunch together.
S'ils avaient de l'argent, ils voyageraient.
If they had money, they would travel.

Vocabulary

dépenser *to spend*
avoir les moyens de *to be able to afford*
faire un effort *to make an effort*
se rendre compte de *to realize*
gros lot (masc.) *top prize in the lottery*
importance (fem.) *importance*
tant de *so much, so many*

B2 EXAMPLES *(Dreams)* (CD)

1. **Si je gagnais le gros lot, je serais millionnaire.**
2. **Que ferais-tu si tu étais riche ?**
3. **Moi, je dépenserais tout !**
4. **Moi, je ferais des cadeaux à tout le monde.**
5. **Si j'en avais les moyens, j'achèterais des tableaux.**
6. **Si j'avais beaucoup d'argent, j'ouvrirais un compte en banque en Suisse.**
7. **Si je n'avais pas besoin de gagner ma vie, je passerais mon temps à lire.**
8. **Si c'était possible, j'arrêterais de travailler.**
9. **Si j'étais riche, je n'aurais pas besoin de travailler.**
10. **S'ils se rendaient compte de l'importance des problèmes, les pays riches aideraient les pays pauvres.**
11. **Si tout le monde faisait un effort, on trouverait des solutions.**
12. **Les gens seraient peut-être plus heureux si l'argent n'avait pas tant d'importance.**

36 What would you do if you were rich?

B3 COMMENTS

Grammar

- Note that when the infinitive ends with an **e**, the **e** is dropped in the conditional. Ex.:

lire	*to read*	**je lirais**	*I would read*
écrire	*to write*	**j'écrirais**	*I would write*
prendre	*to take*	**je prendrais**	*I would take*
descendre	*to go down*	**je descendrais**	*I would go down*

Conditional of:	*to have*	*to be*	*to do*	*can*
	avoir	**être**	**faire**	**pouvoir**
	I would have etc.	*I would be* etc.	*I would do* etc.	*I could* etc.
je, j'	aurais	serais	ferais	pourrais
tu	aurais	serais	ferais	pourrais
il, elle	aurait	serait	ferait	pourrait
nous	aurions	serions	ferions	pourrions
vous	auriez	seriez	feriez	pourriez
ils, elles	auraient	seraient	feraient	pourraient

- The conditional of **pouvoir** is used in questions to make orders more polite. Ex.: **Pourriez-vous me passer le pain ?**
  Could you pass me the bread?
- Note that the subordinate clause needn't be repeated (see B2, 3 and 4).

B4 TRANSLATION

1. If I won the top prize in the lottery, I would be a millionaire.
2. What would you do if you were rich?
3. I would spend all my money!
4. I would give everybody presents.
5. If I could afford it, I'd buy paintings.
6. If I had a lot of money, I'd open a bank account in Switzerland.
7. If I didn't need to earn my living, I'd spend my time reading.
8. If it were possible, I'd stop working.
9. If I were rich, I wouldn't need to work.
10. If they realized the importance of the problems, the rich countries would help the poor countries.
11. If everybody made an effort, we could find solutions.
12. People would perhaps be happier if money weren't so important.

C1 EXERCISES

A. Put the verb in the correct tense :

1. Si mon ami avait un mois de vacances, il (partir) en Grèce.
2. Si vous faisiez un discours, que (dire)-vous ?
3. Anne ne (être) pas toujours en regard si elle se levait plus tôt !
4. Si vous (rester) chez moi, nous écouterions des disques.

B. Translate into French :

1. If your son phoned the doctor now, he would have an appointment for next Monday.
2. If we were famous singers, we would earn a lot of money.
3. They would learn a lot of things if they talked more with Pierre.
4. If you spoke less quickly, I would understand !
5. If you came to Paris, you could meet my students.

C2 ANSWERS

A. 1. Si mon ami avait un mois de vacances, il partirait en Grèce.
2. Si vous faisiez un discours, que diriez-vous ?
3. Anne ne serait pas toujours en retard si elle se levait plus tôt !
4. Si vous restiez chez moi, nous écouterions des disques.

B. 1. Si ton/votre fils téléphonait au docteur maintenant, il aurait un rendez-vous pour lundi prochain.
2. Si nous étions des chanteurs célèbres, nous gagnerions beaucoup d'argent.
3. Ils/elles apprendraient beaucoup de choses s'ils/si elles discutaient plus avec Pierre.
4. Si vous parliez/tu parlais moins vite, je comprendrais !
5. Si vous veniez/tu venais à Paris, vous pourriez/tu pourrais rencontrer mes étudiants.

C3 DEPARTMENT STORES

■ From 1830 on, economic development and the requirements of competition were such that Paris merchants bought directly from the producers and stocked the large quantities, which led to the rise of department stores.
■ **A. Boucicaut**, whose name still graces a square, had the **Bon Marché** built in 1852. It was his wife who had the Boucicaut Hospital built in the 15th arrondissement and subsidized the Pasteur Institute.
Le Bon Marché is more upmarket in its fashion collections and home furnishing departments, with newly revamped men's, women's and lingerie sections. The excellent window displays provide a real snapshot of seasonal trends. Shop 2 contains a brilliant food hall, bistro and antique arcade.
■ Galeries Lafayette was started in 1895. Its stores are located on the **Boulevard Haussman** and at Maine Montparnasse as well as in several cities in France and throughout the world : Bangkok, Singapore, New York and Berlin. It receives the visit of the equivalent of the entire population of Paris each month and is the largest perfume and beauty store in the world. **Le Printemps** dates from 1865 and comprises several stores including those devoted to fashion, home furnishings, and men's fashions (**Brummel**). The houseware and stationery sections are worth a look.
■ **La Samaritaine** still shows flashes of original « art nouveau » splendor. It is famous for its huge toy department. From the roof top terrace you can enjoy one of the best views of Paris. The **BHV (Bazar de l'Hôtel de Ville)** is the central Paris alternative to warehouse superstores which are usually to be found in the suburbs of the big cities. It offers a vast range of plumbing, hardware, paint, tools, and electrical goods, although it also stocks the usual fashionable clothing, accessories and beauty aids on the ground floor.

D1 UN NOUVEL EMPLOI (CD)

Marc : Salut Anne. Comment vas-tu ?
Anne : Très bien. J'ai enfin trouvé du travail. Je n'y croyais plus après trois mois de chômage.
Marc : Je suis content pour toi. C'est quel genre de boulot ?
Anne : Un boulot de secrétariat. Mais je vais beaucoup travailler sur ordinateur et si je ne me remets pas à l'informatique tout de suite je vais avoir du mal.
Marc : En cas de besoin n'hésite pas à m'appeler. Je viens de finir un stage de Bureautique.
Anne : Ah si j'en savais autant que toi je n'aurais plus de problème !
Marc : Tu commences quand ?
Anne : Lundi prochain. Bien sûr je n'aurai pas de congés payés cette année mais c'est un travail intéressant et le salaire est correct.
Marc : C'est loin de chez toi ?
Anne : Pas du tout, si je prends le bus je mets un quart d'heure

D2 CELA PRENDRA DU TEMPS *IT'LL TAKE TIME*

- **prendre** + expression of time — *take* + expression of time

Cela prendra deux jours — *It' ll take two days.*
Cela prend des années. — *That takes years.*
Cela a pris beaucoup de temps. — *It took a lot of time.*

- Another way of conveying the same meaning is to use the verb **mettre** :

  On mettra deux jours à peindre les fenêtres.
  We' ll spend two days painting the windows.
  On met des mois à apprendre une langue.
  One spends months learning a language.
  On a mis beaucoup de temps à trouver la solution.
  We spent a lot of time finding the solution.

D 3 A NEW JOB

Marc : Hi, Anne. How are you ?
Anne : I'm fine. I've finally found a job. I was losing faith after three months of unemployment.
Marc : I'm pleased for you. What kind of job ?
Anne : A secretarial job. But I'm going to work on the computer a lot, and if I don't brush up my computer skills right away, I'm going to have a hard time.
Marc : Don't hesitate to call me if you need help. I've just finished a computer training period.
Anne : Oh, if I knew as much as you do, I wouldn't have any problem.
Marc : When are you starting ?
Anne : Next Monday. Of course, I won't have any paid vacation this year, but it's interesting work, and the salary is adequate.
Marc : Is it far from where you live ?
Anne : Not at all ; if I ride the bus, it takes me a quarter of an hour.

D4 HOW TO EXPRESS A CONDITION

- Besides si, other expressions can be used to express conditions.

au cas où **pour le cas où** **dans le cas où**	+	verb in the conditional in the subordinate clause	*in case*
en cas de	+	substantive	*in case of*
à condition de	+	infinitive	*providing*

Au cas où il y aurait des grèves, nous viendrions en voiture.
In case there were strikes, we would come by car.
En cas de grèves, nous viendrions en voiture.
In case of strikes, we would come by car.
À condition de partir tôt, vous serez à l'heure.
Providing you leave early, you'll be on time.

en cas d'urgence	*in case of emergency*
en cas de besoin	*in case you need...*
en cas d'accident	*in case of accident*
en cas de malheur	*in case something terrible happened*

37 On ne peut pas toujours faire ce qu'on veut !

A1 PRESENTATION

Grammar

- The French equivalent of *to want* is **vouloir**. It is used to express either will or wish.

	Présent	**Imparfait**	**Futur**
	I want, etc.	*I wanted*, etc.	*I shall want*, etc.
je	**veux**	**voulais**	**voudrai**
tu	**veux**	**voulais**	**voudras**
il, elle	**veut**	**voulait**	**voudra**
nous	**voulons**	**voulions**	**voudrons**
vous	**voulez**	**vouliez**	**voudrez**
ils, elles	**veulent**	**voulaient**	**voudront**
Past participle: **voulu** *(wanted)*			

Vocabulary

rester — *to be left*
accompagner — *to go with, to accompany*
menu (masc.) — *menu*
plat du jour (masc.) — *the day's special*
comme — *as, whatever*
ensuite — *next*

A2 EXAMPLES *(At the restaurant)* (CD)

1. **Bonjour ! Voulez-vous jeter un coup d'œil au menu ?**
2. **Nous voulions goûter votre plat du jour.**
3. **Qu'est-ce que vous voulez boire ?**
4. **Tu veux encore un peu de viande ?**
5. **Il reste des légumes, tu en veux ?**
6. **Non, merci, je n'en veux plus.**
7. **Qu'est-ce que tu veux faire ensuite ?**
8. **Comme tu voudras !**
9. **Je vais demander à Hélène ce qu'elle veut faire.**
10. **Qu'est-ce que tu veux dire ?**
11. **Je vais lui demander si elle veut nous accompagner.**
12. **On ne peut pas toujours faire ce qu'on veut !**

37 You can't always do what you want!

A3 COMMENTS

■ Grammar

- **vouloir** can be followed by a noun or an infinitive.
  Ex.: **Pierre veut un nouvel appareil photo.**
  Pierre wants a new camera.
  Mes enfants veulent des disques de jazz.
  My children want jazz records.
  Nous voulions partir de bonne heure.
  We wanted to leave early.

- Remember that in reported speech **qu'est-ce que** becomes **ce que**.
  Ex.: (direct speech) **Qu'est-ce que tu veux .**
  What do you want?
  (indirect speech) **Dis-moi ce que tu veux.**
  Tell me what you want.

- **est-ce que** becomes **si**:

Est-ce qu'elles viennent ?	*Are they coming?*
Demande-leur si elles viennent.	*Ask them if they are coming.*

- Note the impersonal form of **il reste...** meaning *...left.*
  Ex.:

Il reste du pain.	*There is some bread left.*
Il reste de la place.	*There is some room left.*
Il reste des places.	*There are some seats left.*
Il ne me reste pas d'argent.	*I have no money left.*
Il ne nous reste pas beaucoup de temps.	*We haven't much time left.*

A4 TRANSLATION

1. Good afternoon! Would you like to have a look at the menu?
2. We would like to try today's special.
3. What would you like to drink?
4. Do you want a little more meat?
5. There are some vegetables left, do you want some?
6. No, thank you, I don't want any more.
7. What do you want to do next?
8. Whatever you like!
9. I'm going to ask Hélène what she wants to do.
10. What do you mean?
11. I'm going to ask her if she wants to go with us.
12. You can't always do what you want!

37 Expliquez-nous ce que vous voudriez faire.

B1 PRESENTATION

Grammar

- **vouloir** in the conditional:

je	**voudrais**	*I*	*would*	*like*
tu	**voudrais**	*you*	*would*	*like*
il, elle	**voudrait**	*he, she*	*would*	*like*
nous	**voudrions**	*we*	*would*	*like*
vous	**voudriez**	*you*	*would*	*like*
ils, elles	**voudraient**	*they*	*would*	*like*

- The conditional is often used:

— to make a request more polite. Ex.:
Je voudrais emprunter ce livre, voudriez-vous me le prêter ?
I would like to borrow this book, would you lend it to me?

— to express a wish. Ex.:
Je voudrais devenir célèbre.
I would like to become famous.

Vocabulary

réussir	*to succeed, to be successful*	**ennui** (masc.)	*trouble, problem*
		avenir (masc.)	*future*
attendre de	*to expect from*	**succès** (masc.)	*success*
atteindre	*to reach*	**but** (masc.)	*goal, purpose*
gâcher	*to ruin*		

B2 EXAMPLES *(Hopes)* CD

1. **Beaucoup de gens voudraient réussir dans la vie.**
2. **Ils voudraient aussi être heureux et faire ce qu'ils veulent.**
3. **Ils ne voudraient pas avoir d'ennuis.**
4. **Les uns voudraient ceci, les autres voudraient cela.**
5. **Certains voudraient tout avoir !**
6. **Et vous, que voudriez-vous faire ? Si vous nous disiez ce que vous attendez de l'avenir ?**
7. **Vous voudriez peut-être avoir du succès ?**
8. **Expliquez-nous ce que vous voudriez faire.**
9. **Dites-nous le but que vous voudriez atteindre.**
10. **Parfois on voudrait pouvoir revenir en arrière.**
11. **On voudrait être et avoir été.**
12. **On ne voudrait pas gâcher sa vie !**

B3 COMMENTS

Grammar

- Note the masculine and feminine forms:

l'un... l'autre / l'une... l'autre	*one... the other*
les uns... les autres / les unes... les autres	*some... others*

- **si** followed by a subject and a verb in the imperfect conveys the meaning of: *what about, how about* followed by a verb. Ex.:
  Si nous partions ? *How about leaving?*
  Si on allait au cinéma ? *What about going to the pictures?*
- **et** followed by a noun or pronoun conveys the meaning of: *what about, how about* followed by a noun or pronoun.
  Ex.: **Et Anne ?** *What about Anne?*
  Et vous ? *What about you?*
  Et toi ? *What about you?*
  Et lui ? *What about him?*
  Et eux ? *What about them?*
- Note that the expression **vouloir bien** has a different meaning according to the tense.
  — **vouloir bien** in the present means: *to be happy to*
  — **vouloir bien** in the conditional means: *would like*
  Ex.: **Je veux bien t'accompagner.**
  I'll be happy to go with you.
  Je voudrais bien t'accompagner.
  I would like to go with you.

B4 TRANSLATION

1. Many people would like to succeed in life.
2. They would also like to be happy and do what they want.
3. They don't want to have problems.
4. Some would like this, others would like that.
5. Some want to have it all!
6. What about you, what would you like to do? How about telling us what you expect from the future.
7. Perhaps you want to be successful?
8. Explain to us what you would like to do.
9. Tell us the goal you would like to reach.
10. Sometimes one wants to be able to go back and start over.
11. One wants to be and to have been.
12. One doesn't want to ruin one's life!

37 Exercises

C1 EXERCISES

A. Fill in the blanks with correct form of <u>vouloir</u> :

1. Mes étudiants… voyager à l'étranger.
2. Sa fille… louer un studio.
3. Téléphone-lui si tu… discuter avec lui.
4. Que… -il comme cadeau de Noël ?
5. Je… visiter ce musée hier.
6. Demande leur s'ils… sortir avec nous.
7. Que…-vous faire aujourd'hui ?
8. Nous… passer par Paris.

B. (CD) Translate into French :

1. Ask them what they want.
2. I wish I were twenty !
3. Would you like to live in France ?
4. Would you lend me your camera, please ?

C2 ANSWERS

A. 1. Mes étudiants veulent/voudraient voyager à l'étranger.
2. Sa fille veut/voudrait louer un studio.
3. Téléphone-lui si tu veux discuter avec lui.
4. Que veut/voudrait-il comme cadeau de Noël ?
5. Je voulais visiter ce musée hier.
6. Demande-leur s'ils veulent sortir avec nous.
7. Que voulez-vous faire aujourd'hui ?
8. Nous voulons/voudrions passer par Paris.

B. 1. Demande-leur ce qu'ils veulent.
Demandez-leur de qu'ils veulent.
2. Je voudrais avoir vingt ans !
3. Voudrais-tu habiter/vivre en France ?
Voudriez-vous habiter/vivre en France ?
4. Voudrais-tu me prêter ton appareil-photo s'il te plaît ?
Voudriez-vous me prêter votre appareil-photo s'il vous plaît ?

C3 MENU OF A RESTAURANT

■ HORS D'ŒUVRES
Green or Mixed Salad
Salade verte ou mélangée
Avocado with Oil and Vinegar Dressing
Avocat vinaigrette
Green Bean Salad
Salade de haricots verts
Homemade Duck Foie Gras
Foie gras de canard maison
Morteau Sausage, Potatoes with Oil
Saucisse de Morteau pommes à l'huile
Homemade Fish Soup
Soupe de poissons maison
Warm Calf's Head Salad
Salade de tête de veau tiède
Six Large Burgundy Snails
Six gros escargots de Bourgogne
■ MAIN DISHES / *ENTRÉES*
(See our dishes of the day on the blackboard.)
(Consultez les plats du jour sur l'ardoise)
Tartar Steak, French Fries (GB : Chips), Green Salad
Steak tartare, pommes frites, salade verte
Grilled Salmon Steak with Béarnaise Sauce
Saumon grillé sauce béarnaise
Fried Scallops à la Provencal
Saint Jacques à la provençale
Grilled Chitterlings Sausage
Andouillette grillée
Veal Kidneys, Fried Potatoes
Rognons de veau, pommes frites
■ CHEESE PLATE / *PLATEAU DE FROMAGES*
■ DESSERT / *DESSERTS*
Pie of the Day / **Tarte du jour**
Choice of Ice Cream/Sherbet (3 scoops)
Choix de glaces et sorbets (3 boules)
Chocolate Cake / **Gâteau au chocolat**
Floating Island / **Île flottante**
Crêpes with Sugar / **Crêpes au sucre**
Profiteroles with Hot Chocolate Sauce
Profiterolles sauce au chocolat chaud

D1 INVITATION (CD)

Marie : Je crois que tout est prêt ! Ah non, j'ai oublié de sortir les apéritifs.

Nicolas : On sonne, ne te dérange pas, j'y vais.... Bonsoir, content de te voir, tu vas bien, entre.

Julien : Je vous ai apporté le petit vin qu'on a goûté l'autre soir.

Marie : Merci. Assieds-toi. Tu veux boire quelque chose ?

Julien : Je prendrais bien un whisky.

Marie : De la glace ?

Julien : Non merci, je le prends sec.

.....(*à table*)

Nicolas : Félicitations Marie, ce gigot est un régal j'en reprendrais bien une tranche. Et toi Julien ?

Julien : Non merci, mais je voudrais bien goûter ces petits légumes.

.....(*en partant*)

Julien : Merci encore, c'était une soirée très agréable. On se revoit chez moi le dix-sept.

Marie : D'accord, merci d'être venu, à bientôt.

D2 JE NE VOULAIS PAS.../*I DIDN'T MEAN TO*

- **Vouloir** in the **imparfait** or **passé composé**, negative form, conveys the meaning of : *didn't mean to, didn't intend to, had no intention of.*

Ex. : **Il n'a pas voulu vous faire mal.**
He didn't intend to hurt you.

Je ne voulais pas vous déranger.
I didn't mean to disturb you.

Je n'ai pas voulu la contrarier !
I didn't mean to annoy her !

D3 A DINNER PARTY

Marie : I think everything's ready. Oh, no, I've forgotten to get the aperitifs out.
Nicolas : Somebody's at the door. Don't bother, I'll get it. Good evening, glad to see you, how are you, come on in.
Julien : I brought you a bottle of that little wine we tasted the other evening.
Marie : Thanks. Sit down. Would you like something to drink ?
Julien : A glass of whiskey would be nice.
Marie : With ice ?
Julien : No, thank you, I take it straight.
.....(*At the table*)
Nicolas : Congratulations, Marie. This leg of lamb is absolutely delicious. I'd love another slice of it. What about you, Julien ?
Julien : No, thank you. But I would like to try those little vegetables.
.....(*On the way out*)
Julien : Thank you again. It was a very pleasant evening. We'll see each other again on the 17th at my place.
Marie : Okay, thanks for coming. See you.

D4 MORE ABOUT *WILL AND WISH*

- **en vouloir à**
  Ex. : **J'en veux à Pierre !** *I've got a grudge against Peter !*
- **ne pas vouloir de**
  Ex. : **Je ne veux pas de ça !** *I won't have it !*

désirer	*to desire*	**désir** (masc.)	*desire*
espérer	*to hope*	**espoir** (masc.)	*hope*
souhaiter	*to wish*	**souhait** (masc.)	*wish*
volonté (fem.)	*will*	**bonne volonté** (fem.)	*willingness*
vœu (masc.)	*wish*		

volontiers	*willingly/with pleasure*
(in)volontairement	*(un)intentionally/on purpose*
à volonté	*at will*
bon gré mal gré	*willy nilly*

38 Certains ne veulent pas que les voitures...

A1 PRESENTATION

■ Grammar

- When **vouloir** is followed by **que** and a subordinate, the verb in the subordinate clause is in a present tense called: **présent du subjonctif.**

  Ex.: **Nous voulons qu'ils écoutent.** *We want them to listen.*
- **Présent du subjonctif:**

Verbs of the 1st and 3rd group		Verbs of the 2nd group	
stem +	-e -es -e -ions -iez -ent	stem +	-isse -isses -isse -issions -issiez -issent

■ Vocabulary

construire	*to build*	**habitant** (masc.)	*inhabitant*
organiser	*to organize*	**maire** (masc.)	*mayor*
agrandir	*to enlarge, to extend*	**école** (fem.)	*school*
		entrée (fem.)	*admission*
interdire	*to forbid*	**marché** (masc.)	*market*
stationner	*to park*	**gratuit**	*free (of charge)*
		au contraire	*on the contrary*

A2 EXAMPLES *(Town management)* (CD)

1. **Les habitants de notre ville veulent que ça change !**
2. **Ils veulent que le maire se rende compte des problèmes.**
3. **Ils veulent que l'on construise un nouvel hôpital.**
4. **Ils voudraient qu'on finisse rapidement les travaux.**
5. **Ils voudraient qu'on agrandisse l'ancienne école.**
6. **Ils ne veulent pas qu'on la ferme.**
7. **Les jeunes voudraient qu'on organise des concerts.**
8. **Les familles voudraient que l'entrée à la piscine soit gratuite.**
9. **Beaucoup de gens voudraient qu'on interdise la circulation dans le centre ville.**
10. **Certains ne veulent pas que les voitures stationnent près du marché.**
11. **D'autres veulent, au contraire, qu'on agrandisse le parking.**
12. **Les commerçants voudraient qu'on agrandisse la zone piétonne.**

38 Some people don't want cars...

A3 COMMENTS

■ Grammar

- Irregular verbs (subjunctive present):

		être	avoir	pouvoir
(que)	je, j'	sois	aie	puisse
"	tu	sois	aies	puisses
"	il, elle	soit	ait	puisse
"	nous	soyons	ayons	puissions
"	vous	soyez	ayez	puissiez
"	ils, elles	soient	aient	puissent

- Note that **vouloir que**, whatever the tense of **vouloir**, is always followed by a subjunctive.
- Remember that **que l'on** is often used instead of **qu'on** in elegant speech.
- The **présent du subjonctif** will be found often in French. It is always used in subordinate clause generally expressing wish or will after verbs such as:

souhaiter (que) *to wish*
espérer (que) *to hope*
vouloir (que) *to want*

A4 TRANSLATION

1. The inhabitants of our town want things to change!
2. They want the mayor to be aware of the problems.
3. They want a new hospital to be built.
4. They want the construction work to be finished rapidly.
5. They want the old school to be extended.
6. They don't want it to be closed.
7. The young people want concerts to be organized.
8. The families want admission to the swimming pool to be free.
9. Many people want traffic to be forbidden in the centre of town.
10. Some people don't want cars to be parked near the market.
11. Others, on the contrary, want the car park to be extended.
12. The shopkeepers want the pedestrian zone to be extended.

38 On n'a pas de temps à perdre, il faut...

B1 PRESENTATION

Grammar

- The **présent du subjonctif** is always used after the expression: **il faut que.**

  Il faut que conveys the idea of obligation, of necessity. It is an impersonal expression similar to *it is necessary that.*

  Ex.: **Il faut que vous partiez.**
  You must leave.
  Il faut que les documents soient prêts à midi.
  The documents must be ready by twelve.

Vocabulary

décider	*to make a decision*
correspondre aux besoins	*to meet the requirements*
besoin (masc.)	*need*
candidat (masc.)	*applicant*
expérience (fem.)	*experience*
CV (curriculum vitae) (masc.)	*CV (*US : *resume)*
entretien (masc.)	*interview*
compétent	*competent*
efficace	*efficient*
au moins	*at least*

B2 EXAMPLES *(A man to meet our requirements)* (CD)

1. **Il faut que nous choisissions un nouveau directeur commercial.**
2. **On n'a pas de temps à perdre, il faut qu'on décide rapidement.**
3. **Il faut que la personne corresponde à nos besoins.**
4. **Il faut que le candidat ait au moins dix ans d'expérience.**
5. **Il faut qu'il soit compétent et efficace.**
6. **Il faut qu'il soit prêt à travailler en équipe.**
7. **Il ne faut pas qu'il ait plus de quarante-cinq ans.**
8. **Il ne faut pas qu'il soit trop jeune non plus.**
9. **S'ils sont intéressés, il faut que les candidats écrivent, il ne faut pas qu'ils téléphonent.**
10. **Il faut qu'ils envoient un CV et une photo.**
11. **Il faut qu'ils puissent se libérer d'ici à un mois.**
12. **Il faut que le P.-D.G. ait un entretien avec chaque candidat.**

B3 COMMENTS

Grammar

- Note that **il faut** can be followed by an infinitive when there is no specific subject.

  Ex.: **Il faut faire attention.**
  One must pay attention. / One must be careful.

  or when the subject is understood as **nous** or **on**.

  Ex.: **C'est trop loin, il faut prendre un taxi.**
  It is too far, we have to take a taxi.

- In the conditional **il faut** becomes **il faudrait** and is followed by a subjunctive.

  Ex.: **Il faudrait que nous partions de bonne heure.**
  We'd have to leave early.

  or an infinitive.

  Ex.: **Il faudrait partir de bonne heure.**
  We'd have to leave early.

Il faudrait is used to give advice.

B4 TRANSLATION

1. We must choose a new marketing manager.
2. There's no time to lose, we have to make a decision quickly.
3. The person must meet our requirements.
4. The applicant has to have at least ten years' experience.
5. He or she has to be competent and efficient.
6. He or she has to be willing to work as a member of a team.
7. The applicant mustn't be more than 45 years old.
8. The applicant mustn't be too young, either.
9. If the job interests them, applicants must write; they mustn't telephone.
10. They must send a CV and a photo.
11. They must be free within a month's time.
12. The President and Managing Director has to interview every applicant.

38 Exercises

C1 EXERCISES

A. Transform the sentences using <u>il faut</u> or <u>il ne faut pas</u> as in the example : Dépêche-toi. Il faut que tu te dépêches.

1. Choisissez une carte. – 2. N'utilise pas la voiture.
3. Repose-toi un peu. – 4. Téléphonez au directeur de l'agence. – 5. Attends quelques minutes. – 6. Ne soyez pas en retard ! – 7. Prépare-toi.

B. (CD) Translate into French :

1. I must send my CV as soon as possible. – 2. They must organize an election to have a new mayor. – 3. Don't park here, you mustn't leave your car in front of the hospital. – 4. Do you want us to wait for you ? – 5. I would like her to avoid the town centre.

D2 VIE PRATIQUE

A. 1. Il faut que vous choisissiez une carte. – 2. Il ne faut pas que tu utilises la voiture. – 3. Il faut que tu te reposes un peu. – 4. Il faut que vous téléphoniez au directeur de l'agence. – 5. Il faut que tu attendes quelques minutes. – 6. Il ne faut pas que vous soyez en retard ! – 7. Il faut que tu te prépares.

B. 1. Il faut que j'envoie mon CV dès que possible. – 2. Il faut qu'ils organisent des élections pour avoir un nouveau maire. – 3. Ne stationnez pas ici, il ne faut pas que vous laissiez votre voiture devant l'hôpital. – 4. Voulez-vous que nous vous attendions ? *or* Est-ce que vous voulez que nous vous (*or* t') attendions ? – 5. Je voudrais qu'elle évite le centre ville.

C3 EMPLOYMENT

■ EMPLOYMENT PROBLEMS

Like most of the other industrialized economies, France has been suffering from chronic unemployment for the past twenty years. Opinion polls show that it is our fellow citizens'major cause for concern. The **ANPE** (the state employment agency) has on its books about three million job seekers (representing 12.5 %) who have not found work. As a sign of these times of crisis, short-term work is increasing : there are those doing temporary work, those with temporary contracts, and part-time employees. Thus, the labor market is divided among those who are protected from unemployment (civil servants, for example), those who are fortunate enough to have permanent contracts, and those who are half way between the world of employment and exclusion. The government is providing incentives to companies who recruit the unemployed, and is attempting to improve the training made available to job seekers.

■ SEASONAL JOBS AND JOB REGULATIONS

Legally, a temporary contract is required for summer holiday jobs. However, nearly 20 % of young people moonlight. The jobs most affected by illegal work are in catering and the hotel business. Moonlighters also work, for example, in beach clubs, windsurfing rentals, hawking, snack stands and night clubs.

Officially, a young person is allowed to work from the age of 16, for no more than 39 hours a week (soon 35 ?), with a compulsory day off. He or she only earns the **SMIC** (literally "minimum inter-professional growth salary", or index-based minimum wage) from the age of 18. Workers' paid holidays represent 10 % of their salary, provided they have a work contract or a letter of appointment and can produce a pay slip. Disputes may be dealt with by bringing in the **Inspection du travail** (a body that enforces the application of labor law), or by turning to the trade unions.

D1 AGENDA (CD)

(*Sylvie et son assistante Catherine organisent le travail de la semaine*)

Sylvie : Il faut que nous décidions d'une date pour la réunion avec les représentants de NOVMOD.

Catherine : Que pensez-vous du mardi vingt-huit ?

Sylvie : Impossible il faut que je sois à Lyon ce jour-là pour présenter nos nouvelles collections.

Catherine : Vous ne voulez pas que j'y aille à votre place ?

Sylvie : Non, Il vaut mieux que nous soyons toutes les deux à la réunion. Proposez le jeudi trente.

Catherine : Dans ce cas il faut que j'annule mon rendez-vous avec M. Dupuis. J'espère qu'il sera d'accord pour que nous remettions le rendez-vous à la semaine d'après.

Sylvie : Je suis sûre que ça ne posera pas de problème. Il faudrait aussi que nous choisissions les photos pour la presse.

Catherine : J'ai déjà fait une sélection, mais il vaut mieux que vous jetiez un coup d'oeil.

C2 J'EN DOUTE/*I DOUBT IT*

- Verbs or verbal expressions conveying an idea of doubt, wish or regret are followed by a subordinate in the subjunctive. Ex. :

Je doute qu'elle soit mariée.
I doubt she is married.

Je ne crois pas qu'elle soit mariée.
I don't believe she is married.

Je ne pense pas qu'il ait plus de trente ans.
I don't think he is more than thirty.

Je n'ai pas l'impression que cela puisse correspondre à nos besoins.
I don't feel it can meet our requirements.

→Note the negation to express doubt.

Je souhaite qu'ils réussissent. *I hope they succeed.*
Je regrette que vous soyez malade. *I am sorry you are ill.*

D3 AGENDA

(*Sylvie and her assistant Catherine are organizing the week's work*).

Sylvie : We have to decide on a date for the meeting with the NOVMOD representatives.

Catherine : What do you think about Tuesday, the 28th ?

Sylvie : Impossible. I've got to be in Lyons that day to present our new collections.

Catherine : Wouldn't you like me to go instead ?

Sylvie : No, it's better that both of us be at the meeting. Suggest Thursday, the 30th.

Catherine : In that case, I'll have to cancel my appointment with Mr. Dupuis. I hope he'll agree to put the appointment off until the following week.

Sylvie : I'm sure that won't be a problem. We also have to choose the photos for the press.

Catherine : I've already made a selection, but you'd better have a look at them.

D4 QUELQUES PANNEAUX D'INTERDICTION *SOME WARNING SIGNS*

Interdit de fumer.	*No smoking.*
Stationnement interdit. / **Interdit de stationner.**	*No parking*
Entrée interdite.	*No entrance.*
Jeux de ballons interdits.	*Ball games forbidden.*
Feux interdits.	*No fires.*
Il est interdit de marcher sur les pelouses.	*Keep off the grass.*
Ne pas se pencher au dehors.	*Do not lean out of the window.*
Défense d'entrer.	*No trespassing.*
Défense d'afficher.	*Post no bills.*
Défense de déposer des ordures.	*No dumping.*

In 1968, you could read graffiti on the walls of Paris/
«Il est interdit d'interdire. » *"It is forbidden to forbid."*

39 Pouvez-vous lui dire de me les apporter...

A1 PRESENTATION

Grammar

- When there are two personal pronouns (a direct and an indirect object) in a sentence, the pronouns must be placed before the verbal form in a given order: indirect object + direct object. Ex.:

Pierre nous donne un livre. *Pierre gives us a book.*
Pierre nous le donne. *Pierre gives it to us.*

- When the indirect object pronoun is **lui** or **leur** this rule doesn't apply. The order is: direct object + indirect objet. Ex.:

Pierre donne un livre à son amie. *Pierre gives a book to his friend.*
Pierre le lui donne. *Pierre gives it to her.*
Pierre donne un livre aux enfants. *Pierre gives the children a book.*
Pierre le leur donne. *Pierre gives it to them.*

Vocabulary

envoyer	*to send*	**hebdomadaire** (m.)	*weekly*
montrer	*to show*	**abonnement** (masc.)	*subscription*
rendre	*to turn in, to give back*	**rédacteur en chef** (masc.)	*editor*
exemplaire (masc.)	*copy*	**article** (masc.)	*article*
numéro (masc.)	*issue*	**d'urgence**	*urgently*

A2 EXAMPLES *(A weekly paper)* CD

1. **Un libraire demande dix exemplaires du dernier numéro.**
2. **Il faut les lui envoyer d'urgence.**
3. **Est-ce qu'on a envoyé un exemplaire du nouvel hebdomadaire à tous les clients ?**
4. **Est-ce qu'on le leur a envoyé avec des formulaires d'abonnement ?**
5. **Si le facteur apporte du courrier, vous devez le donner à Mme Martin.**
6. **Vous le lui donnerez dès qu'il sera arrivé.**
7. **Quand va-t-on montrer les photos au rédacteur en chef ?**
8. **Il faut les lui montrer dès qu'elles arriveront.**
9. **Il faut que les journalistes nous rendent leurs articles avant cinq heures.**
10. **Il ne faut pas qu'il nous les rendent plus tard.**
11. **Pouvez-vous dire à la secrétaire de m'apporter les articles qu'elles a tapés ?**
12. **Pouvez-vous lui dire de me les apporter immédiatement ?**

A3 COMMENTS

■ Grammar

- **Vous le lui donnerez dès qu'il sera arrivé.**

The compound tense used here is called **futur antérieur**.
It is used in a subordinate clause when the main clause is in the future. It refers to an action which will happen in the future but before the main action.

Ex.: **Quand il aura fini, il rendra son article.**
When he has finished, he'll turn in his article.
(Literally: When he will have finished, he'll turn in his article.)

- The **futur antérieur** is formed with:

avoir or **être** in the future	+	past participle of the verb

- The **futur antérieur** is very much like the **passé composé**. **Avoir** is used with most verbs, but with some of them (see list in lesson 25, C2), **être** is necessary.

Ex.: **Je lirai son roman quand il l'aura écrit.**
I'll read his novel when he has written it.
Dès qu'il sera parti, quelqu'un prendra sa place.
As soon as he leaves, someone will take his place.

With **être** the past participle agrees with the subject.

Ex.: **Dès qu'elle sera partie, quelqu'un prendra sa place.**
As soon as she leaves, someone will take her place.

A4 TRANSLATION

1. A bookseller wants ten copies of the last issue.
2. They must be sent to him urgently.
3. Did we send a copy of the new weekly to all the customers?
4. Did we send it to them with the subscription forms?
5. If the postman brings the mail, you must give it to Mrs. Martin.
6. Give it to her as soon as it arrives.
7. When are we going to show the photos to the editor?
8. We must show them to him as soon as they arrive.
9. The journalists must turn their articles in to us before five o'clock.
10. They mustn't give them in to us any later.
11. Can you tell the secretary to bring me the articles that she typed?
12. Can you tell her to bring them to me immediately?

39 Ne le leur dis pas, même s'ils insistent.

B1 PRESENTATION

Grammar

- With an imperative form, the pronouns must be placed after the verb; the order is : direct object / indirect object.

  Ex.: **Envoyez-le-moi.** *Send it to me.*

- With a negative command, the pronouns are placed before the verb and the order is inverted.

  Ex.: **Ne me l'envoyez pas.** *Don't send it to me.*
  Ne nous les envoyez pas. *Don't send them to us.*

- But with **lui** and **leur** this rule doesn't apply; the order must be:

  ne + indirect object + direct object + verb

  Ex.: **Ne le lui envoyez pas.** *Don't send it to him/her.*
  Ne le leur envoyez pas. *Don't send it to them.*

Vocabulary

insister	*to insist*	**réveillon** (masc.)	*Christmas*
aller	*to fit*	**(de Noël)**	*Eve party*
renvoyer	*to send back*	**(du 1er de l'an)**	*New Year's Eve party*
plaire*	*to please*		
ne pas se gêner (pour)	*not to hesitate, to feel free to*	**gilet** (masc.)	*cardigan*
		même	*even*
ennuyer	*to bother, to annoy*	**en recommandé**	*registered post*

* see C4.

B2 EXAMPLES *(Granny and Grandpa can't come for Christmas)* CD

1. **Nous ne pourrons pas venir pour Noël, explique-le aux enfants.**
2. **Explique-le-leur.**
3. **Ne leur montre pas les cadeaux.**
4. **Ne les leur montre pas encore.**
5. **Ne leur dis pas ce que c'est.**
6. **Ne le leur dis pas, même s'ils insistent.**
7. **Donne-les-leur le soir du réveillon.**
8. **Essaye le gilet que je t'ai fait; s'il ne te va pas, renvoie-le-moi.**
9. **Ne me le renvoie pas trop tard, s'il te plaît.**
10. **S'il ne te plaît pas, dis-le-moi, ne te gêne pas.**
11. **N'oubliez pas de prendre des photos, envoyez-les-nous vite.**
12. **Envoyez-les-nous en recommandé, si cela ne vous ennuie pas.**

39 Don't tell them, even if they insist.

B3 COMMENTS

■ Grammar

- **Ne leur dis pas ce que c'est. Ne le leur dis pas.**
  Note that in **Ne le leur dis pas,** *Don't tell them,*
  or **Dis-le-leur,** *Tell them,*
  Dis-le-moi, *Tell me,*
  Dis-le-lui, *Tell him/her,*
  le, meaning *it*, summing up a whole sentence, has no equivalent in the English expression, but it should not be omitted in French although you may sometimes hear **Dis-lui** or **Dis-leur** in familiar speech.
- **S'il ne te plaît pas beaucoup...** *If you don't like it very much...*
  But remember that *very* has no equivalent here, **très** doesn't appear in the French sentence.
  Ex.: **Merci beaucoup !** *Thank you very much!*
- **Si cela ne vous ennuie pas.** *If it's not too much bother/trouble.*
  (Literally: if it doesn't annoy you.)
  Note the construction of the French expression.
- For verbs ending in **-oyer** or **-uyer** in the infinitive (ex.: **envoyer, ennuyer**), there is a change of spelling when the ending of the conjugation is a silent **e**: **e / es / ent**.
  Ex.: **Tu envoies, ennuies / il envoie, ennuie**
  elles envoient, ennuient.

B4 TRANSLATION

1. We can't come for Christmas; explain this to the children.
2. Explain it to them.
3. Don't show them the presents.
4. Don't show them to them yet.
5. Don't tell them what they are.
6. Don't tell them, even if they insist.
7. Give them to them on Christmas Eve.
8. Try on the cardigan that I made for you; if it doesn't fit, send it back to me.
9. Don't send it back to me too late, please.
10. If you don't like it, tell me so, don't hesitate to be frank.
11. Don't forget to take photos, send them to us quickly.
12. Send them to us by registered post, if it's not too much bother.

39 Exercises

C1 EXERCISES

A. Replace the nouns by pronouns :

1. Ne montre pas cette lettre à ton fils.
2. Donnez les résultats des élections aux journalistes.
3. Ne vends pas ta voiture à cette personne.
4. Apporte ces fleurs à tes parents.
5. Ne loue pas ton appartement à cet homme.
6. Achetez-nous les billets.

B. (CD) Translate into French :

1. When you have finished your article, we'll go and see the editor.
2. If he doesn't like your article very much, he'll tell you at once.
3. Send me a copy of your new novel, if it's not too much bother.
4. I am going to meet some journalists, I would like to show it to them.

C2 ANSWERS

A. 1. Ne la lui montre pas.
2. Donnez-les-leur.
3. Ne la lui vends pas.
4. Apporte-les-leur.
5. Ne le lui loue pas.
6. Achetez-les-nous.

B. 1. Quand tu auras (vous aurez) fini ton (votre) article, nous irons voir le rédacteur en chef.
2. Si ton (votre) article ne lui plaît pas beaucoup, il te (vous) le dira tout de suite.
3. Envoie (envoyez)-moi un exemplaire de ton (votre) dernier roman, si cela ne t'(vous) ennuie pas.
4. Je vais rencontrer des journalistes, je voudrais le leur montrer.

C3 IMMIGRATION

■ France has always been a land that welcomes populations of diverse origins. At the end of the 19th century, a decrease in population growth incited employers to have recourse to immigrant workers. Later, White Russians fleeing the Communist Revolution, and, twenty years after that, Spanish Republicans forced to leave their country came in great numbers to France, taking advantage of the right to political asylum. Still, it was mainly the need for a masculine workforce which has been and remains the major cause for the transfer of foreign populations to French territory.

■ There are today more than four and one half million immigrants, forming a important component of the population. In a Europe with a decreasing, aging population, this aspect of the question cannot be ignored. There is frequently a confusion between "immigrant" and "foreigner". Some of the immigrants, around ten thousand per year, become French citizens through naturalization and thus drop out of the population of four million foreigners. The reform of the law on the acquisition of French nationality stipulates that "Any foreigner born in France of foreign parents may, from the age of 16 to the age of 21, acquire French nationality on the condition that he expresses the desire to do so, that he resides in France at the date when he indicates this desire, and that he can justify having habitually resided in France during the five years which precede the request" (Article 44).

■ The presence of numerous foreigners as well as of numerous immigrants fuels a political and occasionally passionate debate for they are, in a time of crisis, undesirable, and they are presented by the far right as "threatening national identity". Their integration, one of the major stakes in French domestic politics, is impeded by a variety of obstacles : the action of certain foreign governments which encourage their citizens to maintain their nationality, the instability of bachelors who have kept family ties in their country of origin, the constitution of ghettos which perpetuate values linked to the country of origin, etc. On the contrary, the action of school, marriage, and political and trade union activism are all factors which tend to promote assimilation.

D1 MESSAGE SUR REPONDEUR (CD)

Nathalie : Tiens tu es là Bruno !
Bruno : Oui, j'arrive à l'instant.
Nathalie : Est-ce que tu as écouté le répondeur ?
Bruno : J'allais le faire.
Bonjour ici Pierre. Mercredi six heures, j'appelle à propos de l'article que tu nous a promis. S'il est prêt envoie-le moi tout de suite, il faut que je le fasse photocopier et que j'en donne un exemplaire à Gérard. Il en a besoin d'urgence. Merci d'avance. A bientôt.
Bruno : Zut ! Il me l'a déjà demandé hier cet article. Il faut absolument que je le lui porte ce soir.
Ce message est pour Nathalie Brifard : la montre que vous nous avez laissée en réparation est prête. Vous pouvez passer la prendre dès demain. Merci.
Nathalie : Enfin, ils me l'ont réparée !
Bonjour. C'est Marie, Désolée pour le dîner de samedi, je suis obligée de l'annuler. Je vous rappellerai.....

D2 NOM, PRÉNOM
NAME, FIRST NAME

- Remember that to introduce oneself or somebody else, the commonly used expression is :

Je m'appelle *...	*My name is...* (literally : *I call myself...*)
Tu t'appelles *...	*Your name is...*
Il, elle s'appelle *...	*His, her, its name is...*
Nous nous appelons...	*Our names are...*
Vous vous appelez...	*Your names are..., your name is...*
Ils, elles s'appellent *...	*Their names are...*

- **Comment vous appelez-vous ?**
  Comment tu t'appelles ?] *What's your name ?*

* Notice the double **l** : in that case, the first **e** is pronounced like e in *pet.* In **appelons** and **appelez**, only one **l** and the **e** is glided over.

D3 MESSAGE ON THE ANSWERING MACHINE

Nathalie : Oh, you're there, Bruno !
Bruno : Yes, I just came in.
Nathalie : Have you listened to your answering machine ?
Bruno : I was going to.
Hello, this is Pierre. Wednesday, six o'clock. I'm calling about the article you promised us. If it's ready, send it to me right away ; I've got to have it photocopied and give a copy to Gérard. He needs it urgently. Thanks in advance. See you soon.
Bruno : Darn ! He already asked me yesterday for that article. I've absolutely got to take it to him this evening.
This message is for Nathalie Brifard : the watch you left us to be repaired is ready. You can come pick it up anytime after today. Thank you.
Nathalie : They've finally fixed it for me !
Hello, this is Marie. Sorry about the dinner on Saturday, but I'm obliged to call it off. I'll call you back.

D4 CE LIVRE VOUS PLAÎT ? *DO YOU LIKE THIS BOOK ?*

- The verb **plaire** is frequently used in French to convey the meaning of *to like*.

Ex. :

Ce livre me plaît.	*I like this book.*
Cet appartement leur plaît.	*They like this flat.*
Vous lui plaisez.	*He/she likes you.*
Il ne me plaît pas.	*I don't like him.*
Est-ce que ça vous plaît ?	*Do you like it ?*

- **plaire** is found in the different tenses.

Ex. :

Est-ce que ça vous a plu ?	*Did you like it ?*
Vous lui plaisiez beaucoup.	*He liked you very much.*
Comme il vous plaira.	*As you like it.*

- It is also found of course in : **s'il te plaît, s'il vous plaît.**

40 Il faut un slogan simple pour que les gens...

A1 PRESENTATION

Grammar

- **Pour que, pour qu'...** conveys the meaning of *so that*.
  Bien que, bien qu'... conveys the meaning of *though*.
- Both conjunctions are followed by the **subjonctif** in French.
  Ex.: **Je lui écris pour qu'elle vienne à Noël.**
  I am writing to her so that she comes at Christmas.
  Bien qu'il soit très jeune, il a réussi son examen.
  Though he is very young he passed his exam.

Vocabulary

passer devant	*to walk by*
faire attention	*to pay attention*
attirer l'attention	*to draw attention*
se souvenir	*to remember*
remarquer	*to notice*
slogan (masc.)	*slogan*
œuvre d'art (fem.)	*work of art*
efficace	*effective*
vif (masc.)/**vive** (fem.)	*bright*
presque	*nearly*
donc	*therefore*

A2 EXAMPLES *(Posters)* (CD)

1. **Que faut-il pour que les affiches soient efficaces ?**
2. **Bien qu'il y en ait presque partout dans les villes, les gens ne les voient pas toujours.**
3. **Bien qu'ils passent devant plusieurs fois par jour, ils n'y font pas attention.**
4. **Pour qu'on les voie que faut-il faire ?**
5. **Que faut-il faire pour qu'on s'en souvienne ?**
6. **Bien que les gens ne les regardent pas vraiment, elles doivent attirer leur attention.**
7. **Elles doivent attirer leur attention pour qu'ils achètent.**
8. **Il faut donc des couleurs vives pour qu'on les remarque.**
9. **Il faut un slogan simple pour que les gens s'en souviennent.**
10. **Pour qu'on puisse le lire vite et facilement.**
11. **Il vaut mieux qu'il soit drôle pour plaire à tous.**
12. **Bien qu'elles soient faites pour vendre, les affiches peuvent être des œuvres d'art.**

A3 COMMENTS

■ Grammar

- Note that, with **pour**, when the subject is the same in the main clause and in the subordinate, the infinitive is used, not the subjunctive. Ex.:

  Il nous écrit pour donner des nouvelles.
  He is writing to tell us how he is.

  but **Il nous écrit pour que nous donnions de nos nouvelles.**
  He is writing us to know how we are.
  (Literally: *So that we give news.*)

- Remember that **être fait pour** is the French equivalent of *to be meant for* or *to be fit for.*

  C'est fait pour être vu. *It is meant to be seen.*
  Il n'est pas fait pour ce travail. *He's not fit for this job.*

- **vif, vive:** all adjectives ending in **f** in the masculine change into **ve** in the feminine. Ex.: **naïf, naïve**.

- We have already seen words which are the same in French and in English; **slogan** is another one; so are: **sandwich, barman, babysitter, interview...**
  But some words borrowed from English have been slightly altered:
  parking means *car park,*
  camping " *camp ground, site.*

A4 TRANSLATION

1. What is necessary for posters to be effective?
2. Though they are nearly everywhere in the cities, people don't always see them.
3. Though they walk by them several times a day, they don't pay any attention to them.
4. What must be done so that they are seen?
5. What must be done so that they are remembered?
6. Though people don't really look at them, they must draw their attention.
7. They must draw people's attention so that they buy.
8. Therefore they need to have bright colours so that they are noticed.
9. They need a simple slogan so that people can remember it.
10. So that people can read it quickly and easily.
11. It is better if it is funny so that everyone likes it.
12. Though they are meant to sell, posters can be works of art.

40 Ils joueront jusqu'à ce que tout le monde s'en aille.

B1 PRESENTATION

■ Grammar

- **avant que** conveys the meaning of *before* followed by a subordinate clause;
  en attendant que, jusqu'à ce que both convey the meaning of *till, until*.
  Both conjunctions are followed by the **subjonctif** in French.
  Ex.: **Je prépare tout avant qu'ils ne soient là.**
  I prepare everything before they are there.
  Jouons aux cartes en attendant qu'ils viennent.
  Let's play cards till they come.

■ Vocabulary

décorer	*to decorate*	**tombée** (fem.)	*fall*
bavarder	*to chat*	**feu d'artifice** (masc.)	*fireworks*
façade (fem.)	*front*	**foule** (fem.)	*crowd*
drapeau (masc.)	*flag*	**bal** (masc.)	*ball, dance*
défilé (masc.)	*parade*	**fête** (fem.)	*feast, holiday*
rang (masc.)	*row*		
		en attendant	*meanwhile*

B2 EXAMPLES *(Bastille Day, July 14th)* (CD)

1. **Les façades sont décorées de drapeaux avant que les cérémonies n'aient lieu.**
2. **Le matin, un défilé est organisé dans chaque ville ; les gens sont déjà là avant qu'il ne commence.**
3. **Tout le monde se dépêche pour être au premier rang avant que passe le défilé.**
4. **Il ne commencera pas avant que le maire ne soit là.**
5. **Les gens bavardent en attendant.**
6. **Il y aura des feux d'artifice après la tombée de la nuit.**
7. **La foule se promène dans les rues en attendant qu'il fasse nuit.**
8. **S'il y a un orage on attendra jusqu'à ce qu'il ne pleuve plus !**
9. **Il y a aussi des bals presque partout ; les musiciens bavardent en attendant que les gens arrivent.**
10. **Ils joueront jusqu'à ce qu'il n'y ait plus personne.**
11. **Ils joueront jusqu'à ce que tout le monde s'en aille.**
12. **On entendra de la musique jusqu'à ce que la fête finisse.**

40 They will play till everyone goes.

B3 COMMENTS

Grammar

- **Les façades sont décorées de drapeaux. Un défilé est organisé**, those sentences are in the passive.
  Its construction is: subject + **être** + past participle.
  This form is less often used in French than it is in English as **on** and an active voice usually express what is expressed in English by a passive.
  Ex.: **On a volé un tableau célèbre.**
  A famous painting has been stolen.
  However, the passive is found in French to emphasize the result of an action.
- **avant que passe le défilé**, note that the verb can precede the subject.
- **avant qu'il ne commence, avant que le maire ne soit là.**
  Note that, even in a statement, you can find **ne** between the subject and the verbal form in subordinate clauses introduced by **avant que**.
- Note that **en attendant que** is followed by a subjonctive.
  Ex.: **En attendant qu'il vienne.**

  en attendant de is followed by an infinitive.
  Ex.: **En attendant de partir.**

B4 TRANSLATION

1. The house fronts are decorated with flags before the ceremonies take place.
2. In the morning, a parade is organized in every city; people are already there before it starts.
3. Everyone hurries to be in the front row before the parade passes by.
4. It won't start before the mayor is there.
5. Meanwhile people are chatting.
6. There will be fireworks after nightfall.
7. The crowd strolls in the streets till it is dark.
8. If there is a storm, they will wait until it stops raining.
9. There are also balls nearly everywhere; the musicians chat while waiting for people to come.
10. They will play till there is no one left.
11. They will play till everyone goes.
12. Music will be heard until the holiday's over.

C1 EXERCISES

A. Put the verb int he correct form :

1. Téléphone-leur avant qu'ils ne (partir) de chez eux. – 2. Le client doit attendre jusqu'à ce qu'on lui (donner) sa carte de crédit. – 3. Restons là en attendant qu'il (faire) beau. – 4. J'envoie un colis aujourd'hui pour qu'elle l'(avoir) avant mardi. – 5. Bien qu'elle n'(aller) pas très loin, elle prendra l'avion.

B. Put the verb in the right form :

1. Une nouvelle étoile vient d'être (découvrir). – 2. Ces lettres ont été (écrire) il y a cent ans. – 3. Une église va être (construire) près de la gare. – 4. La circulation devrait être (interdite) ici. – 5. Est-ce que la piscine est (ouvrir) le dimanche ? – 6. Les listes n'ont pas encore été (faire).

C2 ANSWERS

A. 1. Téléphone-leur avant qu'ils ne partent de chez eux.
2. Le client doit attendre jusqu'à ce qu'on lui donne sa carte de crédit.
3. Restons là en attendant qu'il fasse beau.
4. J'envoie un colis aujourd'hui pour qu'elle l'ait avant mardi.
5. Bien qu'elle n'aille pas très loin, elle prendra l'avion.

B. 1. Une nouvelle étoile vient d'être découverte.
2. Ces lettres ont été écrites il y a cent ans.
3. Une église va être construite près de la gare.
4. La circulation devrait être interdite ici.
5. Est-ce que la piscine est ouverte le dimanche ?
6. Les listes n'ont pas encore été faites.

C3 CINEMA

■ In 1895, the **Lumière** brothers shot the first moving pictures. Since that time, France has always been considered the land of the "Seventh Art." **Meliès and Max Linder** were its pioneers. Among the great directors in the period before World War II, **Marcel Pagnol** should be mentioned : he successfully transferred his theatrical productions to film with movies such as **Marius, Fanny,** and **César**, and produced the films that **Fernandel** and **Raimu** made so successful. **Carné** with "The Evening Visitors", **Prévert**, and **Renoir** with "Children of Paradise," illustrated what was called "poetic realism".

■ By the beginning of the sixties, the arrival of television was partially responsible for a major crisis in cinema. During that period, **Bresson** and **Tati** refused to be identified with a "school". Rejection of conventional screenplays coupled with a need to find a new cinematic voice gave birth to the New Wave represented by **Alain Resnais** («Hiroshima, My Love, » 1959), **François Truffaut** («The 400 Blows »), **Jean Luc Godard** («Breathless »), and **Claude Chabrol**. The French tradition of cinéma d'auteur continues, even if production constraints are increasingly heavy.

■ Today, France has 4400 movie theaters, the second largest number in Europe after Russia, which draw some 130 million spectators per year. It produces each year around one hundred feature films, a third of which are debuts, putting it in third place world wide after the United States and India. Close to a third of movie goers in France got to see French films. Directors such as **Bertrand Tavernier, Bertrand Blier, Maurice Pialat, Luc Besson** (**Le Grand Bleu, Le 5**[e] **élément**), **Jean Jacques Beinex** (**Diva**), **Jean Jacques. Annaud** (the Bear) or **Patrice Chéreau** are very successful. Since 1946, the city of **Cannes** has hosted the renowned Cannes Film Festival, perhaps the most important annual gathering of the entertainment industry, which includes an ever-increasing number of retrospectives or homages celebrating the body of work of different directors or actors.

D1 AU CINEMA (CD)

Bastien : J'irais bien au cinéma. Qu'est-ce qu'on joue dans le quartier ?

Fabienne : Je crois qu'il y a de bons films. Jette un coup d'oeil sur le programme en attendant que je me prépare.

Bastien : Voyons.... On donne un western à l'Escurial.

Fabienne : Ça ne m'emballe pas. J'aimerais mieux un polar.

Bastien : On redonne « Le Cercle Rouge » au Palace.

Fabienne : Bien que ce soit un excellent film, je préférerais voir quelque chose de plus nouveau.

Bastien : Un film de science fiction ?

Fabienne : Pourquoi pas ? Mais il faut se décider sinon on va rater le début de la séance.

Bastien : Je te propose le film qui a eu la Palme d'Or au Festival de Cannes. Il a un succès fou

Fabienne : Il va falloir faire la queue, alors ?

Bastien : Tant pis, ça doit valoir la peine.

D2 IL ÉTAIT UNE FOIS.../ *ONCE UPON A TIME*

Plusieurs fois par jour is the equivalent of *several times a day*; note the presence of **par** and the absence of an article (literally : *several times by day*). Similar expressions :

Une fois par an	*Once a year*
Deux fois par semaine	*Twice a week*
Dix fois par jour	*Ten times a day*

Expressions :

Combien de fois ?	*How many times ?*
Encore une fois	*Once more*
À la fois	*For once*
Une fois pour toutes	*Once and for all*

D3 AT THE MOVIES

Bastien : I'd like to go to the movies. What's playing in the neighborhood ?

Fabienne : I think there are some good films. Have a look at the program while I get ready.

Bastien : Let's see. There's a western at the Escurial.

Fabienne : I don't feel like seeing a western. I'd rather see a thriller.

Bastien : They're playing « The Red Circle » again at the Palace.

Fabienne : Even though it's an excellent film, I'd rather see something more recent.

Bastien : A science fiction film ?

Fabienne : Why not ? But we have to decide or we're going to miss the beginning of the show.

Bastien : I suggest the movie that won the Golden Palm at the Cannes Festival. It's a really big hit.

Fabienne : Are we going to have to stand in line (GB : to queue up), then ?

Bastien : Never mind, it should be worth it.

D4 PRENDRE CONGÉ…
TO TAKE LEAVE…

In addition to au **revoir**, here are some expressions to take leave of someone/

Je vous laisse, je vous quitte.	*I'm leaving (you).*
Adieu	*Farewell*
À bientôt	*See you soon*
Au plaisir de vous revoir	*I hope we shall meet again*

Complete with a, b, c or d : (There is only one correct answer for each item)

1. Nous ——— en train de parler du match d'hier.
   a) était
   b) étais
   c) étions
   d) étaient

2. Elles ne nous ——— pas attendre.
   a) feront
   b) ferons
   c) fera
   d) ferez

3. Je ——— contente quand tu ——— ton examen.
   a) sera aura
   b) serai auras
   c) serez aurez
   d) serons auras

4. Est-ce que tu as du café ? Non, ———
   a) je n'ai pas
   b) je n'y ai pas
   c) je n'en ai pas
   d) je n'ai

5. Si tu rencontrais Pierre, tu ——— l'inviter.
   a) pourras
   b) peux
   c) pouvais
   d) pourrais

6. Demande leur ce qu'ils ———.
   a) veut
   b) voulons
   c) veulent
   d) voulez

7. Il faut que tu ——— à l'heure.
   a) es
   b) être
   c) soyez
   d) sois

8. Ne montre pas ce livre à Marie. Ne ——— pas
   a) le lui montre
   b) lui le montre
   c) montre le lui
   d) montre lui le

9. Nous attendrons jusqu'à ce que le spectacle ———
   a) finir
   b) finit
   c) finisse
   d) finissait

10. Pourquoi lui écris-tu ? Pour qu'elle ——— où je suis.
   a) savoir
   b) sait
   c) savait
   d) sache

CORRECTION DES TESTS :

KEYS TESTS - LESSONS 1 TO 10

1. b) 2. d) 3. a) 4. b) 5. c)
6. b) 7. c) 8. d) 9. a) 10. b)

KEYS TESTS - LESSONS 11 TO 20

1. a) 2. b) 3. c) 4. b) 5. d)
6. a) 7. b) 8. c) 9. c) 10.c)

KEYS TESTS - LESSONS 21 TO 30

1.a) 2. c) 3. c) 4. b) 5. d)
6. b) 7. d) 8. c) 9. b) 10. d)

KEYS TESTS - LESSONS 31 TO 40

1. c) 2. a) 3. b) 4. c) 5. d)
6. c) 7. d) 8. a) 9. c) 10. d)

GRAMMAR SUMMARY

Content .... pages

1 - STATEMENTS

As far as the construction of simple statements is concerned, there are few differences between French and English.

Ex.: **Pierre est français.** *Pierre is French.*
Il habite à Paris. *He lives in Paris.*

Of course the structures can be more complex and this grammar summary will help you to construct them.

2 - NEGATIVE STATEMENTS

Negative statements are formed with **ne ... pas** on either side of the verb.

Ex.: **Je ne fume pas.** *I don't smoke.*
Ce n'est pas* difficile. *It isn't difficult.*

* **n' ... pas** is used when the verb starts with a vowel or **h**.

Ne/n' ... rien, *not anything* **ne/n' ... plus,** *no more/no longer* **ne/n' ... jamais,** *never,*
are used in the same way.

Ex.: **Je n'achète rien.** *I don't buy anything.*
Nous ne travaillons plus. *We no longer work.*
Ils ne sortent jamais. *They never go out.*

3 - QUESTIONS

To turn a statement into a question:

1. You may simply modify the intonation of the statement without changing the structure (see lesson 3, A3).
   Ex.: **Tu chantes ?** *Do you sing?*
2. **Est-ce que** can be placed at the beginning of the statement.
   Ex.: **Est-ce que tu chantes ?** *Are you singing?*
   Est-ce que c'est cher ? *Is it expensive?*
3. When the subject is a pronoun, the subject and the verb can be inverted (mostly with: **vous, il, elle, ils, elles**).
   Ex.: **Chantez-vous ?** *Are you singing?*
   Prennent-ils le train ? *– Do they take the train?*
   When the verb is inverted, it is joined to the pronoun by a hyphen.
   Ex.: **Parlez-vous français ?** *Do you speak French?*
   If the verb ends with a vowel, **t** is introduced between the verb and **il** or **elle**.
   Ex.: **Parle-t-elle français ?** *Does she speak French?*

4. In more elegant French, you can find both a subject and a pronoun which recalls it following the verbal form:

subject + verbal form + pronoun + ...

Ex.: **Pierre va-t-il parler ?**
Is Pierre going to speak?
Ta sœur vient-elle demain ?
Is your sister coming tomorrow?

---

4 - NOUNS

■ GENDER

- All nouns in French are either masculine or feminine. For persons or animals this corresponds to male or female.
- For things or concepts, there is no real rule; for instance, trains are masculine and cars are feminine; it is therefore best to learn the gender when you learn the word. In this book, (masc.) or (fem.), after the noun, indicate the gender. This will help you to memorize the noun with an article. For nouns indicating persons or animals, the feminine can be formed:

  1. by adding **e** to the masculine.
  Ex.: **ami - amie** (the pronunciation doesn't change);
  client - cliente, candidat - candidate (the final consonant is heard);
  chat - chatte (the final consonant is doubled and heard);

  2. by changing the ending.
  Ex.: **directeur - directrice** *manager*
  chanteur - chanteuse *singer*

- Some nouns remain the same in the masculine and the feminine.
  Ex.: **secrétaire, journaliste, artiste.**
  secretary, journalist, artist.
- Some are completely different.
  Ex.: **homme - femme** *man - woman*
  mari - femme *husband - wife*
  frère - sœur *brother - sister*

■ NUMBER

- The plural of nouns is generally formed by adding **s** to the singular:
  un ami - des amis - une amie - des amies,
  a friend - friends
  un livre - des livres
  a book - books
- For most nouns ending with **eau, eu, x** is added instead of **s**.
  Ex.: **un oiseau - des oiseaux** *a bird - birds* **un cheveu - des cheveux** *a hair - hairs*

- For most nouns ending with **al** or **ail** the ending changes into **aux** in the plural.

  Ex.: **un cheval - des chevaux** *a horse - horses*
  un travail - des travaux *work - works*

- Nouns ending with **s, z,** and **x** in the singular do not change in the plural.

  Ex.: **un nez - des nez** *a nose - noses*
  un repas - des repas *a meal - meals*
  un prix - des prix *a price - prices*

- Generally family names do not change in the plural.

  Ex.: **les Lenoir, les Martin.**

5 - ARTICLES

In French the article agrees in gender and number with the noun it accompanies.

■ DEFINITE AND INDEFINITE ARTICLES

	Indefinite		Definite		
	masc.	fem.	masc.	fem.	contract. (with à & de) masc. fem.
sing.	**un**	**une**	**le (l')**	**la (l')**	**à + le = au** **de + le = du**
plur.	**des**		**les**		**à + les = aux** **de + les = des**

Remember that it is practically impossible to use a noun alone in French, an article (or a partitive, possessive, demonstrative, numeral, etc.) is almost always necessary.

■ PARTITIVE ARTICLES

The partitive construction requires: **de** + the appropriate singular definite article:

AFFIRMATIVE		NÉGATIVE
fem.	masc.	masc. fem.
de la salade **de l'**eau	**du** vin **de l'**argent	pas **de** café pas **d'**eau

In the plural, only one possibility:

des légumes **pas de légumes**
des enfants **pas d'enfants**

In English the partitive article is often omitted; in French it must <u>always</u> be expressed. Ex.: **Nous avons du vin et de l'eau.**
We have got wine and water.

6 - NUMBER AND QUANTITY

- To ask a question about either a number or a quantity, the interrogative word is: **combien de/d'** *how many / how much?*

Countable nouns

For a large number	For a small number
beaucoup de/d' + plur. *a lot of, many*	**peu de/d'** + plur. *few* **quelques** + plur. *a few, some*

Non-countable nouns

For a large quantity	For a small quantity
beaucoup de/d' + sing. *a lot of, much*	**peu de/d', un peu de/d'** + sing. *little, a little*

- A subjective judgment about a number or a quantity can be expressed by:

trop de/d' *too many, too much*
assez de/d' *enough*
pas assez de/d' *not enough*

Ex. **beaucoup d'amis, peu d'amis, quelques amis, beaucoup de courage, peu de courage, pas assez de courage.**

7 - ADJECTIVES

AGREEMENT

- The adjective always agrees in gender and number with the noun it accompanies.

Ex.: **un hiver froid, une nuit froide**
a cold winter, a cold night
des hivers froids, des nuits froides
cold winters, cold nights

- When an adjective refers to several nouns, and at least one of them is masculine, the form of the adjective is masculine plural.

FEMININE

- To form a feminine adjective, the usual rule is to add **e** to the masculine form.

Ex.: **joli - jolie** *pretty*
bleu - bleue *blue*

(The pronunciation doesn't change.)

- When the masculine adjective ends with an **e** there is no change in the feminine.

Ex.: **jeune** *young*
moderne *modern*

- When the masculine adjective ends with a consonant which is not heard, the rule applies and the final consonant is then heard, the **e** is glided over.

Ex.: **grand - grande** *big, great*
intelligent - intelligente *intelligent*

- If the final consonant is an **x**, it generally turns into **se** in the feminine.

Ex.: **joyeux - joyeuse** *merry*
délicieux - délicieuse *delicious*

(But **doux - douce** *soft, mild.*)

- If the final consonant is an **f** it generally turns into **ve** in the feminine.

Ex.: **vif - vive** *bright*
neuf - neuve *new*

- Other minor changes of spelling (ex.: final consonant doubled in **gentil - gentille**) are systematically indicated when a new adjective appears in the lessons.

- Here are some adjectives with a particular feminine form:

beau - belle *beautiful*
nouveau - nouvelle *new*
vieux - vieille *old*

■ PLURAL

- To form the plural of an adjective, the usual rule is to add **s** to the singular, whether masculine or feminine.

Ex.: **joli - jolis** *pretty*
jolie - jolies *pretty*
triste - tristes *sad*

(Remember that the final consonant is not heard.)

- Adjectives ending with **eau** in the singular add **x** instead of **s** in the plural.

Ex.: **beau - beaux** *beautiful*
nouveau - nouveaux *new*

- Adjectives ending with **s** or **x** in the singular do not change in the plural.

Ex.: **gris - gris** *grey*
vieux - vieux *old*

■ PLACE

Most adjectives are placed after the noun they accompany. However some short, commonly used adjectives are placed before the noun. Here are the most frequently met:

masc.	fem.	
bon	**bonne**	*good*
cher	**chère**	*dear*
grand	**grande**	*tall, big, great*
jeune	**jeune**	*young*
joli	**jolie**	*pretty*
long	**longue**	*long*
mauvais	**mauvaise**	*bad*
petit	**petite**	*little*
vieux/vieil	**vieille**	*old*
nouveau	**nouvelle**	*new*

8 - ADVERBS

Most adverbs are formed by adding **ment** to the feminine adjective.

Ex.: masc. sing.	fem. sing.	adverb
lent *(slow)*	**lente**	**lentement** *(slowly)*
rapide *(fast)*	**rapide**	**rapidement** *(fast)*

But not all adverbs end in **ment**, especially adverbs of:

time:	**souvent**	*often*
	maintenant	*now*
	parfois	*sometimes*
place:	**ici**	*here*
	là	*there*
	loin	*far*
and	**bien**	*well*
	mal	*badly*

All adverbs are invariable.

■ PLACE

Adverbs are usually placed after the verb they modify.

Ex.: **Elle parle lentement.**
She speaks slowly.
Ils viennent souvent.
They often come.
Tu danses bien.
You dance well.

9 - COMPARATIVES AND SUPERLATIVES

■ COMPARATIVES

With adjectives and adverbs the comparative form is as follows:

+	**plus**	adjective/adverb	**que/qu'**
=	**aussi**	....	**que/qu'**
–	**moins**	....	**que/qu'**

Ex.: **Pierre est plus jeune que Louis.**
Pierre is younger than Louis.

Il est plus intelligent que Louis.
He is more intelligent than Louis.

Anne est aussi jolie qu'Hélène.
Anne is as pretty as Hélène.

Louis est moins riche que Pierre.
Louis is less rich than Pierre.

The pronoun after **que/qu'** must be a strong pronoun: **moi, toi, lui, elle, eux.**

Ex.: **Pierre est plus petit que moi.** *Pierre is smaller than me.*

With nouns the comparative form is as follows:

+	**plus**	**de/d'**	+ noun
=	**autant**	**de/d'**	....
–	**moins**	**de/d'**	....

Ex.: **plus d'argent, autant d'argent, moins d'argent**
more money, as much money, less money.

■ SUPERLATIVES

The superlative is formed by placing:

le, la, les plus... *the most*
le, la, les moins... *the least*

before the adjective.

Ex.: **C'est la plus intelligente.**
She is the most intelligent.
C'est le plus drôle.
He is the funniest.
Ce livre est le moins cher.
This book is the least expensive.

After a superlative, the complement is introduced by **de** or the contracted form **du**.

Ex.: **le plus grand immeuble de la ville.**
the tallest building in town.
la plus belle fille du monde.
the most beautiful girl in the world.

■ IRREGULAR COMPARATIVES AND SUPERLATIVES

bon *(good)*:
meilleur (masc. sg.) **... que,** **meilleure** (fem. sg.) **... que**
meilleurs (masc. pl.) **... que,** **meilleures** (fem. pl.) **... que**
= *better than...*
le, la, les meilleur(e)(s) = *the best...*

bien *(well)*: **mieux que** = *better... than*
le mieux = *the best*

mauvais *(bad)*: **pire que** = *worse than* (both masc. and fem.)
le pire = *the worst*

10 - DEMONSTRATIVES

■ ADJECTIVES

	masc.	fem.	
sg.	**ce**	**cette**	***this / that***
plur.	**ces**		***these / those***

Ex.: **ce garçon** *this (that) boy*
cette femme *this (that) woman*
ces amis *these (those) friends*

Ce becomes **cet** before a vowel or **h**: **cet ami, cet homme.**

■ PRONOUNS

The demonstrative pronoun agrees in gender and number with the noun it refers to:

(masc. sg.) **celui** (fem. sg.) **celle**
(masc. pl.) **ceux** (fem. pl.) **celles**

-ci can be added to the pronoun
celui-ci **celle-ci** *this (one)*
ceux-ci **celles-ci** *these (ones)*

-là can be added to the pronoun
celui-là **celle-là** *that (one)*
ceux-là **celles-là** *those (ones)*

Ex.:
Est-ce que vous utilisez un ordinateur ? **Oui, celui-ci.**
Are you using a computer? *Yes, this one.*
Est-ce que vous avez une voiture ? **Oui, c'est celle-ci.**
Have you got a car? *Yes, it is this one.*

Ceci is the French equivalent of *this* used alone.

Cela is the French equivalent of *that* used alone.
In colloquial French **cela** is frequently contracted to **ça**.

Ex.: **Je n'aime pas cela/ça.** *I don't like that (it).*

11 - POSSESSION

In French, possession is generally expressed with the preposition **de** followed by the name of the possessor.
There is no form corresponding to the possessive case.

Ex.: **la voiture de Pierre** *Peter's car*
le sac de la secrétaire *the secretary's bag*

It is comparable to « the car of Peter », « the bag of the secretary ».

À qui ? is the equivalent of *whose?*

Ex.: **À qui est la voiture ?** *Whose car is it?* (literally: to whom is the car?)
À qui sont ces vêtements ? *Whose clothes are they?*

Être à is commonly used to answer a question starting with **À qui.**

Ex.: **À qui est ce livre ?** *Whose book is it?*
Il est à Pierre. *It is Peter's.*

■ POSSESSIVE ADJECTIVES

The French possessive adjective agrees in gender and number with the noun it accompanies:

masc. sg.	fem. sg.	masc. & fem. plural	
mon **ton** **son** **notre** **votre** **leur**	**ma** **ta** **sa** **notre** **votre** **leur**	**mes** **tes** **ses** **nos** **vos** **leurs**	*my* *your* *his, her, its* *our* *your* *their*

ma, ta, sa change into **mon, ton, son** when preceding a vowel or **h.**

Ex.: **mon amie, son histoire** *my friend, his/her story*
(**amie, histoire** are feminine nouns.)

■ POSSESSIVE PRONOUNS

le mien, la mienne **les miens, les miennes**	à moi	*mine*
le tien, la tienne **les tiens, les tiennes**	à toi	*yours*
le sien, la sienne **les siens, les siennes**	à lui, à elle	*his, hers, its*
le nôtre, la nôtre **les nôtres**	à nous	*ours*
le vôtre, la vôtre **les vôtres**	à vous	*yours*
le leur, la leur, les leurs	à eux, à elles	*theirs*

Ex.:

Ce livre est à elle ; c'est <u>le sien</u>. *It is hers.*
Ces livres sont à elle ; ce sont <u>les siens</u>. *They are hers.*
Ce livre est à nous ; c'est <u>le nôtre</u>. *It is ours.*
Ces livres sont à nous ; ce sont <u>les nôtres</u>. *They are ours.*

12 - PERSONAL PRONOUNS

		Subject	Direct object	Indirect object (without preposition)	Indirect object (with preposition)
SING.	1re	**je/j'**	**me, m'**	**me**	**moi**
	2e	**tu**	**te, t',**	**te**	**toi**
	3e	**il** **elle** **on****	**le, l', se*, s'*** **la, l', se*, s'*** **le, la, l', se, s'**	**lui, se** **en, y**	**lui** **elle** **lui, elle, soi**
PLUR.	1re	**nous**	**nous**	**nous**	**nous**
	2e	**vous**	**vous**	**vous**	**vous**
	3e	**ils** **elles**	**les, se, s'**	**leur, se** **en, y**	**eux** **elles**

Remember that **tu/te/toi** are used for a child, a person you know very well, a relative or a friend.

* **se/s'** is a reflexive pronoun.

Ex.: **Il <u>se</u> lave.** *He washes (himself).*

** **on** is an impersonal pronoun used when the subject is unknown or when the speaker is more interested in *what is/was done* than in *who does/did it*; it is therefore a frequent equivalent of the English passive.

Ex.: **On vient.** *Someone is coming.*

On a ouvert un nouveau musée.
A new museum has been opened.

In colloquial French **on** is often used instead of **nous.**

Ex.: **On part à 5 heures.** *We are leaving at 5 o'clock.*

- Remember that **quelqu'un** = *somebody, anybody,* **personne** = *nobody* are indefinite personal pronouns.
- **En** and **y** can be indefinite personal pronouns used as indirect objects.

Ex.: **Il parle de sa femme, il en parle.**
He speaks about her.
Il pense à son avenir, il y pense.
He thinks of it.

PLACE AND ORDER

1	2	3	
je, tu **on, il, elle** **nous, vous** **ils, elles**	**me, m', te, t'** **nous, vous** **le, la, les** **lui, leur** **m', t', nous, vous**	**le, la, les** **en** **lui, leur, en** **en**	verb

Ex.:
Je te le donne, nous le lui donnons, elles vous les donnent
I give it to you, we give it to him/her/it, they give them to you

For the order with the imperative see lesson 39, B1, B3.

13 - RELATIVE PRONOUNS

The relative pronouns which are most often used are:

		simple forms	compound forms	
subject	**qui**	*who, that, which*	**ce qui**	*what*
direct object	**que/qu'**	*whom, that, which*	**ce que**	*what*

qui and **que** may refer to a masculine or feminine, singular or plural noun. Both may refer to persons or things. Ex.:

Écoute l'homme qui parle. *Listen to the man who is speaking.*
L'homme que vous voyez est anglais.* *The man you see is English.*
Donne-moi le livre qui est là. *Give me the book which is there.*
Où est le livre qu'Anne lisait ?* *Where is the book Anne was reading?*
Regarde ce qui est ici. *Look what is here.*
Regarde ce que j'ai. *Look what I've got.*

* Remember that **que/qu'** cannot be omitted in French.

14 - INTERROGATIVE WORDS

ADJECTIVES

masc. sing. masc. plur.	**quel** **quels**	fem. sing. fem. plur.	**quelle** **quelles**	*what, which* *what, which*

- Remember that, in French, adjectives always agree with the noun they accompany.

Ex.:

Quel livre lis-tu ? *Which book are you reading?*
Quels livres lis-tu ? *Which books are you reading?*
Quelle voiture préfères-tu ? *Which car do you prefer?*
Avec quelles amies pars-tu ? *Which friends are you going with?*

PRONOUNS

	Persons	Things
subject	**qui ?** *who*	**qu'est-ce qui ?** *what*
direct object	**qui ?** *who*	**que ?** *what*
indirect object (with preposition)	**qui ?** *who*	**quoi ?** *what*

Ex.:

Qui est-ce ? *Who is it?*
Qui est-ce qui parle ? *Who is talking?*
Qui regardent-ils ? *Who are they looking at?*
Qui est-ce que tu préfères ? *Who(m) do you prefer?*
À quoi est-ce que vous pensez ? *What are you thinking about?*
Que manges-tu ?
Qu'est-ce que tu manges ? → *What are you eating?*

- The interrogative pronoun corresponding to **quel** is **lequel**, it also agrees in gender and number with the noun it refers to.

masc. sing. **lequel** fem. sing. **laquelle**
masc. plur. **lesquels** fem. plur. **lesquelles**

Ex.: **Lequel préfères-tu ?** *Which one do you prefer?*
Lesquelles préfères-tu ? *Which ones do you prefer?*

ADVERBS

combien ? *how much, how many?*
comment ? *how?*
où ? *where?*
pourquoi ? *why?*
quand ? *when?*

15 - VERBS

Regular French verbs belong to:

the 1st group ending in **er**: **parler**;

the 2nd group ending in **ir**: **finir**;

the 3rd group: other endings: **répondre, entendre, ouvrir**.

Verbs of the same group have the same conjugation.
In French, the endings of verbs vary according to the subject.

- **Présent** - *Present tense*

	1st group	2nd group	3rd group		
	Parler *(to speak)*	**Finir** *(to finish)*	**Voir** *(to see)*	**Entendre** *(to hear)*	**Ouvrir** *(to open)*
je, j'	parle	finis	vois	entends	ouvre
tu	parles	finis	vois	entends	ouvres
il, elle, on	parle	finit	voit	entend	ouvre
nous	parlons	finissons	voyons	entendons	ouvrons
vous	parlez	finissez	voyez	entendez	ouvrez
ils, elles	parlent	finissent	voient	entendent	ouvrent

The French **présent** corresponds to the English simple present as well as to the progressive present.

- **Impératif** - *Imperative*

Only 3 persons, no subject (see lessons 1 and 2).

Ex.: **parle, parlons, parlez.**

■ TO REFER TO A PAST EVENT

- **Imparfait** - *Imperfect*

A past tense used to express what was taking place or what used to happen.
It is formed by dropping the ending **ons** of the 1st person plural of the present tense and adding: **-ais**
-ais
-ait
-ions
-iez
-aient
to the stem.

Ex.: **je marchais, tu finissais, nous prenions.**

It is the same for all verbs, except **être**.

- **Passé composé**

  It corresponds to the English simple past as well as to the English present perfect. For most verbs it is formed with the present tense of

  avoir + past participle

  Ex.: **Il a travaillé hier.** *He worked yesterday.*
  Il n'a jamais travaillé.* *He has never worked.*

* In compound tenses, the negation is placed on either side of the auxiliary.

- For some verbs (see list in lesson 25, C2) the **passé composé** is formed with

  être + past participle

  Ex.: **Il est resté, il est parti.**

  With this auxiliary, the past participle agrees with the subject.

  Ex.: **Elle est restée, elle est partie.**

- **Plus-que-parfait** - *Pluperfect*

  It is formed like the **passé composé** with

  imperfect of **être** or **avoir** + past participle

  The **plus-que-parfait** is the same in usage as the pluperfect in English.

  Ex.: **Il avait fini quand elle a appelé.**
  He had finished when she called.
  Nous étions partis quand vous êtes arrivés.
  We had left when you arrived.

  As for the **passé composé**, the past participle agrees with the subject when the auxiliary is **être**.

  The endings of the past participles are:
  é for all the verbs in **er** **(parler - parlé)**
  i for most verbs in **ir** **(finir - fini)**
  u for most verbs in **oir** or **re (voir - vu, entendre - entendu)**
  But some verbs are irregular.

■ MAIN IRREGULAR PAST PARTICIPLES

aller → allé
apprendre → appris
asseoir (s') → assis
attendre → attendu
avoir → eu
boire → bu
choisir → choisi
comprendre → compris
conduire → conduit
connaître → connu
construire → construit
croire → cru
découvrir → découvert
devenir → devenu
devoir → dû
dire → dit
dormir → dormi
écrire → écrit
entendre → entendu
être → été
faire → fait
falloir → fallu
finir → fini
interdire → interdit
lire → lu
mettre → mis
mourir → mort
offrir → offert
ouvrir → ouvert
partir → parti
perdre → perdu
permettre → permis
plaire → plu
pleuvoir → plu
pouvoir → pu
prendre → pris
recevoir → reçu
répondre → répondu
réussir → réussi
rire → ri
savoir → su
sentir → senti
sortir → sorti
vendre → vendu
venir → venu
vivre → vécu
voir → vu
vouloir → voulu

■ TO EXPRESS A FUTURE ACTION

- **Aller** + infinitive.

  It is the equivalent of *to be going to* + infinitive.

  Ex. **Je vais acheter une nouvelle voiture.**
  I am going to buy a new car.

- **Futur** - *Future*

  Its construction is infinitive + **-ai**
  -as
  -a
  -ons
  -ez
  -ont

  Ex.: **Je sortirai, tu parleras, il jouera, nous finirons.**

  When the infinitive ends in **re**, the **e** is dropped.

  Ex.: **conduire - je conduirai.** *I'll drive.*
  prendre - tu prendras. *you'll take.*

- The **futur antérieur** is used for a future action preceding another future action (see lesson 39).

  Ex.: **Dès qu'il sera parti, quelqu'un prendra sa place.**
  As soon as he leaves, someone will take his place.

  It is formed with
  être or **avoir** in the future + past participle.

- **Conditionnel** - *Conditional*

  The conditional is formed with the infinitive + **-ais**
  -ais
  -ait
  -ions
  -iez
  -aient

  Ex.: **Il parlerait, nous dormirions.**

- When the infinitive ends with an **e**, it is dropped in the conditional.

  Ex.: **lire** **je lirais**
  prendre **je prendrais**

- The present tense of the conditional is used when the condition is expressed in the **imparfait**.

  si/s' + subordinate clause + main clause

  Ex.: **Si vous veniez à midi, nous déjeunerions ensemble.**
  If you came at noon, we would have lunch together.

- **Présent du subjonctif**

	1st and 3rd group		2nd group
stem +	**e**	stem +	**isse**
	es		**isses**
	e		**isse**
	ions		**issions**
	iez		**issiez**
	ent		**issent**

Ex.: **Que vous parliez, que tu finisses, qu'ils entendent.**

It is mainly used after **vouloir que/qu'** *to want someone to*
il faut que/qu' *it is necessary that*

after conjunctions such as

avant que/qu'	*before*
en attendant que/qu'	*till*
pour que/qu'	*so that*
bien que/qu'	*though*

and to express an idea of *doubt, wish* or *regret* (see lessons 38, 39, 40).

Ex.: **Je veux que vous veniez.** *I want you to come.*
Il faut que vous partiez. *You have to go.*

16 - CONJUGATIONS

■ 1st GROUP - **Aimer** *(To love)*

INDICATIF		SUBJONCTIF
Présent *I love* j' **aime** tu **aimes** il **aime** nous **aimons** vous **aimez** ils **aiment**	**Passé composé** *I loved, I have loved* j' ai aimé tu as aimé il a aimé nous avons aimé vous avez aimé ils ont aimé	**Présent** *I love* que j' **aime** que tu **aimes** qu'il **aime** que nous **aimions** que vous **aimiez** qu'ils **aiment**
Imparfait *I loved* j' **aimais** tu **aimais** il **aimait** nous **aimions** vous **aimiez** ils **aimaient**	**Plus-que-parfait** *I had loved* j' avais aimé tu avais aimé il avait aimé nous avions aimé vous aviez aimé ils avaient aimé	**IMPÉRATIF** **Présent** *love* **aime** **aimons** **aimez**
	PARTICIPE	**CONDITIONNEL**
Futur *I'll love* j' **aimerai** tu **aimeras** il **aimera** nous **aimerons** vous **aimerez** ils **aimeront**	**Participe passé** *loved* aimé **Participe présent** *loving* aimant	**Présent** *I would love* j' **aimerais** tu **aimerais** il **aimerait** nous **aimerions** vous **aimeriez** ils **aimeraient**

■ 2nd GROUP - **Finir** *(To finish)*

INDICATIF		SUBJONCTIF
Présent *I finish, I am finishing* je **finis** tu **finis** il **finit** nous **finissons** vous **finissez** ils **finissent**	**Passé composé** *I finished, I have finished* j' ai fini tu as fini il a fini nous avons fini vous avez fini ils ont fini	**Présent** *I finish* que je **finisse** que tu **finisses** qu'il **finisse** que nous **finissions** que vous **finissiez** qu'ils **finissent**
Imparfait *I was finishing* je **finissais** tu **finissais** il **finissait** nous **finissions** vous **finissiez** ils **finissaient**	**Plus-que-parfait** *I had finished* j' avais fini tu avais fini il avait fini nous avions fini vous aviez fini ils avaient fini	**IMPÉRATIF** **Présent** *finish* **finis** **finissons** **finissez**
Futur *I'll finish* je **finirai** tu **finiras** il **finira** nous **finirons** vous **finirez** ils **finiront**	**PARTICIPE** **Participe passé** *finished* fini **Participe présent** *finishing* finissant	**CONDITIONNEL** **Présent** *I would finish* je **finirais** tu **finirais** il **finirait** nous **finirions** vous **finiriez** ils **finiraient**

■ 3rd GROUP - **Ouvrir** *(To open)*

INDICATIF		SUBJONCTIF
Présent *I open, I am opening* j' **ouvre** tu **ouvres** il **ouvre** nous **ouvrons** vous **ouvrez** ils **ouvrent**	**Passé composé** *I opened, I have opened* j' ai ouvert tu as ouvert il a ouvert nous avons ouvert vous avez ouvert ils ont ouvert	**Présent** *I open* que j' **ouvre** que tu **ouvres** qu'il **ouvre** que nous **ouvrions** que vous **ouvriez** qu'ils **ouvrent**
Imparfait *I was opening* j' **ouvrais** tu **ouvrais** il **ouvrait** nous **ouvrions** vous **ouvriez** ils **ouvraient**	**Plus-que-parfait** *I had opened* j' avais ouvert tu avais ouvert il avait ouvert nous avions ouvert vous aviez ouvert ils avaient ouvert	**IMPÉRATIF** **Présent** *open* ouvre ouvr**ons** ouvr**ez**
Futur *I'll open* j' **ouvrirai** tu **ouvriras** il **ouvrira** nous **ouvrirons** vous **ouvrirez** ils **ouvriront**	**PARTICIPE** **Participe passé** *opened* ouvert **Participe présent** *opening* ouvrant	**CONDITIONNEL** **Présent** *I would open* j' **ouvrirais** tu **ouvrirais** il **ouvrirait** nous **ouvririons** vous **ouvririez** ils **ouvriraient**

■ AUXILIARIES

• Être *(To be)*

INDICATIF

Présent — *I am*

je	suis
tu	es
il	est
nous	sommes
vous	êtes
ils	sont

Passé composé — *I was, I have been*

j'	ai	été
tu	as	été
il	a	été
nous	avons	été
vous	avez	été
ils	ont	été

Imparfait — *I was*

j'	étais
tu	étais
il	était
nous	étions
vous	étiez
ils	étaient

Plus-que-parfait — *I had been*

j'	avais	été
tu	avais	été
il	avait	été
nous	avions	été
vous	aviez	été
ils	avaient	été

Futur — *I'll be*

je	serai
tu	seras
il	sera
nous	serons
vous	serez
ils	seront

SUBJONCTIF

Présent — *I am*

que je	sois
que tu	sois
qu'il	soit
que nous	soyons
que vous	soyez
qu'ils	soient

IMPÉRATIF

Présent — *be*

sois
soyons
soyez

PARTICIPE

Participe passé — *been*

été

Participe présent — *being*

étant

CONDITIONNEL

Présent — *I would be*

je	serais
tu	serais
il	serait
nous	serions
vous	seriez
ils	seraient

• Avoir *(To have)*

INDICATIF

Présent — *I have*

j'	ai
tu	as
il	a
nous	avons
vous	avez
ils	ont

Passé composé — *I had, I have had*

j'	ai	eu
tu	as	eu
il	a	eu
nous	avons	eu
vous	avez	eu
ils	ont	eu

Imparfait — *I had*

j'	avais
tu	avais
il	avait
nous	avions
vous	aviez
ils	avaient

Plus-que-parfait — *I had had*

j'	avais	eu
tu	avais	eu
il	avait	eu
nous	avions	eu
vous	aviez	eu
ils	avaient	eu

Futur — *I'll have*

j'	aurai
tu	auras
il	aura
nous	aurons
vous	aurez
ils	auront

SUBJONCTIF

Présent — *I have*

que j'	aie
que tu	aies
qu'il	ait
que nous	ayons
que vous	ayez
qu'ils	aient

IMPÉRATIF

Présent — *have*

aie
ayons
ayez

PARTICIPE

Participe passé — *had*

eu

Participe présent — *having*

ayant

CONDITIONNEL

Présent — *I would have*

j'	aurais
tu	aurais
il	aurait
nous	aurions
vous	auriez
ils	auraient

■ IRREGULAR VERBS

• Aller *(To go)*

INDICATIF

Présent — *I go, I am going*

je	vais
tu	vas
il	va
nous	allons
vous	allez
ils	vont

Passé composé — *I went, I have gone*

je	suis	allé
tu	es	allé
il	est	allé
nous	sommes	allés
vous	êtes	allés
ils	sont	allés

Imparfait — *I was going*

j'	allais
tu	allais
il	allait
nous	allions
vous	alliez
ils	allaient

Plus-que-parfait — *I had gone*

j'	étais	allé
tu	étais	allé
il	était	allé
nous	étions	allés
vous	étiez	allés
ils	étaient	allés

Futur — *I'll go*

j'	irai
tu	iras
il	ira
nous	irons
vous	irez
ils	iront

SUBJONCTIF

Présent — *I go*

que j'	aille
que tu	ailles
qu'il	aille
que nous	allions
que vous	alliez
qu'ils	aillent

IMPÉRATIF

Présent — *go*

va
allons
allez

PARTICIPE

Participe passé — *gone*

allé

Participe présent — *going*

allant

CONDITIONNEL

Présent — *I would go*

j'	irais
tu	irais
il	irait
nous	irions
vous	iriez
ils	iraient

• Boire *(To drink)*

INDICATIF

Présent — *I drink, I am drinking*

je	bois
tu	bois
il	boit
nous	buvons
vous	buvez
ils	boivent

Passé composé — *I drank, I have drunk*

j'	ai	bu
tu	as	bu
il	a	bu
nous	avons	bu
vous	avez	bu
ils	ont	bu

Imparfait — *I was drinking*

je	buvais
tu	buvais
il	buvait
nous	buvions
vous	buviez
ils	buvaient

Plus-que-parfait — *I had drunk*

j'	avais	bu
tu	avais	bu
il	avait	bu
nous	avions	bu
vous	aviez	bu
ils	avaient	bu

Futur — *I'll drink*

je	boirai
tu	boiras
il	boira
nous	boirons
vous	boirez
ils	boiront

SUBJONCTIF

Présent — *I drink*

que je	boive
que tu	boives
qu'il	boive
que nous	buvions
que vous	buviez
qu'ils	boivent

IMPÉRATIF

Présent — *drink*

bois
buvons
buvez

PARTICIPE

Participe passé — *drunk*

bu

Participe présent — *drinking*

buvant

CONDITIONNEL

Présent — *I would drink*

je	boirais
tu	boirais
il	boirait
nous	boirions
vous	boiriez
ils	boiraient

IRREGULAR VERBS (continuation)

• Connaître *(To know)*

INDICATIF		SUBJONCTIF
Présent *I know*	**Passé composé** *I knew, I have known*	**Présent** *I know*
je connais	j' ai connu	que je connaisse
tu connais	tu as connu	que tu connaisses
il connaît	il a connu	qu'il connaisse
nous connaissons	nous avons connu	que nous connaissions
vous connaissez	vous avez connu	que vous connaissiez
ils connaissent	ils ont connu	qu'ils connaissent
Imparfait *I knew*	**Plus-que-parfait** *I had known*	**IMPÉRATIF**
		Présent *know*
je connaissais	j' avais connu	
tu connaissais	tu avais connu	connais
il connaissait	il avait connu	connaissons
nous connaissions	nous avions connu	connaissez
vous connaissiez	vous aviez connu	
ils connaissaient	ils avaient connu	
	PARTICIPE	**CONDITIONNEL**
Futur *I'll know*	**Participe passé** *known*	**Présent** *I would know*
je connaîtrai	connu	je connaîtrais
tu connaîtras		tu connaîtrais
il connaîtra	**Participe présent** *knowing*	il connaîtrait
nous connaîtrons		nous connaîtrions
vous connaîtrez	connaissant	vous connaîtriez
ils connaîtront		ils connaîtraient

• Devoir *(Must - Have to)*

INDICATIF		SUBJONCTIF
Présent *I must, I have to*	**Passé composé** *I had to*	**Présent** *I must, I have to*
je dois	j' ai dû	que je doive
tu dois	tu as dû	que tu doives
il doit	il a dû	qu'il doive
nous devons	nous avons dû	que nous devions
vous devez	vous avez dû	que vous deviez
ils doivent	ils ont dû	qu'ils doivent
Imparfait *I had to*	**Plus-que-parfait** *I had had to*	**IMPÉRATIF**
		Présent
je devais	j' avais dû	dois
tu devais	tu avais dû	devons
il devait	il avait dû	devez
nous devions	nous avions dû	
vous deviez	vous aviez dû	
ils devaient	ils avaient dû	hardly used
	PARTICIPE	**CONDITIONNEL**
Futur *I'll have to*	**Participe passé** *had to*	**Présent** *I would have to*
je devrai	dû	je devrais
tu devras		tu devrais
il devra	**Participe présent** *having to*	il devrait
nous devrons		nous devrions
vous devrez	devant	vous devriez
ils devront		ils devraient

• Dire *(To say - To tell)*

INDICATIF

Présent
I say, I tell
I am saying, I am telling

je	dis
tu	dis
il	dit
nous	disons
vous	dites
ils	disent

Passé composé
I said, I told
I have said, I have told

j'	ai	dit
tu	as	dit
il	a	dit
nous	avons	dit
vous	avez	dit
ils	ont	dit

Imparfait
I was saying, I was telling

je	disais
tu	disais
il	disait
nous	disions
vous	disiez
ils	disaient

Plus-que-parfait
I had said, I had told

j'	avais	dit
tu	avais	dit
il	avait	dit
nous	avions	dit
vous	aviez	dit
ils	avaient	dit

Futur
I'll say, I'll tell

je	dirai
tu	diras
il	dira
nous	dirons
vous	direz
ils	diront

SUBJONCTIF

Présent
I say, I tell

que je	dise
que tu	dises
qu'il	dise
que nous	disions
que vous	disiez
qu'ils	disent

IMPÉRATIF

Présent
say, tell

dis
disons
dites

PARTICIPE

Participe passé
said, told

dit

Participe présent
saying, telling

disant

CONDITIONNEL

Présent
I would say, I would tell

je	dirais
tu	dirais
il	dirait
nous	dirions
vous	diriez
ils	diraient

• Écrire *(To write)*

INDICATIF

Présent
I write, I am writing

j'	écri**s**
tu	écri**s**
il	écri**t**
nous	écri**vons**
vous	écri**vez**
ils	écri**vent**

Passé composé
I wrote, I have written

j'	ai	écrit
tu	as	écrit
il	a	écrit
nous	avons	écrit
vous	avez	écrit
ils	ont	écrit

Imparfait
I was writing

j'	écri**vais**
tu	écri**vais**
il	écri**vait**
nous	écri**vions**
vous	écri**viez**
ils	écri**vaient**

Plus-que-parfait
I had written

j'	avais	écrit
tu	avais	écrit
il	avait	écrit
nous	avions	écrit
vous	aviez	écrit
ils	avaient	écrit

Futur
I'll write

j'	écri**rai**
tu	écri**ras**
il	écri**ra**
nous	écri**rons**
vous	écri**rez**
ils	écri**ront**

SUBJONCTIF

Présent
I write

que j'	écri**ve**
que tu	écri**ves**
qu'il	écri**ve**
que nous	écri**vions**
que vous	écri**viez**
qu'ils	écri**vent**

IMPÉRATIF

Présent
write

écri**s**
écri**vons**
écri**vez**

PARTICIPE

Participe passé
written

écrit

Participe présent
writing

écrivant

CONDITIONNEL

Présent
I would write

j'	écri**rais**
tu	écri**rais**
il	écri**rait**
nous	écri**rions**
vous	écri**riez**
ils	écri**raient**

■ **IRREGULAR VERBS** (continuation)

• Faire *(To do - To make)*

INDICATIF		SUBJONCTIF
Présent *I do, I make* *I am doing, I am making*	**Passé composé** *I did, I made* *I have done, I have made*	**Présent** *I do, I make*
je fais	j' ai fait	que je fasse
tu fais	tu as fait	que tu fasses
il fait	il a fait	qu'il fasse
nous faisons	nous avons fait	que nous fassions
vous faites	vous avez fait	que vous fassiez
ils font	ils ont fait	qu'ils fassent
Imparfait *I was doing, I was making*	**Plus-que-parfait** *I had done, I had made*	**IMPÉRATIF** — **Présent** *do, make*
je faisais	j' avais fait	fais
tu faisais	tu avais fait	faisons
il faisait	il avait fait	faites
nous faisions	nous avions fait	
vous faisiez	vous aviez fait	
ils faisaient	ils avaient fait	
Futur *I'll do, I'll make*	**PARTICIPE** — **Participe passé** *done, made*	**CONDITIONNEL** — **Présent** *I would do, I would make*
je ferai	fait	je ferais
tu feras		tu ferais
il fera	**Participe présent** *doing, making*	il ferait
nous ferons	faisant	nous ferions
vous ferez		vous feriez
ils feront		ils feraient

• Mettre *(To put)*

INDICATIF		SUBJONCTIF
Présent *I put, I am putting*	**Passé composé** *I put, I have put*	**Présent** *I put*
je mets	j' ai mis	que je mette
tu mets	tu as mis	que tu mettes
il met	il a mis	qu'il mette
nous mettons	nous avons mis	que nous mettions
vous mettez	vous avez mis	que vous mettiez
ils mettent	ils ont mis	qu'ils mettent
Imparfait *I was putting*	**Plus-que-parfait** *I had put*	**IMPÉRATIF** — **Présent** *put*
je mettais	j' avais mis	mets
tu mettais	tu avais mis	mettons
il mettait	il avait mis	mettez
nous mettions	nous avions mis	
vous mettiez	vous aviez mis	
ils mettaient	ils avaient mis	
Futur *I'll put*	**PARTICIPE** — **Participe passé** *put*	**CONDITIONNEL** — **Présent** *I would put*
je mettrai	mis	je mettrais
tu mettras		tu mettrais
il mettra	**Participe présent** *putting*	il mettrait
nous mettrons	mettant	nous mettrions
vous mettrez		vous mettriez
ils mettront		ils mettraient

• **Pouvoir** *(Can - To be able to)*

INDICATIF		SUBJONCTIF
Présent *I can* je peux je puis tu peux il peut nous pouvons vous pouvez ils peuvent	**Passé composé** *I have been able to* j' ai pu tu as pu il a pu nous avons pu vous avez pu ils ont pu	**Présent** *I can* que je puisse que tu puisses qu'il puisse que nous puissions que vous puissiez qu'ils puissent
Imparfait *I could, I was able to* je pouvais tu pouvais il pouvait nous pouvions vous pouviez ils pouvaient	**Plus-que-parfait** *I had been able to* j' avais pu tu avais pu il avait pu nous avions pu vous aviez pu ils avaient pu	**IMPÉRATIF** pas d'impératif
Futur *I'll be able to* je pourrai tu pourras il pourra nous pourrons vous pourrez ils pourront	**PARTICIPE** **Participe passé** *been able to* pu **Participe présent** *being able to* pouvant	**CONDITIONNEL** **Présent** *I would be able to* je pourrais tu pourrais il pourrait nous pourrions vous pourriez ils pourraient

• **Prendre** *(To take)*

INDICATIF		SUBJONCTIF
Présent *I take, I am taking* je prends tu prends il prend nous prenons vous prenez ils prennent	**Passé composé** *I took, I have taken* j' ai pris tu as pris il a pris nous avons pris vous avez pris ils ont pris	**Présent** *I take* que je prenne que tu prennes qu'il prenne que nous prenions que vous preniez qu'ils prennent
Imparfait *I was taking* je prenais tu prenais il prenait nous prenions vous preniez ils prenaient	**Plus-que-parfait** *I had taken* j' avais pris tu avais pris il avait pris nous avions pris vous aviez pris ils avaient pris	**IMPÉRATIF** **Présent** *take* prends prenons prenez
Futur *I'll take* je prendrai tu prendras il prendra nous prendrons vous prendrez ils prendront	**PARTICIPE** **Participe passé** *taken* pris **Participe présent** *taking* prenant	**CONDITIONNEL** **Présent** *I would take* je prendrais tu prendrais il prendrait nous prendrions vous prendriez ils prendraient

■ IRREGULAR VERBS (continuation)

• Savoir *(To know)*

INDICATIF		SUBJONCTIF
Présent *I know* je sais tu sais il sait nous savons vous savez ils savent	**Passé composé** *I knew, I have known* j' ai su tu as su il a su nous avons su vous avez su ils ont su	**Présent** *I know* que je sache que tu saches qu'il sache que nous sachions que vous sachiez qu'ils sachent
Imparfait *I knew* je savais tu savais il savait nous savions vous saviez ils savaient	**Plus-que-parfait** *I had known* j' avais su tu avais su il avait su nous avions su vous aviez su ils avaient su	**IMPÉRATIF** **Présent** *know* sache sachons sachez
	PARTICIPE	**CONDITIONNEL**
Futur *I'll know* je saurai tu sauras il saura nous saurons vous saurez ils sauront	**Participe passé** *known* su **Participe présent** *knowing* sachant	**Présent** *I would know* je saurais tu saurais il saurait nous saurions vous sauriez ils sauraient

• Tenir *(To hold)*

INDICATIF		SUBJONCTIF
Présent *I hold, I am holding* je tiens tu tiens il tient nous tenons vous tenez ils tiennent	**Passé composé** *I held, I have held* j' ai tenu tu as tenu il a tenu nous avons tenu vous avez tenu ils ont tenu	**Présent** *I hold* que je tienne que tu tiennes qu'il tienne que nous tenions que vous teniez qu'ils tiennent
Imparfait *I was holding* je tenais tu tenais il tenait nous tenions vous teniez ils tenaient	**Plus-que-parfait** *I had held* j' avais tenu tu avais tenu il avait tenu nous avions tenu vous aviez tenu ils avaient tenu	**IMPÉRATIF** **Présent** *hold* tiens tenons tenez
	PARTICIPE	**CONDITIONNEL**
Futur *I'll hold* je tiendrai tu tiendras il tiendra nous tiendrons vous tiendrez ils tiendront	**Participe passé** *held* tenu **Participe présent** *holding* tenant	**Présent** *I would hold* je tiendrais tu tiendrais il tiendrait nous tiendrions vous tiendriez ils tiendraient

All verbs ending in **enir** have the same conjugation.

- **Vivre** *(To live)*

INDICATIF		SUBJONCTIF
Présent *I live, I am living* je vis tu vis il vit nous vivons vous vivez ils vivent	**Passé composé** *I lived, I have lived* j' ai vécu tu as vécu il a vécu nous avons vécu vous avez vécu ils ont vécu	**Présent** *I live* que je vive que tu vives qu'il vive que nous vivions que vous viviez qu'ils vivent
Imparfait *I was living* je vivais tu vivais il vivait nous vivions vous viviez ils vivaient	**Plus-que-parfait** *I had lived* j' avais vécu tu avais vécu il avait vécu nous avions vécu vous aviez vécu ils avaient vécu	**IMPÉRATIF** **Présent** *live* vis vivons vivez
Futur *I'll live* je vivrai tu vivras il vivra nous vivrons vous vivrez ils vivront	**PARTICIPE** **Participe passé** *lived* vécu **Participe présent** *living* vivant	**CONDITIONNEL** **Présent** *I would live* je vivrais tu vivrais il vivrait nous vivrions vous vivriez ils vivraient

- **Voir** *(To see)*

INDICATIF		SUBJONCTIF
Présent *I see* je vois tu vois il voit nous voyons vous voyez ils voient	**Passé composé** *I saw, I have seen* j' ai vu tu as vu il a vu nous avons vu vous avez vu ils ont vu	**Présent** *I see* que je voie que tu voies qu'il voie que nous voyions que vous voyiez qu'ils voient
Imparfait *I saw* je voyais tu voyais il voyait nous voyions vous voyiez ils voyaient	**Plus-que-parfait** *I had seen* j' avais vu tu avais vu il avait vu nous avions vu vous aviez vu ils avaient vu	**IMPÉRATIF** **Présent** *see* vois voyons voyez
Futur *I'll see* je verrai tu verras il verra nous verrons vous verrez ils verront	**PARTICIPE** **Participe passé** *seen* vu **Participe présent** *seeing* voyant	**CONDITIONNEL** **Présent** *I would see* je verrais tu verrais il verrait nous verrions vous verriez ils verraient

■ IRREGULAR VERBS (continuation)

• Vouloir *(To want)*

INDICATIF		SUBJONCTIF
Présent *I want* je veux tu veux il veut nous voulons vous voulez ils veulent	**Passé composé** *I wanted. I have wanted* j' ai voulu tu as voulu il a voulu nous avons voulu vous avez voulu ils ont voulu	**Présent** *I want* que je veuille que tu veuilles qu'il veuille que nous voulions que vous vouliez qu'ils veuillent
Imparfait *I wanted* je voulais tu voulais il voulait nous voulions vous vouliez ils voulaient	**Plus-que-parfait** *I had wanted* j' avais voulu tu avais voulu il avait voulu nous avions voulu vous aviez voulu ils avaient voulu	**IMPÉRATIF** **Présent** veux (veuille) voulons (veuillons) voulez (veuillez*) * is the only form used.
Futur *I'll want* je voudrai tu voudras il voudra nous voudrons vous voudrez ils voudront	**PARTICIPE** **Participe passé** *wanted* voulu **Participe présent** *wanting* voulant	**CONDITIONNEL** **Présent** *I would want* je voudrais tu voudrais il voudrait nous voudrions vous voudriez ils voudraient

■ IMPERSONAL VERBS

• Falloir (to express necessity or obligation)

INDICATIF		SUBJONCTIF
Présent il faut	**Passé composé** il a fallu	**Présent** qu'il faille
Imparfait il fallait	**Plus-que-parfait** il avait fallu	**IMPÉRATIF** Pas d'impératif
Futur il faudra	**Participe passé** fallu	**CONDITIONNEL** **Présent** il faudrait

• Pleuvoir *(To rain)*

INDICATIF		SUBJONCTIF
Présent *it is raining, it rains* il pleut	**Passé composé** *it rained, it has rained* il a plu	**Présent** *it rain* qu'il pleuve
Imparfait *it was raining* il pleuvait	**Plus-que-parfait** *it had rained* il avait plu	**IMPÉRATIF** Pas d'impératif
Futur *it'll rain* il pleuvra	**Participe passé** *rained* / plu **Participe présent** *raining* / pleuvant	**CONDITIONNEL** **Présent** il pleuvrait

LEXIQUE FRANÇAIS • ANGLAIS

FRENCH/ENGLISH VOCABULARY
Gender : (m) = *masculine*, (f) = *feminine*
Number : (pl) = *plural*

à *at, in, to*
à bientôt *see you soon*
à cause de *because of*
à côté *next door*
à droite *on the right*
à gauche *on the left*
à l'étranger *abroad*
à l'heure *on time*
à louer *to let* (US *to rent, for rent*)
à partir de *from*
à propos de *about*
à temps *in time*
à vrai dire *to tell the truth*
abandonner *to give up*
abonnement (m) *subscription*
absent (e) *absent, not at home*
absolument *absolutely*
accepter *to accept*
accident (m) *accident*
accompagner *to go with, to accompany*
acheter *to buy*
acompte (m) *deposit*
actuellement *presently*
adieu *farewell*
adorer *to love, to adore*
adresse (f) *address*
aéroport (m) *airport*
affaire (f) *case, matter*
affaires (f pl) *business*
affiche (m) *poster*
agence de voyages (f) *travel agency*
agent de police (m) *policeman*
agrandir *to enlarge, to extend*
agréable *pleasant*
aider *to help*
aimer *to love*
aimer beaucoup *to be very fond of*
aimer bien *to like*
album (m) *album*
Allemagne *Germany*
aller *to go*
allumer *to switch on*
ambulance (f) *ambulance*
améliorer *to improve*
ami (e) (m/f) *friend*
an (m) *year*
anglais (e) *English*
Angleterre *England*
animal (m) *animal*
année (f) *year*
annuler *to cancel*
août (m) *August*
apéritif (m) *aperitive*
appareil ménager (m) *domestic appliance*
appareil photo (m) *camera*
appartement (m) *flat* (US *apartment*)
appeler *to call*
apporter *to bring*
apprendre *to learn*
approcher *to get near*
après *after*
après-demain *the day after tomorrow*
après-midi (m) *afternoon*
argent (m) *money*
arrêt (m) *stop*

arrêter *to stop*
arriver *to come, to arrive,*
arriver à *to reach*
article (m) *article*
artiste (m) *artist*
ascenseur (m) *lift* (US *elevator*)
assez (de) *enough*
assiette (f) *plate*
assurance (f) *insurance*
atteindre *to reach*
attendre *to wait*
attendre de *to expect from*
attentivement *carefully*
attirer l'attention *to draw attention*
au bord de la mer *at the seaside*
au contraire *on the contrary*
au fur et à mesure *as, progressively*
au lieu de *enstead of*
au moins *at least*
au moment où *the moment whe*
au revoir *good bye*
au-dessus *above*
aucun (e) *no*
aujourd'hui *today*
aussi *too*
aussitôt que *as soon as*
autobus/bus (m) *bus*
automne (m) *Autumn*
autoroute (f) *motorway*
autre *other*
autre chose *something/anything else*
autrefois *in the past, formerly*
avant *before*
avec *with*
avec inquiétude *anxiously*
avec joie *with pleasure*
avec peine *with difficulty*
avec plaisir *with pleasure*
avenir (m) *future*
avenue (f) *avenue*
aveugle *blind*
avion (m) *plane*
avoir *to have*
avoir besoin de *to need*
avoir chaud *to be hot*
avoir confiance *to trust*
avoir de la chance *to be lucky*
avoir du mal *to have trouble, difficulty*
avoir envie de *to feel like*
avoir faim *to be hungry*
avoir froid *to be cold*
avoir honte de *to be ashamed*
avoir l'air *to look, to sound*
avoir l'habitude *to be used to*
avoir le droit de *to have the right to*
avoir les moyens de *to be able to afford*
avoir lieu *to take place*
avoir peur de *to be afraid*
avoir raison *to be right*
avoir soif *to be thirsty*
avoir tort *to be wrong*
avril (m) *April*
bagage (m) *luggage*
bagarre (f) *fight*
baguette (f) *(long French loaf of bread)*
bal (m) *ball, dance*
baladeur (m) *walkman*
baleine (f) *whale*
ballon (m) *ball*
banlieue (f) *suburbs*
banque (f) *bank*
bateau (m) boat
bavarder *to talk, to chat*
beau/belle *beautiful*
beaucoup de *a lot of*

bébé (m) *baby*
beige *beige*
Belgique *Belgium*
besoin (m) *need*
beurre (m) *butter*
bien *well*
bien que *though, although*
bien sûr *of course*
bientôt *soon*
bière pression (f) *draught beer* (US *draft beer*)
billet (m) *ticket, note*
bizarre *odd, strange, funny*
blanc/blanche *white*
blessé (m) *enjured*
bleu (e) *blue*
blond (e) *fair*
bois (m) *wood*
boisson (f) *drink*
boîte (f) *firm, company (colloq)*
boîter *to limp*
bon marché *cheap*
bon, bonne *good*
bonjour *good morning*
bonne nuit *good night*
bonsoir *good evening, good night*
bord (m) *side*
bouche (f) *mouth*
boucherie (f) *butcher's*
boulangerie (f) *baker's*
boulot (m) *job (colloquial)*
bouteille (f) *bottle*
boutique (f) shop
bras (m) *arm*
bronzé *tanned*
brouillard (m) *fog*
bruit (m) *noise*
brûler *to burn*
brun (e) *dark haired*
bureau (m) *office, desk*
bureau de change (m) *foreign exchange office*
but (m) *goal, purpose*
c'est à dire *that is to say*
c'est ça *that's it*
ça *that*
ça dépend *it depends*
ça suffit *it's enough*
ça va *everything's fine*
cabine (f) *phone box* (US *booth*)
cadeau (m) *present*
café (m) *coffee*
caisse (f) *cash desk*
calculatrice (f) *calculator*
campagne (f) *country, countryside*
campagne électorale (f) *election campaign*
candidat (m) *candidate*
caramel m *caramel*
carnet (m) *note book*
carotte (f) *carrot*
carrefour (m) *intersection, cross-roads*
carte (f) *card, map*
carte de crédit (f) *credit card*
carte de vœux (f) *greeting card*
carte postale *postcard*
cassette (f) *cassette*
ce *this, that*
ceci *this*
ceinture *belt*
ceinture (f) *that*
célèbre *famous*
celle-ci, celle-là *this one, that one*
celles-ci, celles-là *these ones, those ones*
celui-ci, celui-là *this one, that one*
cent *hundred*
centaine (f) *hundred*
cérémonie (f) *ceremony*

certain (e) s *some*
certainement *certainly*
ces *these, those*
cet/cette *this, that*
ceux, ceux-ci *these*
chaîne (f) *channel*
chaîne stéréo (f) *stereo equipment*
chaise (f) *chair*
chaleur (f) *heat*
chambre (f) *bedroom*
champ (m) *field*
champignon (m) *mushroom*
champion (m) *champion*
changer *to change*
chanson (f) *song*
chanter *to sing*
chaque *each*
chat (m) *cat*
château (m) *castle*
chaud (e) *hot, warm*
chaussure (f) *shoe*
chemin (m) *way*
chemise (f) *shirt*
chèque (m) *cheque*
chèque de voyage (m) *travellers'cheque*
chéquier (m) *cheque book*
cher, chère *dear, expensive*
chercher *to look for, to fetch*
cheval (m) *horse*
cheveux (m, *usually plural*) *hair*
cheville (f) *ankle*
chez moi *at home*
chien (m) *dog*
chiffre (m) *figure*
choc (m) *shock*
choisir *to choose*
chômage (m) *unemployment*
ciel (m) *sky*
cigarette (f) *cigarette*
cinéma (m) *cinema*
cinq *five*
cinquante *fifty*
circulation (f) *traffic*
clef or clé (f) *key*
client (m) *customer*
code (m) *code*
coin (m) *corner*
colis (m) *parcel*
combien *how much*
combien de *how much, how many*
combien de temps *how long*
commander *to order*
comme *like, as*
commencer *to begin, to start*
comment *how*
commerçant (m) *shopkeeper*
compétent (e) *competent*
comprendre *to understand*
comptable (m/f) *accountant*
compte en banque (m) *bank account*
compter sur *to rely on*
concert (m) *concert*
conduire *to drive*
confortable *comfortable*
congés payés (m, pl) *paid holidays*
connaissance (f) *acquaintance*
connaître *to know*
conseiller *to advise*
construire *to build*
content (e) *glad, happy*
continuer *to go on, to continue*
contraire (m) *contrary, opposite*
contrat (m) *contract*
copain (m) *friend (colloq)*
corps (m) *body*
côte (f) *coast*

coton (m) *cotton*
cou (m) *neck*
couche d'ozone (f) *ozone layer*
coucher de soleil (m) *sunset*
coup (m) *blow*
couple (m) *couple*
couramment *fluently*
courir *to run*
courrier (m) *mail*
course (f) *race*
court (e) *short*
cousin (m) *cousin*
coûter *to cost*
couverture (f) *blanket*
crainte (f) *fear*
crème (f) *cream*
crier *to shout*
croire *to believe*
croiser *to come across*
croisière (f) *cruise*
croissant (m) *croissant*
cuir (m) *leather*
cuisine (f) *kitchen, cookery*
CV (m) *CV*
d'accord *all right*
d'autre *else*
d'habitude *usually*
d'ici *from here*
d'urgence *urgently*
Danemark (m) *Denmark*
dangereux/se *dangerous*
danois (e) *Danish*
dans *in*
dater *to date*
de *of, from*
de bonne heure *early*
de moins en moins *less and less*
de nouveau *again*
de plus en plus *more and more*
de toute façon *anyway*
débat (m) *debate*
décembre (m) *December*
déchet (m) *waste*
décidément *decidedly*
décider *to decide*
déclarer *to declare*
décoller *to take off*
décorer *to decorate*
découvrir *to discover*
décrocher *to lift the receiver*
déçu *disappointed*
défilé (m) *parade*
dégât (m) *damage*
déjà *already*
déjeuner *to have lunch*
délicieux/se *delicious*
demain *tomorrow*
demander *to ask*
démarrer *to start*
demi-heure (f) *half hour*
demie (f) *half*
démocratie (f) *democracy*
dépenser *to spend*
depuis *since, for*
député (m) *Member of Parliament*
dernier/ère *last*
derrière *behind*
dès que *as soon as*
descendre *to go down*
désir (m) *desire*
désirer *to desire*
désolé (e) *sorry*
dessin humoristique (m) *cartoon*
dessous *below*
détester *to hate*
deux *two*
devant *in front of*
devenir *to become*
devoir *must, to owe*
devoir (m) *duty*

devoirs (m pl) *homework*
dictionnaire (m) *dictionary*
différent (e) *different*
dimanche (m) *Sunday*
dire *to say, to tell*
directeur (m) *manager*
dis donc ! dites donc ! *say*
discours (m) *speech*
discuter *to discuss*
disque (m) *record*
distributeur automatique (m) *cash dispenser*
dix *ten*
docteur (m) *doctor*
document (m) *document*
doigt (m) *inger*
donc *therefore*
donner *to give*
dossier (m) *file*
doucement *softly*
douze *twelve*
drapeau (m) *flag*
droit de vote (m) *right to vote*
drôle *funny*
du premier coup *on the first try*
durer *to last*
eau (f) *water*
éclater *to break out*
école (f) *school*
écouter *to listen*
écrire *to write*
écrivain (m) *writer*
écurie (f) *stable*
efficace *efficient.*
égalité (f) *equality*
église (f) *church*
électeur (m) **électrice** (f) *voter*
élection (f) *election*
éléphant (m) *elephant*
elle *she, her*
elles *they, them*
embouteillage (m) *traffic jam*
émission (f) *broadcast*
emmener à *to take to*
employé (e) (m/f) *employee*
emporter *to take (away)*
en *in*
en attendant *meanwhile*
en cas de *in case of*
en ce moment *at the moment*
en face *opposite*
en forme *fit*
endroit (m) *place*
enfance (f) *childhood*
enfant (m/f) *child*
ennui (m) *trouble, problem*
ennuyer *to bother, to annoy*
énorme *huge*
énormément *immensely*
ensemble *together*
ensuite *then*
entendre *to hear*
enthousiaste *enthusiastic*
entre *between*
entrecôte (f) *steak (rib)*
entrée (f) *admission, entrance*
entreprise (f) *firm*
entrer *to go in, to enter*
entretien (m) *interview*
envoyer *to send*
épagneul (m) *spaniel*
épaule (f) *shoulder*
épeler *to spell*
épicerie (f) *grocer's*
éponger *to mop up*
équipe (f) *team*
escalope (f) *escalope*
espace (m) *space*
Espagne (f) *Spain*
espagnol (e) *Spanish*

espérer *to hope*
espoir (m) *hope*
essayer *to try*
essence (f) *petrol*
Est (m) *East*
et *and*
étage (m) *floor*
étagère (f) *shelf*
été (m) *Summer*
étoile (f) *star*
étouffer *to suffocate*
étourdi *stunned,*
étranger (m) *foreigner*
étranger/ère *foreign*
être *to be*
être le/la bienvenu (e) *to be welcome*
être pressé (e) *to be in a hurry*
étude (f) *study*
étudiant (e) (m/f) *student*
éviter *to avoid*
exactement *exactly*
exagérer *to exagerate*
examen (m) *exam*
exemplaire (m) *copy*
expéditeur (m) *sender*
expérience (f) *experience*
expliquer *to explain*
expression (f) *expression*
extraordinaire *extraordinary*
façade (f) *front*
facile *easy*
facteur (m) *postman*
faculté (f) *college*
faible *weak*
faire *to do, to make*
faire attention *to pay attention*
faire beau *to be fine*
faire confiance *to trust*
faire le plein *to fill up*
faire ses études *to study*
faire signe *to wave*
faire un discours *to make a speech*
faire un effort *to make an effort*
faire une promenade *to go for a walk, a ride*
faits divers (m pl) *news in brief*
famille (f) *family*
fatiguant *tiring*
fatigué *tired*
femme (f) *woman, wife*
fenêtre (f) *window*
fer (m) *iron*
ferme (f) *farm*
fermer *to shut, to close*
fête (f) *feast*
feu d'artifice (m) f*ireworks*
feuilleton (m) *serial, series*
février (m) *February*
fiche (f) *form, card*
fidèle *faithful*
fille (f) *girl, daughter*
fils (m) *son*
fin (f) *end*
finir *to end*
fleur (f) *flower*
fois (f) *time*
forêt (f) *forest*
formulaire (m) *form*
formule (f) *formula*
fort (e) *strong*
fortune (f) *fortune*
fou/folle *mad, crazy*
foule (f) *crowd*
frais/fraîche *fresh*
franc (m) *franc*
français (e) *French*
France *France*
frapper *to strike, to hit*
frère (m) *brother*

frigo (m) *fridge*
frite (f) *chips* (US *French fries*)
froid (e) *cold*
fromage (m) *cheese*
front (m) *forehead*
fruit (m) *fruit*
fuite (f) *leak*
fumer *to smoke*
gâcher *to ruin, to waste, to spoil*
gagner *to win, to earn*
gant (m) *glove*
garage (m) *garage*
garçon (de café) (m) *waiter*
gardien (m) *keeper*
gare (f) *station*
gâteau (m) *cake*
génération (m) *generation*
genre (m) *gender*
genre (m) *sort, kind*
gens (m, pl) *people*
gentil/gentille *nice*
gigot (m) *leg of lamb*
gilet (m) *cardigan, waistcoat* (US *vest*)
glacé *iced*
glace (f) *ice*
goûter *to taste*
goutte (f) *drop*
gouvernement (m) *government*
gouverner *to govern*
grâce à *thank to*
grand (e) *tall, big, large, great*
grands-parents (m, pl) *grandparents*
gratuite (e) *free*
grave *serious*
grec/grecque *Greek*
Grèce *Greece*
grève (f) *strike*
gris (e) *grey*
gros/grosse *big*
gros lot *top prize in the lottery*
groupe (m) *group*
guerre (f) *war*
guichet (m) *position* (US *wicket*)
guide (m) *guide*
habitant (m) *inhabitant*
habiter *to live in*
haricot vert (m) *French beans*
hebdomadaire (m) *weekly*
héritier (m) *heir*
heure (f) *time, hour*
heureusement *fortunately*
heureux/heureuse *happy*
heurter *to bump into*
hier *yesterday*
histoire (f) *story, history*
hiver (m) *Winter*
homme (m) *man*
hôpital (m) *hospital*
horaire (m) *time table*
hors d'oeuvre (m) *hors d'œuvre, starter*
hors service *out of service*
hôtel (m) *hotel*
huile (f) *oil*
huit *eight*
humour (m) *humour*
ici *here*
idéal *ideal*
idée (f) *idea*
il fait bon *it is warm*
il fait chaud *it is hot*
il fait froid *it is cold*
il fait jour *it is daylight*
il fait mauvais *the weather is bad*
il fait nuit *it is dark*
il fait sec *it is dry*
il fait soleil *it is sunny*
il y a there *is, there are, ago*

il/ils *he they*
île (f) *island*
imagination (f) *imagination*
immense *huge*
immeuble (m) *building*
imperméable (m) *raincoat.*
importance (f) *importance*
incroyable *incredible*
indiquer *to show, to indicate*
infirmière (f) *nurse*
inondation (f) *flood*
inquiète/inquiète *anxious*
insister *to insist*
intact *intact*
intelligent (e) *intelligent, clever*
interdire *to forbid*
intéressant (e) *interesting*
intérieur *inside*
inutile *useless*
invité (m) *guest*
inviter *to invite*
irlandais (e) *Irish*
Irlande *Ireland*
Italie *Italy*
italien/italienne *Italian*
j'en ai assez *I'm fed up*
jambe (f) *leg*
janvier (m) *January*
jardin (m) *garden*
jardinage (m) *gardening*
jaune *yellow*
je, j' *I*
jeter un coup d'oeil à *to have a look at*
jeu (m) *game*
jeudi (m) *Thursday*
jeune *young*
joli (e) *pretty*
joue (f) *cheek*
jouer *to play*
jouet (m) *toy*
joueur (m) *player*
jour (m) *day*
jour de l'An (m) *New Year's Day*
journal (m) *newspaper*
journaliste (m or f) *journalist*
journée (f) *day*
joyeux/joyeuse *merry*
juillet *July*
juin *June*
jusqu'à quand *until when*
juste *just*
juste à temps *just in time*
justement *precisely*
kiosque (m) *kiosk*
la *the*
là *there*
là-bas *over there*
laine (f) *wool*
laisser *to let, toleave*
lait (m) *milk*
laitue (f) *lettuce*
lampe (f) *lamp*
langue (f) *language, tongue*
large *broad*
lavabo (m) *washbasin*
le *the*
léger/légère *light*
légume (m) *vegetable*
lendemain (m) *day after*
lentement *slowly*
lequel, laquelle *which*
les *the*
lesquels, lesquelles *which*
lettre (f) *letter*
leur, leurs *their*
liberté (f) *freedom, liberty*
librairie (f) *bookshop*
libre *free*
ligne (f) *line*

limitée *limited*
lion (m) *lion*
liquide (m) *cash, liquid*
lire *to read*
liste (f) *list*
livre (m) *book*
loin *far*
long/longue *long*
longtemps *a long time*
louer *to rent*
lundi *Monday*
lune (f) *moon*
lunette (f) *telescope*
lunettes (f, pl) *glasses*
lutte (f) *struggle, wrestling*
lycée (m) *grammar school*
ma *my*
machine (f) *machine*
madame *madam, Mrs*
mademoiselle *miss*
magasin (m) *shop, store*
magazine (m) *magazine*
magnifique *magnificent*
mai (m) *May*
main (f) *hand*
maintenant *now*
maire (m) *mayor*
mais *but*
maison (f) *house*
majorité (f) *majority*
mal *badly*
mal à la tête (m) *headache*
malade *sick*
maladie (f) *sickness, disease*
malheur (m) *misfortune*
malheureusement *unfortunately*
manger *to eat*
manifestation (f) *demonstration*
manquer *to miss*
manteau (m) *coat*
marche (f) *walking*
marché (m) *market*
marcher *to walk*
mardi (m) *Tuesday*
mari (m) *husband*
mariage (m) *wedding, marriage*
marié *married*
marquer *to score (a goal)*
marrant *funny (colloq)*
marron *brown*
mars (m) *March*
match (m) *match*
math *math*
matin (m) *morning*
matinée (f) *morning*
mauvais (e) *bad*
me *me*
médicament (m) *medicine*
meilleur (e) *best*
mélodramatique *melodramatic*
même *same*
menthe (f) *mint*
menton (m) *chin*
menu (m) *menu*
mer (f) *sea*
merci *thak you*
mercredi (m) *Wednesday*
mère (f) *mother*
mes *my*
message (m) *message*
mesure (f) *measure*
métier (m) *job*
métro (m) *tube* (US *subway*)
mettre *to put*
meuble (m) *piece of furniture*
midi *noon*
mieux que *better than*
mille *thousand*
milliard (m) *milliard* (US billion)
milliardaire (m) *multimillionaire*

millier (m) *thousand*
million (m) *million*
ministre (m) *minister*
minuit *midnight*
minute (f) *minute*
mission (f) *mission*
mode (f) *fashion*
modèle (m) *model*
moderne *modern*
moment (m) *moment*
mon *my*
monarchie (f) **monarchy**
monde (m) *world, people*
moniteur (m) *instructor*
monnaie (f) *change*
monsieur (m) *sir, Mr*
montagne (f) *mountain*
monter *to go up*
montre (f) *watch*
montrer *to show*
moquette (f) *carpet*
mort (e) *dead*
moto *motorcycle*
mots croisés (m, pl) *crosswords*
mourir *to die*
moyen/moyenne *average*
moyenne (f) *average*
musée (m) *museum*
musicien (m) *musician*
musique (f) *music*
n'importe comment *anyhow, carelessly*
n'importe quand *any time*
n'importe qui anybody, *anyone*
n'importe quoi *anything*
naître *to be born*
natation (f) *swimming*
nature (f) *nature, wildlife*
nausée (f) *nausea*
navette (f) *shuttle*
navré (e) *sorry*
ne. quittez pas *hold the line*
ne... jamais *never*
ne... pas *not*
ne... pas encore *not yet*
ne... plus *no more*
ne... rien *nothing, not anything*
neige (f) *now*
neuf *nine*
neuf/neuve *new*
nez (m) *nose*
Noël (m) *Christmas*
noir (e) *black*
nom (m) *name*
nombre (m) *number*
nommer *to nommer*
non *no*.
Nord (m) *North*
normalement *in the ordinary course of things*
nos *our*
noter *to mark, to give mark*
notre *our*
nous *we, us*
nouveau/nouvelle *new*
nouvelles (f, pl) *news*
novembre (m) *November*
nuage (m) *cloud*
nuit (f) *night*
numéro (m) *number*
objets trouvés (m, pl) *lost property*
occupé *busy*
octobre (m) *October*
œil (m) *eye*
œuf (m) *egg*
œuvre d'art (f) *work of art*
offrir *to offer*
oiseau (m) *bird*
oncle (m) *uncle*
onze *eleven*

opposition (f) *opposition*
or (m) *gold*
orage (m) *storm*
ordinaire *ordinary*
ordinateur (m) *computer*
ordonnance (f) *prescription*
oreille (f) *ear*
organiser *to organise*
original *original*
ou *or*
où *where*
oublier *to forget*
Ouest (m) *West*
oui *yes*
ours (m) *bear*
ouvrier (m) *worker*
ouvrir *to open*
P. D. G. *M D (managing director)*
pain (m) *bread*
paix (f) *peace*
pâle *pale*
pané *coated with breadcrumbs*
panne (f) *breakdown*
panneau (m) board, road *sign*
pantalon (m) *trousers*
Pâques *Easter*
paquet (m) *parcel*
par exemple *for instance, for example*
par hasard *by chance*
par ici *this way*
par là *that way*
parapluie (m) *umbrella*
parasol (m) *sunshade*
parce que *because*
pardon *pardon*
parent (m) *parent*
parfait *perfect*
parfois *sometimes*
parking (m) *parking place*
parler *to speak*
parti (politique) (m) *party*
particulier *special*
partir *to leave*
partout *everywhere*
pas cher *cheap, unexpensive*
pas mal *not bad*
passer (le temps) *to spend*
passer devant *to walk by*
passer par *to go via*
pâtes (f, pl) *pasta*
patience (f) *patience*
patienter *to wait, to be patient*
patron (m) *boss*
pauvre *poor*
payer *to pay*
pays (m) *country*
Pays-Bas *Netherlands*
paysage (m) *landscape*
péage (m) *toll*
pêche (f) *fishing*
pendant *for, during*
penser *to think*
perdre *to lose*
perdre connaissance *to faint*
père (m) *father*
période (f) *period*
périphérique (m) *ring road*
permettre *to allow*
permis de conduire (m) *driving license*
persil (m) *parsley*
personne *nobody*
personne (f) *person*
petit déjeuner (m) *breakfast*
petit (e) *small, little*
petite-fille (f) *grand-daughter*
petites annonces (f, pl) *ads (classified)*
peu de *little, few*

peut-être *maybe, perhaps*
pharmacie (f) *chemist's*
photo (f) *photo, picture*
pièce (f) r*oom, play, coin*
pied (m) *foot*
piéton (m) *pedestrian*
pile (f) *battery*
pire que *worse than*
piscine (f) *swimming pool*
piste (f) *trail*
place (f) *seat, room*
plage (f) *beach*
plaindre *to pity*
plaire *to please*
plaisanter *to joke*
planche à voile (f) *surf board*
planète (f) *planet*
plante (f) *plant*
plastique (m) *plastic*
plat (m) *dish*
pleuvoir *to rain*
plomberie (f) *plumbing*
plombier (m) *plumber*
pluie (f) *rain*
plus tard *later*
plusieurs *several*
plutôt *rather*
pneu (m) *tyre*
poche (f) *pocket*
poireau (m) *leek*
poisson (m) *fish*
poissonnerie (f) *fishmonger's*
politique (f) *politics, policy*
pollution (f) *pollution*
pomme de terre (f) *potato*
pont (m) *bridge*
portable (téléphone) (m) *cell phone*
porte (f) *door*
porter *to carry, to wear*
portugais (e) *Portuguese*
Portugal *Portugal*
poser *to put,*
posséder *to own*
possible *possible*
poste (f) *post office*
poster *to post*
pouce (m) *thumb*
pour *for*
pour que *so that*
pourquoi *why*
pourtant *yet*
pouvoir *can, to be able to, may*
pratiquer *to practise*
préférer *to prefer*
premier/première *first*
prendre *to take*
prendre contact *to contact*
prénom (m) *first name*
préparer *to prepare*
près *near*
présenter *to present*
président (m) *president*
presque *nearly, almost*
prêt (e) *ready*
principal *main*
printemps (m) *Spring*
prix (m) *price, prize*
problème (m) *problem*
prochain (e) *next*
programme (m) *programme*
projet (m) *plan*
promenade (f) *walk, ride*
proposer *to propose*
prudent (e) *prudent, careful*
public (m) *public, audience*
publicité (f) *advertising*
puis *then*
quai (m) *platform*
quand *when*

quand même *all the same, nevertheless*
quarante *forty*
quart (m) *quarter*
quartier (m) *ditrict, area*
quatorze *fourteen*
quatre *four*
quatre-vingt dix *ninety*
quatre-vingts *eight*
quel, quels *what, which*
quelle heure est-il ? *what time is it ?*
quelle, quelles *what, which*
quelqu'un *somebody, someone,*
quelque *some*
quelque chose *something, anything else*
quelquefois *sometimes*
questions (f) *questions*
queue (f) *queue*
qui *who*
quinze *fifteen*
quitter *to leave*
quoi *what*
quotidien (m) *daily*
raccrocher *to hang up*
rang (m) *row*
ranger *to tidy*
rapide *fast, quick*
rapidement *fast quickly*
rappeler *to call back*
rapporter *to bring back*
rarement *rarely, seldom*
rayure (f) *stripe*
récent (e) *recent*
recevoir *to receive, to get*
recommandé *registered (post)*
reçu (m) *receipt*
recyclage (m) *recycling*
rédacteur en chef (m) *editor*
régal (m) *treat*
regarder *to look, to watch*
régler *to settle*
regretter *to regret*
régulièrement *regularly*
reine (f) *queen*
relevé (m) *statement (bank)*
remarquer *to notice*
remettre *to post pone*
remplir *to fill, to fill in*
rencontrer *to meet*
rendez-vous (m) *appointment, date*
rendre *to turn in, to give back*
renoncer *to drop, give up*
renseignement (m) *information (a piece of)*
rentrer *to go home, to come back*
renverser *to run over*
renvoyer *to send back*
réparer *to repair, to mend*
repartir *to go back*
repas (m) *meal*
répondeur (m) *answering machine, answerphone*
répondre *to answer, to reply*
représentant (m) *representativesalesman*
représenter *to represent*
république (f) *republic*
réserver *to book, to reserve*
respecter *to respect*
resplendissante *radiant*
rester *to stay, to remain*
retourner *to return*
retrait (m) *withdrawal*
réunion (f) *meeting*
réussir *to succeed, to be successful*
rêve (m) *dream*
réveillon (m) *Christmas Eve party*
revenir *to come back*
rêver *to dream*

réviser *to revise*
revue (f) *magazine, review*
riche *rich*
rideau (m) *curtain*
rien *nothing*
robe (f) *dress*
robinet (m) *tap*
rocher (m) *rock*
roi (m) *king*
roman (m) *novel*
rose (f) *rose*
roue (f) *wheel*
rouge *red*
rouler *to drive*
roux *red haired*
rue (f) *street*
ruisseau (m) *brook*
s'amuser *to have fun, to enjoy oneself*
s'appeler *to be called*
s'arrêter *to stop*
s'asseoir *to sit*
s'échapper *to escape*
s'habiller *to dress, to dress up*
s'il te plaît/s'il vous plaît *please*
s'occuper de *to look after, to take care of*
sa *his, her, its*
sac (m) *bag*
sacré (Fam) *damned*
saignante (viande) *rare*
salade (f) *salad*
salaire (m) *salary*
salle (f) *room*
salle à manger (f) *dining room*
salle de bains (f) *bathroom*
salle de conférences (f) *conference room*
salon (m) *drawing room* (US *living room*)
salut *Hello, Hi*
samedi (m) *Saturday*
sans *without*
sans arrêt *endlessly*
sans peine *easily, painlessly*
sauf *except*
savoir *to know*
se baigner *to bathe*
se coucher *to go to bed*
se dépêcher *to hurry*
se déplacer *to move*
se déranger *to go to trouble*
se disputer *to quarrel, to argue*
se distraire *to have fun*
se faire mal *to hurt oneself*
se laver *to wash*
se lever *to get up*
se libérer *to free oneself*
se passer *to happen*
se perfectionner *to improve*
se poser *to land*
se préparer *to get ready*
se promener *to go for a walk*
se raser *to shave*
se régaler *to have a real treat*
se rendre compte de *to realise*
se renseigner *to ask for information*
se reposer *to rest*
se réveiller *to wake up*
se revoir *to meet again*
se servir de *to use*
se souvenir *to remember*
se tordre (la cheville) *to twist (one's ankle)*
se tromper *to be mistaken*
se tromper de *to take the wrong..*
séance (f) *show, performance*
sec, sèche *dry*
secrétaire (m, f) *secretary*

seize *sixteen*
séjour (m) *living room, stay*
sélectionner *to select*
semaine (f) *week*
sembler *to seem*
sentir *to smell, to feel*
sept *seven*
septembre (m) *September*
serpent (m) *snake*
serre (f) *greenhouse*
serrée *tight*
serviette (f) *napkin, towel*
ses *his, her, its*
seul (e) *alone*
sévèrement *strictly*
short (m) *pair of shorts*
si *if*
signaler *to report*
signer *to sign*
singe (m) *monkey, ape*
sinon *otherwise*
six *six*
skier, faire du ski *to ski*
slogan (m) *slogan*
sœur (f) *sister*
soigner *to take care, to treat*
soir (m) *evening, night*
soirée (f) *evening*
soixante *sixty*
soixante-dix *seventy*
solde (bank) (m) *balance*
soleil (m) *sun*
sombre *dark*
somme (f) *amount, sum*
son *his, her, its*
sondage (m) *poll*
sonner *to ring*
sortir *to go out*
soudain *suddenly*
souffle (m) *breath*
souhait (m) *wish*
sourire (m) *smile*
sous *under*
sous peu *before long*
souvent *often*
spécialiste (m, f) *specialist*
spectaculaire *spectacular*
spendide *splendid*
sport (m) *sport*
stade (m) *stadium*
stationne *to park*
stylo (m) *pen*
succès (m) *siccess*
sucre (m) *sugar*
Sud (m) *South*
suivre *to follow*
superbe *superb*
supplément (m) *supplement*
sur *on*
sûr *sure*
sûrement *surely*
sympatique *nice*
syndicat (m) *trade union*
ta *your*
table (f) *table*
tableau (m) *painting*
taille (f) *size*
talent (m) *talent*
tant de' *so much, so many*
tant pis *too bad*
taper à la machine *to type*
tapis (m) *carpet*
tard *late*
tarder *to be long*
tarif (m) *fee*
taxi (m) *taxi*
te *you*
technologie (f) *technology*
tee-shirt (m) *tee-shirt*
teinturerie (f) *cleaner's*

télégramme (m) *telegramme*
téléphone (m) *telephone*
téléviseur (m) *television set*
télévision (f) *television*
tellement *so much, so many*
témoin (m) *witness*
tempête (f) *storm*
temps (m) *weather, time*
terre (f) *earth*
terrible *terrible*
tes *your*
tête (f) *head*
théâtre (m) *theatre*
tiers (m) *third*
tigre (m) *tiger*
timbre (m) *stamp*
titre (m) *title*
tomate (f) *tomato*
tombée de la nuit (f) *nightfall*
tomber *to fall*
ton *your*
tôt *early*
toujours *always*
touriste (m, f) *tourist*
tourner *to turn*
tout *all, the whole*
tout à coup *all of a sudden*
tout à fait *quite*
tout à l'heure *in a moment*
tout de suite *straight away, immediately*
tout le monde *everybody*
tracteur (m) *tractor*
train (m) *train*
traitement de texte (m) *word processor*
tranche (f) *slice*
tranquille *quiet*
transistor (m) *transistor*
travail (m) *work*
travailler *to work*
travaux (m, pl) *road works*
traverser *to cross*
treize *thirteen*
trempée *soaked*
trente *thirty*
très *very*
triste *sad*
trois *three*
trop *too*
trop de *too much, too many*
trouver *to find, to think*
tu *you*
tunnel (m) *tunnel*
un (e) *a, an, one*
urgence (f) *emergency*
usine (f) *factory*
utile *useful*
utiliser *to use*
vacances (f, pl) *holidays* (US *vacation*)
vague (f) *wave*
valable *valid*
valise (f) *suitcase*
valoir *to be worth*
valoir mieux *to be better*
vélo (m) *bike*
vendre *to sell*
vendredi *Friday*
venir *to come*
venir de *have just + verb*
vent (m) *wind*
vérifier *to check*
verre (m) *glass*
vers *to, towards*
verser *to pour*
vert (e) *green*
vêtements (m, pl) *clothes*
viande (f) *meat*
vide *empty*

vie (f) *life*
vieillir *to get old*
vieux, vieil/vieille *old*
vif/vive *bright*
villa (f) *cottage, house*
village (m) *village*
ville (f) *town*
vin (m) *wine*
vinaigrette (f) *French dressing*
vingt *twenty*
violent *violent*
violet (te) *purple*
visage (m) *face*
visiter *to visit*
vite *fast, quick*
vitesse (f) *speed*
vitrine (f) *shop window*
voici *here is, here are*
voie (f) *railway*
voir *to see*
voisin (m) *neighbour*
voiture (f) *car*
voix (f) *voice*
vol (m) *theft*
voler *to steal*
volonté (f) *will*
volontiers *willingly, with pleasure*
vos *your*
voter *to vote*
votre *your*
vouloir *to want*
vous *you*
voyage (m) *trip, journey*
voyage (m) **de noces** *honeymoon*
voyager *to travel*
vrai (e) *true*
vraiment *really*
y *there*
yeux (m, pl) *eyes*

LEXIQUE ANGLAIS • FRANÇAIS

a long time longtemps
a lot of beaucoup de
a, an, one un (e)
about à propos de
above au-dessus
abroad à l'étranger
absent,
not at home absent (e)
absolutely absolument
accept (to) accepter
accident accident (m)
accountant comptable (m/f)
acquaintance connaissance (f)
address adresse (f)
admission, entrance entrée (f)
ads (classified) petites annonces (f, pl)
advertising publicité (f)
after après
afternoon après-midi (m)
again de nouveau
airport aéroport (m)
album album (m)
all of a sudden tout à coup
all right d'accord
all the same, nevertheless quand même
all, the whole tout
alone seul (e)
already déjà
always toujours
ambulance ambulance (f)
amount, sum somme (f)
and et
animal animal (m)
ankle cheville (f)
answer (to), reply (to) répondre
answering machine, answerphone répondeur (m)
anxious inquiète/inquiète
anxiously avec inquiétude
any time n'importe quand
anybody, anyone n'importe qui
anyhow, carelessly n'importe comment
anything n'importe quoi
anyway de toute façon
aperitive apéritif (m)
appointment, date rendez-vous (m)
April avril (m)
arm bras (m)
article article (m)
artist artiste (m)
as soon as aussitôt que, dès que
as, progressively au fur et à mesure
ask (to) demander
ask (to) for information se renseigner
at home chez moi
at least au moins
at the moment en ce moment
at the seaside au bord de la mer
at, in, to à
August août (m)
Autumn automne (m)
avenue avenue (f)
average moyen/moyenne
average moyenne (f)
avoid (to) éviter
baby bébé (m)

bad **mauvais (e)**
badly **mal**
bag **sac (m)**
baker's **boulangerie (f)**
balance **solde (bank) (m)**
ball **ballon (m)**
ball, dance **bal (m)**
bank **banque (f)**
bank account **compte en banque (m)**
bathe (to) **se baigner**
bathroom **salle de bains (f)**
battery **pile (f)**
be (to) afraid **avoir peur de**
be (to) **être**
be (to) able to afford **avoir les moyens de**
be (to) ashamed **avoir honte de**
be (to) better **valoir mieux**
be (to) born **naître**
be (to) called **s'appeler**
be (to) cold **avoir froid**
be (to) fine **faire beau**
be (to) hot **avoir chaud**
be (to) hungry **avoir faim**
be (to) in a hurry **être pressé (e)**
be (to) long **tarder**
be (to) lucky **avoir de la chance**
be (to) mistaken **se tromper**
be (to) right **avoir raison**
be (to) thirsty **avoir soif**
be (to) used to **avoir l'habitude**
be (to) very fond of **aimer beaucoup**
be (to) welcome **être le/la bienvenu (e)**
be (to) worth **valoir**
be (to) wrong **avoir tort**
beach **plage (f)**
bear **ours (m)**
beautiful ***beau/belle***
because ***parce que***
because of **à cause de**
become (to) **devenir**
bedroom **chambre (f)**
before **avant**
before long **sous peu**
begin (to), start (to) **commencer**
behind **derrière**
beige **beige**
Belgium **Belgique**
believe (to) **croire**
below **dessous**
belt **ceinture**
best **meilleur (e)**
better than **mieux que**
between **entre**
big ***gros/grosse***
bike **vélo (m)**
bird **oiseau (m)**
black **noir (e)**
blanket **couverture (f)**
blind **aveugle**
blow **coup (m)**
blue **bleu (e)**
board, road sign **panneau (m)**
boat **bateau (m)**
body **corps (m)**
book **livre (m)**
book (to), reserve (to) **réserver**
bookshop **librairie (f)**
boss **patron (m)**
bother (to), annoy (to) **ennuyer**
bottle **bouteille (f)**
bread **pain (m)**
break out (to) **éclater**

breakdown **panne** (f)
breakfast **petit déjeuner** (m)
breath **souffle** (m)
bridge **pont** (m)
bright **vif/vive**
bring (to) **apporter**
bring back (to) **rapporter**
broad **large**
broadcast **émission** (f)
brook **ruisseau** (m)
brother **frère** (m)
brown **marron**
build (to) **construire**
building **immeuble** (m)
bump into (to) **heurter**
burn (to) **brûler**
bus **autobus/bus** (m)
business **affaires** (f pl)
busy **occupé**
but **mais**
butcher's **boucherie** (f)
butter **beurre** (m)
buy (to) **acheter**
by chance **par hasard**
cake **gâteau** (m)
calculator **calculatrice** (f)
call (to) **appeler**
call back (to) **rappeler**
camera **appareil photo** (m)
can, be (to) able to, may **pouvoir**
cancel (to) **annuler**
candidate **candidat** (m)
car **voiture** (f)
caramel **caramel** m
card, map **carte** (f)
cardigan, waistcoat (US **vest** **gilet** (m)
carefully **attentivement**
carpet **moquette** (f)
carpet **tapis** (m)
carrot **carotte** (f)
carry (to), wear (to) **porter**
cartoon **dessin humoristique** (m)
case, matter **affaire** (f)
cash desk **caisse** (f)
cash dispenser **distributeur automatique** (m)
cash, liquid **liquide** (m)
cassette **cassette** (f)
castle **château** (m)
cat **chat** (m)
cell phone **portable (téléphone)** (m)
ceremony **cérémonie** (f)
certainly **certainement**
chair **chaise** (f)
champion **champion** (m)
change **monnaie** (f)
change (to) **changer**
channel **chaîne** (f)
cheap **bon marché**
cheap, unexpensive **pas cher**
check (to) **vérifier**
cheek **joue** (f)
cheese **fromage** (m)
chemist's **pharmacie** (f)
cheque **chèque** (m)
cheque book **chéquier** (m)
child **enfant** (m/f)
childhood **enfance** (f)
chin **menton** (m)
chips (US *French fries*) **frite** (f)
choose (to) **choisir**
Christmas **Noël** (m)
Christmas Eve party **réveillon** (m)
church **église** (f)

cigarette **cigarette** (f)
cinema **cinéma** (m)
cleaner's **teinturerie** (f)
clothes **vêtements** (m, pl)
cloud **nuage** (m)
coast **côte** (f)
coat **manteau** (m)
coated with breadcrumbs **pané**
code **code** (m)
coffee **café** (m)
cold **froid** (e)
college **faculté** (f)
come (to) **venir**
come (to), arrive (to) **arriver**
come across (to) **croiser**
come back (to) **revenir**
comfortable **confortable**
competent **compétent** (e)
computer **ordinateur** (m)
concert **concert** (m)
conference room **salle de conférences** (f)
contact (to) **prendre contact**
contract **contrat** (m)
contrary, opposite **contraire** (m)
copy **exemplaire** (m)
corner **coin** (m)
cost (to) **coûter**
cottage, house **villa** (f)
cotton **coton** (m)
country **pays** (m)
country, countryside **campagne** (f)
couple **couple** (m)
cousin **cousin** (m)
cream **crème** (f)
credit card **carte de crédit** (f)
croissant **croissant** (m)
cross (to) **traverser**
crosswords **mots croisés** (m, pl)
crowd **foule** (f)
cruise **croisière** (f)
curtain **rideau** (m)
customer **client** (m)
CV **CV** (m)
daily **quotidien** (m)
damage **dégât** (m)
damned **sacré** (Fam)
dangerous **dangereux/se**
Danish **danois** (e)
dark **sombre**
dark haired **brun** (e)
date (to) **dater**
day **jour** (m) **journée** (f)
day after **lendemain** (m)
dead **mort** (e)
dear, expensive **cher, chère**
debate **débat** (m)
December **décembre** (m)
decide (to) **décider**
decidedly **décidément**
declare (to) **déclarer**
decorate (to) décorer
delicious **délicieux/se**
democracy **démocratie** (f)
demonstration manifestation (f)
Denmark **Danemark** (m)
deposit **acompte** (m)
deposit (to) **verser**
desire **désir** (m)
desire (to) **désirer**
dictionary **dictionnaire** (m)
die (to) **mourir**
different **différent(e)**
dining room **salle à manger** (f)
disappointed **déçu**

discover (to) **découvrir**
discuss (to) **discuter**
dish **plat** (m)
ditrict, area **quartier** (m)
do (to), make (to) **faire**
doctor **docteur** (m)
document **document** (m)
dog **chien** (m)
domestic appliance **appareil ménager** (m)
door **porte** (f)
draught beer (US *draft beer*) **bière pression** (f)
draw attention (to) **attirer l'attention**
drawing room (US *living room*) **salon** (m)
dream **rêve** (m)
dream (to) **rêver**
dress (to) **robe** (f)
dress (to), dress up (to) **s'habiller**
drink **boisson** (f)
drive (to) **conduire**
drive (to) **rouler**
driving license **permis de conduire** (m)
drop (to) **goutte** (f)
drop (to), give up (to) **renoncer**
dry **sec, sèche**
duty **devoir** (m)
each **chaque**
ear **oreille** (f)
early **tôt, de bonne heure**
earth **terre** (f)
easily, painlessly **sans peine**
East **Est** (m)
Easter **Pâques**
easy **facile**
eat (to) **manger**
editor **rédacteur en chef** (m)
efficient. **efficace**
egg **œuf** (m)
eight **huit**
eight **quatre-vingts**
election **élection** (f)
election campaign **campagne électorale** (f)
elephant **éléphant** (m)
eleven **onze**
else **d'autre**
emergency **urgence** (f)
employee **employé** (e) (m/f)
empty **vide**
end **fin** (f)
end (to) **finir**
endlessly **sans arrêt**
England **Angleterre**
English **anglais** (e)
enlarge, extend **agrandir**
enough **assez** (de)
enthusiastic **enthousiaste**
equality **égalité** (f)
escalope **escalope** (f)
escape (to) **s'échapper**
evening **soirée** (f)
evening, night **soir** (m)
everybody **tout le monde**
everything's fine **ça va**
everywhere **partout**
exactly **exactement**
exagerate (to) **exagérer**
exam **examen** (m)
except **sauf**
expect from (to) **attendre de**
experience **expérience** (f)
explain (to) **expliquer**
expression **expression** (f)

extraordinary **extraordinaire**
eye **œil** (m)
eyes **yeux** (m, pl)
face **visage** (m)
factory **usine** (f)
faint (to) **perdre connaissance**
fair **blond** (e)
faithful **fidèle**
fall (to) **tomber**
family **famille** (f)
famous **célèbre**
far **loin**
farewell **adieu**
farm **ferme** (f)
fashion **mode** (f)
fast quickly **rapidement, vite**
fast, quick **rapide,**
father **père** (m)
fear **crainte** (f)
feast **fête** (f)
February **février** (m)
fee **tarif** (m)
feel like (to) **avoir envie de**
field **champ** (m)
fifteen **quinze**
fifty **cinquante**
fight **bagarre** (f)
figure **chiffre** (m)
file **dossier** (m)
fill (to), fill in (to) **remplir**
fill up (to) **faire le plein**
find (to), think (to) **trouver**
finger **doigt** (m)
fireworks **feu d'artifice** (m)
firm **entreprise** (f)
firm, company (colloq) **boîte** (f)
first **premier/première**
first name **prénom** (m)
fish **poisson** (m)
fishing **pêche** (f)
fishmonger's **poissonnerie** (f)
fit **en forme**
five **cinq**
flag **drapeau** (m)
flat (US *apartment*) **appartement** (m)
flood **inondation** (f)
floor **étage** (m)
flower **fleur** (f)
fluently **couramment**
fog **brouillard** (m)
follow (to) **suivre**
foot **pied** (m)
for **pour**
for instance, for example **par exemple**
for, during **pendant**
forbid (to) **interdire**
forehead **front** (m)
foreign **étranger/ère**
foreign exchange office **bureau de change** (m)
foreigner **étranger** (m)
forest **forêt** (f)
forget (to) **oublier**
form **formulaire** (m)
form, card **fiche** (f)
formula **formule** (f)
fortunately **heureusement**
fortune **fortune** (f)
forty **quarante**
four **quatre**
fourteen **quatorze**
franc **franc** (m)
France **France**
free **gratuite** (e)
free **libre**

free oneself (to) **se libérer**
freedom, liberty **liberté** (f)
French **français** (e)
French beans **haricot vert** (m)
French dressing **vinaigrette** (f)
French loaf of bread **baguette** (f)
fresh **frais/fraîche**
Friday **vendredi**
fridge **frigo** (m)
friend **ami** (e) (m/f)
friend (colloq) **copain** (m)
from **à partir de**
from here **d'ici**
front **façade** (f)
fruit **fruit** (m)
funny **drôle**
funny (colloq) **marrant**
future **avenir** (m)
game **jeu** (m)
garage **garage** (m)
garden **jardin** (m)
gardening **jardinage** (m)
gender **genre** (m)
generation **génération** (m)
Germany **Allemagne**
get near (to) **approcher**
get old (to) **vieillir**
get ready (to) **se préparer**
get up (to) **se lever**
girl, daughter **fille** (f)
give (to) **donner**
give up (to) **abandonner**
glad, happy **content** (e)
glass **verre** (m)
glasses **lunettes** (f, pl)
gloven **gant** (m)
go (to) **aller**
go back (to) **repartir**
go down (to) **descendre**
go for a walk (to) **se promener**
go for a walk (to), a ride **faire une promenade**
go home (to), come back (to) **rentrer**
go in (to), enter (to) **entrer**
go on (to), continue (to) **continuer**
go out (to) **sortir**
go to bed (to) **se coucher**
go to trouble (to) **se déranger**
go up (to) **monter**
go via (to) **passer par**
go with (to), accompany (to) **accompagner**
goal, purpose **but** (m)
gold **or** (m)
good **bon, bonne**
good bye **au revoir**
good evening, good night **bonsoir**
good morning **bonjour**
good night **bonne nuit**
govern (to) **gouverner**
government **gouvernement** (m)
grammar school **lycée** (m)
grand-daughter **petite-fille** (f)
grandparents **grands-parents** (m, pl)
Greece **Grèce**
Greek **grec/grecque**
green **vert** (e)
greenhouse **serre** (f)
greeting card **carte de vœux** (f)
grey **gris** (e)
grocer's **épicerie** (f)
group **groupe** (m)
guest **invité** (m)

guide **guide** (m)
hair **cheveux** (m, *usually plural*)
half **demie** (f)
half hour **demi-heure** (f)
hand **main** (f)
hang up (to) **raccrocher**
happen (to) **se passer**
happy **heureux/heureuse**
hate (to) **détester**
have (to) **avoir**
have (to) the right to **avoir le droit de**
have a look at (to) **jeter un coup d'œil à** *have a real treat (to)* **se régaler**
have fun (to) **se distraire**
have fun (to), enjoy oneself (to) **s'amuser**
have just + verb **venir de**
have lunch (to) **déjeuner**
have trouble (to), difficulty **avoir du mal**
he, they **il/ils**
head **tête** (f)
headache **mal à la tête** (m)
hear (to) **entendre**
heat **chaleur** (f)
heir **héritier** (m)
Hello, Hi **salut**
help (to) **aider**
here **ici**
here is, here are **voici**
his, her, its **sa**
his, her, its **ses**
his, her, its **son**
hold the line **ne quittez pas**
holidays (US *vacation*) **vacances** (f, pl)
homework **devoirs** (m pl)
honeymoon **voyage** (m) **de noces**
hope **espoir** (m)
hope (to) **espérer**
hors d'œuvre, starter **hors d'œuvre** (m)
horse **cheval** (m)
hospital **hôpital** (m)
hot, warm **chaud** (e)
hotel **hôtel** (m)
house **maison** (f)
how **comment**
how long **combien de temps**
how much **combien**
how much, how many **combien de**
huge **énorme, immense**
humour **humour** (m)
hundred **cent, centaine** (f)
hurry (to) **se dépêcher**
hurt oneself (to) **se faire mal**
husband **mari** (m)
I **je, j'**
I say **dis donc ! dites donc !**
I'm fed up **j'en ai assez**
ice **glace** (f)
iced **glacé**
idea **idée** (f)
ideal **idéal**
if **si**
imagination **imagination** (f)
immensely **énormément**
importance **importance** (f)
improve **améliorer, se perfectionner**
in **dans, en**
in a moment **tout à l'heure**
in case of **en cas de**

in front of **devant**
in the ordinary course of things **normalement**
in the past, formerly **autrefois**
in time **à temps**
incredible **incroyable**
information (a piece of) **renseignement** (m)
inhabitant **habitant** (m)
injured **blessé** (m)
inside **intérieur**
insist (to) **insister**
instead of **au lieu de**
instructor **moniteur** (m)
insurance **assurance** (f)
intact **intact**
intelligent, clever **intelligent** (e)
interesting **intéressant** (e)
intersection, crossroads **carrefour** (m)
interview **entretien** (m)
invite (to) **inviter**
Ireland **Irlande**
Irish **irlandais** (e)
iron **fer** (m)
island **île** (f)
it depends **ça dépend**
it is cold **il fait froid**
it is dark **il fait nuit**
it is daylight **il fait jour**
it is dry **il fait sec**
it is hot **il fait chaud**
it is sunny **il fait soleil**
it is warm **il fait bon**
it's enough **ça suffit**
Italian **italien/italienne**
Italy **Italie**
January **janvier** (m)
job **métier** (m)
job (colloquial) **boulot** (m)
joke (to) **plaisanter**
journalist **journaliste** (m or f)
July **juillet**
June **juin**
just **juste**
just in time **juste à temps**
keeper **gardien** (m)
key **clef or clé** (f)
king **roi** (m)
kiosk **kiosque** (m)
kitchen, cookery **cuisine** (f)
know (to) **connaître, savoir**
lamp **lampe** (f)
land (to) **se poser**
landscape **paysage** (m)
language, tongue **langue** (f)
last **dernier/ère**
last (to) **durer**
late **tard**
later **plus tard**
leak **fuite** (f)
learn **apprendre**
leather **cuir** (m)
leave **partir**
leave **quitter**
leek **poireau** (m)
leg **jambe** (f)
leg of lamb **gigot** (m)
less and less **de moins en moins**
let (to), leavet **laisser**
letter **lettre** (f)
lettuce **laitue** (f)
life **vie** (f)
lift (US *elevator)* **ascenseur** (m)
lift the receiver (to) **décrocher**
light **léger/légère**
like (to) **aimer bien**

like, as **comme**
limited **limitée**
limp **boîter**
line **ligne** (f)
lion **lion** (m)
list **liste** (f)
listen (to) **écouter**
little, few **peu de**
live in (to) **habiter**
living room, stay **séjour** (m)
long **long/longue**
look (to), sound (to) **avoir l'air**
look (to), watch (to) **regarder**
look after (to), take care of (to) **s'occuper de**
look for (to), fetch (to) **chercher**
lose (to) **perdre**
lost property **objets trouvés** (m, pl)
love (to) **aimer**
love (to), adore (to) **adorer**
luggage **bagage** (m)
M D (managing director) **P. D. G.**
machine **machine** (f)
mad, crazy **fou/folle**
madam, Mrs **madame**
magazine **magazine** (m)
magazine, review **revue** (f)
magnificent **magnifique**
mail **courrier** (m)
main **principal**
majority **majorité** (f)
make a speech (to) **faire un discours**
make an effort (to) **faire un effort**
man **homme** (m)
manager **directeur** (m)
March **mars** (m)
mark (to), give marks (to) **noter**
market **marché** (m)
married **marié**
match **match** (m)
math **math**
May **mai** (m)
maybe, perhaps **peut- être**
mayor **maire** (m)
me **me**
meal **repas** (m)
meanwhile **en attendant**
measure **mesure** (f)
meat **viande** (f)
medicine **médicament** (m)
meet (to) **rencontrer**
meet again (to) **se revoir**
meeting **réunion** (f)
melodramatic **mélodramatique**
Member of Parliament **député** (m)
menu **menu** (m)
merry **joyeux/joyeuse**
message **message** (m)
midnight **minuit**
milk **lait** (m)
milliard (US *billion*) **milliard** (m)
million **million** (m)
minister **ministre** (m)
mint **menthe** (f)
minute **minute** (f)
misfortune **malheur** (m)
miss **mademoiselle**
miss (to) **manquer, rater**

mission mission (f)
model modèle (m)
modern moderne
moment moment (m)
monarchy monarchie (f)
Monday lundi
money argent (m)
monkey, ape singe (m)
moon lune (f)
mop up éponger
more and more de plus en plus
morning matin (m)
morning matinée (f)
mother mère (f)
motorcycle, moto
motorway autoroute (f)
mountain montagne (f)
mouth bouche (f)
move (to) se déplacer
multimillionaire milliardaire (m)
museum musée (m)
mushroom champignon (m)
music musique (f)
musician musicien (m)
must, owe (to) devoir
my ma
my mes
my mon
name nom (m)
name (to) nommer
napkin, towel serviette (f)
nature, wildlife nature (f)
nausea nausée (f)
near près
nearly, almost presque
neck cou (m)
need besoin (m)
need (to) avoir besoin de
neighbour voisin (m)
Netherlands Pays-Bas
never ne… jamais
new neuf/neuve, nouveau/nouvelle
New Year's Day jour de l'An (m)
news nouvelles (f, pl)
news in brief faits divers (m pl)
newspaper journal (m)
next prochain (e)
next door à côté
nice gentil/gentille
nice sympatique
night nuit (f)
nightfall tombée de la nuit (f)
nine neuf
ninety quatre-vingt dix
no aucun (e)
no non
no more ne… plus
nobody personne
noise bruit (m)
noon midi
North Nord (m)
nose nez (m)
not ne… pas
not bad pas mal
not yet ne… pas encore
note book carnet (m)
nothing rien
nothing, not anything ne… rien
notice (to) remarquer
novel roman (m)
November novembre (m)
now maintenant
number nombre (m)

number **numéro** (m)
nurse **infirmière** (f)
October **octobre** (m)
odd, strange, funny **bizarre**
of course **bien sûr**
of, from **de**
offer (to) **offrir**
office, desk **bureau** (m)
often **souvent**
oil **huile** (f)
old **vieux, vieil/vieille**
on **sur**
on the contrary **au contraire**
on the first try **du premier coup**
on the left **à gauche**
on the right **à droite**
on time **à l'heure**
open (to) **ouvrir**
opposite **en face**
opposition **opposition** (f)
or **ou**
order (to) **commander**
ordinary **ordinaire**
organise (to) **organiser**
original **original**
other **autre**
otherwise **sinon**
our **nos, notre**
out of service **hors service**
over there **là-bas**
own (to) **posséder**
ozone layer **couche d'ozone** (f)
paid holidays **congés payés** (m, pl)
painting **tableau** (m)
pair of shorts **short** (m)
pale **pâle**
parade **défilé** (m)
parcel **colis** (m), **paquet** (m)
pardon **pardon**
parent **parent** (m)
park (to) **stationner**
parking place **parking** (m)
parsley **persil** (m)
party **parti (politique)** (m)
pasta **pâtes** (f, pl)
patience **patience** (f)
pay (to) **payer**
pay attention (to) **faire attention**
peace **paix** (f)
pedestrian **piéton** (m)
pen **stylo** (m)
people **gens** (m, pl)
perfect **parfait**
period **période** (f)
person **personne** (f)
petrol **essence** (f)
phone box (US *booth*) **cabine** (f)
photo, picture **photo** (f)
piece of furniture **meuble** (m)
pity (to) **plaindre**
place **endroit** (m)
plan **projet** (m)
plane **avion** (m)
planet **planète** (f)
plant **plante** (f)
plastic **plastique** (m)
plate **assiette** (f)
platform **quai** (m)
play (to) **jouer**
player **joueur** (m)
pleasant **agréable**
please **s'il te plaît s'il vous plaît**
please (to) **plaire**
plumber **plombier** (m)

plumbing **plomberie** (f)
pocket **poche** (f)
policeman **agent de police** (m)
politics, policy **politique** (f)
poll **sondage** (m)
pollution **pollution** (f)
poor **pauvre**
Portugal **Portugal**
Portuguese **portugais** (e)
position (US *wicket*) **guichet** (m)
possible **possible**
post (to) **poster**
post office **poste** (f)
postcard **carte postale**
poster **affiche** (m)
postman **facteur** (m)
postpone (to) **remettre**
potato **pomme de terre** (f)
practise (to) **pratiquer**
precisely **justement**
prefer (to) **préférer**
prepare (to) **préparer**
prescription **ordonnance** (f)
present **cadeau** (m)
present (to) **présenter**
presently **actuellement**
president **président** (m)
pretty **joli** (e)
price, prize **prix** (m)
problem **problème** (m)
programme **programme** (m)
propose (to) **proposer**
prudent, careful **prudent** (e)
public, audience **public** (m)
purple **violet** (te)
put (to) **mettre, poser**
quarrel (to), argue (to) **se disputer**
quarter **quart** (m)
queen **reine** (f)
questions **questions** (f)
queue **queue** (f)
quiet **tranquille**
quite **tout à fait**
race **course** (f)
radiant **resplendissante**
railway **voie** (f)
rain **pluie** (f)
rain (to) **pleuvoir**
raincoat. **imperméable** (m)
rare **saignante** (viande)
rarely, seldom **rarement**
rather **plutôt**
reach (to) **arriver à, atteindre**
read (to) **lire**
ready **prêt** (e)
realise (to) **se rendre compte de**
really **vraiment**
receipt **reçu** (m)
receive (to), get (to) **recevoir**
recent **récent** (e)
record **disque** (m)
recycling **recyclage** (m)
red **rouge**
red haired **roux**
registered (post) **recommandé**
regret (to) **regretter**
regularly **régulièrement**
rely on (to) **compter sur**
remember (to) **se souvenir**
rent (to) **louer**
repair (to), mend (to) **réparer**
report (to) **signaler**
represent (to) **représenter**
representative, salesman **représentant** (m)
republic **république** (f)

respect (to) respecter
rest (to) se reposer
return (to) retourner
revise (to) réviser
rich riche
right to vote droit de vote (m)
ring (to) sonner
ring road périphérique (m)
road works travaux (m, pl)
rock rocher (m)
room salle (f)
room, play, coin pièce (f)
rose rose (f)
row rang (m)
ruin, waste, spoil gâcher
run (to) courir
run over (to) renverser
sad triste
salad salade (f)
salary salaire (m)
same même
Saturday samedi (m)
say (to), tell (to) dire
school école (f)
score (to) (a goal) marquer
sea mer (f)
seat, room place (f)
secretary secrétaire (m, f)
see (to) voir
see you soon à bientôt
seem (to) sembler
select sélectionner
sell (to) vendre
send (to) envoyer
send back (to) renvoyer
sender expéditeur (m)
September septembre (m)
serial, series feuilleton (m)
serious grave
settle (to) régler
seven sept
seventy soixante-dix
several plusieurs
shave (to) se raser
she, her elle
shelf étagère (f)
shirt chemise (f)
shock choc (m)
shoe chaussure (f)
shop boutique (f)
shop window vitrine (f)
shop, store magasin (m)
shopkeeper commerçant (m)
short court (e)
shoulder épaule (f)
shout (to) crier
show (to) montrer, indiquer
show, performance séance (f)
shut (to), close (to) fermer
shuttle navette (f)
sick malade
sickness, disease maladie (f)
side bord (m)
sign (to) signer
since, for depuis
sing (to) chanter
sir, Mr monsieur (m)
sister sœur (f)
sit (to) s'asseoir
six six
sixteen seize
sixty soixante
size taille (f)
ski (to) skier, faire du ski
sky ciel (m)
slice tranche (f)
slogan slogan (m)
slowly lentement

small, little **petit (e)**
smell (to), feel (to) **sentir**
smile **sourire (m)**
smoke (to) **fumer**
snake **serpent (m)**
snow **neige (f)**
so much, so many **tant de**
so much, so many **tellement**
so that **pour que**
soaked **trempée**
softly **doucement**
some **certain (e) s**
some **quelque**
somebody, someone, **quelqu'un**
something/anything else **autre chose**
something, anything else **quelque chose**
sometimes **parfois**
sometimes **quelquefois**
son **fils (m)**
song **chanson (f)**
soon **bientôt**
sorry **désolé (e)**
sorry **navré (e)**
sort, kind **genre (m)**
South **Sud (m)**
space **espace (m)**
Spain **Espagne (f)**
spaniel **épagneul (m)**
Spanish **espagnol (e)**
speak (to) **parler**
special **particulier**
specialist **spécialiste (m, f)**
spectacular **spectaculaire**
speech **discours (m)**
speed **vitesse (f)**
spell (to) **épeler**
spend **dépenser, passer (le temps)**
splendid **spendide**
sport **sport (m)**
Spring **printemps (m)**
stable **écurie (f)**
stadium **stade (m)**
stamp **timbre (m)**
star **étoile (f)**
start (to) **démarrer**
statement (bank) **relevé (m)**
station **gare (f)**
stay (to), remain (to) **rester**
steak (rib) **entrecôte (f)**
steal (to) **voler**
stereo equipment **chaîne stéréo (f)**
stop **arrêt (m)**
stop (to) **arrêter, s'arrêter**
storm **orage (m), tempête (f)**
story, history **histoire (f)**
straight away, immediately **tout de suite**
street **rue (f)**
strictly **sévèrement**
strike **grève (f)**
strike (to) hit (to) **frapper**
stripe **rayure (f)**
strong **fort (e)**
struggle, wrestling **lutte (f)**
student **étudiant (e) (m/f)**
study **étude (f)**
study (to) **faire ses études**
stunned, **étourdi**
subscription **abonnement (m)**
suburbs **banlieue (f)**
succeed (to), be successful (to) **réussir**
success **succès (m)**
suddenly **soudain**

suffocate (to) étouffer
sugar sucre (m)
suitcase valise (f)
Summer été (m)
sun soleil (m)
Sunday dimanche (m)
sunset coucher de soleil (m)
sunshade parasol (m)
superb superbe
supplement supplément (m)
sure sûr
surely sûrement
surf board planche à voile (f)
swimming natation (f)
swimming pool piscine (f)
switch on (to) allumer
table table (f)
take (away) (to) emporter
take (to) prendre
take care (to), treat (to) soigner
take off (to) décoller
take place (to) avoir lieu
take the wrong..(to) se tromper de
take to (to) emmener à
talent talent (m)
talk (to), chat (to) bavarder
tall, big, large, great grand (e)
tanned bronzé
tap robinet (m)
taste (to) goûter
taxi taxi (m)
team équipe (f)
technology technologie (f)
tee-shirt tee-shirt (m)
telegramme télégramme (m)
telephone téléphone (m)
telescope lunette (f)
television télévision (f)
television set téléviseur (m)
tell the truth à vrai dire
ten dix
terrible terrible
thank to grâce à
thank you merci
that ça
that ceinture (f)
that is to say c'est à dire
that way par là
that's it c'est ça
the la, le, les
the day after tomorrow après-demain
the moment when au moment où
the weather is bad il fait mauvais
theatre théâtre (m)
theft vol (m)
their leur, leurs
then ensuite, puis
there là, y
there is, there are, ago il y a
therefore donc
these ceux, ceux-ci
these ones, those ones celles-ci, celles-là
these, those ces
they, them elles
think penser
third tiers (m)
thirteen treize
thirty trente
this ceci
this one, that one celle-ci, celle-là, celui-ci, celui-là
this way par ici
this, that cet/cette

though, although **bien que**
thousand **mille, millier** (m)
three **trois**
thumb **pouce** (m)
Thursday **jeudi** (m)
ticket, note **billet** (m)
tidy (to) **ranger**
tiger **tigre** (m)
tight **serrée**
time **fois** (f)
time table **horaire** (m)
time, hour **heure** (f)
tired **fatigué**
tiring **fatiguant**
title **titre** (m)
to advise **conseiller**
to allow **permettre**
to let (US *to rent, for rent*) **à louer**
to, towards **vers**
today **aujourd'hui**
together **ensemble**
toll **péage** (m)
tomato **tomate** (f)
tomorrow **demain**
too **aussi trop,**
too bad **tant pis**
too much, too many **trop de**
top prize in the lottery **gros lot**
tourist **touriste** (m, f)
town **ville** (f)
toy **jouet** (m)
tractor **tracteur** (m)
trade union **syndicat** (m)
traffic **circulation** (f)
traffic jam **embouteillage** (m)
trail **piste** (f)
train **train** (m)
transistor **transistor** (m)
travel (to) **voyager**
travel agency **agence de voyages** (f)
travellers'cheque **chèque de voyage** (m)
treat **régal** (m)
trip, journey **voyage** (m)
trouble, problem **ennui** (m)
trousers **pantalon** (m)
true **vrai** (e)
trust (to) **avoir confiance, faire confiance**
try (to) **essayer**
tube (US *subway*) **métro** (m)
Tuesday **mardi** (m)
tunnel **tunnel** (m)
turn (to) **tourner**
turn in (to), give back (to) **rendre**
twelve **douze**
twenty **vingt**
twist (to) (one's ankle) **se tordre (la cheville)**
two **deux**
type (to) **taper à la machine**
tyre **pneu** (m)
umbrella **parapluie** (m)
uncle **oncle** (m)
under **sous**
understand (to) **comprendre**
unemployment **chômage** (m)
unfortunately **malheureusement**
until when **jusqu'à quand**
urgently **d'urgence**
use (to) **se servir de, utiliser**
useful **utile**
useless **inutile**
usually **d'habitude**

valid valable
vegetable légume (m)
very très
village village (m)
violent violent
visit (to) visiter
voice voix (f)
vote (to) voter
voter électeur (m) électrice (f)
wait (to) attendre
wait (to), be patient patienter
waiter garçon (de café) (m)
wake up (to) se réveiller
walk (to) marcher
walk by (to) passer devant
walk, ride promenade (f)
walking marche (f)
walkman baladeur (m)
want (to) vouloir
war guerre (f)
wash (to) se laver
washbasin lavabo (m)
waste déchet (m)
watch montre (f)
water eau (f)
wave vague (f)
wave (to) faire signe
way chemin (m)
we, us nous
weak faible
weather, time temps (m)
wedding, marriage mariage (m)
Wednesday mercredi (m)
week semaine (f)
weekly hebdomadaire (m)
well bien
West Ouest (m)
whale baleine (f)
what quoi
what time is it ? quelle heure est-il ?
what, which quel, quels, quelle, quelles
wheel roue (f)
when quand
where où
which lequel, laquelle, lesquels, lesquelles
white blanc/blanche
who qui
why pourquoi
will volonté (f)
willingly, with pleasure volontiers
win (to), earn (to) gagner
wind vent (m)
window fenêtre (f)
wine vin (m)
Winter hiver (m)
wish souhait (m)
with avec
with difficulty avec peine
with pleasure avec joie
with pleasure avec plaisir
withdrawal retrait (m)
without sans
witness témoin (m)
woman, wife femme (f)
wood bois (m)
wool laine (f)
word processor traitement de texte (m)
work travail (m)
work (to) travailler
work of art œuvre d'art (f)
worker ouvrier (m)
world, people monde (m)
worse than pire que

write (to) écrire
writer écrivain (m)
year an (m), année (f)
yellow jaune
yes oui
yesterday hier
yet pourtant
you tu, te, vous
young jeune
your ta, ton, tes, vos, votre

TOPIC INDEX (numbers refer to pages)

GRAMMAR INDEX

Instant French

POCKET

Fast access to basic French

Impression réalisée sur Presse Offset par

CPI
Brodard & Taupin

43820 – La Flèche (Sarthe), le 02-10-2007
Dépôt légal : novembre 1997
Suite du premier tirage : octobre 2007

POCKET – 12, avenue d'Italie - 75627 Paris cedex 13

Imprimé en France